10 —

THE CIVILIZATION OF THE AMERICAN INDIAN SERIES

CORN IS OUR BLOOD

sintli ne toeso
"corn is our blood"

CORN IS OUR BLOOD

CULTURE AND ETHNIC IDENTITY
IN A
CONTEMPORARY AZTEC INDIAN VILLAGE

BY ALAN R. SANDSTROM

UNIVERSITY OF OKLAHOMA PRESS : NORMAN AND LONDON

By Alan R. Sandstrom

The Image of Disease: Medical Practices of Nahua Indians of the Huasteca (Columbia, Mo., 1978)
Traditional Curing and Crop Fertility Rituals among Otomi Indians of the Sierra de Puebla, Mexico: The Lopez Manuscripts (Bloomington, Ind., 1981)
Traditional Papermaking and Paper Cult Figures of Mexico (with Pamela Effrein Sandstrom) (Norman, 1986)
Corn is Our Blood: Culture and Ethnic Identity in a Contemporary Aztec Indian Village (Norman, 1991)

Publication of this book as made possible in part by a grant from the offices of the Dean of the School of Arts and Sciences and of the Vice Chancellor for Academic Affairs at Indiana-Purdue University at Fort Wayne, and in part with the assistance of the National Endowment for the Humanities, a federal agency which supports the study of such fields as history, philosophy, literature, and languages.

Sandstrom, Alan R.
    Corn is our blood : culture and ethnic identity in a contemporary Aztec Indian village / by Alan R. Sandstrom.—1st ed.
      p.   cm.—(The Civilization of the American Indian series : v. 206)
    Includes bibliographical references and index.
    ISBN 0-8061-2399-0
    1. Nahuas—Ethnic identity.   2. Nahuas—Religion and mythology.
3. Nahuas—Social life and customs.   4. Veracruz (Mexico : State)—
Case studies.   I. Title.   II. Series.
F1221.N3S258   1991
972'.62—dc20   91-50307
                                            CIP

Jacket design by Bill Cason

Dedicated to
Esther Plançon Sandstrom
and to the memory of
J. Russell Sandstrom

NA NI INDIO

Na ni indio:
pampa ijkinoj nech tokajtijkej koyomej
kemaj asikoj ipan ni yankuik tlatipaktli.

Na ni indio:
pampa mokajkayajkej koyomej
kemaj asikoj kampa tlanauatiayaj nokoluaj.

Na ni indio:
pampa ijkinoj nech manextijkej koyomej
para uelis nopan nejnemisej uan nech pinajtisej.

Na ni indio:
pampa ijkinoj tech tokajtijkej koyomej
nochi timaseualmej tlen ni yankuik tlaltipaktli.

Na ni indio:
uan namaj ika nimotlakaneki ni tlajtoli
tlen yaluaya ika nechpinajtiayaj koyomej.

Na ni indio:
uan namaj ayok nij pinauia ma ijkinoj nechilikaj
pampa nij mati para mokuapolojkej koyomej.

Na ni indio:
uan namaj nij mati para nij pixtok
no neluayo uan no tlajlamikilis.

Na ni indio:
uan namaj nij mati para nij pixtok
no ixayak, no tlachialis uan no nemilis.

Na ni indio:
uan namaj nij mati melauak ni mejikano
pampa ni tlajtoua mejikano, tlen inintlajtol nokoluaj.

Na ni indio:
uan namaj tlauel ni yolpaki
pampa ualaj se yankuik tonatij, se yankuik tlanextli.

Na ni indio:
uan namaj nij machilia tlamisa kuesoli
sampa uelis niyolpakis uan nimoyolchikauas.

Na ni indio:
uan namaj sampa yeyektsij nij kaki
ayakachtlatsotsontli xochitlatsontsontli.

Na ni indio:
uan namaj sampa nikinita
uan nikintlakakilia ueuetlakamej.

Na ni indio:
uan namaj sampa nech neluayotia tlaltipaktli,
tonana tlatipaktli.

I AM INDIAN

I am Indian:
because the white men named me thus
when they arrived in this new land.

I am Indian:
because of an error of the white men
when they arrived in the land governed by my grandparents.

I am Indian:
because that is how the white men labeled me
in order to crush me and discriminate against me.

I am Indian:
because that is what the whites called us
all the people of this continent.

I am Indian:
and now this word fills me with pride
the word which yesterday the white men used to jeer us.

I am Indian:
and now it causes me no pain that they call me this
because I know the historical error of the whites.

I am Indian:
and now I know that I have my own roots
and my own thoughts.

I am Indian:
and now I know that I have my own face
my own look and my own feelings.

I am Indian:
and now I know that I am truly Mexican
because I speak the Mexican language, the language of my grandparents.

I am Indian:
and now my heart is happy
because a new day is coming, a new dawn.

I am Indian:
and now I feel that this sadness will soon end,
again my heart will be able to laugh and be stronger.

I am Indian:
and now I can contemplate the beauty of the dance,
and hear the music and the song.

I am Indian:
and now I can see and hear
anew the elders.

I am Indian:
and now the earth returns to give me roots,
our mother earth.

By José Antonio Xokoyotsij, pseudonym of Natalio Hernández Hernández, a Nahua born in the *municipio* of Ixhuatlán de Madero (1986:50–51).

CONTENTS

ILLUSTRATIONS

FIGURES

MAPS

TABLES

PREFACE

THE ancient Aztecs of Mexico are the most famous of the Nahua Indians, almost a million of whom today continue to speak their native language, grow corn, and practice religious traditions tracing back to pre-Hispanic days. Although the Nahuas are one of the most populous and important Native American groups, few people recognize their name or realize their connection to the great pre-Hispanic civilizations of Middle America. Fewer still are familiar with basic Nahua cultural features. This work is an ethnographic sketch of the contemporary Nahua village of Amatlán (a pseudonym), written with a minimum of anthropological jargon for the interested nonspecialist. I hope that the work will also be of value to anthropologists, other social scientists, and students in social science courses interested in ethnicity, culture change, and the processes by which traditional people adapt to the conditions of life in a modern nation.

I gathered most of the information on Amatlán through participant observation, the research methodology favored by most anthropologists who study living communities. Participant observation is a method in which the researcher is required to spend long periods of time living among the people he or she wishes to study. During my many months of residence in Amatlán, I was often physically uncomfortable, occasionally fearful, and usually in a state of some confusion, but I was never bored. Long-term research of this type is filled with problems and opportunities, and it is always conducted at the pleasure of one's hosts. In the pages that follow I will attempt to communicate something of what it is like to do this type of research in a Nahua village for those interested in learning more about the mysteries of the fieldwork experience. Despite its shortcomings as a scientific methodology, I remain convinced that participant observation is one of the most powerful tools we have for increasing our understanding of the human condition.

To improve readability, I have used in-text citations sparingly.

However, I have deviated from this practice in the instances where I make use of an interesting source of ethnographic information. In the late 1970s, the Mexican government, under the auspices of the Secretary of Public Education and the National Indigenous Institute, established a program to make graduate training in ethnolinguistics available to bilingual Indian schoolteachers. One requirement for completion of the program was that each candidate write a thesis based on ethnographic research among his or her own people. The works were then published in 1982 in a special series entitled Etnolingüística. Six of the candidates were Nahuas who wrote about villages in and around the southern Huasteca, the region where Amatlán is located. These schoolteachers produced works that are rare in the ethnographic record in that they contain descriptions of a culture by informed members of the culture itself. The names of the six researchers are Juan de la Cruz Hernández, Rosendo Hernández Cuellar, Joel Martínez Hernández, Agustín Reyes Antonio, Rosa Reyes Martínez, and Joaquin Romualdo Hernández. Because their works contain valuable cultural information from the vantage point of insiders, I have cited these authors often, either to confirm an ethnographic point I wish to establish or to refer the reader to additional information on a topic. All works consulted in the writing of this book are listed at the end.

I have organized much of the descriptive material to clarify several key questions that underlie this study. How have the Nahuas managed to survive as a group after nearly 500 years of conquest and domination by Europeans? What are the reasons for the continuities we see in Nahua culture, and why have certain changes occurred? How are villages like Amatlán organized to resist intrusion of the national culture, and what internal distortions of village life are caused by the marginal position occupied by Indian communities in Mexico?

The answer to these and related questions lies in the complex process by which the Nahuas have forged and maintained their identity as Indians. Here we enter the realm of paradox. The policy of the Spanish, and later the Mexican government, was to assimilate the Native Americans into an essentially European system. But by suppressing native populations and attempting to exercise total control over them, the Spaniards virtually guaranteed that Indian culture would survive. Ethnicity, to some extent, can be understood as an effective defense on the part of a subordinated group against social, political, economic, or military domination. My purpose in this book, in addition to describing features of life in Amatlán, is to examine how Nahua ethnic identity has adapted native peoples to life under domination. I will not be concerned with the phenomenological problems of understanding what it is to be a Nahua, how Nahuas see themselves relative to others, or how it feels to be an Indian in Mexico, although these are topics that I do not completely ignore. Instead, I want to specify some of the concrete advantages that being a Nahua confers on the people living in a particular village. I hope to uncover some of the underlying motives that lead people to be active in creating an identity for themselves both as a defense against alien elites and as a strategy for creating opportunities for themselves.

Some scholars today object to the use of the word *Indian* to refer to the Native Americans. They point out that an Indian is a person who fits a social category created by colonialism, a person who has suffered conquest and domination by foreign elites. They further argue that most native peoples do not refer to themselves as Indians. An additional problem is that it has proven exceedingly difficult to attach a precise definition to the term *Indian*. Nevertheless, I use the term in this book because I believe that it is useful for distinguishing Hispanically oriented peoples from those who look to their pre-Hispanic traditions as their legitimate history. The Nahuas call Native Americans *masehualmej*, which means "countrymen" or "Indian farmers," a term that seems too restricted to cover the range of Native American cultures. I do not intend my use of the word *Indian* to be demeaning or to perpetuate the pejorative categorization of human beings deriving from a dehumanizing colonial past. I use the term because it is familiar to most people, it is found throughout the social scientific literature, and it retains analytical validity if used with care.

Given the danger and potential harm that publicity can pose to traditional people, I have chosen to use a pseudonym for the village. Also, to protect villagers from possible embarrassment or even danger, I have not used their real names. The world has changed significantly since the first trained anthropologists journeyed to exotic locales the world over to bring back early scientific information about other cultures. Since then traditional cultures and ethnic groups have been increasingly caught up in international power struggles, and they have often been pawns and victims of unscrupulous governments, multinational economic conglomerates, missionaries, and other groups pursuing their own agendas without regard for the human cost. In this context, information gathered by anthropologists has become poten-

tially useful to powerful interest groups. The village, the people, and
the events I have recorded are real, and the descriptions are as accurate
as I can make them. I have changed only the names of people and
selected locations.

ALAN R. SANDSTROM

Fort Wayne, Indiana

ACKNOWLEDGMENTS

IT is my pleasure to express appreciation to some of the people and organizations who made this study possible. Greatest thanks of course goes to the people of the village of Amatlán who accepted me and my family into their community. The Nahuas are not saintlike, but if I catalogued all of the kindnesses both large and small they showed over the years it would fill a volume larger than this one.

An incident occurred in 1986 that will reveal something of what I mean. One day the eminent French anthropologist Guy Stresser-Péan and his wife, Claude, visited us in Amatlán. Neither I nor the villagers expected them, and in any event there was no way that our visitors could have let us know they were coming. At the time they entered the village, my family and I were attending a curing ritual, and some men came to inform us that my "parents" had arrived. We were delighted that they had come and invited them to witness the close of the ritual. Being experienced fieldworkers, the Stresser-Péans had come prepared with supplies of food; however, by the time we all returned to our quarters a couple of hours later, a child was waiting with freshly made tamales. Every several hours during the two days that the Stresser-Péans were with us a different child would appear with food for us and our guests. No one ever acknowledged that they had sent food and no payment was ever asked. The dishes that people sent were the most valued and delicious examples of Nahua cuisine, requiring much preparation time. Obviously many families were cooperating in this effort and the Stresser-Péans had no need to use any of their supplies. This expression of sincere kindness and generosity on the part of individuals with no thought of direct reward was a common occurrence in my years in Amatlán.

Many individuals in the village took a personal interest in my attempts to understand their culture and way of life. They spent hours talking with me as I asked question after question about topics that to them must have seemed obvious and boring. Still, throughout it all, most people appreciated the high comedy of the situation and tolerated me and my family with grace and humor. As I will demonstrate shortly, they were as curious about me as I was about them, and I like to think that, in our interactions, they discovered something worth knowing about American culture. It is a sad commentary on the world we live in that I feel I cannot thank people by name for fear this will cause them trouble, either from local authorities or from foreign missionary groups.

To my wife, Pamela Effrein Sandstrom, I owe especial thanks for her unwavering support in this long-term effort. Pamela and our son, Michael, have accompanied me on all recent field trips to Amatlán. They are both natural ethnographers with abundant curiosity and a love of adventure. But Pamela is remarkable in the ease with which she adapts to the often difficult and dangerous conditions of life far from any familiar conveniences. She has proven herself outstanding at generating rapport even across a significant cultural and language gap. She made lasting friends among village women and was able to help me understand better their points of view. She also made significant contributions to the hard work of census-taking and mapping the village.

But Pamela's efforts did not stop when we left Amatlán after our last visit. She has also worked tirelessly to help in the editing of this work. She carefully read the manuscript several times and her excellent suggestions will be appreciated, even if unconsciously, by anyone who reads this book.

I also owe many thanks to my longtime friend John A. Mead for his meticulous editing of previous drafts of this work. John wrote many pages of corrections and suggestions based on his editing abilities and his extensive knowledge of anthropology. John contributed the glossary, and his efforts have significantly improved the quality of this work. I want to thank James M. Taggart for his extremely thoughtful suggestions on an earlier draft of the book. The anonymous reviewer for the University of Oklahoma Press also made many valuable suggestions. Finally, I want to thank my brother, John E. Sandstrom, for his worthy comments on the manuscript.

I want to extend thanks to Alfonso Medellín Zeníl and Alfonso Gorbea Soto of the Instituto de Antropología, Universidad Veracruzana, for sharing the institute's data with me and for arranging permissions for traveling and working in northern Veracruz. Thanks also to our friend, linguist Román Güemes Jímenez of the University of Veracruz, whose mastery of Nahuatl and whose knowledge of the

Huasteca was of great help to us. Román accompanied us to the village on several occasions and he transcribed and translated much of the Nahuatl text that appears in this work. Thanks also to Virginia Oliveros, who worked for a time as our research assistant.

I want to express appreciation to Domingo Cabrera Hernández, schoolmaster and administrative director of the school in Amatlán when I arrived there in 1970. He and his family showed me every hospitality and actively aided in the research. The late Patricio Hernández, schoolmaster in Amatlán in more recent years, and his family also were hospitable during our residence in the village. I also want to thank our friends Manuel Torres Guévara and Julio and Ana de Keijzer for making visits to Xalapa a pleasure. A note of appreciation is due to Luis Reyes García and Punciano Ortiz. And finally, for introducing me to the area, Christina Boilès and the late Carlos Boilès deserve special mention.

I wish to acknowledge the assistance of Frances Karttunen for her help with the Nahuatl. She gave generously of her time and did me the favor of introducing me to Geoffrey Kimball, an expert on Huastecan Nahuatl. Geoffrey spent many hours going over each of the terms included in the text and helped in translating some of the more difficult words. William Klemme generously offered his invaluable assistance in improving my translations of Spanish texts. Frans J. Schryer helped a great deal by sending me copies of data he collected among Nahuas in the Huasteca Hidalguense. Richard Bradley was kind enough to forward a copy of his dissertation based on research he conducted in southern Veracruz. To Georgia and Mark Ulmschneider I owe many thanks for their contributions leading to our acquisition of a four-wheel drive vehicle for our 1985–86 research.

I wish to thank Kenneth Balthaser, director of the Learning Resource Center (LRC) at Indiana-Purdue University at Fort Wayne (IPFW) for his generous assistance over the years. Ken has done everything possible to facilitate my research, and his efforts have improved the quantity and quality of my results. To photographer Elmer Denman of LRC, I owe a debt of gratitude for his assistance over the years. James Whitcraft, an artist at LRC, did an excellent job finalizing details on the charts and maps that appear in this work. I want to thank my sister, Susan E. Sandstrom, and Robert Bradley for visiting us in Amatlán and for their support in this work. And for the numerous times they offered their help, Edwin and Dorothea Effrein deserve many thanks.

I also want to extend thanks to John N. Drayton, Editor-in-Chief of the University of Oklahoma Press, for his support, as well as to the various staff members of the Press who have become our friends.

The research was supported by a number of grants from different organizations. I wish to acknowledge the United States government NDFL Area Studies Program, and the following Indiana University programs: Center for Latin American and Caribbean Studies; Office of Research and Advanced Studies; President's Council on International Programs; President's Council on the Social Sciences; and the IPFW Grants for Summer Research Program. I also received major funding to support the fieldwork phases of the work in the form of a Fulbright Post-doctoral Research Fellowship (award #1035214) and an Organization of American States Research Fellowship (award #F96735).

THE TRANSCRIPTION AND USAGE OF
SPANISH, NAHUATL, AND ENGLISH TERMS

THE Nahuas speak an Uto-Aztecan language called Nahuatl and as such it is related to several North American Indian languages including Ute, Paiute, Hopi, and Comanche. English has borrowed many familiar words from Nahuatl, for example, the terms *chocolate, tomato, chile, peyote, coyote, ocelot,* and *shack.* I have included many Nahuatl terms in this book, and my methods of transcription and translation require some explanation.

My knowledge of the language is mostly in the spoken form and, although I have studied Nahuatl grammar, I claim no expertise as a linguist. Throughout my research in Amatlán I have relied on bilingual informants for the transcription of words and texts. Most Nahuas of this region of Mexico do not read or write their language, and in fact only an occasional schoolmaster or Nahua who has been able to attend urban educational institutions has any facility with written Nahuatl. At this point there exists no standardized transcription system agreed upon by literate Huastecan Nahuas. Beller and Beller are linguists who have recently published a method for Huastecan Nahuatl (1984), but it is clear that they are dealing with a slightly different dialect from that spoken in Amatlán. Stiles (1976–79) has a brief course for beginners including a dictionary of yet another dialect, and I only recently discovered a grammatical sketch by Kimball (1980) of the Huazalinguillo dialect of Huastecan Nahuatl.

Because I believe that the Nahuas have the right to set the transcription standards of their own language, I have relied heavily on the systems employed by my bilingual research assistants. Although this system only approximates the actual sounds of the spoken language, it has the advantage of being far more accessible to the nonspecialist than would a literal transcription. I would like to add here that the absence of a standardized system for transcribing Huastecan Nahuatl and my reliance upon various bilingual research assistants over the years has produced a degree of inconsistency in my published renderings of Nahuatl. In fact, linguists who have worked on Huastecan Nahuatl have not always been consistent either, which compounds the problems of ethnographic researchers like myself. In any case, anyone familiar with the language should have little trouble recognizing words and phrases that I have transcribed in this and previously published works. Where there are inconsistencies or clear errors in the transcriptions of words, I have relied on the work of the Bellers to make corrections. Where I have had difficulty translating a Nahuatl word or phrase into English I have included a more literal translation in parentheses following my English rendering. Finally, I acknowledge the contribution of two linguists who are experts on Nahuatl who have kindly checked all of my transcriptions and translations.

In general the letters used to transcribe Nahuatl words are equivalent in sound value to their Spanish counterparts. Following are exceptions to the Spanish pattern:

"x" is equivalent to "sh" as in shop.

"j" is like the English "h" as in house.

"tl" is a single sound with the "l" released simultaneously on both sides of the tongue.

"u" followed by a vowel has a "w" sound as in Spanish, but a silent "h" appears before the "u" when it begins a syllable or when it is between vowels; thus the word "cuahuitl" (tree or wood) is pronounced "kwawitl."

The glottal stops occuring in the Amatlán dialect of Nahuatl are predictable and I have not marked them. A glottal stop occurs before all vowel-inital words, between any two vowels that have a morpheme break between them, and following a final vowel in a word. Final "n" is generally devoiced but it is retained in certain words such as "apan" (water place) and "mictlan" (death place).

In general, stress in Nahuatl is on the penultimate syllable. Exceptions are indicated with an acute accent mark (´). Vowel length is a feature of Nahuatl, but I, along with my research assistants and most linguists who have worked in the Huasteca region, do not mark it. It is apparently not necessary to mark vowel length in the overwhelming number of cases. In certain transcription systems, double letters are used to indicate the internal structure of words. Again following the practices of the Bellers and my local assistants, I do not use this method. To avoid prejudging the significance of concepts in my ethnographic descriptions, I have not used capital letters in Nahuatl words. When quoting Nahuatl words published by others, I have retained their spellings and translations. Finally, when I write "in Nahuatl" throughout the text to distinguish indigenous words, please read "in this particular dialect of Nahuatl" because I do not wish to imply that what is spoken in Amatlán is necessarily representative of the language as a whole.

I have used the *Random House Dictionary of the English Language*, second edition unabridged (1987), as my authority for word usage in English. Both Nahuatl and Spanish words are set off by italics the first time they appear in the text. Certain Spanish terms, however, such as "arroyo" and "mestizo" have, according to the editors, entered the English language to the point that it is no longer necessary to write them in italics. When in doubt, I have followed their editorial judgment in these matters.

CORN IS OUR BLOOD

CHAPTER 1

ENTERING THE FIELD

ON the evening of December 24, 1972, I was seated in the corner of a small thatch-roofed shrine deep in the tropical forests of northern Veracruz, Mexico. The shrine is located in Amatlán, a Nahua Indian village of just under 600 people and the site of my first anthropological fieldwork. I was in a state of high anticipation as I watched people make preparations for a major ritual dedicated to *tonantsij*, a mother deity associated with fertility. Although I had lived in Amatlán for several months, this was the first time people had invited me to witness an important village event.

Outside, men wearing colorful headdresses constructed from bamboo, folded paper, long ribbons, and mirrors shook rattles as they performed traditional dances mimicking planting and harvesting. Off to one side, men and boys squatted around glowing beeswax candles and a smoking incense brazier preparing palm and marigold adornments for the main altar inside the shrine. More and more people began to arrive, each bearing food offerings or additional palm leaves and marigolds for the adornment makers. Inside, two pairs of musicians played the lilting and eerily beautiful sacred music of the Nahuas on guitar and violin. Thick clouds of copal incense smoke perfumed the air, obscuring the yellow light given off by the dozens of beeswax candles that lined the altar.

As helpers adorned the altar, men, women, and children entered the shrine, faced the altar, and walked down its length bowing. Suddenly, out of the darkness appeared Reveriano, the tall, imposing, and slightly mysterious head shaman of Amatlán. I had tried to contact him on several previous occasions without success. He peered at me long and hard through the swirling activity and then squatted down to chant before the altar. Assistants brought in four chickens, and the shaman, after censing them and chanting, quickly wrung their necks. As he laid the still-fluttering bodies of the chickens down in front of the altar, helpers brought him his sisal carrying bag. Out of it he

3

carefully removed a pair of scissors and a folded stack of colored tissue paper.

Reveriano was a man of powerful personality and great assurance of movement. He proceeded to select sheets of paper, fold them, and cut out intricate figures that, when unfolded, resembled small human beings with their hands raised by the sides of their heads. They were fantastic creations with headdresses that resembled animal horns, benign facial expressions, and patterns of holes cut from the body. While the shaman worked I tried to contain my excitement and remain inconspicuous as I began to realize what I was witnessing. Ritual paper cutting was practiced extensively by the pre-Hispanic civilizations where it played a major part in religious observances. The craft was suppressed by the Spaniards and later by missionaries who associated it with the Native American religions they were trying to eliminate. And yet here in Amatlán, almost 500 years after the Conquest, ritual paper cutting was apparently a central feature of religious practices (see Lenz 1973, 1984, and Sandstrom and Sandstrom 1986).

The shaman, who suddenly took notice of me again, raised his hand, and shouted for the musicians to stop playing. I became uneasy, unsure of what was to follow. He picked up a smoking brazier filled with red-hot coals and, while the hushed crowd look on, walked over to where I was sitting. He stood over me and began to blow incense smoke up and down until I was enveloped in a rosiny, pine-scented cloud. He then led me to the center of the shrine, and as we squatted he began to explain the ritual. He told me about tonantsij and about the offerings that would be made later that night. He explained why each house in the village was visited by a procession during the first days of the religious observance. Finally, he pointed to the neat stack of paper figures and revealed that they represented malevolent wind spirits that viciously attack people and cause disease and death. The figures would be used to cleanse the shrine before the main offering to tonantsij. After these explanations, the shaman waved his arm, the musicians resumed their playing, and the ritual continued until 10 o'clock the following morning.

On that memorable night in December, my position in Amatlán changed forever. Instead of dangerous intruder, I would now be treated more as a harmless ignorant outsider. This is a big step in the fieldwork enterprise. After the tonantsij ritual, I had shared a significant experience with the people, and it gave us a common ground for interaction. But at the time, of course, my main feeling was of relief. I was pleased that I had not been escorted out of the inner sanctum of the shrine, and I was amazed that Reveriano had taken the trouble to explain what he was doing. This was touched with a feeling of embarrassment at the thought that I had interrupted what seemed to be the most sacred part of the ritual. As I was invited to more events, I learned that Nahua rituals are characterized by a sense of informality and that such interruptions are easily tolerated.

At the same time I had the overwhelming feeling that night that I had been privileged to witness something rare and absolutely amazing. Here was a ritual, deeply felt by the people in attendance, that traced back to the days before the Conquest. I was struck by the continuity with the past and the fact that cultural systems are far from ephemeral. The ritual contained elements from Spanish Catholicism to be certain; Nahua culture is far from static. But as I hope to show in this book, the core of Nahua religion and world view is Native American and not European. I want to show that the people of Amatlán have used their traditions to forge a cultural identity for themselves that has allowed them to survive as a people. They, along with the other Indian groups of Mesoamerica, blended the old with the new to create a remarkable and resilient cultural system that over the centuries has allowed them to overcome conquest, near extermination, bloody war, and exploitation by European and native-born masters. Nahua culture is not a quaint survival; it is a subtle and powerful instrument wielded by a people who wish to endure and thrive.

Nahua Indians first came into contact with Europeans in 1519 shortly after Hernán Cortés and his Spanish soldiers landed on the shore of what is today the state of Veracruz on the east coast of Mexico. The Nahuas were united by a common language (although it was separated into several dialects) and a common Mesoamerican cultural tradition. Most of them lived in the central highlands of Mexico where the massive Sierra Madre Occidental and the Sierra Madre Oriental mountain ranges meet. But the Nahuas were divided into a number of sometimes mutually hostile groups, the most well known of which were the Colhua-Mexica, better known as the Aztecs, and their implacable enemies, the Tlaxcalans. With the help of the Tlaxcalans, Cortés conquered the Aztec capital on August 13, 1521, thus ending Nahua hegemony and initiating the colonial period of Mexican history.

Under Spanish domination the Native Americans of Mesoamerica withstood one of the most brutal colonial regimes in history. Within 100 years of the Conquest the region's population was reduced by as much as 95%. Entire areas were depopulated. Disease claimed most lives, but the Spaniards, through neglect, forced labor, and outright murder, were to blame. Over the centuries the decimated Indian populations began to increase, and in isolated pockets the people began to reconstruct their cultural traditions. Today there are approximately 800,000 people who speak Nahuatl, the Nahua language, many of them continuing to live in small villages or towns in the central highlands of Mexico (Horcasitas de Barros and Crespo 1979:29).

The village of Amatlán is located in the lowlands of northern Veracruz, to the north and east of the central highlands and thus outside of the main Nahua population concentration. Village and regional history will be sketched in a subsequent chapter, but the inhabitants of Amatlán are historically, linguistically, and culturally connected to the ancient Aztecs. Ethnohistorical sources affirm that several Aztec emperors launched invasions into the region, and large tracts of coastal territory had already been conquered before the arrival of the Spaniards. More direct evidence of Aztec heritage comes from the village itself. A man from Amatlán refers to himself as a *mexijcatl*, the same word an ancient Aztec would have used to identify his group affiliation. In fact the name "Mexico" means "place of the Mexijcaj (or Aztec) people," a name that recognizes their political, military, and economic dominance in this region of the New World.

BACKGROUND AND AIMS OF THE STUDY

Few contemporary American anthropologists go to the field with the aim of writing a generalized description of the culture being investigated. Most field research in cultural anthropology is problem oriented in that it seeks to accumulate information that will be useful in solving or at least casting light on a specific theoretical issue. Problem orientation is a legacy of earlier fieldworkers such as Margaret Mead, who was one of the first to realize that general descriptions are of limited use in the formulation and testing of sociocultural theories. In any case, total descriptions are impossible to achieve. All cultures are infinitely complex, and all descriptions entail theoretical assumptions on the part of the researcher even though they may be unstated or even unconscious.

My original purpose in going to Amatlán was to analyze Nahua magico–religious beliefs and practices in relation to ecological adaptation and economizing behavior. The goal was to explain as much of the ritual and symbolic system as possible with reference to its effect upon and derivation from horticultural practices and other production activities and the ways villagers chose to allocate their scarce resources.

I found that much of Nahua behavior in Amatlán could be understood in terms of social and economic exchange and that even rituals were viewed by the villagers as a form of exchange between humans and spirit entities. These initial findings formed the basis of my doctoral dissertation.

The work presented here develops from that original research program. Before stating my present aims, however, I would like to explain the scientific problems I plan to examine and provide the context for the approach that will clarify these problems. What follows, therefore, is a summary; most of the issues presented will be considered in greater detail later in the book. A key question underlying this study is how and why do traditional cultures persist in the face of massive worldwide change? Traditional cultures the world over have risen to meet the challenge of modernization, industrialization, and Westernization, and, just like many Indian groups in Mexico, they have managed to survive to a remarkable degree. Before the crash of the international oil market in 1982, Mexico had one of the fastest growing economies in the world. Yet thousands of villages like Amatlán persist all over the country. In this book I will examine the part that villagers themselves have played in maintaining their cultural identity.

In attempting to understand the persistence of traditional cultures, I am led to consider other related questions. How do communities like Amatlán fit into the nation as a whole? What role do they play in national life? As we will see later in this chapter, anthropologists and other social scientists have struggled to understand the place of the Indian community in rapidly developing Mexico (and the persistence of traditional communities in other parts of the world). Often traditional peoples survive as subjugated minorities, ruthlessly exploited by a dominant group. Why do villagers perpetuate traditions and lifestyles that can be used to justify exploitation? How are Indian communities organized to perpetuate traditional culture? What features of village life encourage the continuance of tradition, and how do villagers insulate themselves from outside influence? The issues involved are extremely complex, and there is little agreement among experts on how to clarify them. Finally, how are certain features of village life distorted by social, political, and economic forces that originate at the regional, national, and international levels? Even the most remote village is linked to the rest of the world by a network of ties and must respond to forces generated outside itself.

None of these questions admit of easy answers. The most I can hope to accomplish in a single study is to clarify some of the key issues and suggest fruitful appoaches to the problems. Two conclusions from my study of Amatlán must be kept in mind from the start, however. Although these conclusions may appear self-evident, I believe that many scholars have failed to grasp them and that this failure has contributed to the difficulties of understanding the place of the traditional community in Mexico. The first is that the villagers are quite capable of acting rationally on their own behalf. There is no need to invoke blind obedience to strange customs to account for their behavior. This assertion will become clear in the discussion of Nahua farming practices and the relation of the village to the market system. The second conclusion is that Indian culture is neither static nor opposed to change, and in fact many changes in village life have been self-generated and achieved through traditional means. But if the villagers make rational decisions and they are not opposed to change, how do we explain the persistence of traditional cultures within a modern nation-state?

I believe that we can make progress in understanding the enduring presence of Indian communities in Mexico (and traditional communities throughout the world) by focusing on the processes by which ethnic groups are forged and maintained. Traditional cultures like that of the Nahuas often exist as ethnic enclaves within larger nation-states. In a sense, ethnicity is the response of a group of people to the threats and opportunities they face in a world they do not control. People are motivated to create and maintain an ethnic identity for specific reasons. I will examine Nahua ethnicity to find out how being a Nahua in a nation of non-Nahuas confers advantages upon the inhabitants of Amatlán.

I will discuss the concept of ethnicity in the next chapter, but here it suffices to state that ethnicity clearly has to do with culture and differentiation. Members of ethnic groups consider themselves to be culturally distinct from other groups. Of necessity, ethnicity is based on contrast and requires at least two groups to have any real meaning. Ethnic identity emerges, then, where two or more groups interact with each other on the basis of perceived cultural differences. In some cases ethnicity is ascribed to people against their will by the members of a dominant group, although in fact there has been no previously established ethnic identity. It is rare, however, for the subordinate group to remain passive in this circumstance, and in most instances members of suppressed populations will respond by developing an ethnic identity. In this book I am not directly concerned with ascribed ethnicity, although I will return to the topic in the concluding chapter. I am more interested in showing how and why a group in a population creates an identity by which it distinguishes itself from other groups.

Nahua culture as it exists today undoubtedly derives from processes of ethnicity that have their origin in the colonial period. Ethnic identity was also important in pre-Hispanic Mexico, but the cataclysm of the Conquest altered forever the old social arrangements. Nevertheless, the Nahuas possess a culture that is based to a large extent on traditions tracing back to the pre-Hispanic era. Like all ethnic groups, the Nahuas often define themselves in contrast to other groups and in particular to the Hispanically oriented and dominant mestizos (see Chapter 2). Nahuas differ culturally from mestizos in a number of important ways, including language, motor habits, living arrangements, technology, and most significantly, religion. When in public, however, a man communicates his identity through his striking white costume, tire-tread sandals, and sheathed steel machete hung at his side. A woman proclaims her Indian identity with her spectacularly embroidered blouse, colorful skirt, and strips of bright cloth braided into her hair. These symbols say, "I am an Indian" to all the world and yet, paradoxically, every one of these items is of Hispanic origin. This fact implies that Indian culture is not a simple survival of pre-Hispanic traditions in remote villages. Rather it suggests that Indian identity is actively and creatively pursued by villagers, that it is a rational response to the conditions of their lives.

It is instructive to examine what the Nahuas of Amatlán choose *not* to use as an ethnic marker. As we will see in Chapter 6, Nahua religion is quite distinct from what most North Americans and most mestizos would recognize as standard Roman Catholicism. Nahua religious beliefs and practices derive largely from pre-Hispanic traditions and thus set the Nahuas apart from mestizos. Yet villagers are careful to identify themselves to outsiders as Catholics. Villagers clearly recognize the distinction between their own religion and standard Catholicism, and still they call themselves Catholics. In fact the one clear test of whether an individual is an Indian or mestizo is whether or not the person participates in traditional rituals. There are historical and political reasons why Indians do not wish to identify as non-Catholics, but the point I want to make is that villagers make an active choice in the symbols of their ethnic status. They are not passively carrying forward fragments of some remote pre-Hispanic past.

The core of this work is a description of selected aspects of life in Amatlán. Following a venerable anthropological tradition I will trace the effect of macroscopic forces originating on the national and international levels on the lives of real people. I will chart village-level responses to the social forces of our time as well as the great cataclysms of history. I will examine how the Nahuas of Amatlán respond to their place in Mexico and the world. In my description I will attempt to link specific features of village life to the strategies the people have developed to forge and maintain their identity as Nahuas. Finally, I will document recent changes that have overtaken the village, changes that threaten the status quo and promise to undermine Nahua identity. I will show, for example, how the workings of the Nahua political and kinship systems are subverted by a land shortage imposed by outside forces. In my descriptions of village life, I will not attempt to distinguish in a systematic way pre-Hispanic features from those that were imported by the Spaniards. As we have just seen, in establishing their Indian identity the villagers themselves do not seem concerned over questions of aboriginal authenticity.

The majority of data presented here were gathered between 1970 and 1977. These years constitute the ethnographic present of my description of Nahua life in Amatlán. However, each time I return to the field I discover new information, and I increase my total grasp of village life. Thus, although the ethnographic data were collected for the most part in the early- to mid-1970s, they are organized and analyzed according to my most recent understanding of Nahua culture. When I make an observation or present data from the period after 1977 I will specify the years to which the observation or data pertain. Information I gathered after 1977 appears, for the most part, in the last two chapters.

Fieldwork is a never-ending process, and any field report is a temporary resting point in time and space in a continuous struggle to understand cultural processes. Although the focus of this work is a small village of fewer than 600 people, village life—like human life everywhere—is exceedingly complex. Despite the restricted scope of this study, it is an axiom of anthropological research that global processes are best isolated and analyzed as they are reflected in the lives of real people. My work there will never be complete, but I hope that in this endeavor to make sense of the microcosm of Amatlán we may gain an increased understanding of village life and its transformations everywhere.

Several classic ethnographic studies of the Nahuas have been published by anthropologists over the years. Redfield (1930) wrote a well-known community study of the small town of Tepoztlán located near Cuernavaca, in the state of Morelos. In his study he focused on

Tepoztlán as an example of a relatively homogeneous folk community. Lewis (1951) provoked a debate within anthropology with his restudy of Tepoztlán in which he disputed many of Redfield's interpretations of Nahua culture. Madsen (1960) studied San Francisco Tecospa, a small Nahua community near Mexico City and was able to connect many practices and beliefs he documented with those recorded in the ethnohistorical literature. Nutini has written a number of detailed studies of highly Hispanicized Nahua communities in the state of Tlaxcala focusing on kinship (1968), ritual kinship (with Bell 1980, and 1984), and the religious observance of All Saints (1988).

Montoya Briones (1964) published a study of the Nahua community of Atla located in the Sierra Norte de Puebla (in Puebla state), an area adjacent to the Huasteca region and Amatlán. He describes a conservative community in which many beliefs had survived, sometimes in modified form, from the pre-Hispanic era. Chamoux (1981b) has written a community study of Teopixca, a Nahua village located near the city of Huauchinango in the Sierra Norte de Puebla. She examines Nahua identity in the context of Indian–mestizo interaction and shows how being an Indian is functional for individuals on a number of levels. Focusing on Indian communities also located in the northern Sierra de Puebla, Taggart has produced studies of Nahua kinship (1975b) and gender relations as reflected in oral narratives (1983). He found that kinship is an important factor in Nahua social organization and that gender relations are affected by historic as well as socioeconomic factors. Nutini and Isaac have written a survey of contemporary Nahua communities in the Tlaxcala–Puebla region (1974), and Madsen (1969) summarizes what is known about Nahua Indians in general.

Very little work has been published on Nahuas of the Huasteca. Provost (1975) has written a dissertation on the village of Tizal in the southern Huasteca in which he analyzes Nahua cultural principles. My own dissertation (1975) focused on the interpretation of Nahua ritual in Amatlán. Reyes García published a study of Carnival in a Huastecan Nahua community (1960) and has summarized features of Nahua culture in the region (1976). This listing does not exhaust the published works on contemporary Nahua culture, but it gives an idea of the range of studies undertaken. My work in Amatlán adds to the published research on the Nahuas by presenting information on a highly traditional community that has managed to retain its Indian identity to a high degree. Amatlán shares many cultural features with other Nahua communities reported upon by researchers, but the small village study remains relatively rare in anthropological scholarship on Mexico. My work in Amatlán is intended to help fill this gap in our knowledge and add a further dimension to our scientific understanding of Nahua culture during a period of rapid change.

ANTHROPOLOGY AND THE STUDY OF CULTURE

The study of Nahua ethnicity is, in the end, about culture and about how culture persists and is transformed. In this section, therefore, I will briefly discuss the concept of culture along with some of the methods and motivations that have guided anthropological research. Culture in its anthropological sense is the evolving totality of learned behavior, ideas, and values shared by members of social groups. The first scientific formulation of the concept of culture was made in the latter part of the nineteenth century by the early English anthropologist Edward B. Tylor. The concept was used to help explain what the Europeans of the day regarded as the exotic or quaint practices of foreign peoples. The concept of culture took on a new significance in this century when trained scholars began to conduct on-site field research and publish reliable information on non-Western peoples. Although nothing about anthropology required that researchers restrict their studies to non-Western peoples, the discipline developed that reputation early and retains it to this day. The purpose of cross-cultural study was (and is) to obtain a better sample of the range of human behavior so that social scientific theories will be objective and universal in scope. For this purpose all cultures are equally valid expressions of human nature, and thus all cultures contribute equally to our increasing understanding of human conduct.

The early contact that fieldworkers had with people from alien cultural traditions paid unforeseen dividends. Fieldworkers returned home with a whole new level of respect for traditional cultures. Often arrogantly dismissed by other Western scholars, traditional cultures proved to be coherent, complex, and often elegant solutions to the problems of being human. Long-term immersion in foreign cultures led early scholars to improve our understanding of the phenomenon of culture itself. It led to the creation of powerful new concepts that elucidate sociocultural systems. Equally important, it caused social scientists to view our own cultural system in a new light, to view the familiar as strange and thus render it amenable to analysis. How else would we know that most Anglo-Americans use an Eskimo-type kinship terminology or that a wedding is a rite of passage?

The research method most used by anthropologists is called participant observation. It requires that the researcher live among the people
being studied and that he or she participate in daily life while at the
same time making systematic observations. It may sound easy but it
is not. The project is long term, usually over 1 year, it involves learning
the native language, and it means living a life that is unfamiliar and
not always pleasant. Fieldwork is hard work in an alien context. But
that is the whole point; to let the newness of the situation work its
magic and allow the researcher to see what even the people living the
culture often cannot.

Participant observation is a general approach to social research that
is composed of a variety of specific methodologies. Fieldworkers must
undergo training to learn such techniques as mapping, using aerial
photography, census taking, conducting structured and unstructured
interviews, linguistic analysis, administration of psychological tests,
sampling techniques for all types of observations, eliciting kinship
data, and using a variety of equipment such as still and movie cameras
and tape recorders in data gathering. There are also several techniques
for eliciting highly specialized kinds of cultural information. These
include the creation and administration of questionnaires (if the field
situation allows it) and highly developed procedures for gathering data
on cognitive categories. The most successful field projects use a variety
of these techniques both to retrieve new data and to check earlier
observations. Many books have appeared in recent years on the subject
of methods and techniques in anthropological research, including Bernard 1988, Collier 1967, Naroll and Cohen 1973, Pelto and Pelto 1978,
Spradley 1979, 1980, Vogt, 1974, and Werner and Schoepfle 1987.

In participant observation, the trained fieldworker is the instrument
of research, and herein lies a problem. Culture is pervasive and largely
unconscious in human beings, and this includes the researcher. Therefore the researcher brings to the field a set of orientations and values
that affect the information being gathered. In addition, the fieldworker
is trained in the Western scientific tradition that in turn will affect the
selection of data gathered. This is a problem faced by all sciences, but
it is particularly acute in cross-cultural studies. Many techniques have
been developed to lessen the influence of the observer upon the data
he or she finds, but no complete solution to the problem exists. When
reading this account of the Nahuas it should never be forgotten that
I am giving my own version of their culture. What I have written is
probably not identical to what the Nahuas themselves would have
written, but, on the other hand, they do not have the advantage of

being outsiders and hence of being somewhat objective about their own culture.

Despite the many advantages of participant observation in contributing to a scientific understanding of culture, it would be misleading to imply that ethnographic fieldwork in anthropology is motivated solely by intellectual curiosity or the desire to obtain a better sample of the range of human behavior. There is a less tangible factor involved that affects the kinds of information retrieved and the development of explanatory theories in anthropology. Fieldwork has a mystique and romance about it that can transcend its scientific purpose.

Most cultural anthropologists are partially motivated by a sense of adventure in travel and in living in circumstances that are out of the ordinary. Perhaps it is a legacy from the earliest fieldworkers who often caused a sensation when they returned home with information about faraway peoples. But the image of the intrepid explorer meeting strange new peoples is also a theme in Euro-American history and strikes a chord in contemporary popular culture. Both true and fictionalized accounts of expeditions into the unknown provide themes for movies, television shows, books, and magazines and are always popular fare among the public. Cultural anthropology is part of that adventure-seeking tradition and has even helped to define it.

Ethnographic fieldwork based on participant observation provides the romantic mystique that tantalizes anthropologists and the general public alike. We imagine the lone scientist living in some remote mountain or jungle village interviewing people about esoteric aspects of rituals or kinship. Margaret Mead in Samoa, Bronislaw Malinowski in the Trobriands, and Franz Boas among the Eskimos give cultural anthropologists a self-definition and job description that separates them from generalized social science. The experience of fieldwork is considered a necessary rite of passage for students before they can legitimately claim to be professional anthropologists. In the wake of cutbacks of funds supporting research during the 1980s, this criterion of professionalism is weakening, but it is still strong.

Part of the negative results of this romantic side of ethnographic fieldwork is an inclination to emphasize the more exotic discoveries or the behavior that deviates most from familiar Western practices. Here is one reason why anthropological accounts often stress ritual cannibalism, food taboos, matrilineality, blood sacrifice, and bizarre sexual practices. These are interesting customs calling out for description and explanation, but they can overshadow everyday behavior that may be less dramatic but more important scientifically. Although it is true that one of the contributions anthropology can make is to document the complete range of human behavior (hence justifying the stress on the exotic), the overall goal of the discipline is identical to that of all social sciences: to propose and test scientific explanations for human behavior.

The romance of fieldwork in anthropology is thus a necessary part of the discipline, but it can interfere with its scientific mission. It is part of the "cultural baggage" brought along with the fieldworker mentioned earlier. But critics of the participant-observation method and of cross-cultural studies in general often have a false view of ethnographic fieldwork and of all science. Anthropological fieldwork is a systematic attempt to gather information on another culture. It is the search for cultural data that can be verified or falsified by others. Wherever possible information is quantified, photographed, taped, or video recorded. The fieldworker is faced with a chaos of information coming in bits and pieces, and it is his or her task to propose a way to construct a version of the culture in a coherent fashion. No scientific presentation should be considered the final word on a subject. Ethnography, like all science, produces a tentative formulation subject to revision, and it is self-correcting through critical evaluation by peers.

The aura that surrounds ethnographic fieldwork is a key to understanding a core value of contemporary cultural anthropology. Fieldwork is an adventure, and it has its moments of high drama. It involves hardship and the thrill of discovery, both central elements in stories and myths. Most of all, it is an experience with deep psychological and emotional implications that can change the life of the fieldworker. The relationship between the researcher and his or her subjects in participant observation is unique in all the social sciences. The people being studied become friends or at least allies in the study of their own culture. Attachments formed in the field are particularly intense and often last a lifetime. In the end, most fieldworkers develop a strong admiration for the people and the culture they have come to know so intimately. Leaving the field can be far more traumatic than entering it. It is small wonder that fieldwork itself is surrounded by stories and myth.

None of this invalidates ethnographic information nor the methods by which it is collected. The fieldworker must become personally involved in the research because of the nature of the methods being used. Separating out various sources of bias is a problem to be faced and cannot be avoided by simply depersonalizing the data collecting techniques. Anthropologists learn techniques of objective observation as part of their training, and like all scientists they succeed to varying degrees. What is important is that anthropologists' cultural accounts are documented and open to correction and that readers of their work are aware of the problems of human beings studying human beings.

MY INTRODUCTION TO THE NAHUAS

My first encounter with the Nahuas occurred in the summer of 1970. It is a meeting I shall never forget. At the time I was a graduate student in anthropology, and I was chosen to participate in a pilot field school in Mexico. I was not particularly enthusiastic because Mexico was not a major interest of mine, but I was anxious to experience fieldwork and the thrill of getting to know an alien culture firsthand. The director of the project was a firm believer in the "sink-or-swim" method of field training, and thus it did not trouble him that I spoke very little Spanish and not a word of Nahuatl.

There were four graduate students selected to go to Mexico, and we were each to be placed in Indian villages widely separated from each other in the remote reaches of northern Veracruz. Once every 2 weeks we were scheduled to meet in a small, centrally located market town to discuss our progress and problems. No matter that maps of the region did not exist, that there was no communication in or out of the area, or that most of the people had seen few foreigners before. Our group assembled in the city of Xalapa, capital of Veracruz state, for a final round of preparatory seminars and to obtain the official permissions necessary to travel into the rural areas. We departed by bus a week later and traveled toward the north all night, arriving in the frontier oil town of Poza Rica the next morning. We transferred to an overcrowded third-class bus with little intact flooring and no glass in the windows for the trip to the interior. After leaving paved roads, we crossed the broad Río Pantepec on a rickety ferry and left urban civilization behind.

The bus bounced over the ruts for hours as the tropical sun turned the vehicle into an oven. We passed through streams and flooded areas left by the seasonal rains as the road deteriorated into a trail. I began to feel a mild panic that we were getting too far into the interior where escape would be no easy matter. After several hours most of the remaining passengers were Indians heading back to their villages after attending to some business in town. It was amusing to see people board and do double takes as they first caught a glimpse of the group of dirty and exhausted Anglos in their midst. At midafternoon the bus lurched to a stop, unable to pass a quagmire created by the previous rain. We grabbed our equipment and proceeded on foot as the bus slowly turned around and abandoned us. The other passengers, accustomed to such inconveniences, disappeared into the forest carrying their belongings.

We slowly trudged along in the broiling heat, catching an occasional glimpse of a thatch-roofed Indian house in the forest. Smaller trails led off into the brush on either side, but we stayed on the main road, hoping to reach the tiny market town of Ixhuatlán de Madero by nightfall. It was at this inopportune moment that several of us experienced equipment failure. One colleague broke a thong on her hiking sandal and had to proceed barefooted. The strap on my backpack snapped, turning the pack into an awkward bundle that was extremely difficult to carry. Actually, I was glad it happened because the straps had cut deeply into my shoulders and I could not have endured them much longer anyway. We walked for 3 hours before reaching the Río Vinazco. We arrived overheated, injured, and deeply fatigued. I was absolutely amazed at how quickly we had become truly miserable and demoralized. But then our luck changed.

As we sat at the river's edge, wondering how we would get to the other side of its broad expanse, a man approached and offered to pole us across in his dugout canoe. The trip across was death defying as the canoe dipped and spun in the raging current. Once across we faced a 3-hour walk to our destination. After we had traversed about half of the distance, a pickup truck from a local cattle ranch stopped to offer us a ride. We gladly accepted and arrived in Ixhuatlán at dark. We found room in the only boarding house in town, and by that time even the plank bed looked wonderfully inviting. But sleep was not to be ours that night. A local meeting of rural schoolteachers turned into a riotous party that lasted until dawn.

The next morning, after gathering information and necessary permissions from local authorities, our director took the other 3 students and accompanied them in search of likely villages for their research. I remained in town with his Mexican wife that day, awaiting his return. The director arrived that evening, and the next morning the three of us departed along the road we had traveled the day before. They had planned to return that evening and so carried no equipment with them. Only I was burdened with my defective pack and a carrying bag. Our destination was Amatlán, a Nahua village listed by the Ixhuatlán authorities and suggested by state anthropologists back in Xalapa as a representative village of its type. Although no one had studied Amatlán or any villages in the vicinity, a Mexican anthropologist had passed nearby while on an exploratory mission in the mid-1950s (Medellín Zenil 1979, 1982). He reported that Amatlán appeared to be laid out in the pre-Hispanic pattern and that pre-Hispanic statues were still being venerated in neighboring villages. This was certainly intriguing information. As we walked along that day it suddenly occurred to me that the villagers may have managed to maintain their fascinating traditions by rejecting all intrusions by strangers.

The fieldschool director and his wife assumed background positions and forced me to handle any eventualities that arose. We met very few people as we walked but whenever we did, I asked directions to Amatlán. What I did not know at the time is that people in this region have a complex attitude toward direct questions. If they do not know the answer to a question, they consider it rude to say so. Rather than insult the questioner they will simply tell the person what they think he or she wants to hear. Once you become aware of this practice, it is fairly easy to determine that the person you are asking is groping for the answer to your question. The slight hesitation or the overly enthusiastic response are dead giveaways. But at the time I was unaware of this custom, and so I tended to believe what people told me. At one man's suggestion we turned into the forest near the river and were instantly engulfed by an eerie green silence.

According to our last informant, Amatlán was supposed to be about 15 minutes along this particular trail. After walking for half an hour we began to grow anxious. Tropical forest trails are not as idyllic as one might imagine them to be. Rather than sunny thoroughfares, they are more like narrow tunnels—branching, labyrinthine, dark, and suffocating tunnels that make retracing your steps an impossibility. We longed to meet somebody again to ask directions but then, with bitter irony, I reflected, "what good would that do?" We had been walking for 6 hours at this point, since leaving Ixhuatlán that morning. The temperature was over 100 degrees, and the humidity was stifling. We came upon a rushing stream that cut across the trail. Removing shoes and socks we carefully picked our way across the slippery bottom. In the next hour we crossed a total of six such streams, some of them almost waist deep.

Two hours after we had entered the forest we were all becoming panicked. We had not seen a single house or human being on the trail. Evening was approaching, and none of us relished a night alone in the forest. It was with some relief then that I spotted a small board attached to a tree with the words "Comunidad de Amatlán." I later learned that the village schoolmaster had placed the sign there so that visitors would not get lost. My relief was immediately tempered by the thought of the next problem, namely what should I say to the people I was about to encounter. I had rehearsed this moment in my mind a hundred times, but all of that left me as we walked on, soaking wet from the stream crossings, filthy dirty, thirsty, and exhausted.

The trail led to a cleared area in the forest with four horses grazing on the thick tangled grass. At the far end of the clearing were some small low buildings with mossy ceramic-tile roofs. Nearby was a larger building with a corrugated iron roof, undoubtedly the schoolhouse. In the thick forest that surrounded the clearing, I could see Indian houses with tall, peaked thatched roofs. The atmosphere smelled of cooking fires, and a haze of smoke hung over the forest. Dogs began to bark and the horses started, but so far not a soul was in evidence.

We approached the school buildings, but no one appeared to greet us. Finally, I sat on my pack and waited as my companions left to wash and cool off in a nearby stream. I began to wonder if the village had recently been abandoned. In about half an hour a small man dressed in dazzling white and carrying a Collins machete with a 30-inch blade in a dark leather sheath appeared at the edge of the forest. He approached me with determination in his step, and I began to get an uneasy feeling. I stood erect as he walked up to me. He looked at me and said in broken Spanish, "What are you doing here?" I must admit at that moment I was not sure of the answer, and the canned response I had rehearsed seemed totally out of place. I told him that I had come from the United States to ask permission to live in Amatlán for a while in order to study the customs of the people there. I said that I was interested in studying how corn is grown and how houses are built. None of this made the slightest impression on him. Finally, I got lucky when I added that I want to study Nahuatl so that I could talk to people. He perked up and said, "You want to learn Nahuatl?" I said yes and handed him the letter of introduction from the local authorities. He held it upside down, examined the official seal, and then turned around and walked back into the forest.

Five minutes later the man reappeared leading several dozen men, each wearing the traditional white tunic and pants and carrying a sheathed machete. Apparently they had retreated into the forest to observe our approach. They surrounded me and my companions, who had just returned from the stream, and the man, who was seemingly the village leader, asked why I wanted to learn Nahuatl. I explained that I wanted to learn the language so that I could talk to people and that many Mexicans speak Nahuatl and that therefore it is an important language to learn. It did not make any sense to me either, but the headman repeated it in Nahuatl and the men entered into discussion among themselves. I could not tell how it was going, but I did notice that it was getting dark. Darkness comes fast in the tropics, and the night is remarkably black a hundred miles from the nearest electric lights. The headman asked what I had in the pack and indicated that the crowd wanted to see. I opened it and everyone examined the contents, passing my things around amid intense discussion.

Admittedly I did not have much of interest or value having lightened my load several times in the previous three days. But I did not like the feeling of having a group of strangers passing my possessions around and discussing them in a language I did not understand. Apparently they could see that I was getting anxious, and everyone carefully handed the things back to me. At this point I did not know what to do next. I know that if it had been possible for me to leave and to return to the United States at that moment I would have done it. I wondered why I was there and whether I was cut out for this work. I was miserable and wanted everyone to leave me alone, and yet I was the one who had come to Amatlán. I had intruded on these people, and I resented them for it. At that black moment four figures mounted on horseback emerged from the forest and headed in our direction.

It was the schoolmaster and his wife and sons returning from the market. I witnessed yet another classic double take as they rode over. They introduced themselves and asked what we were doing there. I explained, and then the headman, the schoolmaster, and several other men held a conference. The schoolmaster read the letter of introduction to the assembled men and a brief conversation ensued. They decided that I could spend the night in one room of the two-room schoolhouse because school was out of session for the summer. My companions were to sleep in an abandoned hut attached to the school. They opened the door to the schoolhouse and I carried my pack inside. The room was small, but it had a stone floor and would do for one night. I made no arrangements for obtaining a more permanent residence nor for having food prepared because I was firmly committed to the plan of leaving the next day, never to return. As I was trying to unpack by flashlight, the schoolmaster carried in a makeshift cot made of burlap bags. He said casually that I probably should not sleep on the floor because of the tarantulas and scorpions. The blackness seemed to close around me as I gratefully accepted the cot.

As I sat there trying to think of alternative careers for myself, I realized how completely exhausted I was. I had gotten drinking water from the schoolmaster's wife, and I could actually sweat again. The heat was oppressive and took away any desire for food. Sleep was all I could think of when out of the darkness more than 100 men, every one of them carrying a machete, crowded into the small schoolroom and stood there silently. I lighted a small candle stub I found and tried to assume a casual air as I arranged and rearranged my things. Finally I took a risk and announced that I was tired and that I was going to sleep. There was a pause, and then one man repeated my statement in Nahuatl. A conversation broke out, and the headman approached holding out his hand. I grabbed it thinking that a vigorous handshake was in order. His hand withdrew rapidly and went for the black machete handle at his side. He came forward again and indicated that a proper handshake is to touch fingertips lightly. The men lined up, and I touched everyone's fingers in the proper manner. They all laughed, said "tomorrow" in Nahuatl, and left. I had just had my first lesson in Nahua etiquette.

That night it rained so hard that I thought the building would collapse. The beating on the tin roof was like the roar of a locomotive, and the lightning and thunder were spectacular. At dawn the headman came and stood outside of my door without making a sound. This was another lesson in Nahua protocol, and it was only by accident that I happened to open the door to find him there. Nahua visitors do not make their presence known right away in order to avoid interrupting the household they are visiting. I later developed the skill to be able to tell when someone was silently waiting outside. I learned that my companions had left several hours before in the pre-dawn hours without telling me. I remember feeling abandoned and alone. The headman asked for the packets of rice and beans I had brought with me. He placed them in his carrying bag and then invited me to follow him to his house. I could barely keep up with him on the trail even though I was a foot taller than he was. Upon arriving at his house I was treated to more Nahua hospitality—a special tiny visitor's chair set out for guests.

As several women prepared food over a smoky fire, the headman said that there would be a meeting of the village household heads that evening to decide whether or not I could remain. In the meantime he offered to have food prepared for me and to show me where it was safe to bathe in the arroyo that nearly encircles Amatlán. He wanted to know how long I intended to stay. I did not know what to say, but I heard my voice respond two months. The previous night I had planned to leave immediately, but that morning I realized that I was not in physical shape to face the long trail back loaded with my supplies and equipment. I needed some time to recover and besides, where would I go? I decided to give it a few days to see what developed. The interaction was somewhat friendly but formal and guarded. It was clear they did not know what to make of me, but I was grateful that the headman had set about solving the problem of my living arrangements.

I spent the day in the vicinity of the schoolhouse. It was not necessary for me to wander throughout the village to meet people because everyone seemed to have business on my front porch that day. At first I thought it was some kind of meeting, but I soon realized that I was the attraction. It was interesting being the center of attention for about the first hour, but then it became a burden. There was lots of laughing and staring and a few unsatisfying attempts at interaction, but it was exhausting trying to communicate across the language and culture barriers. Finally I decided to close the door and go to the arroyo to bathe. To my horror most of the crowd followed me and sat on shore to watch the proceedings. This lack of privacy was to prove one of the most difficult aspects of fieldwork and one to which I never quite became accustomed. In any event, the crowd was friendly, and they only cast occasional glances in my direction.

That evening men slowly gathered in the clearing in front of the schoolhouse. They were the heads of households meeting to discuss my case, and I counted 110 individuals who showed up. The meeting was yet another lesson in Nahua culture. There appeared to be no organization nor any formal procedures being followed. As some men lounged around holding private conversations, others stood up and spoke with no one seeming to listen. Sometimes two or three men would stand and speak simultaneously. The audience remained inattentive, even when the headman rose and held up the letter of introduction. After about 45 minutes of seeming pandemonium, most of the men got up and drifted away as slowly as they arrived. I was convinced there was a serious problem regarding my case, and I made mental preparations to leave on the following day. The crowd dispersed, leaving only a few hangers-on smoking homemade cigars engaged in quiet conversation. An hour later the headman and several other men came to break the news. They informed me that it was decided unanimously that I could stay, and that furthermore I could continue my residence in the schoolhouse. A widow was found who agreed to cook for me for the wage of 50 pesos (then $4 U.S.) per week. I also learned that several other important items of business were decided that night, all by unanimous vote.

The surprise decision meant that I could stay if I wanted. The big question remaining now was, Did I want to? Over the next few days as I developed a routine and as I was able to explore the village and surrounding area, I developed a curiosity about Amatlán that was to prove decisive. What was going on beneath the placid exterior of this place? The village was dotted with pre-Hispanic ruins covered with thick undergrowth. What was their history? I could see that the village was arranged in groupings of beautiful thatch-roofed houses scattered widely in the tropical forest. How was the village organized? What were the people like, and how did they see the world? It was like an enticing mystery waiting to be solved. After a few weeks the mystery deepened as I discovered flower-covered shrines built over freshwater springs in the forest. Once, while going to bathe, I surprised two men standing in the arroyo holding candles. Standing between them was a naked 10-year-old boy, and one man was rubbing his back with smooth stones from the water. What were they up to? I stayed on 2 months and vowed as I left to come back to the village as soon as possible.

The pilot field school was never funded, and so no further expeditions have been sent into the region. I returned to Amatlán for over a year in 1972–73 to conduct research for my doctoral dissertation and again for several shorter periods in subsequent years. In 1985–86, I went back to Amatlán for 1 year, this time accompanied both by my wife and 3-year-old child. Finally, the three of us spent several months in the village in the spring of 1990. The outcome of an initial field encounter with people from an alien culture hinges on many factors. The personalities of the local leaders, whether or not there has been recent political infighting, and the availability of housing are all circumstances outside of the control of the fieldworker. Success takes perseverance to be sure, but luck plays a major role. It is impossible to develop the natural curiosity that is necessary to conduct field research if living arrangements cannot be made or if the initial experience in the field site is overwhelmingly negative. Of the four graduate students to participate in the pilot project I was the only one to return to the region.

THE INCIDENT AT CHOTE

The following case study provides an introduction to some of the features of village life to be described and analyzed in later chapters.

It dramatically illustrates the deep divisions that can tear apart the social fabric of even remote villages. The incident reveals the dangerous passions that can be aroused as national and international issues become linked to local conflicts and are fought out among villagers. Most of all the tragedy at Chote brings out into the open what is often obscured. The incident vividly demonstrates the subordinate position of the Indian village in the nation and world.

In early 1977, Pedro Martínez from Amatlán was murdered as he walked with a friend to the distant town of Ixhuatlán de Madero. I was not in the village at the time of the killing, but I was able to piece together what had happened by interviewing witnesses and participants in the events surrounding the tragedy. By luck I was able to read the sentencing document prepared by the judge who heard the case and so had access to the findings of the official investigation. The court document was written in Spanish, the language of the trial, and it contained quoted testimonies of the defendants and witnesses. I present this case for what it reveals about village dynamics in the politico–economic realm. A traumatic event such as this reveals what is often hidden and brings to the foreground what lies just out of sight and consciousness. Small villages often are the stages upon which life and death struggles are enacted, the ultimate causes of which derive from national-level political and economic forces far removed from the awareness and scrutiny of the actors in the local drama.

When I first entered Amatlán, I was struck by its isolation and almost idyllic serenity. With no electricity or motorized vehicles, and with the dense forest muffling every sound, life seemed peaceful and calm, quite unlike the often raucous chaos of daily existence in a Mexican city or town. I knew about the violence of the colonial era with its genocidal reduction of Indian populations. I also knew about the brutality that led up to the Mexican Revolution, and the unbelievable devastation it produced in the cities and countryside. I was aware that city newspapers often reported on contemporary violent struggles over land in the southern Huasteca. But all of that seemed far away from village life where peaceful afternoons were only disturbed by a single high-flying jet that the Indians said was loaded with gringos going to Mexico City. It was only after several months in residence that I began to realize how much violence and fear form a part of villagers' lives.

The incident directly involved five men, but in the end most people in the village became participants. At the center of the action was Pedro Martínez, a well-proportioned young man with a handsome face. Pedro was a leader with a quick mind who never shrank from a fight. Quietly confident, he was a compelling speaker who could produce in his listeners the same outrage at perceived injustice that he felt so strongly himself. To his enemies he was a troublemaker; to his allies he was perceptive and courageous. I often saw him walking with one of his children on the way to market or to visit with friends. His brother, Gregorio, shared Pedro's quick mind and striking appearance, but he projected more of an air of aggressiveness. His temper flared at the hint of insult, and he seemed to be hiding a grudge or some deep personal injury. He possessed a charismatic personality and took great pride in being an Indian farmer. He had much energy and provided well for his family.

The third protagonist was Lorenzo Hernández, a man of about 35 years with a stocky build and the air of a man accustomed to command. I knew Lorenzo better than the others, and I found him to be somewhat grim but highly intelligent and quick-witted. He was very friendly to me, but at the same time he struck me as someone who would make a dangerous adversary. He was politically minded and a prominent sponsor of village rituals. Of all the people I knew in Amatlán, Lorenzo was the most direct in his speech and at times he appeared almost brusque. He was one of those people of powerful personality who can intimidate with a look and who does not mind pointing out to people when they have made a mistake. The last two men involved in the incident played relatively minor roles. One, a teenage boy named Martín, accompanied Pedro on that fatal morning. Martín was a quiet person, accustomed to being in the background. I had the impression that he joined Pedro Martínez's group because of the attention he received from the older men rather than from commitment to any political cause. The final figure is Lorenzo's nephew, a man I knew quite well and who, in this case, seemed to be a victim of circumstance.

Pedro Martínez held the village office of Presidente del Consejo de Vigilancia at the time of his death. The Consejo de Vigilancia is a committee of local men elected to oversee village affairs and to insure that the will of the majority is carried out by officials. Pedro's brother Gregorio occupied the important village post of Presidente del Comisariado Ejidal during this period. The Comisariado Ejidal is a committee that oversees important aspects of village internal affairs particularly as they relate to land issues (see Chapter 4 for a more detailed explanation of these committees and their officers). Under normal circumstances, having brothers occupy important village offices tends to smooth local operations. In this case, however, the two brothers were deadly enemies who often fought in the presence of others.

Pedro was the elder brother and thus had inherited most of the land owned by his father. Land was in short supply, and Gregorio fell into a bitter dispute with his brother over a parcel passed down by their father. Moreover there were political differences between the two brothers. Pedro had worked for a short time in a restaurant in Mexico City and had become active in socialist politics. He returned to Amatlán a confirmed member of the Partido Socialista de los Trabajadores (Socialist Workers Party, or PST), and he began to attract a following among the villagers. Gregorio was a member of the mainstream Partido Revolucionario Institucional (Party of the Institutionalized Revolution, or PRI). One might think that political differences of this type would have little meaning in an Indian village that is so far removed from the centers of national power. In this case, however, the stakes in the battle between the PST and the PRI were more than symbolic.

The self-appointed PRI spokesman in the village was Lorenzo Hernández, whose better than average command of Spanish qualified him to represent people to higher authorities. He formed a faction, which included Gregorio Martínez, composed of men who had no land of their own or who had insufficient land to support a family. He collected money from these men and went to the city to plead with party and government officials that more land be allocated to the people of Amatlán. Bureaucracy in Mexico can be remarkably slow in acting, and the solicitations went on for many years. Initially, Pedro Martínez was a supporter of Lorenzo in his efforts and even became his ritual kinsman when Lorenzo's wife gave birth to a child. Over the years, however, resentment began to grow among villagers, and a rumor circulated that Lorenzo and his friends were stealing the money given to them. On one occasion Lorenzo and two friends were observed eating in a restaurant in the provincial town of Alamo when they were supposed to be in the state capital meeting with PRI officials.

Pedro Martínez became leader of the opposition to Lorenzo's faction, and the stage was set for tragedy. The event that apparently triggered the killing was a dispute over village land distribution. According to law, land is to be distributed evenly among household heads in the village. This law is sometimes circumvented in a number of ways, and Lorenzo was accused by his growing opposition of having more than his share of property. He denied guilt, but Pedro took up the cause and proposed that all land be redistributed evenly in accord with the law. This proposal must have threatened more village land-holders than just Lorenzo, and the controversy, fueled by numerous other rumors, standing disagreements, and outright confrontations, reached the boiling point.

Two versions of what happened predominate, one from Lorenzo Hernández and the other from the victim's brother, Gregorio Martínez. According to Lorenzo, Gregorio became increasingly agitated over the actions of his brother. Following is a translation of Lorenzo's testimony as it was recorded in court documents at his trial for murder. I have edited sections to improve readability.

> Yes, it is true that on various occasions Gregorio Martínez said to me that we should do something to his brother, to kill him, because he is becoming so troublesome. He said this to me because Gregorio was Comisariado Ejidal and Pedro was Consejo de Vigilancia but they were never in accord. Gregorio was PRI and Pedro was PST and they were never in accord in the running of the village.
>
> On Friday the 14th of that month Gregorio came to my house at about 6:30 in the evening. He told me that on the following morning his brother, Pedro, was going to leave to have a meeting with fellow party members. He confided that he feared Pedro was contracting with others to have him killed. He said that he was sick and tired of his brother, that it would be best to get him out of the way, and that he wanted me to accompany him. I figured since Gregorio wanted to kill his own brother that if I went along I would be considered less responsible for what happened than he would. Gregorio asked if I would borrow a gun for him to use. That is why at about 7:00 o'clock that same evening I went to my nephew's house to borrow his shotgun. He only had one cartridge left, and I told him that I would pay for it later if I used it. I told him I wanted the gun to shoot ducks.
>
> The next morning at about 7:00 o'clock Gregorio returned to my house, whistled for me to come outside and meet him, and said that we must go because it was already late. At this time I handed him the shotgun. We hurried to the place called Chote near where the trail goes down a steep decline and hid ourselves in a thicket. In a little while Pedro came walking along with his friend Martín and passed close to us. Gregorio stood up, bending underneath the bushes and shot his brother in the face with the single cartridge. Martín, splattered with Pedro's blood, was dumbstruck and stood there a moment before running away as fast as he could.
>
> Gregorio, seeing that Martín was far away, jumped out of the thicket and went over to his brother who was already dead. So that no one would suspect what happened, Gregorio robbed the body. We left Pedro on the trail, his face torn apart by the shotgun and his blood soaking into the dry earth. Upon returning to the village, Gregorio said that we should go to

our houses and say nothing. I returned the gun to my nephew, and after a while I went to the weekly communal work party that was assembling at the schoolhouse.

Later Martín came to the village and reported where the body was and we all went to Chote. People immediately recognized that the deceased was Pedro, and Gregorio, my nephew, and I became suspects. The police came from Ixhuatlán de Madero and took us to jail. It is true that I confessed to many things in Ixhuatlán but what I said is not what really happened. I was beaten by the police and then dunked in a tank of ice-cold water until I told them what they wanted to hear. The fact is that I was there in the ambush but Gregorio, Pedro's very own brother, was the one who pulled the trigger.

Gregorio's story differs from that of Lorenzo. According to the court document he stated that he did not really know who killed his brother. He claimed that several witnesses could prove that he was at the schoolhouse work party at the time of the murder. Further, he stated that Lorenzo and his brother were deadly enemies and that Lorenzo was vehemently opposed to having the plots of land measured and allocated to each household head. He, too, renounced his earlier confession that he claimed was elicited by police torture. In short, Gregorio turned the suspicion back on Lorenzo even though they were former allies against Pedro and the PST faction.

An investigation was held over the next several months while Lorenzo, his nephew, and Gregorio were held in jail. Martín, the murder victim's companion, refused to testify for fear that the killers or their friends would retaliate. The villagers lined up in their testimony according to which faction they supported. Witnesses swore that Gregorio was at the work party during the murder and that he could not have committed the crime. Others swore that Lorenzo was with them at the time of the murder and that he could not have done it. It was even stated that Lorenzo did not really borrow the shotgun from his nephew. At the end of the initial investigation, the picture was confused and seemingly without resolution. Many villagers were beginning to think that Pedro was killed by gunmen hired by local ranchers. Ranchers were in fact worried that Pedro was succeeding in his efforts to have ranch land redistributed to local Indian villages.

All three men were charged with murder, and a trial was held to determine the varying degrees of responsiblity each had for the crime. A break in the case occurred when Martín was convinced by the police to testify about what he witnessed on the day of the murder. Following is his testimony on the day of the trial that I have translated from the court document. Again, I have edited the statement to improve readability.

> Out of fear I did not testify before about who fired the shot that killed my companion Pedro Martínez. But the truth is as follows: on the day of the crime I accompanied my friend Pedro until we reached the place called Chote. I heard a shot from a shotgun come from our left. My companion fell mortally wounded face up on the trail. From surprise I stopped for a moment and turned toward the place from where the shot came. I can now give account that the man who fired the shot was Lorenzo Hernández. I could see perfectly well because it was daytime and I know him perfectly well. I can say this with no fear of confusing him with someone else. Knowing full well that Lorenzo is an extremely dangerous individual I fled from that place swearing to myself never to reveal who killed Pedro Martínez.
>
> Now I am testifying because the authorities have guaranteed my personal safety. I have decided to tell the truth even though I have fear of being a victim of reprisal. I further state that I saw no companion of Lorenzo at the time of the shooting.

The judge listened to the case and evaluated all of the confusing and contradictory evidence. The judgment was necessarily based on a weighing of various testimonies rather than the attempt to ascertain some absolute truth in the matter. Lorenzo was found guilty of homicide with some extenuating circumstances. He was given 15 years in prison. Both Gregorio and Lorenzo's nephew were absolved of the crime and were freed following the trial. Lorenzo was released from prison after about 9 years, and he returned to Amatlán to resume his life. In fact he returned to the village in 1986 while my family and I were in the field. He invited us to eat at his house "for old time's sake" and informed me that he plans to devote his energies to cultivating his crops and to the celebration of the traditional rituals. He made me ritual kinsman of his 12-year-old son and he confided to me late one night that he did not kill Pedro Martínez.

This murder case even in the simplified version I have presented reflects the complexity and convoluted nature of village politics. More importantly it mirrors some of the dynamics that underlie village life. Paramount among these is the struggle for land. In a sense, competition over land began when the Spaniards first stepped ashore in Veracruz almost half a millenium ago. Even though serious long-term land distribution began after the Mexican Revolution, as this case reveals, the struggle between the Indians and the ranchers and among the Indians themselves is far from over. Land shortage is a problem that permeates village life. Witness the altercation between Pedro and his brother Gregorio over their inheritance. Their animosity may have begun in conflicts they had during their childhoods, but what is interesting is that their enmity is expressed through a heated quarrel over land. Most villagers interpret any fight between brothers as the result of a land dispute. The land shortage that leads to inheritance customs that divide brothers against each other is one of the underlying causes of this and many other tragedies in the southern Huasteca region.

A key feature revealed by this case is the relative helplessness of the village in the face of outside forces. Lorenzo is selected to represent landless villagers because his Spanish is more acceptable to urban lawyers and bureaucrats. The language and culture barrier between Indians and those in positions of power on a national or regional level can be used against the villagers. They are constantly put in a position of pleading or even begging official authorities for considerations that are often their right by law. Notice also how local police and militia are alleged to torture suspects in order to elicit "confessions." The judge in the murder trial casually mentioned the beatings and water torture in his sentencing document with no indication that such things should be halted or even investigated. Occasionally, the marginal position occupied by Indians in Mexican society works in an individual's favor. One reason that Lorenzo was convicted of murder with extenuating circumstances was that the judge noted Lorenzo's "low level of culture," that is, he was "only" an Indian and thus was not to be held fully responsible for his actions. Most often, though, being Indian means powerlessness and third-class citizenship in the eyes of the power elite.

But, paradoxically, there can be a certain power in being powerless, as I will demonstrate in subsequent chapters. Unfortunately the case of Pedro Martínez reveals a key obstacle that prevents villagers from expressing what power they have in an effective manner. Despite their mutual identity as Indians in a hostile world not of their own making, the villagers are divided among themselves. They do not speak with the same voice, and so their message is garbled and undermined by the lack of consensus. As is often the case, violence deriving from social inequality is directed inward, against other victims of an unfair system. The people of Amatlán had to suffer the double agony of having within their community a murder victim and a murderer, not to mention a village hopelessly divided against itself. The struggle was a confrontation between brothers and village factions; small communities almost always fight among themselves over specific local issues. But the pretext of the battle was expressed as a fight between the capitalist PRI and the socialist PST, two political philosophies rooted in urban Mexico and deriving from a European tradition basically alien to the Indians. Village conflicts in Mexico and throughout much of the developing world are increasingly phrased in the idiom of global struggles over abstract philosophical principles. The war between these political systems is really being waged in the national and international arenas, but as the case of Amatlán demonstrates, we are seeing it begin to penetrate small villages far from the centers of urban power. The philosophical issues may be abstract, but injury and death are concrete, and it is often rural villagers who suffer the wounds and do the bleeding (see Wolf 1967:314).

THE VILLAGE IN THE NATION AND THE WORLD

To clarify the dynamics of village life, we must reach an understanding of the place of the Indian community in Mexico. This understanding has proven difficult to achieve. The first problem is in distinguishing Indians from non-Indians. In this section let us call an Indian a person who identifies as an Indian by orienting to cultural systems deriving largely from the pre-Hispanic traditions of Mexico, but, as we have seen, including elements of European origin. I will call mestizos, those people who identify as mestizos by orienting to the national culture, which, although it includes a few elements borrowed from pre-Hispanic traditions, is essentially of Western European origin. More precise definitions along with a discussion of the difficulties of distinguishing these social categories appear in Chapter 2.

Many scholars over the years have attempted to analyze the complex interactions and structural relations among villages of Indians and the regional, national, and international forces that affect them. Virtually the only area of agreement to come out of this effort is that the Indian or so-called peasant populations of Mexico are at a tremendous social, economic, and political disadvantage in their dealings with representatives of the national economy and government. The sometimes contradictory approaches to understanding the place of small agricultural communities in Mexican society that I describe in this section are not simply arid academic exercises. Government policy and even one's political stance on such issues as exploitation, poverty, the global population crisis, human rights, and cultural plurality are determined to a large extent by assumptions about how small agricultural communities relate to individual nations and the world. I include capsule summaries of various of these approaches to focus attention away from the microcosm of village life to see the village's place in the national and international arena.

One of the earliest formulations was proposed by Robert Redfield in the 1940s. Redfield was one of the first anthropologists to focus attention on peasants, and he is well known for his studies conducted in the Nahua town of Tepoztlán and in various communities in the Yucatán peninsula (1930, 1934, 1941, 1950, 1953, and 1960). Basing his insights on the work of earlier social thinkers, notably Maine, Durkheim, and Tönnies, Redfield visualized a folk–urban continuum in which villages, towns, and cities form a developmental series. At one extreme of the sequence are the folk communities like Amatlán, which are isolated, small, homogeneous, and family based. To the people in these "little communities," according to Redfield, the social and natural world is permeated with a sense of the sacred, and the universe is governed by a powerful moral order. At the other end of the continuum are the cities and towns that display opposite character- istics. Moving along the continuum from village to urban center, the culture becomes increasingly heterogeneous and loses coherence and organization. The social and natural worlds become secularized, and the moral order of the universe disintegrates. Finally, with the breakup of large families in urban centers, the communal orientation of villagers is destroyed and they become individualized.

As conceived by Redfield, the folk–urban continuum reproduces the historical stages through which small villages have moved on their way to becoming cities. The folk–urban continuum is also a model of acculturation that charts changes in village life as the influences of the city overwhelm local traditions. For Redfield the direction of culture change is unilineal, with villages becoming more like the dominant urban centers as economic development allows the city to reach further into the rural areas. Indian culture survives in Mexico in isolated "little communities" like Amatlán, located far from cities. Indian culture is linked to village life in a fundamental way, and as the little communi- ties are absorbed into urban Mexico, remaining pre-Hispanic traditions and ethnic identities will eventually disappear.

Redfield was interested in peasants, and he wanted to determine whether or not they represent a worldwide social type. Following Eric Wolf (1955), he characterized peasants as people who live in small rural communities and who cultivate crops as a part of their traditions and not as businesses for profit. He added that peasants exhibit a strong traditional attachment to the land and that in some way peasants control the fields they work. A key factor in understanding peasants, according to Redfield, is that they exist only in relation to urban centers. There were no peasants before cities, and the city dominates the political, economic, and social life of all peasant peoples. Peasants are a kind of rural work force that supplies the city with food through barter or small-scale selling of surplus crops, but the peasant–city relationship is asymmetrical with the urban center retaining all of the power and prestige.

In order to clarify the relation between peasantries and cities, Redfield developed the concepts of "great and little traditions" (1960:41ff.) Peasants possess a little tradition rooted in village life that lacks the systematizing influence of professional scholars and codifiers. Cities produce sophisticated philosophies, religions, and aesthetic forms that become the great traditions characterizing an entire nation or state. Following Alfred Kroeber (1948:284), Redfield writes that peasants are "part societes with part cultures": they are incomplete in themselves and exist only as a little tradition dependent upon but unable fully to participate in a great tradition. Peasants share some social and cultural features with the city; they are the folk end of the folk–urban continuum, but they participate in the total social system as mere bit players in the national and international drama.

On the surface, Redfield's model has much to commend it. Besides organizing into a coherent scheme masses of information on Mexican villages, towns, and cities, it also attempts to define peasantry and account for processes of modernization and Westernization. Yet like many initial formulations, it has proved inadequate in explaining the complex relation between village and state in Mexico. One immediate problem for understanding peasantries throughout Latin America is that the Spanish Conquest replaced the great traditions of the Indians with one of European origin. The discontinuity between the Spanish great tradition and the little traditions found in Indian villages, not to mention discontinuities of language and custom, led Redfield to call Indians semipeasants. This means that the thousands of Indian villages throughout Mexico and Latin America fall outside of the strict definition of peasantry.

More serious flaws in Redfield's scheme are revealed as anthropologists apply the folk–urban continuum concept to the real-life situations they study. Many small villages located close to urban centers have retained their Indian character, whereas remote villages in rural regions have undergone dramatic changes. Redfield's assertion of the homogeneity of the little community is contradicted by numerous studies showing that Indian villages can be characterized by significant internal differences in levels of wealth and political power. The murder in Amatlán recounted above is an example of fundamental divisions and discord that should be absent in an ideal little community.

Further complications arise when one examines some of the developments in Mexico that are overlooked by the folk–urban continuum. Urban centers can in fact be the settings for movements to revive some version of Indian identity. Anthropologists have documented city dwellers, far removed in time and space from village life, who expend a great deal of time and money in reestablishing their cultural and linguistic ties to their Indian ancestors (e.g., Royce 1975). In the small villages, Indian culture is far from the passive, evanescent pre-Hispanic survival that, as portrayed by Redfield, is doomed to extinction by the urban onslaught.

The Indians have developed responses to deal with the changing world including the creation of whole new rituals based on their pre-Hispanic heritage. The *chicomexochitl* cult celebrating the sacred nature of corn is an example of one such ritual that will be discussed in Chapter 6. In fact, a major purpose of this book is to document that, despite their disadvantageous position relative to urban Mexico, rural Indians are far from passive players in the national drama. They, too, have their strategies for getting what they want and for asserting themselves in the struggle with the national economy and government over the distribution of resources.

Like Redfield, Eric Wolf ties the survival of Indian culture to a particular type of rural social group that he calls the "closed corporate community" (1955, 1957; see also 1960). According to Wolf, the appearance of the closed corporate community in Mexico is the result of certain historical forces, particularly those that conditioned the relations between Spain and its New World colonies, and later those that influenced economic and political development of postcolonial society. The key characteristics of these communities derive from their former need in colonial Mexico to organize in order to meet tribute payments and to supply corvée labor. In the nineteenth century, the communities were reorganized to meet the need for periodic wage labor and a work force that was self-sufficient and could be used for Mexico's developing capitalist enterprises.

Wolf's closed corporate community is characterized by community control over land resources, mechanisms for pressuring individuals to redistribute excess wealth, values that extol "shared poverty," prevention of outsiders from joining the community, and mechanisms for discouraging members from developing social ties outside of the community. Internal and external features of these communities thus serve to isolate them from the larger society and the potential for change that it represents. According to Wolf, Indian culture has persisted in Mexico and elsewhere because it exists in conjunction with closed corporate communities.

Amatlán retains its Indian character and seemingly exhibits many corporate features. Yet this study will show that additional features of village life do not fit Wolf's typology very well. For example, there are real, long-term differences in wealth and political power within Amatlán. Individuals at the cattle-owning level of the village economy are substantially better off than other community members and yet they are not the object of public scorn nor are they subject to magico–religious sanctions due to envy. In addition, villagers have always periodically left the southern Huasteca to work in neighboring regions, and several have worked as far away as Mexico City. Almost everyone has relatives who live permanently in cities throughout northern Mexico, and these people return to the village regularly, most often for ritual observances. Based on my findings, Wolf overstates the homogeneity and closedness of traditional Indian communities. Moreover, as I will show, he underestimates the degree to which Indians actively participate in the national economy. The people of Amatlán differ more in the style of that participation than in substance. When one is at the bottom, being perceived as an Indian can have its advantages in economic and political pursuits.

But if being an Indian can be an economic benefit and if villages can create and maintain their own internal elites, then why do the Indians and peasant peoples of Mexico consistently occupy the lowest rung of the socioeconomic ladder? This is a complex question that has been answered in different ways by different scholars. The theories of Arturo Warman (1976) and Rodolfo Stavenhagen (1975, 1978, and 1980) focus upon historical factors and upon ongoing social, political, and economic dynamics within modern Mexican society. Following the Conquest, the Spaniards set up a colonial regime whose purpose was to extract wealth from the colony and transfer it to Spain. In the early part of the nineteenth century Mexico won its independence, and the national elites introduced the capitalist mode of production both in industry and agriculture. It was, however, a peculiar variant of capitalism that was totally dependent on the more mature European and North American economies. What resulted is the dualistic economic system found in Mexico today. In the cities and on the large ranches and farms, modern capitalist enterprises predominate, whereas in the rural areas peasants and Indians practice production techniques that have changed little from colonial or even pre-Hispanic days.

The dual economic system that characterizes Mexico deprives the Indian and peasant sector of outside investments and the application of modern technology that it would need to participate as an equal partner in the nation. In fact, the dual economy is set up to extract wealth from the small horticulturalists and transfer it to the developing capitalist sector. This is accomplished in a variety of ways. In a place like Amatlán, surplus produce, usually corn, is sold in local markets to professional middlemen who transport it to urban markets for resale. The prices offered to the villagers are usually well below the national average, but, given the lack of transport, the Indians have no choice but to sell locally. This pricing mechanism controlled by monopolistic middlemen thus effectively transfers wealth from the village to the national economy.

Additional ways that wealth is transferred from the village to the capitalist sector of the economy include unequal inflationary processes rendering agricultural products increasingly worthless relative to manufactured items, monopolies on transportation facilities allowing exhorbitant fees to be charged, the trend toward decreasing size of individual land holdings due to population increases, and agribusiness competition with Indians and peasants for remaining arable land. In effect, what has happened since Mexico's independence is that the peasant and Indian peoples have become internal colonies, plundered now by their fellow countrymen in the cities and on the agribusiness farms and ranches.

According to Warman and Stavenhagen, in the dependent capitalist system such as that found in Mexico and throughout much of Latin America, wealth produced locally is siphoned off to the more mature economies of North America and Europe. For example, each year billions of dollars are transferred from the Mexican economy to the United States, often in the form of interest payments on debts. Investment funds for local industry and agribusiness are desperately needed in Mexico and are obtained by increasing the exploitation of the peasant and Indian sector of the economy. Because village horticulture is labor intensive, the villagers have responded to the pressure in the only way possible: by increasing their numbers. This population boom eventually exacerbates the problem because land resources are limited and an ever-growing body of peasants and Indians are forced to seek work outside of their villages for part of the year. Wages paid to these intermittent workers are extremely low, which effectively transfers even more wealth to the national capitalist sector.

Many urban Mexicans share with international development experts the view that village horticulture with its traditional ancient technology such as that found in Amatlán is an obstacle to general economic development. Warman and Stavenhagen both point out that, to the contrary, it is the surpluses produced by the village farmers that power Mexican capitalism. Warman goes so far as to state that Mexican "industry [is] made of corn" (1976:176). Both scholars show that the poverty of the villages is, in fact, caused by the excessive wealth extracted by the dependent capitalist sector of the Mexican economy. They point out the ultimate irony of the claims made by representatives of the very system causing economic backwardness in Mexico's rural areas who contend that peasant and Indian villages are actually hindering economic expansion.

We can conclude from the work of Warman and Stavenhagen that it is in the interest of the power elites in Mexico to maintain a substantial population of small-village agricultural producers. Far from constituting an obstacle to economic development, such an arrangement has many short-term advantages for the capitalist sector. Rural populations provide a much needed source of surplus wealth for investment and a pool of inexpensive labor. They also do not demand expensive social services, such as social security or unemployment compensation, because they can always return to their villages in times of need. Labor-intensive farming practices in villages absorb enormous numbers of people who would otherwise exacerbate Mexico's chronic urban unemployment problem. Finally, keeping people in the countryside stabilizes the entire social system by diffusing political movements that demand change.

Stavenhagen points out, however, that in the end an impoverished peasantry will hinder economic growth in Mexico because poor people will be unable to purchase industrial goods produced in cities. This in turn will make the capitalist sector more dependent on the United States and Europe, which will result in even greater levels of poverty among peasants and Indians. Warman illustrates the impossible situation of the peasants by examining cycles of corn production in the state of Morelos. Contrary to all apparent economic logic, he found that as the price of corn rose, production fell and that as the price fell, production rose. This is the reverse of what economists expect to happen, and the situation has reaffirmed the opinion of some experts who see peasant production activities as irrational. Actually, the distortion is caused by the poverty of peasant farmers and not the reverse. Corn is the staple crop and as agricultural prices decline, peasants fall back on corn to ensure their food supply. As agricultural prices rise, peasants switch to more profitable crops including a variety of vegetables and cut back on corn production. Thus once again the pricing system and the price cycles of crops effectively prevent peasant producers from entering the national economy on an equal footing with other producers.

Warman and Stavenhagen, then, explain the persistence of peasant and Indian populations in modern Mexico as due to the critical role these play in the maintenance of the dominant capitalist system. From their viewpoint, the key factors in understanding the place of the village in modern Mexico are to be found by examining the historical processes that led to the current socioeconomic situation and by unraveling the complex and sometimes contradictory nature of Mexico's dependent capitalism. For their purposes, the regional- or national-level study best reveals the forces linking villagers to the total system. But both analysts recognize that inhabitants of small villages are not passive bystanders in the national and international system of which they are a part. Villagers have their own strategies and agendas, and the larger processes that Warman and Stavenhagen elucidate are played out in particular places by real people. The process of social incorporation works both ways, and villagers develop their own means of dealing with the prevailing political and economic powers.

The Mexican anthropologist Gonzalo Aguirre Beltrán (1979) has developed an influential and compelling perspective on Indians of Latin America that differs in emphasis from the viewpoints presented above. He recognizes that contemporary Indian peoples are the remnants of pre-Hispanic cultures and that as such they are more than just economically underdeveloped farmers. Indians are ethnically (but not racially) distinct from representatives of the national culture. Indian culture has survived in what he calls "regions of refuge"—hostile and inaccessible environments that are unattractive to capitalist developers.

Through a phenomenon that Aguirre Beltrán calls the "dominical process" (*proceso dominical*, see Hunt 1979:1), the economically and technologically advanced centers of the nation are able to dominate Indians living in the regions of refuge. The dominical process includes such elements as political control, economic subordination, unequal distribution of social services, maintenance of social distance, and missionary activities that encourage Indians to be submissive and to accept and even embrace their low status.

Within these regions of refuge Indian people live in small rural villages and form a type of caste in relation to the mestizo representatives of the nation who, for the most part, live in provincial cities. He uses the term *caste* instead of class to emphasize the archaic and extremely rigid social hierarchy characterizing Indian–mestizo relations. The Indians are subsistence farmers operating in a precapitalist microeconomy based on reciprocity and redistribution of goods, whereas the mestizos are part of the national capitalist economy oriented to making profits. This dual economy, like the dominical process in general, is a legacy of the colonial history of Mexico.

Aguirre Beltrán stresses the mechanisms that keep the Indians separate and unequal. Representatives of the national culture actively resist admitting Indians into the national mainstream. Local mestizos themselves are near the lowest reaches of the national status hierarchy, and having a caste of Indians beneath them often serves their interests. Mestizos maintain their position relative to the Indians through force and by an elaborate system of false consciousness that mystifies the true nature of mestizo–Indian interaction. Thus, from the mestizo viewpoint, Indians need mestizo expertise to provide an element of rationality in their economic and work lives. For their part, the Indians actively resist forces of assimilation that they realize would mean the destruction of their traditional cultures. Their political system, language, religion and world view, strong identification with the land and local environment, and negative experiences in dealing with mestizos leads Indians to close their communities to outside influences.

Central to Aguirre Beltrán's perspective on the place of the Indians in the nation is the idea that colonial-type conditions characterizing the regions of refuge prevent Indian communities from evolving beyond their pre-Hispanic and precapitalist stage of development. He states that while Indians may behave rationally within their own cultural systems, their economic life is not guided by the same principles of rationality that underlie modern capitalism. He argues that land, labor, production, and consumption are not regulated by the market principle and thus the Indian economy will always be dominated by the more rational capitalism of the national economy. The perspective developed by Aguirre Beltrán is activist and political in that he advocates the dismantling of barriers to assimilation so that the Indians can be integrated into the national economy. This, he believes, is the only way that Indians will achieve social, political, and economic equality with other citizens of Mexico.

Indian culture, according to Aguirre Beltrán, persists because it has been prevented from evolving into a more modern form that could play an active role in Mexican national life. Like Warman and Stavenhagen, he concludes that the hyperexploitation of the Indian population and perpetuation of the dual economy serve the interests of the economic elite of the country. He is in agreement with Wolf about the closed nature of the Indian community and with Redfield regarding the role of social and physical isolation in the maintenance of Indian culture. The perspective of Aguirre Beltrán departs somewhat from the others in attributing an active role to the Indians themselves in closing their communities and thereby maintaining their traditions intact. In addition, he is overt about what the others only suggest: that the Indians must lose their culture to win their freedom.

Problems with the viewpoint of Aguirre Beltrán parallel those suggested for Redfield and Wolf. Communities located near cities can retain a strong Indian character, and remote Indian villages are not always as closed as they seem. Information from Amatlán reveals persistent and substantial differences in wealth among Indians themselves, and some individuals have become affluent relative even to local mestizos. But the most serious shortcoming in the perspective of Aguirre Beltrán, and the one that is shared by the others, is the way he misconstrues the nature of the Indian economy. Village economic activity is portrayed as essentially irrational or, at best, rational within an irrational cultural system. Although it is true that land cannot be bought and sold in Amatlán, that there is no access to major credit, and that much productive activity is accomplished on the basis of reciprocity, it is a gross misconception to conclude that villagers do not, therefore, plan, economize, and participate in profit-making enterprises. I will return to this misperception shortly and again in subsequent chapters.

All of the perspectives presented above assume the existence of an Indian population whose cultural content differs from that of the dominant Hispanic group in Mexican society. Some scholars, however, conclude that what was left of Indian culture after the Spanish Conquest was obliterated during the long period of colonization. What remains of the pre-Hispanic past are a few remnants of culture such as language and some widely scattered elements of dress or religious belief that have been incorporated into what is now a thoroughly

Hispanicized system. From this viewpoint, the whole idea of the Indian as a person of differing culture is simply an aspect of the false consciousness created by a society that succeeds through ruthless exploitation of the vast majority of its citizens.

Judith Friedlander (1975) takes this position when she writes of her ethnographic work in the Nahua town of Hueyapan in the state of Morelos. The people of Hueyapan have lost most of their Indian traditions, with the notable exception of the Nahuatl language, and yet they have been forced by government officials, schoolteachers, media representatives, and local mestizos to adopt a definition of themselves as Indians. Indians are considered by the Hispanic population at large to be backward, stupid, and inept—the antithesis of the civilized and sophisticated urban Mexican. When asked about their Indianness, most people of Hueyapan were negative, listing what they did not have or could not do. In essence, being Indian for them meant being poor. Friedlander writes that the people of Hueyapan are simply rural Mexicans who have been forced to accept an Indian identity. The government, through its various programs, has managed to "integrate yet segregate" the people from the national culture (Friedlander 1975:153). The purpose is to maintain the dual economy that, as we have seen, benefits urban elites.

Roger Bartra (1977) examines how interethnic relations based on forced Indian indentity are transformed into the ideological mechanisms that perpetuate capitalism. He claims that native culture has been so thoroughly "submerged, distorted, and dominated" by institutions of the ruling elites that it has been destroyed in its fundamental aspects (1977:421). The traditional economy of the Indians has been overwhelmed by the national capitalist economy, and the Indians have simply been incorporated as the poor people in the system. In fact, Bartra writes that for the new representatives of the national economy "it is sufficient for a man simply to be in rags and tatters and need to sell his labor for him to fall into the category of an Indian" (1977:442). Thus, according to Bartra, Indian culture was first destroyed and then the category "Indian" resurrected by representatives of the national culture as an explanation and justification for poverty and exploitation. In the ideology of the exploiters, Indians, due to their inferiority, have failed to succeed in the national economy and are incapable of integrating themselves into the larger society. In a tragic irony, the profound failure of the national capitalist economy to eliminate poverty is foisted on the poor by this ideology through the "myth of the non-integrated native" (1977:442).

Friedlander and Bartra depart from the other theorists discussed in that they see the "Indian" economy as simply part of the larger capitalist economy of Mexico. Indians as a category of people with distinct cultural traditions simply do not exist, and, therefore, their precapitalist economies organized along principles that differ from the national economy by extension do not exist. True, there are people who call themselves Indians, but these are people of essentially Hispanic culture who have been brainwashed into believing the myths created by the national elites so that they will more easily accept their low status. In this conception, so-called Indian traits such as language, religious rituals, or dress are markers used by the national elites and the people themselves to label the rural poor as natives set apart from the larger Hispanic society. By implication, anthropologists or other scholars who study traditional cultures in Mexico are effectively in collusion with the national elites in their efforts to label and segregate the rural poor and exploit them economically. The whole concept of the dual economy is false according to this perspective, and scholars who write of the opposition between the Indian and dominant capitalist economies are also contributing to the exploitation of the rural poor.

These five perspectives on the place of the village in Mexican society run the gamut from Redfield's view of the Indian as a member of a distinct culture, enclosed in a folk community with its own world view, social system, and values, to that of Friedlander and Bartra who see villagers as the lumpenproletariat in an exploitative system that labels the rural poor as Indians so as to plunder them more effectively. The differing viewpoints highlight a peculiarity of social scientific research: theoretical formulations are based upon a certain view of humanity, and they contain within them values about the human condition and, by extension, implicit recommendations for solving social problems. For Redfield, traditional Indian culture survives only because modern urban culture has not yet arrived in the remote villages. In other words, it is weakly held by the people and will easily disintegrate upon contact with a more appealing alternative. Although he appeared to have a kind of romantic attachment to life in the little community, he saw clearly that the trajectory of development in Mexico is toward the city and that the loss of traditional Indian culture is all but inevitable.

Wolf ties Indian life to the closed corporate community that he views as a social entity formed in response to outside influences and subject to forces originating at the regional and national level. Inside, the community is a kind of refuge from the onslaught of industrialization and the brutal struggle for profits. Like Redfield, Wolf appears to see the Indian as a kind of precapitalist person, more interested in perpetuating harmony with nature and with his fellows than in winning the contest for profits. Aguirre Beltrán shares much with the views of Redfield and Wolf, although he stresses the way that regional- and state-level mechanisms have blocked natural development of Indian communities. He notes the resistance that Indians have mounted against influences from the mestizo world, but he does not see this as a rejection of social and economic progress. According to Aguirre Beltrán, what Indians want is to avoid being incorporated into the national system at the lowest, most exploited level. For him, Indian culture is an anachronism in a developing country like Mexico, and he actively advocates programs to integrate the Indians into the national mainstream.

Warman and Stavenhagen, along with Redfield, Wolf, and Aguirre Beltrán, see the Indians and peasants as victims of an unfair system, based on the dual economy. Warman and Stavenhagen link the dual economy to Mexico's form of dependent capitalism. The rural poor have ethnic and class barriers that are impossible to overcome because of ongoing mechanisms that usurp their surpluses and redirect them to the developing capitalist sector. For them, the Indians and peasants are trapped in a quagmire and can only be extricated by a fundamental change in national development policy. Warman and Stavenhagen see the Indians and peasants as perpetual victims of exploitation, plundered first by the colonial powers and now by national elites. Friedlander and Bartra share this view but expand it to where they see Mexico as a single capitalist economy and villagers as simply a form of rural proletariat. So devastating is the condition of these people, in their view, that nothing short of radical political transformation will correct the system.

The perspectives on Mexican Indians presented here are a sample of the large number of viewpoints that have emerged since the Mexican Revolution. Even in summary form, they convey some of the complexities in developing a coherent picture of Indian culture and its relation to the national whole. Human social life is extraordinarily complex wherever it is found, but the situation in Mexico is compounded by its colonial history, its relation to the more developed economies of the world, and the sheer number of diverse Indian cultures within its borders. Unfortunately, from a scientific perspective, the viewpoints presented above do not differ sufficiently for us to evaluate clearly which best explains the situation. They overlap a great deal and are based on a different selection of variables. For scientific progress to occur, differing theoretical stances must provide alternative explanations for the same set of observations. Researchers can then devise tests based on further field research to determine the most effective theory.

Elements from each of these perspectives help elucidate the situation in Amatlán and improve our understanding of how the village fits into the national and international scheme. In many ways the village is like Redfield's little community and Wolf's closed corporate community. There is no question that village surpluses are expropriated by the artificially low prices paid for village produce and village labor, as Warman and Stavenhagen point out. Aguirre Beltrán is correct in characterizing the almost colonial-like conditions such as found in the southern Huasteca, that effectively prevent villages like Amatlán from developing economically. And there are villagers who do behave like rural proletarians during certain times of the year when they seek work on regional cattle ranches. But many elements do not apply in Amatlán, and some positively falsify the real situation.

One area of disagreement among social scientists surrounds the nature of the economic system in an Indian village. As suggested above, many scholars view village economics as precapitalist, meaning that it is a nondynamic system based on something other than the profit motive. Thus, for example, villagers may grow corn out of a sense of tradition rather than as a rational strategy to maximize their income. Other scholars view village economics as a kind of "penny capitalism" (Tax 1972 [1953]), identical in kind but different in scale from capitalist enterprises in the cities. These two points of view contain within them important assumptions about the nature of non-Western society and the basis of human behavior. It is crucial to reach an understanding about village economics, not only for scientific reasons but also because government programs aimed at helping the Indians succeed or fail depending on how they match up with the realities of village life.

A second source of disagreement that must be resolved is whether or not certain rural villagers are truly people with customs that are distinct from those of Hispanic city dwellers. The traditional peoples of Mexico have been ruled over by an Hispanic elite for close to 500 years, and so there is no one in the country completely free from Western European influence. However, it is wrong to conclude that Indian culture is therefore dead. Pre-Hispanic traditions have disappeared from certain areas of Mexico, and Friedlander's Hueyapan and the Valle de Mezquital studied by Bartra may indeed be two of them. But the people of Amatlán and the large region surrounding it must be considered Indian by any criteria including language, culture, village organization, and self-identification.

In my description of the Amatlán Nahuas, I will emphasize the active role they play in creating and maintaining their Indian ethnic identity. To a great extent, contemporary Nahua culture derives from pre-Hispanic antecedents, but it has played in the past and continues to play in the present a dynamic part in adapting the villagers to the opportunities, liabilities, and contingencies of life in Mexico. In this view, a significant part of Nahua culture survives and is perpetuated in the activities of villagers as they negotiate their statuses with dominant mestizos. It is neither closed villages nor distance from urban influence in regions of refuge that provide the real dynamic of ethnic Indian survival. The dynamic of Nahua ethnic identity is found in the ways that people have been able to use their traditions to succeed materially in an unfair politico–economic system and, at the same time, to create meaningful, culturally coherent lives for themselves.

I intend to show that Indian culture is far from backward or unprogressive and that Nahuas, despite overwhelming odds against them, work hard, engage in planning, follow strategies, and generally attempt to cut costs and increase benefits for themselves and their families. In this view I depart from researchers who see a qualitative difference between traditional Indian economic behavior and the economizing of capitalist mestizos. Indians may play the game somewhat differently from the mestizos in part to gain certain advantages in a system that is stacked against them. However, I hope to show that they allocate their resources according to rational principles. One distinction is that they cultivate their Indianness and, by thus separating themselves from mestizo neighbors, change both the rules of the political and economic struggle and the definitions by which success is measured. By showing how the Nahuas engage the world through their ethnic identity, I want to affirm the authenticity of Indian culture both as a coherent system of meanings and as a dynamic strategy for survival.

In any event, questions about the nature of the village economy, the distinctiveness of Indian culture, and the accuracy of the theoretical perspectives summarized above will best be clarifed by empirical means. The way to resolve the larger abstract issues is to describe and analyze the way real people live their lives.

ECONOMIC DEVELOPMENT IN MEXICO

Small villages like Amatlán are caught in shifting political, economic, and social tides that largely originate at the national and international levels. Some of the historical events and processes that directly affect the village and the southern Huasteca region will be discussed in Chapter 2. Here I would like briefly to sketch some of the global factors that have shaped village life and created the context for the sociocultural features described in subsequent chapters. Mexican history is complex and not easily reduced to a few paragraphs, but some information on the development of the Mexican economy will help in clarifying the wider environment in which the villagers operate. Data presented are taken mostly from Rudolph (1985).

From the beginning of the Wars of Independence in 1810 until the Porfirio Díaz dictatorship in 1876, Mexico experienced a long period of economic stagnation. The war with Spain, internal struggles, two wars with France, and a war with the United States created unstable conditions hindering both economic development and the process of forging a nation from a former colony. During the "Porfiriato" (from 1876 to 1911 when Porfirio Díaz ruled), stability was restored, and the economy sustained a slow but steady growth. Export earnings increased by about 6% annually during this period, based mainly on food crops and raw materials derived from mining and other sources. At the same time, Indians were increasingly dispossessed of their lands as private farms and ranches (haciendas) were established to take advantage of foreign markets. In 1911, following massive civil strife, Díaz was forced to resign. The period from 1910 to 1925, which included the Mexican Revolution and the post-World War I depression, saw the economy devastated, with agricultural production growing a scant 0.1% over the 15-year span.

Just as the economy was recovering in the decade following the Revolution, much progress was reversed by the world depression that began in 1929. In that year and in 1930, land reform was accelerated considerably in Mexico, and many of the largest haciendas were expropriated and the land returned to the Indians. At this time 70% of the economically active population were employed in agriculture, whereas manufacturing employed merely 12%. A short time later, the government acted to diminish the impact of the depression by establishing tariffs, devaluing the peso, and promoting agrarian reform. It created agricultural development banks, invested heavily in agriculture, and in 1938 it nationalized the growing oil industry. Finally, World War II created an enormous demand for Mexican exports, beginning in 1939. Due to these and other factors, the economy grew at a rapid pace in the 1940s. The Gross Domestic Product (GDP) grew at an annual rate of 6.7% in this period, and the population was beginning to increase following the devastation of the Revolution. At this time a change became evident in the direction of the economy. Manufacturing grew by 8.1% per year, whereas agriculture, which previously outstripped manufacturing, grew at a rate of 5.8%.

During the 1950s growth of the GDP slowed a bit to an average of 6.1% per year. But the shift toward manufacturing at the expense of agricultural production became even more pronounced as manufacturing increased at 7.3% annually while agriculture grew at the reduced rate of 4.3% It was in this decade that tourism expanded and became a major Mexican industry, bringing in substantial revenues. At the same time, the population was increasing at the very high rate of 3.1% annually. The shift toward manufacturing is reflected in an exodus from the countryside. By 1960, one-half of the population was living in urban areas. In the 1960s the economy grew at the high rate of 7% per year. Manufacturing grew at 7% per year while agriculture had fallen to a 3.4% growth rate. By 1970, Mexico was self-sufficient in food crops, steel, and most consumer goods. During the 1960s, the government promoted the use of fertilizers, insecticides, and genetically improved seeds, but these programs did not reach remote villages like Amatlán. At the same time, in order to subsidize low wages in the cities, the government artificially maintained low prices on food crops. Investment and production shifted to growing commercial crops for export and industrial use, and the small producer was gradually squeezed out of the national market.

In the 1970s, the boom continued with the GDP growing at an annual rate of over 6%. But trouble in the agricultural sector was reflected in lurching productivity swings. Agriculture started the decade with a 5% increase in productivity, but within a few years declines that ranged from 0.3 to 2.6% were registered. Bad weather contributed to the crisis, and 10 million tons of food had to be imported in 1980. Manufacturing also showed the effects of deepseated problems in the economy. Growth varied between 3.6% and 9% per year, but by the end of the 1970s it was showing vigor. Discovery of the extent of Mexico's oil reserves caused a boom in manufacturing growth from 1978–81, but serious inflation began to appear in 1976 as the peso fell against the U.S. dollar. In 1982, Mexico experienced the worst economic downturn since the depression of the 1930s. Owing to a variety of factors, including a worldwide glut of oil and a recession that affected most nations, the peso had to be devalued three times during 1982 alone. Drought conditions and the recession caused the government to import massive amounts of food in 1984 and to cancel some agricultural programs. Agrarian reform has since assumed a low priority due to the shortage of arable land available to redistribute to peasants and Indians. This has increased the occurrence of land invasions, which in turn have caused a reduction in investments in agriculture by urban financial institutions.

Despite setbacks, Mexican economic growth in general has been remarkable. In 1984, the country ranked as the world's fifteenth-largest economy. The year before, it ranked ninth in the world for productive capacity and fourth in the production and export of oil. Agriculture, for all of its problems, is well diversified, and Mexican cattle herds are among the largest in the world. But the prosperity has not been evenly divided among the population. Farms that produce food for the nation are located in rain-fed regions of the country, whereas agricultural production for export, which has attracted most of the investment money, is concentrated in the arid but irrigated northern regions. Unemployment and underemployment in the rural areas have caused the massive shift of people to the cities who go there seeking seasonal employment.

A few statistics on Mexico's unique program of land distribution will help set the context of the land struggle in Amatlán. In 1910, at the start of the Mexican Revolution, 96% of the population was landless, and 1% of the population owned 97% of the land. One-half of all agricultural land was controlled by 835 haciendas, and 80% of rural villages were tied to the haciendas through debt peonage. Agrarian reform began in 1915, and land redistribution was written into the 1917 Constitution as Article 27. Land was to be returned to the people in the form of the ejido—a parcel of land granted to communities rather than indivduals. A person was required to be a bona fide member of a village to have access to land. The largest redistribution of land occurred during the 1934–40 period when over 17 million hectares were made into ejidos. By 1983, about one-half of the cultivated land in Mexico was held in ejidos. But population growth outstripped land distribution by such an extent that there are now more landless peasants in the countryside than people with ejido rights.

In sum, economic development in Mexico has been uneven and has had little impact on large segments of the population. Those most often left out of the new prosperity are the rural Indians whose lives seem little changed from pre-Hispanic days. As in so many other developing nations, Mexico's experience has laid the groundwork for deep divisions in the population that often lead groups to cultivate their ethnic loyalties. The Nahuas of Amatlán are caught up in these larger processes, and their response has been, in part, to perpetuate their Indianness in the face of continued mestizo domination. In this study I will attempt to illuminate some of the specific local factors that have made ethnic identity an effective strategy for the villagers.

CHAPTER 2

THE VILLAGE IN ITS SETTING

I returned to Amatlán in 1972 for a long-term study of village life. Many months passed before I began to get an accurate picture of how the people structured their lives and to understand the meaning of the events I was witnessing. Part of the problem was overcoming an image I had in my mind about village life in general. Somehow I had pictured a group of small houses, perhaps with thatched roofs, neatly placed on either side of a trail. The people would have a strong sense of community, and there would be suspicion of all outsiders. Everyone would know everything about everyone else, and the village would be conservative, changeless, and a miniature world unto itself. I thought I would find a communal economy based on cooperation, shared work, and reciprocity, with village activities guided by tradition. I expected that there would be factionalism, feuds, and various fault lines in the social structure, but these ultimately would be overcome by the powerful solidarity produced by a simple and communal life.

These preconceptions, which derived in part from published accounts of villages in Mexico and other parts of the world, proved to be an impediment to understanding life in Amatlán. In reality, Amatlán is a much more complex and fascinating place than my earlier stereotypes of village life implied. Far from being bounded, closed, and changeless, Amatlán has proved to be a protean community with few clear borders, internally differentiated, active and ever changing, full of humor and pathos with its inhabitants engaged in confronting a complex and sometimes alien world. In this chapter, following a brief description of how ethnographers adjust to life in the field, I place the village in its geographic, social, and historical context and begin to sketch features of village life.

LIVING AND WORKING IN AMATLÁN

An anthropologist must make a satisfactory adjustment to the field situation if he or she is to succeed at participant observation. The hosts in turn must adjust to a newcomer in their midst and enter into a willing alliance with the anthropologist in the description of their own culture. Everyone involved must adapt to the new, sometimes funny, sometimes painful circumstances produced when individuals from differing cultures meet. I will next examine what happens when individuals leave the relative security of their own society and, risking discomfort and aggravation, choose to live and work among people from a different cultural tradition.

Working in another culture creates a dynamic that affects the quality and quantity of work an investigator can accomplish. A person may go overseas as an individual but can never totally escape his or her own cultural identity. Nor can the people in the host society escape theirs. At least initially, hosts will perceive the outsider not as an individual but as a representative of his culture of origin. The reverse is equally true. The people I first met in Amatlán appeared to me to represent Nahua culture, and I did not know them yet as individuals. Working in another culture, then, is always done in the context of powerful social definitions and forces over which individuals have little control. It is not possible to eliminate these features of contact, but by understanding the dynamic that is created when representatives of distinct cultures meet it becomes possible to avoid many mistakes, to increase cross-cultural understanding, and to achieve our goals beyond expectation.

My adjustment to Amatlán proceeded in three distinct phases that seem to resemble the experiences of many other anthropological fieldworkers with whom I have talked. The first phase I call the "period of attraction." When I returned to the village in 1972 my initial awkward meeting with the Nahuas was softened by the passage of time, and I was overcome by a feeling of excitement, joy, adventure, intense interest in the new surroundings, satisfaction, pleasure, and a strong desire to see everything at once, all combined with a slight but stimulating sense of foreboding. I enjoyed adapting to life without bathrooms, running water, electricity, newspapers, or companions who shared experiences or interests. I could barely sleep at night, and I wrote dozens of pages of enthusiastic notes each day. I think that the villagers also experienced a scaled-down version of attraction as they adjusted to my presence in their midst. Everyone wanted to talk to me, and I recall being exhilarated by all of the attention.

The period of attraction with its sense of adventure and excitement is a necessary part of cross-cultural work, but it cannot be sustained very easily or for very long. This is probably good because it is based on a fairly unrealistic view of the world. The period of attraction is part of the adjustment that individual visitors and hosts make to the new situation. One danger of this period of enthusiasm is that it will lead to a sense of disappointment as routines are established and the fieldworker settles in for the long haul. Care must be taken to balance this "honeymoon" period so that it is not followed by a kind of stunned depression that can seriously hamper successful adaptation and impair the quality of work. Interestingly, I took the best photographs of village life during this period, but my field notes were nearly useless.

During this period of attraction I committed a serious error that almost ended my ability to work in Amatlán. Often, the first people who make an effort to get to know outsiders are those searching for a means to escape from a bad personal situation. I was alone in an alien context, and I made the mistake of becoming immediate friends with three of the first people who presented themselves. I must admit that I was grateful for their company. Even so I wondered why these few men seemed to have so much leisure time when everyone else appeared to be engaged in work. I later learned that they were village deadbeats, and my association with them hampered my work for several weeks. Other people told me later that they avoided me simply because they knew I was in bad company. One must be especially careful to read the social situation correctly during the period of attraction.

The period of attraction with its attendant dangers is often followed by an equally unrealistic phase I call the "period of rejection." I had established a routine of sorts, the novelty of my situation was wearing off, and I began to contemplate the long months ahead. Suddenly much of the charm was gone, the work I came to do seemed pointless, and I felt extremely uncomfortable and out of place. For one thing, I was appalled by the number of snakes I saw when bathing or walking on the trails. I felt repulsed by the scorpions and the huge tarantulas covered with silky black hair that crawled on the walls inside of houses. For another, I measured a foot or more taller than everyone else around me, and I always felt conspicuous. As I entered people's houses I had to bend down to pass under the edge of the thatched roof, and this awkwardness caused great merriment. Whenever I stood in a group I was constantly poked in the back by laughing people who were marking the spot reached by the tops of their heads. Adults and children alike took no pains to hide their curiosity and stared at me wherever I went. I had no privacy at any time night or day.

I was removed from my cultural support system, and I felt isolated, frustrated, clumsy, incompetent, anxious, depressed, and angry; and there were moments when I feared I was becoming emotionally unstable, teetering on the brink of insanity. It is at times like these that one can discover things about oneself that are not very flattering. Frustrations build and can lead to internal outbursts of bigotry, ethnocentrism, and haughty arrogance. I found I could deeply resent the people around me for being different and for their stubbornness in insisting on doing things their way. I became very disturbed at the depths I reached in self-pity and paranoia. I looked on in horror as I became alternately whiny, self-important, petulant, touchy, and uncompromising. During moments of clarity I began to feel that I harbored a monster inside and that I could no longer trust myself. At this point I contracted dysentery, no laughing matter a hundred miles from the nearest bathroom, and I rapidly became weak and overcome with feelings of despair. I felt depressed and alone, and I began to reject everything around me and to dream about how wonderful things were back home. My notes during this period became a compendium of complaints, self-serving observations, and blatant rationalizations.

This is culture shock, and it is one of the most remarkable sensations that a person can experience. It varies in intensity according to the individual and according to the extent of the culture gap. It can last for weeks or months, and some say that one never quite gets over it. Very often, culture shock strikes just when members of the host culture move out of their period of attraction and step back to observe the visitor for a while. Villagers began to ignore me, and I sometimes feared I was being shunned. Considering some of my reactions, although I made great efforts to keep them to myself, it is no wonder that I was not all that popular. This pattern of avoidance or period of rejection is part of the adjustment any group makes toward an intruder as it adapts to the new situation. Somewhere in my confused mind I knew this, and I came to expect that the villagers might try to frighten me away.

One day when I was feeling a little more normal, the village headman came to tell me that cowboys at a local cattle ranch had heard about my presence in Amatlán and in a drunken rage had vowed to kill me. I shrugged off the threat, convinced that this was simply some ploy on the part of the villagers. He looked a little puzzled as I insisted that I was not afraid and that I would stay. About a week later I awakened at about 3:00 A.M. to answer nature's call and ran into a man standing in the total darkness outside my door. He was from Amatlán, and he carried a drawn machete. Apparently he and several other men had been assigned by the headman to guard my place during the night. I suddenly realized that the threat had been real, and I shuddered at how exposed and helpless I was there. At the same time it occurred to me that the villagers were willing to go up against armed cowboys with nothing more than their machetes in order to protect me. The period of rejection is mutual, but it can become exaggerated and cause poor judgment in the mind of the lone fieldworker.

Culture shock can produce a vicious cycle that obstructs work and undermines the entire fieldwork enterprise. Culture shock makes a person feel lost, but it is in fact a hopeful sign that one is in the process of adapting to the new situation. Long-term exposure to another culture loosens your hold upon your own culture, and this alienation from all that is safe and secure is necessary if you are to succeed in embracing the new culture. One response I had to culture shock was escapism. I spent whole days cleaning my camera and checking my tape recorder. In one 3-day period I read a 1,200-page collection of stories I had brought along. I purchased books in the market that under normal conditions I would not dream of reading, and I devoured them in record time. At one point I heard myself make excuses rather than go with people who had invited me to an event.

These and many other practices our clever brains devise serve to increase isolation and abort the process of incorporation in the alien society that culture shock presages. Only knowledge and experience reduce alienation and these both take time. The field research will be as successful as the degree to which the investigator manages to put episodes of culture shock into perspective. Culture shock produces a false view of the world, a view that is distorted by the slow and sometimes painful destruction of your dependence upon your natal culture. Confronting culture shock honestly does little to reduce the pain, but it is the first step toward the development of a whole new perspective on the human condition that is the hallmark of anthropology.

Facing up to culture shock and to one's own shortcomings leads to the final phase that I call the "period of incorporation." In this stage of the cross-cultural encounter, both the hosts and the visitor gradually begin to look upon each other as individual people and less as social representations. When stereotypes fell away, I finally began to get to know individuals. Nahua culture appeared increasingly less strange and foreign to me, and as time passed I began to question why I was there. Local culture appeared reasonable, and I wondered what I was supposed to write about. The period of incorporation continues as long as the outsider is in residence in the host culture. In fact, the periods of attraction and rejection are really the initial phases of an extended period of incorporation, but it rarely appears that way to the person experiencing cross-cultural contact. As incorporation proceeds most people gain a new respect for the host culture, and it is only when this awareness is reached that truly successful fieldwork can begin. Most experienced anthropologists agree that successful adaptation produces a paradox: fieldworkers always feel that they are ready to begin real work just at the point when it is time to return home.

To be successful in another culture, researchers must be aware of cultural differences on the one hand and their reactions to them on the other. Just knowing that culture shock is a normal response to long-term research in another culture helped me to cope. But this type of work is not for everyone. The romantic image of the field experience cannot be preserved in the day-to-day struggle to survive in an alien physical and social environment. When life in Amatlán became rough, I reacted by creating a kind of idealized image of what it was like back home. I pictured lazy summer afternoons, warm showers, familiar food, and a measured pace to my life that I would control for a change.

The glorious day finally arrived, and I said my good-byes. A few days after returning home I knew something was wrong. Somehow my own culture was not exactly as I had remembered it. When I first arrived from Mexico I was surprised at how rapidly everyone walked and gesticulated. I could not stop from greeting people in Nahuatl, and I embarrassed myself by standing goggle-eyed, staring down the aisles of a supermarket. I was suffering from what anthropologists call reverse culture shock. It was weeks before things began to look normal again. But I had changed, and normal was no longer very satisfying. I missed the struggle and sense of discovery that comes from surviving in another culture. It is an addiction that I think is shared by many people who have lived and worked for an extended period cross-culturally. While in the grip of darkest culture shock a month or two after arriving in Amatlán, I solemnly promised myself that I would never again return to that alien (and alienating) place. I thought to myself, "That'll show 'em." Within a few days of returning home, however, I broke that promise and swore to myself that I would go again at the first opportunity.

THE REGION: "A PLACE OF RICH CATTLE RANCHERS AND GUNMEN"

The village of Amatlán is located in the northern part of the state of Veracruz, which stretches its great length along the central Gulf Coast of Mexico. Most of the northern zone of Veracruz is part of a larger region of Mexico covering sections of six states, known as the Huasteca. In addition to its Veracruz component, the Huasteca includes parts of the states of San Luis Potosí, Tamaulipas, Hidalgo, Querétaro, and Puebla (for general works on the Huasteca see Bernal and Dávalos 1952–53; and Stresser-Péan 1979). Experts and local inhabitants disagree on the precise borders of the Huasteca, although there is some agreement that, in Veracruz at least, it is bordered in the south by the Río Cazones and in the north by the Río Pánuco. The western edge of the Huasteca Veracruzana (Veracruz portion of the Huasteca) is dominated by the massive and rugged Sierra Madre Oriental range, which extends southward to join its counterpart from the west coast and form the great central plateau of Mexico. To the east lies the Gulf of Mexico. Between these geographical features we find in the north a flat plain broken only by the island-like Sierra de Otontepec. South of the Otontepec is a vast expanse of choppy hills, the foothills of the Sierra Madre Oriental. It is in the center of this region of sharp, uneven terrain that we find Amatlán. The hills eventually flatten as they reach the coast to the east and the Río Cazones to the south.

The entire state of Veracruz lies below the Tropic of Cancer, but because much of it is mountainous, climate in any region is determined more by elevation than by latitude. Elevations in the state run from sea level to over 5,600 meters at the peak of Mount Orizaba in southern Veracruz. Geographers as well as local inhabitants divide the state into three vertical zones: *tierra caliente* (hot country) from sea level to 800 meters; *tierra templada* (temperate country) from 800 to 1,600 meters; and *tierra fría* (cold country) above 1,600 meters. Each of these regions is characterized by a distinct set of ecological features which have their effect on the cultures within them (see Puig 1976, 1979).

The proximity of mountains, foothills, and the Gulf combine to complicate the climate of northern Veracruz (see Vivó Escoto 1964). Climate and vegetation vary from steamy tropical forest to cool temperatures and stands of evergreen trees as one moves from the Gulf region to the upper reaches of the Sierra. Amatlán, however, lies squarely in the hot country, at an altitude of 180 meters above sea level. Geographers describe the climate of this elevation as hot and humid with abundant rainfall in the summer (Am(f), Am, Am(w) in the modified Köppen system).

The village and its surrounding region receives 2,000 mm (about 78 inches) of rain on the average each year. By comparison, in the United States an agricultural state like Indiana receives about half as much.

However, rainfall in Amatlán is problematic because it is not evenly distributed. Rainfall can vary significantly from place to place and from year to year. Villagers informed me that it is not unusual for one locale to have too much rain, which results in flooded villages and washed out fields, whereas another area 40 kilometers away suffers from drought. This inconsistency of rainfall is one of the most frustrating characteristics of the environment, and it is a constant topic of conversation among villagers. Although mean annual rainfall is high, there is a marked dry season during which it may not rain for several months. The dry season, called *tonamili* in Nahuatl, runs from about mid-November until mid-May. During this time many of the streams and springs will dry completely or be reduced to stagnant pools. The rainy season, or *xopajmili* in Nahuatl, begins in mid to late May and usually continues until about mid-November. The heaviest downpours occur in June, July, and August, when rivers and streams fill to overflowing and low areas often become swamps. Gentle streams become raging torrents, trails and roads are reduced to quagmires, and travel becomes dangerous or impossible for days and weeks at a time in the southern Huasteca.

This extreme seasonality and uneven distribution of rainfall is a major obstacle for horticulturists. On maps of the region, geographers indicate that the soil in the region of Amatlán is good for farming because it retains moisture for a minimum of 11 months out of the year. This finding is contradicted by other geographic maps showing that a very high 24 to 30% of rainwater does not soak into the soil but runs off into the network of streams and rivers. Villagers affirm that most of the rain runs off of their steep fields and that the soil is dry for stretches of time even in the rainy season. In addition, the average annual temperature for the Amatlán region is very high, ranging between 22 and 26 degrees centigrade (71.6 to 78.8 degrees Fahrenheit). Thus, evaporation from fields and the transpiration rate from crops is high, particularly under the broiling tropical sun. The people of Amatlán, like farmers everywhere, are dominated by forces of nature. But due to topography, latitude, and their proximity to the Gulf of Mexico they seem to be caught in an unpredictable cycle of drought and flood. The villagers do not pray for rain; they pray instead for harmony and balance in the extremes of the natural forces they face.

Soils are usually rocky and poor, except for flatlands and the floodplains of rivers and streams that are, for the most part, off-limits to Indian farmers. Villagers recognize three basic soil types whose names in Nahuatl are: *atlali* ("flat earth," or "muddy place," literally "water earth"), found along the banks of rivers and streams and excellent for planting; *cuatlali* ("hilly earth," literally "forest earth"), the major soil type in Amatlán and generally good for cultivation; and *tepetlatl* ("stone mat"), rocky soil found on some hillsides and very poor for cultivation (see De la Cruz 1982:41–42). As in many tropical environments, nutrients are held not in the soil but in the dense vegetation that blankets the whole region. Vegetation in the hot country of the southern Huasteca is classified as "medium sub-evergreen tropical forest." About 25% of the trees are deciduous, and most reach a mature height of less than 20 meters. In the dry season there are many trees and bushes that lose some or all of their leaves, although most plants do retain their foliage throughout the year. Indians have been practicing slash-and-burn horticulture in the southern Huasteca for many hundreds of years, and thus very little of the primary forest now remains. Because nutrients are held in the vegetation, slash-and-burn horticulture is very effective. By cutting down the forest and brush and then burning the dried vegetation, nutrients are returned to the soil for use by domesticated crops.

The forest cover, even though secondary, is thick and verdant and includes many tropical and subtropical species. Represented are species of *ficus* or tropical fig, tropical cedar (white and red), rosewood, brazilwood, bamboo, avocado, mango, banana, zapote, flamboyan, tropical poplar, palms, numerous types of fruit trees, and many grasses, bushes, and other plants (see Puig 1976; Romualdo Hernández 1982:18; and Reyes Antonio 1982:97–105 for the Nahua classification of the various habitats in the region and pages 187–202 in the last work for a list of plants). Larger trees are covered with parasitic flowering plants that bloom brilliantly during certain times of the year. Plant growth is rapid and remarkably dense, particularly during the rainy season. The trails are constantly threatened by encroaching vines and branches, and most people carry a machete with them to clear a path. The climate and soil permits villagers to grow a number of tropical and subtropical crops including sugarcane, coffee, tobacco, yuca (sweet casava?), *camote*, *jícama*, citrus fruits, and many more.

A number of animals and insects that live in the forest have an impact on village life. Those that are most sought after and consumed by villagers are mentioned in the next chapter. The region is known to contain jaguars, although I have never actually observed one. Of more immediate concern are the numerous species of snakes that inhabit the forest and that are sometimes found in the village. The most dangerous is the fer-de-lance (*mahuaquijtli* in Nahuatl), a deadly

snake I often encountered on the trails or while bathing. Several
people in the village were bitten by fer-de-lances while I was in
residence, and I once found one on my cot. There are several other
types, including the tropical coral snake (red and yellow varieties); the
poisonous *metlapili* (in Nahuatl), that resembles a blunt, thick grinding
stone, from which its name derives; and a green species I could not
identify that inhabits the brush along trails and strikes passersby in
the face. Scorpions can be found under logs or rocks, and tarantulas
the size of a man's hand are sometimes seen on trails or inside people's
houses. In my opinion, the most disagreeable creature in the forest
is a remarkable centipede (*pahuaneluatl* in Nahuatl) that is deadly
poisonous and may reach over a foot in length. The creature is unparal-
leled in its ugliness and in the fear that it causes among people.
Villagers told me that the bite is treated by cutting out a large portion
of flesh surrounding the wound with a machete. Finally, there are
many types of biting gnats and mosquitoes, each with their season.
Besides producing bloody and itchy bites, some can carry dangerous
diseases such as malaria and dengue fever. The forest has a real beauty
in its overwhelming greenness and its accents of exotic tropical flowers,
but neither the Indians nor any visitor can forget the many hidden
dangers to be found there (see Reyes Antonio 1982:21; and Romualdo
Hernández 1982:15–18).

The Veracruz portion of the Huasteca is particularly remote and
inaccessible. One well-paved road hugs the coast, connecting the ports
of Tampico in the north and Veracruz to the south. Roads leading to
the interior are surfaced with dirt and river pebbles and are so rough
that vehicular travel is restricted to a 10-mile per hour crawl. Most
interior roads become impassable in heavy rain. Few bridges cross
the hundreds of streams and rivulets that wind their way from the
mountains to the Gulf, and vehicles carrying passengers or produce
are frequently forced to turn back. Third-class buses rattle their way
along many of the interior roads, although, as I discovered, a journey
to most locales usually entails a long final trek on horseback or by foot.
There are only two moderate-sized towns in the Huasteca Veracruzana: Tuxpan on the coast and Pánuco, to the north.

The state of Veracruz is divided into political units called *municipios*,
which are analagous to our counties. Each municipio is run by a local
political leader called the Presidente, who is elected by the population
for a 3-year term. The Huasteca Veracruzana is composed of 33 such
municipios, each of which has its own Presidente and runs its own
internal affairs. The state or national governments always work through

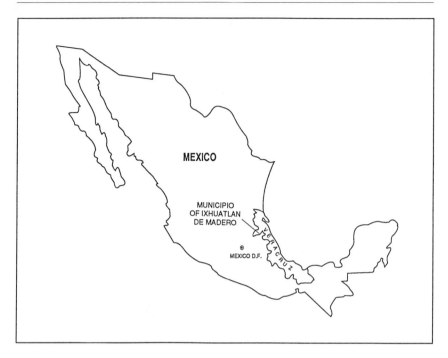

2.1. Mexico showing state of Veracruz and location of municipio of Ixhuatlán de Madero

the municipio structure, and it is this level of political authority that has the greatest direct effect on the lives of the local people. Amatlán lies in the municipio of Ixhuatlán de Madero. The Nahuatl name Ixhuatlán is translated sometimes as "place where plants are born," but in Amatlán people say it means "place of abundant *hoja de papatla*" (a plant with large leaves). Ixhuatlán was the name of a former Indian village that now serves as the administrative center (*cabecera* in Spanish) for the municipio. Thus, the name Ixhuatlán de Madero designates the municipio as a whole as well as the small town that serves as administrative center. The "de Madero" was appended after the Mexican Revolution to call attention to the fact that Ixhuatlán was the center of early support for General Francisco Madero, President of Mexico from 1911–13 (see map 2.1).

The most recently published national census (*X Censo General de Población y Vivienda, 1980*) and the *Statistical Yearbook of Veracruz (Anuario estadístico de Veracruz, 1984*) tells much about Ixhuatlán and the surrounding region. The Huasteca Veracruzana contains 1,003,697 people, 253,506 of which speak Indian languages. This figure represents about 25% of the inhabitants. Of the people speaking Native American languages, fully 67% speak Nahuatl, the language spoken in Amatlán. The municipio of Ixhuatlán de Madero has 53,883 inhabitants, about 1,500 of whom live in the administrative center. The census finds 39,195 speakers of Indian languages in the municipio, 26,793 of whom speak Nahuatl (68%). The remaining languages represented are Otomí (18%), Tepehua (9%), and Huastec (less than 1%).

There are two sources of error in these figures that should be explained. First, many of the values for Indian populations are estimated. Accurate counts of people living in remote villages are hard to achieve, and even resident schoolmasters sometimes grossly miscalculate their estimates of the local populations they serve. Second, when counting speakers of native languages only people 5 years and older are typically included in the census. This acts to underplay the number of Indians relative to non-Indians in the population because, on the average, over 25% of village inhabitants fall below this age cutoff. Taking these potential sources of error into account, we can see that the majority of people in Ixhuatlán de Madero are Indians, based on the criterion of language. The problem of isolating the other features that distinguish Indians from non-Indians will be discussed later in this chapter.

The municipio is about 600 square kilometers in area and lies in the hilly southern reaches of the Huasteca Veracruzana. The administrative center is 306 meters above sea level, placing it well inside of the hot country zone. In fact, despite variation in microclimatic conditions caused by the endless hills and valleys, the whole of Ixhuatlán de Madero can be classed as hot country. There are about 130 villages scattered throughout the municipio, with Nahuatl speakers occupying the northern two-thirds and Otomí and Tepehua speakers living in the southernmost third. On the dividing line between these two areas is situated the administrative center and seat of political control. The center is connected to the outside by a Y-shaped system of unpaved roads. One arm leads in a northwest direction to the neighboring municipio of Benito Juárez, while the other leads to the northeast through the municipio of Temapache and on to Tuxpan and Poza Rica almost 100 miles away. The arms of this road system meet in the market village of Llano de Enmedio (*huextlahuac* in Nahuatl) and proceed southward until reaching the administrative center of Ixhuatlán de Madero. The gravel road stops abruptly in the little town, as if to cut off entrance into the wild sierra that lies beyond.

The Indian population is scattered throughout Ixhuatlán in small villages, most of which range in population from 200 to 800 people. Many of these villages are on communally held plots of land called ejidos. These were established by law all over Mexico following the Revolution of 1910 as a way of returning the land to the large, dispossessed Indian population. Existing villages were allocated a fixed amount of land according to the number of male household heads living there. The holder was granted complete use rights over his land, including that of passing it on to his children or wife after he dies. He is forbidden, however, to sell or in any way dispose of the land outside of the community. The formal internal political structure of the ejido is determined by law, but this structure and the set of rules governing the ejido varies by state and region. Generally, a series of democratically elected community members head various committees that are responsible for the administration of the ejido.

The land tenure situation in the Huasteca region is exceedingly complex and not amenable to easy generalization. The Indians, wealthy landowners, local political leaders, and delegations from state and national governments represent divergent constituencies that are rarely in agreement over the precise nature of various types of land holdings (see Schryer 1986). A significant number of Indians of the region live in villages that have not been officially recognized as ejidos. Most Indians would like to belong to an ejido because of the benefits membership in such a community affords them. Not the least of these advantages is that ejido land is protected by law from being purchased or usurped by local ranchers and land speculators. However, as we have seen, struggles to gain ejido status can be complicated by economic and political divisions among the villagers themselves.

Most of the mestizos in the municipio live and work on the large cattle ranches located in the tracts of land between ejidos. As a rule, the ranches occupy rich and flat bottomland while the villages are located in the hilliest areas. The Huasteca is renowned throughout Mexico as a beef-producing area with many prosperous ranches. Often the ranch owners live in Mexico City or elsewhere, and some even fly in by private plane or helicopter. Despite the pretense of free elections, municipio government is completely in the hands of these mestizo ranch owners or their proxies. They are the ones with the necessary financial backing and connections with state and national politics to run for office. Equally important, they have the cultural and linguistic knowledge to operate among the elite groups of Mexico, none of which are Indian.

Ixhuatlán de Madero has been described by the Mexican anthropologist Roberto Williams García as a "place of rich cattle ranchers and gunmen" (1963:14). This description applies to much of the Huasteca Veracruzana. The mestizo ranch hands and cowboys are seldom without guns, and the Indians are often afraid of these local representatives of the national elites. Traveling through the region is much like returning to the North American West of a hundred years ago. Cowboys on horseback with Winchester rifles in their saddles and pistols stuck in their belts are a common sight. Gunfights between drunken cowboys are not unusual, and a favorite pastime is roping cattle from horseback and then wrestling them to the ground. But the illusion of living in the past is short lived. Occasionally, a traveler on a trail meets an army patrol bristling with machine guns, and this experience serves as a chilling reminder that we live in the twentieth century.

Among city dwellers in Mexico the region is known to be remote and lawless, a place where murder can go unpunished and outsiders are not welcome. A small branch bank that opened in Ixhuatlán de Madero a number of years ago was closed within a few months because it was repeatedly robbed. Little wonder that urban Mexicans were amazed and horrified when I told them that I, a foreigner, was conducting field research in the Huasteca. Several years later when I returned to the area with my wife and child, people thought I was being foolish, and they recommended (in vain) that I buy a gun of my own. The Huasteca is fascinating because it is rich in character. It is a place where the strains of a modernizing Mexico are experienced by the local people and are visible to the careful observer. As the census figures demonstrate, the Huasteca is also a place where Indians live in great numbers. There they follow their traditions and live in a world closely linked to their pre-Hispanic past. They, too, are caught up in the violence of the times as they try to assert their rights in an ever-changing world that is foreign to them. But by their numbers and their very presence, they contribute what is truly unique to the character of the region.

LAND AND PEOPLE

Defining who is an Indian—and who is not—is a surprisingly difficult task. Most Mexicans distinguish between mestizos, people of mixed American Indian and European racial stock who possess a Hispanic cultural outlook, and *indios*, who are identified with the remnants of the traditional American Indian races and cultures that existed at the time of the Conquest. In general, urban Mexicans recognize that rural mestizos share some Indian cultural traits, but they know that mestizo culture is basically that of urban national Mexico. The term *indio* has pejorative connotations for most Mexicans because many urban people consider Indians to be backward, and Indians are overrepresented in the lowest socioeconomic levels of Mexican society. A more neutral phrase in use is *gente indígena*, or indigenous people. Urban Mexicans generally identify these indigenous people as those who live in or originate from small villages, speak Native American languages, and have a traditional culture that differs from theirs. However, this commonly held distinction between people of mixed versus aboriginal heritage is highly misleading.

The first problem is in the use of the term *race*. Virtually all Mexicans are of mixed racial stock. A few people consider themselves "white," claiming to have a pedigree going back to the *peninsulares*, or Spaniards from the Iberian Peninsula, with no Indian admixture. These individuals are exceedingly rare and in most cases probably mistaken. People with Indian features, including black straight hair, dark-brown eyes, brown skin, and relatively short stature, can be found at all levels of Mexican society. This fact has led some observers to claim that Mexico is thus free from racism and that social distinctions are based solely on ethnic and class affiliation. Although it is true that overt racial discrimination such as that often found in the United States is rare and would be impossible to maintain in such a mixed population, definite racial biases exist in Mexico. Indian features are widely held to be unattractive and thus undesirable. Even in Amatlán I found that people admired children born with lighter skin, or brown, as opposed to black, hair. In Mexico to be *güero*, or light complexioned, gives a person advantages over his or her darker peers. But being darker does not necessarily mean the person is more Indian. An Indian can be güero too.

This confusion is not totally eliminated if we focus on strictly sociocultural factors to distinguish Indians from mestizos. In one sense all Mexicans are mestizos and, in fact, scholars and writers sometimes say "we are a nation of mestizos." Indians have influenced many aspects of Mexican urban national culture including diet, art and architecture, language, religious belief, and ritual. In turn, there are virtually no Indians in contemporary Mexico who have escaped the influence of urban, national culture. Thus, from the viewpoint of the outsider, defining what it is to be Indian is a matter of degree rather than of kind. Nor can the criterion of language always distinguish Indians from mestizos. Many rural mestizo people speak Indian languages bilingually, and in some cases Spanish is actually their second language. Individuals who are monolingual in a Native American language, however can almost certainly be said to be Indian by whatever criteria are applied (see Hill and Hill 1986 for a sociolinguistic study of language and ethnicity among Nahuas of central Mexico).

The difficulty of distinguishing Indians from mestizos is a problem faced by the Mexican government as it tries to settle land disputes, develop policies to encourage economic development, and deliver services to Indian populations. In the past, officials needed a quick measure of "Indianness," and they settled on the criterion of footwear as one distinguishing feature. People who wear shoes are mestizos; those who do not are Indians. This solution helps to explain an oddity about the Mexican national census. Like many countries, the federal government conducts a census every 10 years. The surveys normally contained questions regarding language affiliation that were designed to identify Indians. It eventually became obvious that language alone as a measure of Indianness is too crude to be of much use. As a consequence, beginning with the sixth national census in 1943, additional cultural data were collected from people, including whether or not they wore shoes (Marino Flores 1967:17). The question was intended to keep track of the Indian population and measure its growth or decline relative to mestizos. Interestingly, by the 1980 census the question had been deleted (see Castile 1981 for a parallel discussion of Indianness in both North America and Mexico).

The example of Julio Martínez of Amatlán will help to clarify some of the problems in distinguishing Indians from mestizos. Julio was born in the village, and like all other residents learned Nahuatl as his native language. His wife is from a neighboring Indian village and she, too, is a native Nahuatl speaker. Both Julio and his wife speak competent Spanish, and in fact are probably among the most fluent villagers. Julio is a farmer like other villagers, but he is distinguished by being one of the few people who owns cattle as well. His herd is large, and he has constant dealings with neighboring ranchers to assure access to pastures and water. Out of a small counter at the side of his house he runs one of two functioning cantinas in Amatlán. He carries an assortment of dry goods, but most of his business comes from selling cane alcohol to the villagers. His wife peddles bread she bakes in a stone-and-mud bread oven, and his children wait on customers at the cantina counter. Julio is a true entrepreneur who, in addition to his village life, operates a clothing and dry goods stall at the weekly markets in Ixhuatlán de Madero and in Llano de Enmedio. In 1986, when electricity reached Amatlán for the first time, he purchased a small refrigerator that he had transported by burro to the village. He now sells *hielitos*, the Spanish term for popsicle-like frozen bags of water mixed with sugar, coloring, and flavoring, in addition to cold soft drinks and beer.

When I first entered the village in 1970, Julio was one of the few men to wear Western-style clothing as well as shoes. He was curious about the United States and asked many questions about our farming practices and how much farm workers are paid in wages. He is extremely well-off by comparison to the other villagers, and it is clear that he intends the same for his several children. In 1986, his eldest daughter was attending secondary school in a distant town, an expense most villagers cannot afford. In addition to his entrepreneurial activities, Julio had by 1986 become an active force for change in the village. He is on a committee to petition the municipio government to have a road constructed connecting Amatlán to the outside, and he worked diligently to have electricity brought to the village. In sum, his outlook, many economic activities, dress, speech, and other characteristics would seem to link him to the mestizo world. And yet in many ways, he is thoroughly Indian.

Julio and his wife speak Spanish well and yet, for them, Nahuatl is the language of everyday use. With the exception of the refrigerator (purchased in 1986) and the cantina counter, nothing distinguishes their house from any other in the village. In addition, both Julio and his wife participate actively in the communal activities of the village. He never misses a communal work party, and he willingly serves on village committees. Moreover, Julio and his family participate actively in the traditional religion. He has an altar in his house watched over by a paper cutout of a witness spirit, and he calls in traditional curers when a member of his family falls ill. He acts as sponsor to major rituals such as the yearly ceremony to tonantsij, an important fertility spirit. Julio does not appear to engage in these activities to mollify jealous neighbors or fend off criticisms by others less successful than he. He fervently believes in the Nahua pantheon of spirits, follows the traditional customs, and actively participates in his culture. He strives for the benefit of himself and his family, but he does not remain aloof from his neighbors nor attempt to accrue power at their expense. He is one of those rare people little written about in social scientific literature: an Indian who has achieved substantial prosperity, while staying within the Indian system of values.

The complexities of distinguishing Indians from mestizos derive from the fact that no clear and stable dividing lines exist between the two groups. Although the cultural orientations of the two are different, from the perspective of the outsider they shade imperceptibly into one another. As in any sliding scale, the extremes are easy to distinguish. The in-between cases pose the difficulty. I would like to add here that the people of Amatlán do not appear to have any difficulty in determining a person's identity. Only an outsider, unfamiliar with the symbolic means of distinguishing the two groups, has difficulty (see Caso 1971:83ff. for a discussion of the complexities of defining Indians).

For the reader unfamiliar with ethnic divisions in Mexico, I would like to indicate some general features that distinguish Indians from mestizos. Ethnicity is often situational in that people decide when and how to assert their identity using different strategies at different times. An added complicating factor is that over time a group's self-definition changes to meet new challenges, and the symbols people choose to represent their identity may be modified, created anew, intentionally eliminated, or resurrected from a previous period. Thus, any listing of traits poses the danger of oversimplifying and thereby falsifying a complex and constantly shifting multiethnic situation. With these cautions in mind, I will identify some features of Nahua ethnicity recognized by both Indians and mestizos, and also meaningful to the outside observer.

Julio's example provides insight into how we might establish minimal criteria for defining Indian status that are valid for the period of my fieldwork. Such a definition should include the following characteristics: the person must (1) define himself or herself as an Indian; (2) be a native speaker of an indigenous language that is the language of choice in everyday speech; (3) participate freely in the communal activities of a village; (4) revere a pantheon of spirits and participate in rituals that, although influenced to a greater or lesser extent by Spanish Catholicism, derive from Native American traditions; (5) attempt through ritual and other means to enter into a balance or harmony with the social and natural worlds as opposed to striving for strict control over them. This last characteristic is difficult to apply, but it refers to the fact that most mestizos partake of the Euro-American world view, with its injunction to master the natural and social universes. Being Indian is not a state of wealth, nor is it antithetical to entrepreneurship or a progressive outlook that sees some benefits in adopting Western technology. Julio and his family are solidly Indian by their own assessment and by the five characteristics listed above.

(Reck 1986 [1978] has written a novel that seeks to illuminate the distinction between Indian and mestizo world view.)

Two features of this list are important to note. First, none of the criteria are biological. Second, with the possible exception of the first (self-definition as an Indian), each characteristic allows for a range of adherence by the participants. For example, a person may engage in communal village activities in only a minimal way or perhaps remain a background figure during rituals. Individuals divide their time and energies differently, but to be Indian, they must meet to some extent all five criteria. The characteristics cannot be applied rigidly, and each is difficult to measure. However, if one or more of them is not met, the chances are good that the person is on the way to becoming a mestizo. It is mobility from the Indian to the mestizo sector that contributes to the blurring of the distinction between the two social categories. Also, as discussed in Chapter 7, the Indians have an interest in keeping the cultural border area between themselves and the dominant mestizo population ill defined.

Another way to appreciate the differences between Indians and mestizos is to view the situation from a regional perspective. Indians live in villages with distinctive social structures, whereas mestizos live in ranches, towns, or cities. Wherever mestizos live in small, even isolated, farming communities they retain the basic outlook and values of their fellow mestizos who live in the towns. On a regional basis, Indians and mestizos interact under very special conditions. The Indians may work for the ranchers on a temporary basis, or they may trade with mestizo middlemen at the market, but there is virtually no socializing that occurs outside of well-defined situations such as these. Even when Indians invite mestizo cowboys to their villages for a bull-riding event (*jaripeo* in Spanish), the cowboys ride the bulls, and the Indians simply observe from outside the corral. The line separating Indian from mestizo is clearly recognized by the people in the region, and this is reflected in the rules of engagement followed by both groups when they interact.

The people of Amatlán are fully aware of their status as Indians, and this awareness is reflected in the terms they use to describe themselves and outsiders. They call themselves by the general term *masehualmej*, which in Nahuatl means "Indian farmers" or "countrymen." This is the same term used by the ancient Aztecs to refer to commoners, and so the word has an association with pre-Hispanic Mexico (Soustelle 1961 [1955]:70ff.). When wishing to be more specific, the villagers refer to themselves by the Nahuatl term *mexijcaj* (sing. *mexijcatl*) that is the same word used by the ancient Aztecs to refer to themselves. They call all mestizos, whether farmers or not, by the Nahuatl term *coyomej* (sing. *coyotl*) that has been translated by some anthropologists as "gentlemen" but which also has a derogatory connotation. Although James Taggart translates the term as "gentleman," he does point out that the Nahuatl word *coyotl* ("coyote" in English) is an animal the Nahuas view as a mischiefmaker and backbiter as well as being clever and self-serving (1983:260). The coyomej are seen as aggressive and arrogant, people who exploit others when allowed (see Romualdo Hernández 1982:27–30,158; and Reyes Martínez 1982:93,154 for Nahua descriptions of coyomej; also Wolf 1959:237). Older villagers will occasionally use the Spanish–Nahuatl word *caxtiltlacamej* ("Castilians") or the Spanish phrase *gente de razón* ("people of reason") to describe mestizos, obvious legacies of the colonial epoch. Villagers occasionally use the Spanish word *indio* ("Indian") when describing themselves or other non-Nahua Indians, but they will modify the word by adding the diminutive suffix -*ito*. So they may talk about *inditos*, but never *indios*. They use Nahuatl names to refer to their non-Nahua Indian neighbors: *huaxtecatl* for a Huastec, *otomitl* for an Otomí, and *tepehuatl* for a Tepehua. All of these people would be referred to as masehualmej (or "Indian farmers") as well.

The way the villagers use these terms depends largely on the context in which they are speaking. In distinguishing Indians from mestizos, they employ the general terms *masehualmej* and *coyomej*. In other contexts they may choose to distinguish Nahuas from other Indian groups, and they will use the appellation *mexijcaj* . As suggested above, use of these ethnic labels is situational and depends upon the speaker's position relative to his or her listeners and upon how inclusive or exclusive the speaker wishes to be. How villagers use ethnic labels is complicated by the somewhat ambiguous distinctions between Indian and mestizo and the slow but steady migration of Indians into the mestizo world. Local people who relocate to the city always maintain their positive Indian identity in the eyes of those who stay behind. Villagers reserve the disparaging term *otomimej* (sing. *otomitl*) for Indians who disguise themselves by dressing or acting like mestizos in order to put on airs or to take advantage of other Indians (Reyes Martínez 1982:93,176; Romualdo Hernández 1982:158). The use of the term *otomimej* in such a negative context reveals the degree of hostility in interethnic relations among Indians. The most significant social cleavage in the Huasteca, however, is between Indian and non-Indian. In virtually every situation, Indians from differing ethnic affiliations will unite to face the common mestizo threat.

The relationship that people have to the land in the Huasteca Veracruzana is a reflection of the Indian–mestizo distinction. For the most part, the Indians live on ejidos, or in other small settlements or villages. They are likely to be surrounded by several generations of their families and to farm relatively small plots of land. Mestizos may also live in villages and farm small plots, but they are more likely to use the plow and to have access to modern farming technology. For them, farming is seen as a business, an occupation. For the Indians, farming is not only a way to make a living, but it is also a coherent way of life, the central activity that serves as the focus of their social system, as well as their religious beliefs and practices. The people who own independent farms and cattle ranches in the region are always mestizos, and it is this group that dominates local political and economic decision making. Indians and mestizos can live side by side, but they inhabit different worlds. For an Indian to enter the mestizo world with its lure of opportunities for wealth and power, he or she must leave behind much of what is distinctively Indian and embrace an alien culture (see Wolf 1959:235ff. for a discussion of the nature and development of mestizo Mexico).

It is easy to see that despite problems and ambiguities in distinguishing the two groups, there are real differences between Indians and mestizos that have important consequences for the people of the Huasteca. One crucial difference is that Indians generally relate to mestizos from a position of social, political, and economic inequality. Low status, relative powerlessness and poverty, are not expressed directly when Indians interact with mestizos, however. Instead, these and other realities of life for the Indians are submerged in the ethnic distinctions that exist in the region. Indians and mestizos are divided by separate ethnic identities that serve to define in-group cultural values and distinguish them from cultural values of the out-group. Thus one of the most important variables that shapes Indian–mestizo interaction is ethnicity. The processes that determine the internal structures of ethnic groups or that lead to their creation in the first place are exceedingly complex and poorly understood by social scientists. Ethnicity has proven to be such a variable phenomenon with so many different manifestations that experts do not even agree on the precise definition of the phrase "ethnic group."

I define an ethnic group as a population within a larger society whose members identify themselves, for purposes of political, social, or economic advantage, as a distinct group based upon cultural features, such as religion, social character, dress, and perceived common historical origin, that are recognized by group members and outsiders alike. No single feature separates one ethnic group from other groups. As Fredrik Barth states, "It is important to recognize that although ethnic categories take cultural differences into account, we can assume no simple one-to-one relationship between ethnic units and cultural similarities and differences. The features that are taken into account are not the sum of 'objective' differences, but only those which the actors themselves regard as significant" (1969:14). The problem of defining an ethnic group can be at least partially resolved by focusing on the factors that lead people to forge and maintain a distinct identity. We must look at the advantages that accrue as a result of ethnic group membership, advantages that lead ethnic group members to establish boundaries between themselves and others regardless of actual observable cultural distinctions. Individual actors recognize ethnic differences, and we must examine what motivates them to perpetuate those differences through their beliefs and behavior (for a current discussion of ethnicity see Nash 1989).

An important point is that ethnic groups never exist in isolation, but only in relation to other ethnic groups. Thus to some extent, Indian and mestizo ethnic identities owe their existences to one another. Because ethnic groups cannot always be objectively distinguished according to cultural content and because it is impossible to predict which aspects of their culture members will select to distinguish their group, Barth recommends that scholars focus their attention on the boundaries between ethnic groups to see how members create and maintain their identities (1969:15). According to Barth, then, boundaries between Indians and mestizos shape and define their respective ethnic identities. To be an Indian is to participate in a cultural system that everyone in the region agrees is distinctly Indian. The same definition applies to mestizo identity, but because mestizos are more closely linked to the urban mainstream their identity tends to remain implicit. To understand the nature of the boundaries between these groups, we must understand not only what motivates Indians and mestizos to create separate identities for themselves but also how these separate identities influence cross-boundary interaction.

As I will emphasize throughout this work, one way of clarifying the complex ethnic situation in the Huasteca is to view Indian ethnicity as a response to the real-life situations confronting villagers and to recognize that Indian–mestizo interaction is mediated through their respective ethnic identities. Ethnic identity and the formation of ethnic groups will be discussed further in Chapter 7 (see also Tambiah 1989:335–36, for a definition of ethnic group that stresses the "pragmatics of calculated choice and opportunism").

Besides language, the most important overt marker of ethnic identity in the southern Huasteca is dress. Clothing style can distinguish Indians from mestizos as well as the various Indian groups from each other. Even within ethnic groups subtle differences in dress can often identify the village of the wearer. In Amatlán, types of dress are important symbolic markers that link the wearer to certain social categories. I must state at the outset that this system of symbolic classification of people is currently in the process of breaking down. In 1970, when I first went to Amatlán, about 95% of the men and 100% of the women dressed in the traditional style. By traditional I mean dress style identified as Indian, although the styles themselves appear to be primarily based on post-Conquest Spanish peasant dress. In 1986 only 20% of the men and about 75% of the women continued the old pattern. Increasingly, villagers purchase clothes in the mestizo or Euro-American style from secondhand stalls on market day. In fact, the most favored used clothing comes from the United States. On several occasions I was taken aback as I passed someone on the trail wearing, for example, a University of Michigan sweatshirt.

In the traditional system, men and those boys old enough to be working their own fields wear loose-fitting white cotton muslin pants that tie at the waist and ankles. The pants are called *caltsoj* (from the Spanish *calzón*), and like all traditional clothes in the village they are hand sewn by the women from cloth purchased at the market. On top, men wear a very loose-fitting white pullover long-sleeved shirt that reaches to the thigh and is made from the same material. The neck opening extends for about six inches down the front from the neckline and is closed with three or four colored buttons. Some men wear shirts with the cuffs and the area surrounding the buttons embroidered with brightly colored thread. The majority of men rarely wear shoes, although some wear a kind of sandal constructed from a piece of rubber tire—the tire tread or sidewall cut into a shape for the sole—held on with criss-crossed white leather thongs threaded through heavy wire staples. This footwear is called *tecactli* (sing.) in Nahuatl, *huarache* in Spanish. When wading through water or during particularly hot days men may roll their pants legs up above the hem of their long shirts so as to create shorts. Some men keep their sleeves up by wearing a rubberband around each upper arm.

Married women, regardless of age, wear a skirt of a bright solid color that wraps around the waist and falls to the ankles. It is tied on and is frequently made from a heavy satin-type cloth. This skirt, called an *enagua* in Spanish or *cueitl* in Nahuatl, usually has one or two horizontal strips of a contrasting color of cloth or ribbon circling at about knee height. Women wear a short-sleeved blouse called by the Spanish term *camisa* . This beautiful garment is constructed from white muslin that fits tightly under the arms and, through a series of tiny pleats, almost like smocking, hangs loosely down below the waist. Blouses are usually worn tucked into the skirt. The tops of the sleeves and a large rectangle of cloth that serves as the neck of the blouse are sewn on separately. This rectangular yoke, reaching about one-third of the way down the front and back, as well as the sleeve tops are heavily embroidered before they are added to the blouse. Cross-stitch designs portray geometric patterns or flowers, and the embroidery threads used are bright red, yellow, orange, blue, green, and other vivid colors. Around the edging of the sleeves and inside the neck women some-times sew a black ribbon. The border between the embroidered panels and the plain lower two-thirds of the blouse is often set off by a narrow band of bright blue or red embroidery. The sleeves and border areas are sometimes further decorated with a lacelike filagree painstakingly added by the seamstress in white thread. The blouses are strikingly beautiful, and fine handiwork is a source of pride for women. Both women and girls go about barefooted.

Small boys, before they receive land from their fathers, are dressed in a nightshirt-like outfit called a *cotoj* probably from the Spanish *cota* ("blouse"), that hangs to the knee; cloth selected for the *cotoj* is either white or lightly patterned. The young children wear no undergarments and nothing on their feet. At the time when their fathers let them work a small piece of land, usually at about age 9, boys change to adult male dress. Small girls wear a one-piece dress that is usually of a solid bright color. The cloth is often a remnant of the same satiny material used for their mothers' skirts. Young girls' dresses may be decorated at the borders but are plain by comparison to that of the married women. Should a woman not marry, a rare occurrence, she continues to wear the single-piece dress throughout adulthood. Until about the age of 3, infants of both sexes are allowed to go without any clothing whatsoever.

Neither men nor boys adorn themselves beyond the very small amount of embroidery on their shirts. Men very often carry a woven sisal bag over one shoulder that is sparingly decorated with geometric designs. The bag is for general carrying, but it usually contains a red bandana that may be tied around the neck. Young men may carry small bottles of perfume and a mirror in the bag, and they can be observed grooming themselves on occasion. Men rarely leave the house compound without their black-handled Collins machete at their side. This all-purpose tool is carried in a leather sheath, hung on the shoulder, or strapped on the hip by means of a leather thong. Girls have their ears pierced at birth, and thereafter they always wear earrings (sing. *pipiluli* in Nahuatl). As they grow older, girls favor long dangling earrings with inexpensive paste jewels. In addition, girls and women always wear several strands of brightly colored bead necklaces that they acquire at the weekly market.

Women never cut their hair and usually wear it in two long braids. They often weave strips of colored cloth or threads into the braids that may hang down to the back of their legs. Men's hair is kept at medium length, and they have very little or no facial hair. When traveling, women may wear over their heads a black shawllike cloth called a *rebozo* in Spanish. When away from the village, men typically wear a straw hat that they purchase in the market. It is the style of the hat and the way it is trained that identify the wearer as associated with a specific village. The hats also function to protect the wearer from sunstroke or inclement weather on long treks to the market. Clothes are kept scrupulously clean by the women, who spend much of each day doing the washing among the rocks and cool waters of the arroyo. Both men and women wear old and even tattered clothing to do heavy work, but otherwise they are generally neatly dressed and groomed. The women are by far the more colorful in their dress, but the men are quite striking in their flowing white clothes with the machete in its dark-brown sheath hanging by their side.

Clothing worn by the villagers is not only attractive but quite functionally suited to the climate. Loose-fitting, clean cotton clothes are best for humid, hot weather and effectively deter biting insects. During periods of cold, people wear wool poncho-like garments called *jorongos* in Spanish, which are purchased at the market. Sheets of plastic serve as raincoats. As seen, clothes for the Nahuas, as for most people, serve far more than strictly functional ends. Clothes say something about the wearer. In Nahua culture, clothes can indicate a person's sex, marital status, ethnic identity, and village of origin. Interestingly, clothes do not reveal much about the wealth of the wearer; whether well-off or poor, the quality of the clothes among villagers remains about the same.

With the introduction in recent years of purchased urban clothing, both the functional and symbolic systems are rapidly disappearing. Commercially manufactured clothes often fit too snugly and are made from polyester or other synthetic fibers. They are uncomfortable, hot, difficult to clean, cheaply made, and not durable. Arturo Warman has written that the industrial products that make it to the villages are often inferior substitutions for locally produced items. These manufactured goods, therefore, do not contribute to the standard of living and may actually lower it (1976:277). This is certainly true with regard to clothing in Amatlán. What is more, the symbolic message of the clothing has become confused at a fundamental level. The line between Indian and mestizo is blurred, and it becomes even more difficult for Indian and outsider alike to distinguish the two worlds. In my view, the villagers are not changing their clothing from some abstract desire to be viewed as modern. They select uncomfortable and expensive clothing because it confers an advantage upon them in the real-life context in which they operate. For example, villagers who periodically go to cities to work are more successful in dealing with urban mestizos if they discard overt signs that identify themselves as Indians. Having an ethnic identity has advantages and disadvantages, and the Nahuas, like most people, are actively trying to consolidate gains and cut losses. The nature of these advantages and disadvantages will be discussed in a later chapter.

NEIGHBORS

As part of my attempts to understand the significant features in the immediate surroundings of Amatlán, I asked several villagers to help me create a map of the region. Interestingly, their ideas of how to draw a map differed considerably from mine. Rather than outline boundaries around neighboring ejidos or privately owned ranches, they made three or four dots on the paper and identified the points as specific locations within the boundaries of a certain cattle ranch or regional town. They would then make some more dots and identify them as locations in an adjacent ejido. Apparently, they identify a given area of land by key geographic features and not by linear boundaries. When walking around Amatlán the men knew precisely where their land ends and a neighbor's begins, but that is not the way they chose to represent land holdings on paper. After much discussion I was able to get them to agree on the design of a map that included linear boundaries. I then compared their conception with an official map made from aerial photographs. Considering the hilly terrain, I was impressed at how accurate their plan was.

Despite the remote locale and the rugged terrain of the region it is clear that virtually all of the land is claimed by someone. Amatlán is bordered to the north, northeast, south, and southwest by other Nahua ejidos or settlements. To the northwest and southeast are privately owned cattle ranches run by hired managers. Most owners live in major cities throughout Mexico or in mestizo towns elsewhere in the municipio. Surrounding the village further afield are additional Nahua ejidos and private ranches. All of these are connected to each other by a complex network of foot trails and horse paths. Meandering from the northwest to the southeast is an arroyo, an arrestingly beautiful rocky stream that empties into the Vinazco River several kilometers away. On maps, this arroyo is called the Pilpuerta, a mixed Nahuatl-Spanish word meaning "little door" or "little opening." The official designation is not recognized in the villages, however, because they name sections but not the whole arroyo.

Relations among Amatlán and surrounding settlements and ranches are crucial factors in their sociopolitical environment. Generally, the ranches are off-limits and are of service to villagers only as potential sources of temporary wage labor during certain times of the year. Interactions, however, have not always been peaceful. During the days when the government was expropriating land from wealthy ranchers to distribute to the Indians, hostility poisoned relations in the region. The absentee owner of a neighboring cattle ranch directly to the west of Amatlán, and other owners of private land to the south of the village, are each engaged in legal battles to fend off Indians who require more farmland. However, Amatlán is not directly involved in either of these battles.

The relatively fixed land base, coupled with an increasing population, has caused problems for the village. The result has been the formation of daughter villages in the surrounding area. One daughter village of Amatlán applied for and was granted ejido status of its own some years ago. Because the break was amicable, relations between Amatlán and this community have always remained cordial. To the south of Amatlán are two other small daughter villages, both of which fissioned from the main village in the past 15 years. The breaks, however, were not friendly, and there remains a great deal of animosity. Neither of the new villages has yet been granted ejido status, and the inhabitants are in constant danger of losing their houses and crops to an army invasion or to gunmen hired by the landowner. The insecurity of these people led them to invade part of Amatlán just when the latter was negotiating with the state agrarian commission to have its own land base increased. Thus, there is a kind of no-man's-land between Amatlán and its southern neighbors where no one dares to risk planting crops. The invasion was bloody, and hard feelings endure.

Villagers told me that in the late 1970s a fourth daughter village was formed about 4 hours walk to the west. People from Amatlán and several other Nahua villages cleared an unused area belonging to a rancher and planted crops. After 3 years they built houses and began to live permanently in the new village. One fall, as the crops were ready for harvest, the army invaded and burned down all of the houses. Under orders from local commanders, they shot all of the farm animals, burned the ripened crops in the fields, and moved the people out in trucks. The village was obliterated, and the army distributed the homeless families among several distant ejidos. When telling me about this event, villagers expressed their greatest outrage at the way the soldiers wantonly destroyed perfectly good food.

Each village, whether an ejido or not, is engaged in a lone struggle against its Indian and non-Indian neighbors to increase its land base. The struggle is not solely to increase productive capacity but also to accomodate the increase in population. With a fixed amount of land available, many people must leave the village before they become adults with families of their own. The situation is thus not simply Indian pitted against mestizo rancher; it is also Indian against Indian. This complex situation is one reason, I believe, that Indians separate themselves in dress, for example, from local mestizos, as well as from other Indian villagers. A person's support group is focused on the village of residence, and symbolic distinctions are made between members of that village and everyone else.

An important factor to consider here is that the agrarian commission and other governmental agencies are far more likely to distribute land to established villages than to individuals. For this reason, even daughter villages that maintain friendly relations with the mother village find it in their interest to establish their own sense of community and thus distinguish themselves symbolically a short time after separating. As we have seen, the village itself may be divided internally, but nevertheless any effort to increase the land base must originate from and be sustained by members from a common village. Dress is just one way that people establish this sense of common cause. Another more important way this is done is through microvariations in the performance of traditional rituals. This, and additional strategies of establishing community and reasons for doing so, will be discussed in subsequent chapters.

Two cemeteries serve Amatlán; one is shared with a neighboring ejido, and the other is a new one recently opened up in a location that is remote from the houses. The new cemetery was created to relieve overcrowding in the older one. I mention cemeteries in this section on neighbors because, for the Nahuas, they are entrances to the underworld and places inhabited by the souls of the dead. From pre-Hispanic days, the Indians of Mesoamerica have had a significant cultural focus on death. The influence of this heritage has carried into modern Mexico where Day of the Dead celebrations are internationally renowned. For the Nahuas, graves are doors to the underworld, and they see graveyards as sites where the ancestors gather. Villagers generally regard cemeteries as frightening places with powerful emotional significance. They hold elaborate rituals there to make offerings to the dead who, if they are not satisfied, will send disease and death into the village. As we shall see, curing rituals are essentially efforts to establish peace with spirits of the dead, many of whom originate from the graveyard.

Similarly, the Nahuas believe that numerous sacred spots in the vicinity of their villages are residences of spirit entities. As I will explain in Chapters 3 and 6, the Nahuas of Amatlán have a very intimate relationship with the features of the landscape in and around the village. Nahuas hold that the earth is literally alive, and almost every geographical feature plays a role in mythology or folklore, or is the home of a living spirit. In fact, I will argue that Nahua religion has a pantheistic quality in which the universe and everything in it partakes of a living spiritual essence. Thus the peaks of hills, caves, springs, swamps, pre-Hispanic ruins, gorges, and mountain ranges are seen by the Nahuas as local manifestations of a greater animating force. Through rituals and the behavior of shamans, people are brought into almost daily interaction with their geographical surroundings. People offer eggs to the spirit that inhabits the spring when they get water, candles to the spirit of a tree they have just cut down, or food and incense to the field they have just finished planting. The Nahua world includes living spirit entities that, like human neighbors, are part of the social system. Even their physical surroundings are incorporated into a universal spiritual society that far exceeds its human counterpart.

THE MARKETPLACES

One key feature in the setting of a village is its location relative to markets. In many cases access to markets is a decisive factor in village production strategies. A distinction must be drawn between a small store, called by the Spanish term *tienda*, and a weekly market, called *tianquistli* in Nahuatl. Almost all mestizo settlements have one or more permanent stores that are open 6 or 7 days a week. They may sell dry goods, hardware, medicine, or any number of items to serve the local community and surrounding ranches. Indians almost never make purchases at the *tiendas*. Markets are held weekly at selected settlements, and they draw Indian and mestizo customers from miles around. Anyone may set up a display and sell what they wish. The only requirement is that the space be rented from the town. Most of the people selling are mestizo professionals who travel a circuit from market to market. A fair proportion, however, are Indians, many of whom have become professional or semiprofessional merchants.

Amatlán is situated within reach of three regional markets. The first is held on Fridays at *huextlahuac* (its name in Nahuatl; Llano de Enmedio in Spanish), a small mestizo settlement about 1½ hours by foot from Amatlán. People state that prices are slightly higher here than elsewhere, presumably because this is the first regional market of the week and consumer demand is a bit higher. The second market is held at *colatlaj* (Colatlán in Spanish) on Saturdays and is about a 3-hour walk from the village. Colatlán is a larger settlement than Llano de Enmedio, and most cattle business is handled through this market. The last weekly market is in *ixhuatlaj* (Ixhuatlán de Madero in Spanish) and takes place on Sundays. This is by far the largest of the three, and many more items are available for purchase. The town lies across the Vinazco River from Amatlán, about 2 hours walk from the village. The river must be traversed by canoe, or, in the dry season, by horseback, wading, or swimming. The Ixhuatlán market is popular because of its size and because administrative offices of the municipio are there (and open on Sundays). The problem is that the river is an obstacle that prevents animals from crossing, making bulk transport of goods nearly impossible.

These markets are held outdoors beneath crude canvas awnings that protect the sellers and their merchandise from the tropical sun. They are typical of rural marketplaces throughout Mexico and other parts of the world, to an outsider seemingly as much a carnival as a serious place of business. Crowds of people dressed in their best clothing mill around small displays of fruits, vegetables, tools, clothing, toys, and uncountable other commodities. Vendors sit passively or take a more active role in selling by hawking the qualities of their product. People from the villages arrive with loads of produce to sell or trade, and as the day progresses they can be seen leaving with the items they have purchased and perhaps with a small toy or two for their children. Paradoxically, most people seem to be standing around chatting with almost no actual buying and selling going on. By the end of the day, however, everyone in attendance from the villages has transacted some business, and they have caught up on regional news. Relatives from neighboring villages have been contacted, messages have been passed and received, and plans have been made.

The atmosphere of the market hides another key activity on the minds of most people in attendance. Both men and women make it their business to find out the prices paid for key items that week. I was always amazed at how informed everyone in Amatlán was about the going rates for corn, beans, coffee, or other crops and goods. In general, the villagers are very interested in the price of everything, but they are passionate about learning the prices paid for their crops. Prices follow a yearly cycle that, to a certain extent, can be predicted in advance once information becomes available. Prices paid for key commodities are set by regional market conditions, government policy, and professional merchants and thus are outside of village control. During certain times of the year, villagers must buy and sell farm products if they are to remain viable, and the price cycle is an important factor in their success or failure (see Chapter 5).

REGIONAL AND VILLAGE HISTORY: THE LEGACY OF VIOLENCE

Neither the prehistory nor the history of the southern Huasteca is well known. Scholars have neglected the region on the assumption that what happened in the Huasteca is marginal to the spectacular rise of civilizations in the central highlands. Research has focused on the achievements of the Aztecs and Toltecs, and the interesting cultures on the periphery have remained obscure. Part of the problem is that the Spanish conquerors found little to attract them to the region.

There was no gold, valuable minerals were scarce in the Huasteca, the climate was oppressive, and the terrain was forbidding. Few chroniclers wrote about the Huasteca, and thus there is a paucity of ethnohistorical sources on this mysterious region. Information we have often comes from Aztec observers who expressed shock and dismay at the behavior of the Huastec Indians. It is one of the very few areas in Mesoamerica where phallic worship was practiced, and Huastec men were reputed, much to the horror of the puritanical Aztecs, to go about naked. There were also rumors of erotic Huastec fertility rituals, and the Aztec deity Tlazolteotl, goddess of sexual love among other attributes, is believed to have originated in the Huasteca.

We know that in pre-Hispanic times, Maya-speaking Huastec Indians occupied the entire region that today bears their name. Archaeological reconnaissance expeditions carried out in the early 1950s and in the late 1960s have established that Huastec ruins and statuary are found in the southern Huasteca where few Huastec speakers live today (Medellín Zenil 1982:202–4; Wilkerson 1979:41, 44; Ochoa 1979). Amatlán itself is built upon a whole complex of pre-Hispanic stone walls, platform mounds, and enclosed areas, most of which are covered with thick vegetation and forest debris. In the fields northwest of the houses, remains can be seen of a raised stone road of the pre-Hispanic type that proceeds in a straight line westward, directly intersecting the side of a large pointed hill. It continues on the other side of the hill in the direction of a neighboring village several kilometers away. To the west of the houses at a distance of about 2 kilometers, villagers showed me a large complex of ruined temple mounds that were built on a broad, artificially leveled terrace. The site is located on a remote cattle ranch and is used as a pasture. From the summit of the tallest mound I could see Amatlán, and I could also determine that all of the ruins over a several square-kilometer area are part of a single complex.

My preliminary investigation revealed that Amatlán is located in the middle of a major site complex that was unknown to outsiders before the people showed it to me. Most of the site is covered with dense forest, and so it is difficult to determine its extent or layout. In 1986 I sent drawings and photographs to experts in Mexico City, and an archaeologist came to investigate. He collected some pottery fragments and reported that the site is unusually large and almost certainly of Huastec origin. I asked the people of Amatlán about the ruins, which they call by the general term *tetsacual* (sing.) in Nahuatl and *cube* in Spanish. Most people had little opinion about them except to state that they are very old. Some believe that an unknown ancient people built them and then disappeared. Several people told me that an underworld spirit they call *montesoma* in Nahuatl built all of the ruins in addition to the church in Ixhuatlán de Madero. The shamans were in agreement that the ruins are doorways to the underworld. In fact, I have witnessed many curing rituals in which shamans dedicate offerings to disease-causing spirits of the dead at the base of ruined mounds. Everyone I talked to agreed that it is wrong to disturb the stones, although they disagreed in their reasons. Some said that there are poisonous snakes inside of the mounds, whereas others said simply that the ruins are ancient and should be respected.

Preliminary dating of sites in the region has revealed that the Huastecs left their settlements in the southern Huasteca before the arrival of the Spaniards. No one knows why the sites were abandoned, but legendary history recorded in the sixteenth century points to a number of migrations and invasions into the southern Huasteca that may have driven local inhabitants northward. Nahuatl-speaking Toltecs from the highlands are reputed to have entered the southern Huasteca, and there is some archaeological evidence that this occurred. Coastal peoples such as the Totonacs just to the south of the Huasteca are said to have acquired slaves from the central highlands; these slaves may eventually have formed settlements, causing the Huastecs to move north. In addition, sixteenth-century chroniclers recorded pre-Hispanic famines in the highlands during which large numbers of people migrated to the Huasteca lowlands to settle permanently (Kelly and Palerm 1952:16ff.; see Wolf 1959 Chapters 3 and 4 for a general discussion of the migrations of peoples in Mexico including the Gulf Coast).

Due to these and other migrations and invasions, the western and southern portions of the Huasteca have been taken over by Otomís, Tepehuas, and speakers of both Nahuat and Nahuatl dialects. The 1980 census found only 10 Huastec speakers in the entire municipio of Ixhuatlán de Madero, which it will be recalled is located in the southern part of the Huasteca. According to the noted authority on the Huasteca, Guy Stresser-Péan, Nahuas had entered the region by at least the thirteenth century during the final Toltec period and probably much earlier (1971:584–87; see also Stresser-Péan 1952–53). We do not know if the Toltecs came in war or peace nor if they established settlements that persisted until the appearance of the Spaniards. The historical records become more reliable later during Aztec times, and they tell of repeated invasions into the southern Huasteca that were violent and bloody.

In the fifteenth century, Netzahualcoyotl, king of Texcoco (1431–72) and an ally of the Aztecs, conquered parts of the coastal region near the southern Huasteca. As representative of the famed Aztec Triple Alliance, which included the cities of Tenochtitlán, Texcoco, and Tlacopan, Netzahualcoyotl allegedly conquered the southern Huastecan kingdom of Tzicoac as well as the coastal town of Tuxpan. The village of Amatlán is located within the ancient boundaries of Tzicoac, and Tuxpan remains an important coastal town in the region. In an effort to protect themselves, the Totonacs formed alliances with their Huastec neighbors to the north and with the highland Tlaxcalans, enemies of the Aztec alliance. Motecuhzoma (usually called Montezuma) Ilhuicamina, who ruled from 1440 to 1468, launched an invasion into the southern Huasteca in the 1450s and drove a wedge between the Huastecs and their Totonac allies to the south. The Aztec emperors Axayacatl (1468–81), Tizoc (1481–86), Ahuizotl (1486–1502), and finally, Motecuhzoma (Montezuma) Xocoyotl (1502–20) all launched bloody invasions into the southern Huasteca and Totonac region at various times during their reigns. The attacks were carried out either to extend political control or, alternatively, to suppress the frequent revolts of subject populations (Kelly and Palerm 1952:21ff.; Hassig 1988:163,188,204,350).

At the time of the Spanish invasion in 1519 the entire Totonac region, called the Totonacapan, and a portion of the southern Huasteca were firmly held by the Aztecs. Today the distribution of the Indian groups in northern Veracruz reflects these historical occurrences. To the south are located the Totonacs, whom Cortés found to be ready allies in his march against the Aztec capital. Farther to the north, a band of Nahuatl speakers extends from the central plateau to the coastal town of Tuxpan, probably representing the remnants of the Aztec wedge that so effectively separated the Huastecs from their southern allies. Amatlán lies on the southern edge of this Nahua band about 75 kilometers north of the main Totonac population concentration. To the north and south of the band we find small scattered groups of Tepehuas, Otomís, and speakers of the Nahuat dialect. Finally, far to the north are located the Huastecs who continue to occupy what is left of their once vast empire.

Following the defeat of the Aztecs in 1521, Mexico entered its colonial period, and the persecution of the native peoples began in earnest. The brutality of the Spanish occupation is reflected in the drastic population decline that occurred after the Conquest. One authority has written that the population of Mesoamerica in 1519 was 22

million and that within a number of years the total had declined to
fewer than 1 million (Gerhard 1972:23–24). This represents an appall-
ing reduction of over 95%. With regard to the Gulf Coast populations,
the same scholar has written: "In the first decades after the conquest
vast numbers of Indians, probably in the millions, succumbed in the
hot country behind Veracruz" (1972:23–24). William Sanders writes
that the population of the state of Veracruz was almost destroyed
following the Conquest and that the Gulf Coast population declined
to 9% of the 1519 total (1952–53:46; 1971:547). Sherburne Cook and
Lesley Byrd Simpson, in trying to estimate pre-Hispanic population
totals, state that they can provide little information on the southern
Huasteca simply because the population there had practically vanished
by the time records began to be kept (1948:2–3).

The Indians died from disease, forced labor, and neglect, and the
responsibility for this holocaust lies squarely with the Spaniards and
their policies. Following the Conquest, colonial authorities set up a
feudal-type system to reward the conquerors. The Crown made land
grants (which included resident Indians) called *encomiendas* as payment
to soldiers and officials for their exploits. The lands and Indian inhabitants were to be administered by the grantee or *encomendero*. The
encomendero was responsible for his Indian charges, including their
conversion to Christianity, and in return he received free labor and/or
tribute from them. The encomienda system ruthlessly exploited the
Indians, and countless numbers died in the mines and fields belonging
to the conquerors. By the end of the sixteenth-century, encomiendas
were being transformed into haciendas, privately owned ranches run
like businesses, which hired Indian labor. The result was that the
Indians were gradually dispossessed of what land they had managed
to retain, and they were reduced from quasi-independent farmers to
a rural work force. Thus, the process of proletarianization discussed
by Bartra and Friedlander (and outlined in the first chapter) began less
than 100 years after the Conquest.

The Gulf Coast Indians, probably including the Nahuas, reacted to
these depredations by escaping deeper into the inaccessible reaches
of the Sierra Madre range and by continuing to live in small farming
villages, holding most land in common. Decreases in the Indian population, combined with the numbers of families who fled the grasp of
the Spaniards, caused a continuing labor crisis among major landowners and encomenderos. As early as 1592, in the vicinity of Amatlán,
Spanish authorities instituted a policy of *reducciones* ("reductions"),
whereby families were rounded up and forced to live in centralized

locales. It was thought that this policy would make the Indians easier to administer and would help solve the chronic labor shortage. The newly formed settlements resulting from reducciones were called *congregaciones* ("congregations"). Interestingly, Amatlán is classed as a *congregación*, indicating that it may have been created during this early period. Apparently the policy did not work very well, and many Indians continued to escape into the Sierra whenever their situation became intolerable. Ultimately, rural elites solved their labor problem by importing black slaves from Africa to work their lands.

Missionary work in the southern Huasteca began prior to 1530 with the arrival of the Franciscans. A few years later rival Augustinians arrived on the scene, and the southern Huasteca was subjected to one of the longest periods of evangelization in all of Mexico. Early in the sixteenth century, a priest was stationed at Chicóntepec in the heart of Nahua country, several kilometers from Amatlán. Despite the long exposure to missionaries, the southern Huasteca remains a stronghold of pre-Hispanic beliefs and rituals. This lack of success on the part of the missionaries can partially be explained by the scattered nature of the Indian population and the difficulty of travel and communication in the rugged terrain of the region. As missionary pressure became too great, people simply moved further into the Sierra. An additional factor is that the Franciscans and Augustinians were in conflict among themselves and these struggles undoubtedly hampered their missionary work (Kelly and Palerm 1952:30ff.; also see Burkhart 1989 for a discussion of missionary efforts in colonial Mexico and the Nahua response to them).

The early part of the nineteenth century brought the Mexican War of Independence. Surprisingly, the Totonac region and the southern Huasteca became centers for the insurrection, and Indians were active participants in the struggle against Spain. Often armed with bows and stone-tipped arrows, they fought under their own leaders. The greatest oppressors of the Indians were local landowners and government officials, and the fight for independence from Spain was almost solely in the interests of Mexican urban and rural elites. A natural question is why the Indians would fight for a cause that promised to benefit the landowners and not themselves. The paradox of Indian participation in the war is resolved when one realizes that many native fighters continued the struggle long after independence was won. It is clear they felt they were fighting for their own independence and that the campaign included freedom from the newly formed republican government of Mexico. One renowned Totonac Indian leader named

Mariano Olarte fought in the hills around Amatlán for years after independence. Finally in 1838 he was killed by government troops, and many of his Indian followers escaped further into the Sierra. I was not able to determine the extent to which local Nahuas participated in these events, but I assume they played their part. The remote villages established by Indian refugees in order to escape oppression and to retain their cultural integrity were most likely of the closed type suggested by Redfield and Wolf (see Chapter 1).

Even after the war with Spain, much Indian land remained communally held by the village, just as it was in the traditional pre-Hispanic system. In 1856, in order to encourage the development of modern agriculture, the Mexican government passed laws of disentailment (*desamortización*) that were designed to turn communal property into private property. The result was that the Indians lost even more of their lands to hacienda owners and land speculators. In 1864, the French succeeded in installing the Austrian archduke Maximilian as emperor of Mexico (1864–67), and the ensuing struggle carried over to the southern Huasteca and Totonac region. Again the Indians fought, and again the Indians kept fighting the newly formed Mexican government after the French withdrew and Maximilian was executed. The Indians had their own agenda, and it did not include trading one set of oppressors for another. These events lend credence to the position of Aguirre Beltrán, discussed in Chapter 1, who argues that the Indians are almost separate nations within Mexico and that feudal conditions existing in rural areas have arrested their social and economic development and prevented them from participating fully in national life.

An interesting footnote to the history of the southern Huasteca region during this period is that some villages were apparently raided by Comanche warriors coming from what is now the southwestern part of the United States. The Sierra Madre Oriental forms a natural north–south corridor that would have funneled northern raiders into the Huasteca region. Although contemporary villagers have no recollection of these raids, many villages in the region commemorate them in rituals associated with the celebration of Carnival. In Amatlán, disguised young men called *mecos* invade each compound in the village and disrupt normal life by their wild antics (see Chapter 6). The word *meco* may derive from *chichimecaj* that was the general name that pre-Hispanic Aztecs gave to the hunters and gatherers who periodically raided central Mexico from the north. During Carnival celebrations in other villages of the southern Huasteca, young men put on headdresses decorated with turkey feathers or brightly colored paper. They carry bows and arrows in their hands and, like the mecos, scream fiercely while dancing in house compounds. Villagers call these actors *coman-ches* (see Reyes García 1960:54–59,89–92 and Provost 1975:22).

In 1875, the government revived laws of colonization that encouraged entrepreneurs to acquire lands in the region and develop them into modern farms. It was assumed by national leaders that the sparse populations of Indians were insignificant and that potentially productive lands were going to waste. In a few years this policy succeeded in dispossessing the Indians of their remaining lands, and it was not until just before the Mexican Revolution of 1910 that these laws were rescinded. Another development in the late nineteenth century that promised trouble for the Indian population was the discovery of oil in the southern Huasteca. In 1901, the first government concessions were granted to oil companies in the region, but the Mexican Revolution and the subsequent nationalization of the oil industry eclipsed plans of privately owned companies to exploit this important resource. When my family and I returned to Amatlán in 1985, we saw oil-drilling activity less than 60 kilometers from the village. As the search for oil penetrates further into the region, villages like Amatlán will be faced with a new set of circumstances and problems (see Reyes Martínez 1982:128–43 for a description of the negative impact of oil exploration on several Huastecan Nahua communities).

It is difficult to determine what direct role, if any, the people of Amatlán played in these distant historical occurrences. More important for my purposes is to examine the overall pattern of responses to events exhibited by the Indians of the region. Whether Nahua, Totonac, Tepehua, or Otomí, local indigenous people had common interests that made them natural allies. In the struggles to control the southern Huasteca region dating from pre-Hispanic times, the local inhabitants have been active players in the unfolding drama. They took up arms not to serve the interests of conquerors or urban elites but rather to fight for their own freedom from domination. For the most part, they obeyed Indian military leaders and opposed any group that threatened their autonomy, whether foreign invader or representative of republican Mexico. It is interesting to note that people from small villages like Amatlán often play significant roles in major historical transformations, but history rarely records their contributions, much less the agendas that motivated them to participate. The sum total of these and other historical processes led eventually to the great conflagration beginning in 1910 (see Melgarejo Vivanco 1960).

With the Mexican Revolution we arrive at events that are remembered by the oldest villagers. Apparently no one from Amatlán actually participated in the armed struggle, although some were witness to local events (see below). Old people remember when the church in Ixhuatlán de Madero was burned, although they do not know the reasons why it happened or who was engaged in fighting at the time. It appears to have been severely damaged and has only been partially rebuilt. Some people remember hiding in the forest with their parents when soldiers were in the vicinity, but for the most part the Revolution passed by the village. The events of the Mexican Revolution are extremely complex with many competing factions, transitory alliances, and contradictory personalities marking the progress of the struggle. I am certain that very few villagers were fluent in Spanish at that time, and they probably were not fully aware of the sometimes obscure political and philosophical issues at stake (see Schryer 1980 for an historical treatment of the complexities of the Revolution and its aftermath as it occurred in the Huasteca Hidalguense). As will be seen below, however, they were quick to take advantage of new programs to return land to the Indians.

The events of the Revolution were of far less importance to the people of Amatlán than were the agrarian reforms that it produced. The ejido system set up by reformers, a system partially modeled on pre-Hispanic customs of land tenure, gave Indians a chance to regain control of the land. Records from state and local archives reveal that on August 5, 1923, a short time after the end of the Revolution, the people of Amatlán requested from the agrarian reform commission land to be used for cultivation in order "that they might meet the necessities of life." The request was forwarded and appeared in the *Official Journal* published by the agrarian reform commission on September 20, 1923. On April 18, 1932, nine years after the initial request, three representatives of the community presented a petition to the reform commission that contained the results of a census they had taken. At that time there were 178 inhabitants of the village, of which the commission considered 44 to qualify for land. Candidates had to be household heads or married males at least 22 years of age.

The land they were requesting was part of a hacienda named Amatlán where the people lived and worked. The owner was a woman named Felicitas Ramírez de Martínez who owned a total of 727 hectares (the equivalent of just under 1,800 acres). On September 10, 1934, two years after the second petition, the commission allocated 352 hectares on a provisional basis to be divided among the 44 individuals. The community was to be called Ejido de Amatlán. However, the villagers were not satisfied with the land allocation, and they sent official documents to that effect to the commission. Two days later the governor of the state of Veracruz gave them 8 more hectares, bringing the total to 360, with the additional land designated for the building of a schoolhouse. The governor finally agreed to set the allocation at 45 parcels of eight hectares each, with an additional 40 hectares to be used as summer pasturage and forest for the collective use of the community. Four years later, in 1938, the allocation was finally approved, but in the meantime the village had grown to 57 qualified individuals. The total allocation was 400 hectares that, according to documents, left 327 for Dōna Ramírez.

In 1960 the villagers solicited additional lands to accomodate the population growth. Their request was denied because the authorities determined that they were not making good use of the land they possessed. The villagers were already engaged in farming the additional land they had requested, and they were simply seeking to protect themselves legally. Two facts must be emphasized here, both of which will be discussed in greater detail later. The first is that traditional Indian cultivators make radically different use of the land than do modern agriculturists. In Amatlán, although tracts may appear to be in disuse, they are actually going through a necessary fallow period before being planted again, or alternatively they are refuge zones that supply villagers with much-needed raw materials. To most North Americans, efficient use of land implies huge monoculture fields of grain; to a Nahua in the southern Huasteca, efficient land use means a patchwork of fields in varying stages of fallow interspersed with undisturbed forest.

A second important fact is that since the Revolution, the native populations of Mexico have only just recovered from the devastations of the Conquest and colonialism. With increases in population the Indians require yet more land for their methods of farming. From 1932, when the population of Amatlán was 178 individuals, the population grew to about 600 people in 1972. Yet, officially, the land base has remained limited to only about 400 hectares over this period. In response to population pressure, people have been forced to emigrate (see De la Cruz Hernández 1982:13). Only a minority go to the towns and cities; the majority leave, often in family groups, to form new villages on remote, unused lands. Planting on land owned by others but not in apparent use is termed an "invasion" in Mexican law, and it places the perpetrators at considerable risk. Ranchers sometimes call in the army, or with more devastating results they may take the matter into their own hands and hire gunmen to evict the settlers. Despite the serious land shortage, on July 2, 1982, the *Official Journal* reported that 17 household heads from Amatlán had been decertified, deprived of their land rights because they failed to plant for 3 consecutive years. Seventeen new farmers, all of whom were relatives of those who stayed behind and who had been working the abandoned fields anyway, were immediately granted new rights in the village. This process of fissioning, whereby daughter villages are created, will be discussed in greater detail in Chapters 3 and 4.

From the sketch presented above it is clear that the history of the southern Huasteca has been a troubled and bloody one. The Indians have been engaged in a concerted struggle to gain and retain rights over their land since pre-Hispanic days. Only after the Mexican Revolution has the long process of dispossessing Indian lands been permanently reversed. Throughout the years the Indians have responded in a variety of ways ranging from escape to outright rebellion. Despite gains from the Revolution, however, the struggle for land continues to the present. The Huasteca is frequently mentioned in Veracruz newspapers in connection with land invasions, bloody reprisals, and petitions by Indians and mestizos alike to expropriate private ranch lands. The murder and subsequent trial recounted in the previous chapter is one example of a widespread pattern of struggles and tragedies.

The history of the southern Huasteca and of the village of Amatlán is sketchy at best. Like many histories, it contains dates and events but lacks the human element that gives it life. In the course of my fieldwork in Amatlán, I interviewed old people and asked them to recall significant events in village history. The response was interesting. Most remembered people and places in great detail, but no one was able to provide dates. Events were not recounted in a linear order, as presented above, but rather as small groupings of happenings, more or less related to each other. The same events would then be discussed a number of times, with each repetition providing slightly different details. This method of recounting highlights of the past requires a great deal of patience on the part of both teller and listener, but the result is excellent. A picture of past times slowly emerges, and the listener gains a real sense of how and why things happened.

Following is an interview I tape-recorded with two elders of Amatlán. I have edited the dialogue to some extent to improve readability, but it is transcribed largely in their words. One man, whom I shall call

Manuel, is nearly 70 years old. He has a large well-proportioned face and conveys an air of dignity and poise. His thick black hair is only beginning to turn gray and this, combined with the energy in his movements, makes him appear a much younger man. The other man, whom I will call Aurelio, is in his mid-60s and is an important shaman in the village. Aurelio is tall with a handsome face and jet-black hair. Like most people in the village he has an easy laugh and a ready wit. He is known as a person of integrity who has spent a lot of energy and many years learning the techniques to rid the village of sickness and evil. I first met him in 1970 when he was an apprentice curer, and he eventually became one of my most valued and trusted friends. The short history they recount blends into Aurelio's personal history and his brush with death at the hands of the local militia. Again, as always, the issue is land, and Aurelio's story reminds us that even history impartially reported implicates real people. Both men wanted me to record their memories so that they would be written down and would not be lost. They spoke, often with great expression, in Nahuatl.

ETHNOGRAPHER: Now we would like to know who began this village? Where did those who founded it come from? Who built the first houses? Where did the first *masehualmej* ("Indian farmers") who lived here come from? Who were the first in ordering that this village be built?

MANUEL: We have only heard that the first people were the *tetatajmej* ("forefathers"). I still know them as those who lived in the upper village. One of them was called Agriano [local pronunciation of Adrián]. They called him *chinanpixquetl*, that is, the revenue collector or the keeper of the village. He was something like the Comisariado, the one who takes care of the village (see Chapter 4).

This village belonged to Felicitas Ramírez de Martínez. It's upon her property that we're settled. From her comes the land. Later [following the Revolution] the Comisariados arose, and they took the land because they began to think.

Over in [a neighboring municipio] there was a man they called Guada-lupe Osorio. He helped the Indians with papers and red tape. It was he who helped the Comisariados to obtain this land.

Our *patrona* ("patroness" or "landowner") of this place died. Felicitas died, although we never got to know her. So we only heard about it. At that time Don Guadalupe Osorio stood against Raymundo Ortiz Hernán-dez. Ortiz was going around murdering the *tequihuejquej*, the authorities of this village. Although not only in this village, in all of the villages where they were taking back land. Because the authorities and all of us were revolutionaries. They began to take the land back.

In Mirador. . . .

AURELIO: They were killing all of our representatives.

MANUEL: And Guadalupe Osorio defended the Indians, and that is why Raymundo Ortiz got angry. He defended the Indians from Amatlán. Juan Hernández was the representative from here [at that time].

But Raymundo was one of those who liked to kill the Indians; he wanted to finish them. He robbed animals, burros, horses, anything he could find, and that is why he became rich. He used to steal by the cartload: chickens, pigs, horses, cattle. He hauled in all of that.

AURELIO: Yes, that's how this started.

MANUEL: Well, we only heard about where the first ones came from who started the village. The first we know about was Agriano who lived in a house they called *tlajcocali.*

ETHNOGRAPHER: And where was that?

MANUEL: Over there where my *compadre* ("co-father" or "ritual kinsman") Cruz is. We still know the place as *tlajcocali.* There was also a little old man named Agustín who lived in *tlapani,* and over here there was a Nicolás of *tlamaya* house; he was the grandfather of Nicolás [who still lives in the village]. Two brothers were there that we still know about. And from here others, one they called Emiliano, lived at *atlalco,* near to where the man lives who has his hand cut off. And now one of us, the one who arrived first was a little old man who lived down there by Palma Real at a place called *tlalapanco* who we know about. He was a little old man who was not very tall. He settled over there where we are now, and from time immemorial they named the place *tlalapanco.* All of the little pieces of property had names (see Map 3.1).

ETHNOGRAPHER: Okay, then the mestizos murdered them?

MANUEL: Yes, they were killing them, but they did not kill the little old man. He just died, but we got to know about him. But they killed all who were village authorities. The earliest ones just died off one by one; [the mestizos] did not kill them. They killed the rest when that incident began, and it had to do with Máximo [a local rancher] meddling again. Again he went around killing Indians. At that time Raymundo [Ortiz Hernández] was not [yet] walking around as if our land was his. This Máximo had his land in [what is now a neighboring ejido]. Celso Rodríguez was there, and Máximo was his young son. They were three brothers, but two of them did not go around killing people, only Máximo. He began to kill people [in Amatlán], they say, because someone from here wounded him. That is why he began killing people. When he left one day, some people from here stole all of his barbed wire from the ranch, and that is [another reason] why he began to kill them. Afterwards, they began soliciting land. They applied for it and then we were allotted this land here.

AURELIO: But first they planted milpas ("fields") on the lands [now] belonging to the people over there at *cuatsapotl.* Everybody from this village made milpas there. They abandoned the lands belonging to this place because the rich people took them away from us. [The rich mestizos] invaded [and took the land]. They invaded, and they evicted the people from here who had begun to work. The rich people were doing the villagers damage, and it was not possible to recover the land just like that. They were angry, and then we began to get angry. But the Comisariado who used to be here would not move ahead because he was afraid of words.

MANUEL: For 20 years my godfather Tomás served as Comisariado, and it fell upon us to replace him. And when we began [to fight back], they had already taken a lot of land from us. But he was afraid and refused to get involved with the mestizos.

AURELIO: Once when I was still a child I heard him say, "Hmm, why should I push so hard if I don't even have a son? For what reason then, should I involve myself so much? If that is the way it is, then let it be; but I'm not going to push so that others can eat."

I didn't like very much what he said, and when I grew up I went against him. It didn't seem very good to me in any way. There were people who wanted to be Comisariado, and they removed Tomás.

Well, they began to mobilize, to push and push until we knew where it would lead.

MANUEL: The people from Ixhuatlán began to fight us because *tata* ("father") Hilario had purchased property near here. It had been 13 years since he had purchased [the land] when it came my turn to be Comisariado. Then it came about that the municipio started to charge us for 48 hectares that had been added to the village. But it was not true. The [agrarian commission] engineer came and removed us and entered in the record that we had received too much land. From that point on things went badly, and we weren't careful. We all signed [the document], all the members of the ejido, and that is why they took the lands away from us. We are just workers, and we didn't realize what the paper meant; we didn't know, and so we just signed. We thought all of them, Faustino Lagos, Teófilo. . .all of them knew well what they were doing. They all helped each other, but they were not careful. For this reason we later came to have a fight, a cause for anger.

Diego Velasco began to pull us and provoke us. He was an official [in Ixhuatlán].

AURELIO: He was worse than a dog; he was like a snake where he stood, son of a. . . .

MANUEL: He called us in to frighten us. He called us because he wanted to snarl [at us]. We told Velasco and the Presidente of the municipio, "Yes, we are going to pay, but you ought to know that through this plan they have taken [lands] away from us. They have taken a piece away from us and now we end up owing and they have entered in the document that we have been allotted in excess and it isn't true. Because I have studied the records and I have seen how everything stands and I have seen that it is not true. They deceived us."

And that is how we told them, to please give us that land and that yes, we are going to pay. And they didn't give us anything, they ordered us to go to Tuxpan [nearly 160 kilometers away]. There Hilario, who was from [around] here, accused us. There we began. And we also went to Chicóntepec [about 3 hours walk], it was nothing but walking. We would leave here at 5 o'clock in the morning, then we would reach Alamo, all the way on foot and in some places with mud up to here. We would leave here at five in the morning and arrive in Alamo at 6 o'clock at night. An entire day walking. Over there we would accuse them, and they could see that we had come a long way on foot. And we presented the matter of [Gilberto and] Raúl (both local ranchers, see below) and had to go again and again because nothing was resolved.

Then Gilberto bought 70 hectares over there on the river, and Raúl took 80 [hectares] away from us. It was a large amount that they grabbed. It was a spread of land that reached as far as [a neighboring settlement]; that was what we had signed away. There we began, and because we could not resolve [the issue], our representatives started going to Mexico City. They went to Mexico City about 10 times, and that was how we got help from a public attorney who arrived in the zone of Colatlán and who came from Huejutla. He helped us. We always went by foot.

AURELIO: When my compadre Rogelio was Comisariado, it was then that they took two parcels of land in [a neighboring settlement]. Raúl settled in. Then someone else settled in at [another place]. Then this compadre of mine got in with the people [from here in Amatlán]. They settled in the middle of Raúl's 80 hectares and in the middle of Gilberto's 70 hectares. Well, afterwards the rich began to grow angry, and they put us on the line. How? Okay, they began to accuse us. Juta! (an expletive) Then they picked a fight with us verbally. [We decided that it was] better to grab in one fell swoop what belongs to Raúl, seeing that nothing was being resolved. We went there to clear the land, and others planted their milpas. We said that nobody was to back off. But all of us men helped each other equally, equally.

The men began to carry arms. The *tetajmej* ("council of elders") assembled at a spring, gathering around them 20 men with carbines. We took the land with sheer courage. The most valiant was a man called Cruz, *totlayi* ("our uncle") Cruz. Who knows where he might be now, who knows where our lord God might have left him, might have set him down. That man, what a tower of strength! What courage he had, he certainly had courage. He was precisely the one who went about protecting and defending us. At that time we no longer dared to go to market in Ixhuatlán; we went to Colatlán instead where there is also a market.

It was then that José Hernández [who was later found murdered] went there, and they made him a policeman in charge of collecting land rent. At this time they caught me there and tied me up, son of evil! They tied a chain around me here, and they put a lock on it. The police tied me up like a pig. Juta! I stayed there until the men from my village came to

defend me, to get me out. But they did not get me out. The police put
me in a car. At dawn, I was made to sweep the plaza of Colatlán. At 9
o'clock in the morning [the Presidente of the municipio of Ixhuatlán de
Madero] arrived and put me in his car saying, "Let's go to Ixhuatlán."
Well, we came to Ixhuatlán at about 6 o'clock in the evening. "Juta," said
Diego Velasco, "son of the chihuahuas" (an expletive). He was as furious
as a coiled snake.

Then I was there alone. Juta, now you will see, they put me in jail, and
after half a day the policemen and a soldier came to take me out. "Let's
go to the barracks" [they said]. There was no barracks, but rather it was
just a command post where they took me and tied me up, they made me
stand. Some stayed as guards outside the building thinking that I might
[try to] escape and they would be able to beat me. Some came in and
asked me who we [in the village] were, who were the cockiest, and they
said they were going to knock me over and roll me.

[I told my captors,] "What I am going to say to you people is that if you
are going to kill me, kill me; but for certain don't just dump me. Have my
people from Amatlán come pick me up. . . ." [Then I was interrogated.]

"Is is true that you are the brother of Lorenzo?"

"No, he is just my compadre."

"Well, and Nicolás, what relation are you to him?"

"He is just my neighbor."

"And is he the Comisariado?"

"Well, I don't know what he is."

"What do you mean you don't know? That's enough, you'll have to
show us. Who is the leader, the one who goes ahead? Who was the
Comisariado who headed the takeover of Señor Raúl's lands?"

"But those are not his lands, those are the lands of Cormena Corventa."
[And then], juta! he shoots a gun blast by my head that set my ears buzzing.
Again they picked me up, they grabbed me.

"Well, aren't you really going to tell us?"

"Well, I'm not going to tell you anything because I haven't seen anything."

"Well, they say you are the ruler of the roost in Amatlán together with
Lorenzo, with Nicolás, together with Antioco. There are eight of you
together with Esteban."

"It isn't true, I told you."

"What do you mean it isn't true? You are not leaving here [alive] even
though you might think otherwise. Well then, aren't you going to tell us
anything?"

"I won't say anything. Kill me. Here I stand alone with my hands, and
not one strand of hair is standing on end on account of what is going to
happen to me. Here I stand with my mind made up concerning what might
happen to me, here, even though it might seem insignificant to you. And
when I was born, I was alone and that's how I'll die, all alone."

That is how I spoke to the policemen.

"That fellow sure is a *pendejo* ("stupid wimp")," said the policeman. "He believed that he wouldn't tell us anything. And now? Well, let's put him in the can."

Juta, they shoved me so that I would crash against the door. And I thought, "If they beat me I will die." But they didn't beat me, they threw me in jail for about 15 days there in Ixhuatlán. Two men from Pisa Flores were [in the cell] there. They said to me, "They are going to take you out of here some time, but [meanwhile] we are here [with you]. Lie down between us in case they shine a light on you or call you." They defended me.

Juta, at dawn they came and ordered us to speak to Diego Velasco. Juta, about 8 days later they came at 3 o'clock in the morning and got me out. I said to myself, "The time has not come for them to kill me."

I said to the *comandante*, "Please take me over to the church, I am going to light a little candle."

"What?"

"I am going to the church to light a candle."

"Ah well," [he said to his men]. "Take him with you."

"Well," [I said]. "Now I am really happy because you [policemen] are going to take me."

"Well, yes we are going to take you, that is what he ordered us to do."

Well, we left and I met Casiano, together with my uncle Martín. There [in the church] I found them and they had brought tortillas for me. They asked where [the policemen] were taking me.

"Well, I don't know exactly where they will take me."

"Ah," they said. "If they are taking you to [a nearby settlement], then we will go there [to free you]." And truly, over there they were waiting. They were together with my uncle Cruz and others who were present. They were going to kill the *comandante* and the policeman. [My neighbors] had taken shovels and pickaxes so they could bury [the policemen] after they killed them. The [police] took me by way of Tsapoyo and Oxital. At the house of Leobardo they gave me a beer, and they bought a lot of ammunition. The comandante showed it to me and said, "This shall be your inheritance if you try to escape." Pure .38 caliber ammunition.

Well, they gave me a Coca-Cola and I drank it. Then they took me to Corral Viejo, and there was a gentleman who was an Indian. He said, "Now the comandante is gone, he went to see an Indian girl. Now, run for it!" But how was I to escape? The place was a clearing [with no cover] and I was well tied.

When they showed up again they took me with them. We went as far as [a place called] *tecsispaj*, and there in the lower part was a vendor's stand where they stayed drinking. They gave me a Coke and I drank it. That is where Juan Cabrera from Cruz Blanca caught up with me. "Well," he said, "What is happening, Aurelio?"

"Well, here we are, they are taking me to Chicóntepec."

"And what did you do?"

"Well, nothing, it was because of this land problem."

"Ah," he said, "I thought you had killed someone."

Well, we began to climb toward the village of Buenavista when the comandante said, "Take this pig with you, because I have to go see a girlfriend that I have here." He took off. The policeman said to me, "You stay here and keep still, because I am also going to see a piece of meat that I have."

Juan Cabrera said, "They have left you. Take off! Get going!" Juta! He made me flee. When he untied me, I scattered like a deer. I took off and ended up running into a barbed wire fence that was there and I jumped over it and ended up way downhill. I came out where a little old man was bathing, and when I saw him I took off through a coffee plantation. I ended up going around in circles, but I took a direction and went up the face of a slope until I reached the summit.

Juta, when the police were about to find me, I stopped and heard them yelling, "Well, why did you take off?" And they began shooting and shooting, and the bullets went by me here, and here, and here. The branches of a *petlacuahuitl* [tree] kept falling, the branches just kept falling.

Juta, I ended up running into a small abutment that had been built there. I ended up crashing right into it, and the policeman said, "Well, it serves you right for escaping." [As he pointed the gun at me, he said], "To keep you from escaping anymore I've already killed you." But I took off through the middle of the coffee plantation all the way downhill. Afterwards I again climbed up the slope and again ran into the comandante. He shot at me with his pistol, who knows how many times? I ended up sitting down with my knee swollen this much. Well, there I recovered a bit, and I dragged myself to a door which had holes in it. I went in and took shelter. The comandante came this close to me and then he took off.

He went as far as [the place we call] *teponastla* and said to some people, "You, by chance, haven't seen a deer?"

"Not around here. Here, we are building a house."

"Son of a bitch, I'm not asking you if you are building a house. I'm asking you if you haven't seen a bandit pass by."

"Well, nothing has happened here, nobody has passed by." Juuuta! He began to get angry and there I was concealed, observing.

"Sons of whores!" And then he took off. Maybe he took off for Chicóntepec, or I don't know where. Towards afternoon I went through a cleared pasture. There, around *teponastla*, I saw a riverbed and took off along it. I saw a thick little tree and sat down there. Juta, around 10 or 12 o'clock at night they began shooting over there by the village. And thus, daylight began to break and I had slept very little. [Also,] there was a big hog walking around nearby doing damage. I could hear how it was going around eating corn in the milpa.

An animal went by breaking twigs and I took off after it. I ended up on the big trail and followed it as far as [an ejido several hours walk from Amatlán]. There I said I was a courier that wanted them to make a door for someone in Chicóntepec, and that I was going to pay for it. Juta, I ended up stopping there. [Later] I took off along the stream and came out at El Limón. I decided to go along the big trail [and that] I would no longer flee. I was going to surrender so they could kill me.

Well, I stopped where I usually do, at the house of a lady who sells candles. I bought some of her candles and made the sign of the cross. I asked her if she could sell me some tortillas because I was hungry.

"Well, yes," [she said]. "Sit down, even if it's for just a little bite, even if it's just for tortillas."

After eating I realized I had regained my strength. I told her to keep my candles for me. I paid her, and she agreed to do it. Then I set off and went as far as [a place called] *ahuimol*, but it took some effort to get there. My leg was hurting and I bought some pills [for the pain]. Son of a . . . ! And there went Jorge Vargas on his way and I picked up a large rock to defend myself as I passed in front of him. Juta, that's how I approached and we met.

He said, "How are you doing fellow? Are you already back?"

"Yes, I'm on my way back."

"Did you get out already?"

"Yes, I'm already out."

"Ah, that's fine, that's fine."

We merely greeted each other this way. I went as far as Colatlán where I stopped at the house of Othon because he is a very close friend. From there I ended up in Pedro's house. He comes out and asks why they have left me and tells me that my companions are in the vicinity. They were the ones coming from Amatlán. I borrowed a half-liter of *aguardiente* ("cane alcohol") and stayed there until the following day. I sent a message via Gregorio to have the villagers come for me. That is how it came about that they found me. And they came carrying carbines, and afterwards Raúl arrived with his troops.

Raúl said [to me], "You haven't killed me because you really want employment. You haven't killed me because you are really a good person, otherwise, who knows how long ago you would have cut off my ears? I think it is because I have cattle, I have animals." And then he treated me to two beers!

MANUEL: The people from Amatlán began to work those lands. We got them back. The first one for whom we reclaimed the lands was Hilario. We took them from Raúl, then from Gilberto, but he was no *pendejo*; he sold them first. So we took them from the person he sold them to, [from] Narciso.

ETHNOGRAPHER: And what about Máximo, who later did some stealing?

MANUEL: Well that was much earlier and what we are talking about happened more recently. Anyway we had to be careful on the roads whenever we went to market because it was a bitch. . . . I have always had good luck, they never threw me in jail. Twice the policemen came for me, and they couldn't find my house. Twice Raúl brought them but I fled. I took off by way of the entire length of the edge of the arroyo. After that the policemen left.

AURELIO: My compadre Alonso related to me that some of the people [in this region] were Carrancistas (followers of Venustiano Carranza, Mexican revolutionary leader and later, president of Mexico) and others were Villistas (followers of Francisco "Pancho" Villa, Mexican revolutionary leader). He said that the Villistas were Raymundo Ortiz Hernández and his men. He gathered people around him and recounted this story: "Now I'm going to tell how it was that we broke up the haciendas. I knew about it even though I was very little and only tagged along behind the men. The old big trail used to pass by *ayojtlaj*, and through there would pass the Carrancistas looking for the Villistas. We were young, but they armed us until they made us look like troops. When we entered Chicóntepec, everybody stared at us, and the ladies would stare because we were carrying our carbines."

[My compadre Alonso continued,] "Way up there on the slope was a fort. There they had a vantage point and could see if people were coming. There used to be a kind of wall, and it had openings through which to shoot. And there were also some Indians in the fort."

"The [leaders of the fort] came to take us, and they took us to [where we call] *ahuatenoj* and from there to Tantoyuca. From there we went to Potrero del Llano, then to Alamo, and finally here to Llano de Enmedio. The [leaders] said that Don Raymundo was on his way to Llano de Enmedio. Juta, they took us by force. Three representatives from this region came to meet us. But Don Raymundo arrived with his troops and chased us out, and they killed two of the representatives. They were boxed in, and the Indians were leading with their carbines. They came out and the Indians had to retreat and we scattered and they killed our other representative. [There was a lot of fighting] and that is how they put an end to the haciendas. Many of the hacienda owners fled."

[He said,] "One guy they called Acosta and he killed animals. He used to stop over there at the *ayojtlaj* pasture and he would set himself down to watch. He used to kill Raymundo's cattle and so it ended. When Máximo came he would also do some shooting and would steal everything: silverware, machetes, dishes, cups and everything that he could find he would steal. Máximo did as he pleased."

AURELIO: An important point is that when it comes to land we get into it the deepest. We have to follow a straight thread through the thicket. One should not pick a quarrel with the rich but rather do what is correct, what is ordered by law. That is how I spoke to Erón, I told him, "Uncle, don't get into it too deep. I don't know even three or four things concerning the law, but for my part I am telling you not to get into it. You have your certificate of rights [in the ejido], what's your head good for? Leave those others and defend your children, for these lands are going to be for you and tomorrow for your children. It is established in the document."

He replied, "Here, no one gives me advice. You can't do much."

Then I said, "I also know what you know. Be careful how you tread. Don't go around angering the rich, because the rich defend themselves with other rich people, even if [the disagreement] is about a little bit of money." An Indian mustn't wander around just anywhere because they'll kill him. And what I told him happened. Now where is he? They killed him.

Regardless of who is bigger or stronger it doesn't count. There is an order to things, and we must behave like human beings and show respect. I told my namesake Valente that we need more land for the children and that we must follow the application process. We might apply for half of a parcel and pay for the other half to avoid controversy. I considered the matter and told him that I will help and that the village will stick together if we put the request through the legal process. I don't mind dying [if it is necessary], but let's go through procedures of making application and handle the matter in a calm way. Your neighbors from Amatlán and [the neighboring ejido] will help and will work hard at helping if the issue is finding something to eat. We can defend ourselves together. It is nothing to die about. As we are born alone, alone we shall die.

ETHNICITY AND HISTORY

The theme of ethnic identity is a hidden thread winding through the history of the southern Huasteca and the village of Amatlán. In pre-Hispanic times, despite profound similarities among the cultures of Mesoamerica, ethnic identification was all-important. The Huastecs and the Totonacs in uneasy alliance defended their territory in bloody battles against the Aztecs. The Conquest both complicated and simplified the situation. An alien racial and ethnic group became superordinate, in close alliance with certain indigenous groups and in deadly opposition to others. Within a short time, the conquerers lumped all Indians into one socially inferior category. They sneeringly called them *indios*, a name that, for most people, retains pejorative connotations. At first, segregating the Indians from the Spaniards was relatively simple. But soon the population of mixed racial type, the mestizos, began to grow. The importation of black African slaves and their subsequent absorption into the population added to the difficulties faced by the Spaniards in maintaining apartheid in Mexico.

To deal with the problem, the Spanish overlords devised a complicated system of human classification whereby each person was evaluated at birth and assigned a slot in a hierarchy of racial types. Skin color was the primary criterion for locating an individual on the scale, but other factors were used as well. So important was the illusion of racial purity that rumors of past interracial liasons were often enough to ruin a family (Marino Flores 1967:12). After the Revolution, all citizens were declared equal under the law regardless of racial or cultural origin. However, equality has not actually been achieved in social and economic realms, as we have already seen. From the Nahua perspective, they have experienced a long period when they were lumped with a variety of other indigenous ethnic groups into one undifferentiated mass at the bottom of the social pyramid. Long after the Revolution in which many Indians fought and died, they still find themselves at a social, economic, and political disadvantage relative to the mestizos. In short, for the Nahuas of Amatlán there has always existed interethnic conflict. The difference is that following the Revolution, with many legal barriers removed and racial criteria increasingly hard to apply in the thoroughly mixed population, the wall erected between Indian and mestizo developed several gaps. Indians could, under certain circumstances, move in and out of the mestizo world if it suited them.

The incomplete history we have of this region and village shows Indians struggling for land and rights. In the struggle, their foes were Spaniards, mestizos, and other Indians alike. The Indians today continue to fight for the interests of their particular ethnic groups and in so doing, for their own individual interests as well. In the larger picture, it is the powerless against the powerful. But from the Indian perspective it has been more than a simple war of the castes, of downtrodden Indians pitted against mestizo oppressors. This has been, undeniably, an important facet of the struggle, and as Aurelio dramatically relates above, the people of Amatlán have no love for their rich landowning neighbors. But those people who identify as Indians do not automatically hate everything represented by the mestizos. This bind is revealed by Aurelio's adventure. It will be recalled that Aurelio came very close to being killed by a wealthy cattle rancher and then, as if to parody the paradoxical position of the Indian in the national culture, the rich man offered Aurelio a beer and a job! To be Indian is to be a cultivator of the land; anyone or anything interfering with that way of life threatens Indian culture with annihilation. But in the complex world of modern Mexico, the Indians need the mestizo sector of the national economy to sustain many aspects of their village traditions. The mestizo world therefore represents at the same time the oppressors and the safety valve for Indian society.

CHAPTER 3

AMATLÁN AND ITS PEOPLE

LIFE in an Indian village is based on low technology by North American standards. Paradoxically, this does not mean that life is necessarily simpler for the average villager nor that applying a scaled-down technology requires little knowledge or skill. In fact, quite the opposite is often the case. In modern industrial societies technology is increasingly in the hands of specialists, leaving the average citizen with less and less direct knowledge of the tools, machines, and techniques that make the society run. Grim portrayals in movies and novels of what might happen to industrialized nations in the face of a major catastrophe testify to this process. Loss of running water, electricity, gasoline, and grocery stores with frozen-food aisles would place the lives of citizens of economically advanced nations in jeopardy. The villagers, by contrast, are far more self-sufficient in the application of their technology. There is little occupational specialization, and therefore each man and woman must have working knowledge of a wide range of activities that are necessary for the perpetuation of their way of life. These include house building, farming, animal husbandry, fishing, hunting, gathering, birthing techniques, medicine, pottery making, clothes making, basketry, food preparation, and many other subsistence skills (see Chamoux 1981a for an analysis of technical skills and their transmission in a Nahua village).

This is not to imply that Amatlán or any other similar village is self-sufficient and independent of external influences. Nahua villages are linked to and highly dependent upon local, regional, state, and national forces. In addition, low technology increases the importance of local factors when people are engaged in production activities or planning for the future. Villagers must be acutely aware of potential problems with rainfall, crop disease, and soil depletion precisely because they do not have access to irrigation, insecticides, or commercial fertilizers. They must have knowledge of fluctuations in the local market prices offered for their crops, of political tensions with ranchers and

102

neighboring villages, and of new government policies that may affect them. However, as I argue at the end of this chapter, many village features described here must be understood in the context of villagers' desires to maintain a degree of independence from the mestizo-dominated economy.

Before presenting information on Amatlán it might help to list what is *not* found in the village. The absences are a statement about what life is like there and will help to put in relief what we do encounter (see Chapter 7 for technological changes that have occurred in the two decades since 1970). Amatlán has no running water and, until 1986, it had no electricity. There is no road into the village, nor any telephones, telegraph or any other means of communication with the outside. There is no church building and neither a resident nor itinerant priest or minister. No outside representatives of the regional or national government nor police live there. The village lacks a market, stores, a corn-grinding mill, butcher shop, and restaurants. There is no source of gas for cooking or heating, no bathrooms or latrines, nor any boarding houses. A minority of people are able to speak Spanish, the national language of Mexico, with any fluency. Finally, there are no clocks, magazines, newspapers, books, maps (except those used in school or owned by the schoolmaster), industrial machinery of any kind, tractors, or wheeled conveyances. This is a world far removed from urban Mexico and the industrialized West. Now, let us examine what kind of a world it *is*.

THE VILLAGE LAYOUT

The rocky stream, or arroyo, that cuts across the ejido of Amatlán forms a large loop in the center of village lands. The loop surrounds on three sides the central cluster of houses in addition to the lot set aside for school buildings. Although houses are widely scattered, they are concentrated in the relatively flat area along the floodplain of the arroyo. Surrounding the houses on all sides are steep hills, most of which have been stripped of their primary forest growth and are used for cultivation. The small valley containing the houses—the village proper—is heavily forested, and the arroyo winding its way among the large trees and dense foliage creates a picture of tropical beauty. The arroyo has steep banks in certain places, and the water can be several feet deep where it rounds a bend. In general, however, a person can wade across with little trouble save for the treacherously slippery stones that line the bottom. This atmosphere of serenity changes dramatically during the periodic flash floods of the rainy season.

The loop points northward, and houses spill outside of its boundaries to the west and east. At first appearance there seems to be no order to the layout of the village. Groups of houses are widely scattered in the dense tropical forest in no discernible pattern. They are connected by a network of trails that tunnel through the trees and brush. Houses are built in forest clearings that are widely separated and often out of sight of each other. The schoolhouse and its associated buildings occupy one end of a large cleared area that lies at the center of Amatlán. In fact, the school complex, built by the Mexican government and thus somewhat alien to the village itself, seems to be the only focus of village activity. This settlement pattern gives the impression that Amatlán is not a village at all but rather an artificial congregation of houses for the convenience of the government and the school.

Adding to this impression is the way the Nahuas name their villages. They have developed a complex system of labeling subareas within the village that caused me endless confusion during the first year I was in residence. They almost never have need to refer to the entire entity I have been calling Amatlán. In fact the name *Amatlán* refers to only one small cluster of houses just northeast of the school clearing. It is a place where once grew many fig trees, the same species used in pre-Hispanic times to make paper (*amatl* in Nahuatl). Government officials use the appellation Amatlán in their reports to refer to the whole complex, but the people themselves always specify regions within the village or house-site names when talking among themselves. The people do not view the village as a coherent community toward which they owe a great deal of loyalty. However, although the stereotype of the totally integrated village does not apply to Amatlán, the people do identify to an extent with the village as a whole. This identity, how-ever, is due as much to the land rights that are administered by the state through the village political structure as to any deep-seated feeling of solidarity with Amatlán itself.

Names given to subareas of the village are based on geographical features, unusual vegetation, proximity to a distinctive structure such as the schoolhouse, or any other feature that identifies the place for the local inhabitants. The land rises slightly as one moves from the south to the north and west. People thus distinguish the lower from the upper village. Within this division are at least 25 subareas desig-nated by name and these are indicated on map 3.1. It is not possible to provide a definitive list of subareas because variation exists in how people divide up the village. Because residence reflects kinship affiliation, these place names become associated with specific families.

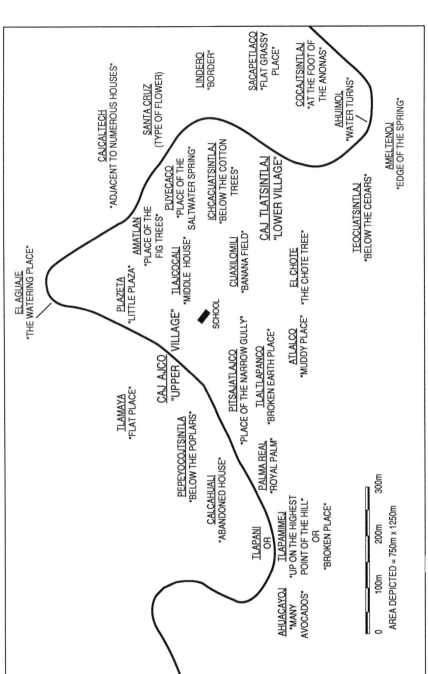

3.1. Named subareas in the village of Amatlán

In addition, if individuals have the same name or nickname, people may use their place name to distinguish among them. Thus, if there are two Juans (and there are many more than that), one may become Juan Atlalco ("muddy place," or "where water passes over a small plain" in Nahuatl), and the other may be called Juan Tlajcocali ("middle house" in Nahuatl). Confusion arises for the outsider when a person or family retains the place name after relocating. Complex systems of toponymy such as this seem to be a feature of Nahua villages throughout Mexico.

Villagers further divide the subareas in Amatlán until they arrive at the individual house cluster or compound. Each compound or often individual house has a house name, or *caltocayotl* in Nahuatl. Names are based on the same type of environmental features used to label village subareas, and the house name may also be assumed by individuals living there. Likewise the location may retain the name long after the house has disappeared. Houses and various distinguishing features of the environment thus come to be known by a profusion of names. For example, although it has no overall name, different sections of the arroyo are labeled. A favorite place to bathe where the water is deep is called *la aguaje*, Spanish for "watering place"; and another section is called *ahuimol*, Nahuatl for "water turns." The system of naming extends outward to include environmental features at some distance from the village. When I showed people maps of the southern Huasteca region they were able to name many villages and specific geographical locales for a radius of about 40 kilometers (25 miles) from the village.

This system of naming, and particularly the use of caltocayotl house names, is found in all Nahua villages and it creates a kind of esoteric cognitive map familiar only to local people. Outsiders, even other Indians, can have no idea where these named places are found nor which families are associated with them. Schoolmasters and municipio government officials often complain about the difficulty of eliciting information about people and places from the Indians because of this practice. A census taker would have to spend months in a village to understand both the lay of the land and residence patterns before getting an accurate count. For this reason, local schoolteachers are usually assigned the annual task of collecting census information, and they complain about how difficult it is and the seeming unwillingness of the Indians to clarify matters. The situation is also complicated by customs followed by the Nahuas in naming people (more will be said on personal naming practices later). In sum, villages are self-contained information networks. Village inhabitants use a system of codes for naming people and geographic features for which only they have the key.

The result of this localization of knowledge is beneficial for the Indians. It carries forward a practice that very likely derives from pre-Hispanic days and thus probably affirms links with their past. It has important implications for their religion, which is organized around a complex sacred geography. It establishes a common cognitive map among villagers, which creates a sense of community and belongingness. Moreover, it always helps to keep potentially dangerous outsiders confused about the precise location of things. The apparent confusion of names keeps interfering schoolmasters, government officials, or police in search of someone at bay. It forces outside officials to deal through the village political authorities, because to go around them would be fruitless. In sum, in a world where Indians are at the bottom of the sociopolitical hierarchy, esoteric systems of dividing and labeling the physical and social worlds give them one measure of control in dealing with outsiders.

The way people use space often reflects something of the underlying social world they inhabit. Nahua villages are no exception, and Amatlán provides an excellent example. The profusion of names and the scattering of houses conceals a definite pattern of residences and an identity the people have with the whole village. Closer examination of house locations reveals that from two to eight houses, usually belonging to patrilineally related males, are clustered in the forest clearings. A group of houses occupying a single clearing is simply called *caltinej*, Nahuatl for "houses." The occupants of each clearing are usually male siblings with their wives and children, along with their elderly father and mother. Other relatives may build in clearings located nearby. Thus residence patterns reflect Nahua social organization.

HOUSES

The Nahuas build into their houses the three main principles of their craftsmanship: functionality, durability, and manufacture from locally available resources. Houses are always small by North American standards and often consist of a single room. In that small space, however, the family prepares and consumes food, stores equipment and produce from the fields, makes ritual offerings, socializes children, sleeps, and carries out the many daily activities of village life.

Buildings in Amatlán are comprised of the government-built school complex, 110 dwellings of active male household heads and their immediate families, and numerous additional structures divided among storage facilities, partially completed houses used as "porches," separate kitchen huts, houses of bachelors who are awaiting marriage, and one shrine. All but a small number of these structures are constructed in the traditional way. Men first clear an area of trees and underbrush. They may do this at a new location, or they may simply enlarge a clearing already containing houses. The normal house, or *cali* in Nahuatl, starts with six beams, usually hand-hewn from tropical cedar, that the builders sink into the ground in two rows of three each. They then lash large poles to the tops of the beams about 7 feet from the ground, to form a closed rectangle. Next, they lash poles across the width of this rectangle so that they overhang each side and then construct the framework for a high, steeply pitched roof. The men extend the base of this roof framework out beyond the beams on all sides by about 3 feet, and connect the short ends of the rectangle by a curved pole. From beneath, the base of the roof frame appears as two parallel sides connected by semicircles on each end.

Next, starting at the bottom edge, the men cover the framework with tightly tied bundles of thatch. There are three types of thatch material, ranging from the leaves of the *xihuitl cali* ("leaf house" in Nahuatl) tree, considered to be the most durable and highest quality roofing material; to the fine grass called *sacatl* ; to the poorest quality material that is sugarcane leaves. After the workers have tied the bundles onto the frame, they halt construction for several weeks to allow the roof to settle and become watertight. At this stage of completion the house is called in Spanish a *ramada* ("thatched shed"), and people often use it like an open-air porch by sitting in its shade at the end of the day. The owner makes adjustments in the thatch until the roof does not leak even in the heaviest downpour.

Once they judge the roof to be waterproof, the men construct the walls. They cut a large number of 5-centimeter (2-inch) diameter straight poles for this purpose. The men stand the poles up vertically and lash them together making sure that they extend up to the cross pieces on top of the beams. They space two or sometimes three poles horizontally and then lash the vertical wall poles to these as well. The builders do not allow for windows in the walls, but they leave a space approximately 3 feet wide for the doorway. They are careful to leave sufficient space above the door to the top of the wall so that a woman can enter carrying a water pot on her head. The owner makes the door either from handmade boards or from poles lashed to a frame. The men leave open the space between the edge of the roof and the top of the walls. Sometimes they pack mud between the vertical wall poles, but more typically they leave the spaces open to allow air passage. Houses have no chimney to vent smoke from cooking fires, and so it collects inside the steep roof. The smoke rises away from people's faces and eventually seeps through the thatch or under the eaves. This arrangement is very effective at ridding the thatch of vermin.

The men pack and smooth an area of earth about 1 foot high both inside and around the outside of the house so that it appears to have been constructed on a low, flat mound. The added height keeps water from running indoors during the rainy season. Houses vary in size, but the average is about 12 by 16 feet with the roof peak rising 14 or 15 feet above the ground. It takes five men about 2 weeks of work to construct a house once the materials have been gathered. According to informants, a house will last between 10 and 25 years with very little upkeep when the thatch is made from the best material. Other buildings such as corncribs, separate kitchens, and shrines are simple variations on the basic house design (see section on the domestic cycle in Chapter 4). Men construct traditional buildings solely from materials gathered from the forest.

There are many variations on this basic design. For example, it is not uncommon for the builders to place one wall so that three support beams are left freestanding under the eave. This creates a kind of narrow porch useful for escape from the tropical sun. A few people have replaced the traditional thatch with roofs made from sheets of corrugated tarpaper. Although there is a certain prestige attached to this type of roof, there are disadvantages associated with it as well. First, its cost is prohibitive ($2.40 a sheet in 1970), and at least 30 sheets are required for an average roof. Second, it requires nails, also expensive by village standards. Third, it is black in color and transforms the inside of the house into an oven during the summer months. Fourth, it does not generally last as long as a thatched roof. The advantages are that construction goes much faster (one man can finish a roof in 2 days), and it eliminates the often burdensome task of gathering hundreds of pounds of thatching material. Alternatives to tarpaper are corrugated sheetmetal or asbestos roofing materials that are making their appearance in some villages in the region and that have some of the same disadvantages as tarpaper.

Inside, all of the dwellings are very similar. Most are single rooms, although some people have built partitions to separate off a sleeping area. Floors are made of packed mud that the women wet down with water at least once a day and sweep using a broom made of twigs. This practice of sprinkling water on the earth floor acts to cool the house even on the hottest days. Against one wall is situated the fire table, a platform-like structure of heavy, handcarved logs covered with a thick layer of dried mud and flat stones. On this, the woman of the house constructs two or three fireplaces, each one marked off by three stones surrounding a blackened area. Called *tenamaxtle* in Nahuatl, these stones house the fire spirit described in Chapter 6. She cooks all meals on the fire table, and it is rare that the stones are ever allowed to cool. On the floor nearby are located two or three additional fireplaces surrounded by larger stones. These are for the bigger cooking tasks, such as boiling large pots of corn in the preparation of cornmeal. Nahua houses may be sparsely furnished and little decorated, but given the climatic conditions they are surprisingly comfortable. They are dry in the rain and quite cool and breezy in the heat. A person sitting inside a house is able to see out through the walls, but it is impossible for passersby to see inside. A new house smells fresh, like mown hay, and is particularly appealing.

Villagers furnish their houses with items that are functional and durable. Family members manufacture most household possessions, although they purchase some things from other villagers or from the market. The kitchen area contains the greatest number of items. Spread over the fire table, hanging from pegs, or placed on one or more crude shelves are the cooking utensils of the household. Largest of these are a series of round-bottomed clay pots, ranging in capacity from less than a quart to several gallons. The pots are handmade by village women using a slab technique, and they sit perfectly on the three stones that surround every fireplace. In addition, each house has two or more griddles made from clay, ranging in diameter from about 15 to 30 inches. Women place these over the fire for greaseless frying. The clay griddle is called *comali* in Nahuatl, and it is used to cook corn tortillas, the Nahua "staff of life."

Besides the clayware, there are also a variety of spoons, scoops, and vessels made from gourds. Each kitchen is also equipped with a knife, usually made from a worn-down machete, a few mass-produced ceramic or metal plates and cups purchased at the market, one or two drinking glasses each of which originally contained a wax votive candle, possibly a blackened iron pan or kettle, one or two crude metal or enamel spoons, and an occasional metal or plastic bucket. Located by the fire table is a three-legged quern with its rolling-pin-sized grinding stone. The grinding stone is called *metlapili* and the quern *metlatl* in Nahuatl (*mano* and *metate* in Spanish), and both items are carved from coarse volcanic rock. The back two legs of the quern are placed on a low shelf or table while the single front leg is set into a free-standing piece of bamboo driven firmly into the ground. This arrangement allows the woman to stand directly over the quern while grinding, thus reducing the strain on her back. Women use this important kitchen implement for grinding a variety of foodstuffs, paramount among which is corn. When not in use, the woman tilts the quern upward onto the two back legs and leans it against the wall of the house.

Other furnishings typically found in a Nahua house include a small, crudely constructed table and several very small, curve-backed chairs (called *botaqui* (sing.) probably from the Spanish *butaca* meaning "easy chair"). On the floor one often finds several small elongated blocks of wood that have been channeled out and are used as seats. These are called *bancos*, a word borrowed from Spanish. Household members build a high narrow shelf against a wall to serve as a religious altar, and upon it they place ritual items such as beeswax candles, purchased pictures of saints, a small wooden cross, a clay incense brazier, and one or more paper cutouts of witness spirits. Villagers hang woven fiber bags and locally made baskets containing clothes, fruit, and other food from roof beams to keep them out of the reach of voracious rodents. At night, people spread palm mats (sing. *petlatl* in Nahuatl) on the floor for sleeping. In the morning they roll up the mats and store them against a wall. One typically finds a cradle made from a wooden hoop with woven palm in the center tied to the roof beams. Parents place newborn babies in the cradle that they can easily set in motion by a gentle tap.

Light is provided by candles that are locally produced from beeswax, or by a small kerosene-burning wick lamp fashioned from a tin can. In addition there are many small and potentially useful items collected by family members such as empty soft-drink bottles, rolls of wire, pieces of rope, sheets of plastic, irregular pieces of iron, newspapers from the market that are useful for wrapping, and so on. A few houses may contain an ax or saw, a nail-studded board used to shell corn, a transistor radio, or a .22-caliber rifle. The house of a musician will contain a violin, guitar, or perhaps a small ukulele-like *jarana*. One also finds tools for farming and fishing stored in each house. A survey of household items that I conducted found that the average house contained between 45 and 55 different items (see Table 3.1). Surpris-

TABLE 3.1. Inventory of Possessions Found in Two Representative Houses in Amatlán

House 1

Bancos (small benches) (2)
Basket containing sewing implements
Baskets, carrying (cuachiquihuitl) (2)
Bateas (carved wooden troughs) (2)
Botaquis (small chairs) (2)
Bowls for chile (2)
Bowls for soup (4)
Bowls, small clay (3)
Bowls, small plastic (2)
Box, small, containing pictures and legal papers
Bucket, metal
Clay jars for water (several)
Clothesline with stored clothes draped over it
Comales (clay griddles) (4)
Copal brazier
Cups, coffee (6)
Fire table
Fishing spear
Fishing weirs (2)
Glass for water
Gourd containers, small (5)

Hammer
Kerosene wick lamp made from tin can
Machetes, worn (2)
Machete case
Maize, stacked
Mano and metate
Mask used in nanahuatili observance
Morrales (sisal carrying bags) used for storage (3)
Paper, small folded packet
Petates (palm sleeping mats) (3)
Pictures of saints (several)
Plates (4)
Pot used for water storage
Pots, large clay (2)
Pots, small clay (5)
Shelf over fire table for holding sugar loaves
Shelf used as altar
Soft drink bottles, empty (6)
Spoons, metal (3)
Stick used as broom handle
Table, small (2)
Wire, small rolls (2)

House 2

Banco (small bench)
Basket containing sewing implements
Baskets, carrying (cuachiquihuitl) (2)
Baskets, large (7)
Basket, small
Bateas (carving wooden troughs) (2)
Botaquis (small chairs) (2)
Bottle for kerosene
Bottles, plastic (4)
Bowls, for chile

Bowls, for soup (4)
Bowls, small plastic (2)
Box, large wooden, for clothes
Box, large wooden, used for pictures and papers
Broom
Bucket, metal large
Bucket, metal medium
Bucket, metal small
Canister for sweets
Chairs, small straight-backed (3)
Clothesline with stored clothes draped over it

TABLE 3.1. *Continued*

Comales (clay griddles) (5)	Paper bag, folded
Copal brazier	*Petates* (palm sleeping mats) (3)
Crib, small round hanging	Pictures of saints (several)
Cups, coffee (9)	Plastic, small sheet
Fire table	Plates (4)
Fishing net	Pots, large clay (2)
Gourd containers, large (several)	Pots, small clay (4)
Jarana (small stringed musical	Pots, small iron (3)
instrument)	Pots with wooden covers used for
Kerosene wick lamp made from	water storage (4)
tin can	Shelf used as altar
Machetes (2)	Soft drink bottles, empty (10)
Machetes, worn (2)	Spoons, wooden (4)
Maize, stacked	Table, small
Mano and *metate*	Tools (metal file, nails, wooden
Mirror	mallet)
Morrales (sisal carrying bags)	
containing sugar loaf (3)	
Morrales, empty (2)	

ingly, the household possessions of wealthier families are practically indistinguishable from those of poorer families in either quality and quantity. Consumption patterns do not seem to be significantly affected by the level of wealth of the household.

Although Nahua houses are the center of much family activity, people spend surprisingly little time inside them. Life in Amatlán is essentially lived outdoors. People spend most of their leisure time seated under a fruit tree in the clearing or perhaps beneath the new roof of a house under construction. Children play outside, and the women sew or embroider in the daylight, often seated under the eaves of their houses. Many of the hundreds of tasks of daily life such as replacing handles on tools, repairing furniture, making toys for children, making pottery or baskets, or constructing an arch in preparation for a ritual are accomplished outdoors. Most cooking, eating, and sleeping activities take place indoors. It is partly a question of climate, but the attitude toward the house goes beyond that alone. A house is a refuge from the weather and from the night. It is a place to eat in privacy, but otherwise it is not where people choose to spend a great deal of their time.

A house represents the largest investment made by a Nahua family. In addition, a man constructing his first house signals that he is about to get married or that he is looking for a spouse. Moreover, the placement of houses in Amatlán provides an important map of the key social relations that underlie village life. Up until the late 1970s men were free to build their houses wherever they pleased. Although it is necessary to petition the ejido authorities for a building site (*solar* in Spanish), permission is never denied to a legitimate member of the community. A few choose to build apart from the rest, perhaps near their fields or pastures. Most, however, build near the houses of people they feel are of significance to them. In most cases this means kinsmen. Where a man builds a house, then, is a sign to other villagers about his kinship identity and the general state of relations within his family. This situation changed in the mid-1980s when local ejido authorities petitioned the government to have electricity brought to the village (see below and Chapter 7).

WHO LIVES IN AMATLÁN?

In the course of fieldwork, I conducted two censuses of the village, one in 1972 and a second in 1986. These were supplemented by censuses taken by the schoolmaster during various years since 1969. I found the process of taking a census to be time consuming and frustrating. The people had granted permission for me to conduct the survey, but early on it became clear that they were not enthusiastic about it. They were not suspicious of me particularly, but I received the impression that they were unaccustomed to giving out information about themselves to outsiders. The various schoolmasters I met over the years shared the same impression, and I noted earlier that some of their censuses invariably contained inaccuracies. One problem that does not usually occur to people who have not tried this type of data gathering is that a population, even a small one, is never static. Over the months of the research people were born or died, and there was a steady movement of people in and out of the village as they left for long periods of wage labor or returned for extended visits.

At the 1986 census, 506 people lived in Amatlán, divided between 260 females and 246 males. This figure does not include the schoolmaster and his family. Using this information as a base, I will examine fluctuations in total population of the village over the years. From archival documents, the population of the village in 1923 can be set at 178 people. National censuses give the following figures for Amatlán: 190 in 1930, 288 in 1940, 343 in 1950, 358 in 1960, and 563 in 1970. My 1972 count found 583 people, which suggests that between

1930 and 1972 village population tripled. Even acknowledging inaccuracies in early censuses, we can conclude that during this period the population increased significantly. The drop in population of 77 people between my first and last census can be attributed to village fissioning; the land resources became too small relative to population levels, forcing the village to split. It is likely that a similar process occurred between 1950 and 1960 that recorded a population increase of only 15 individuals. A daughter village was formed sometime during this period, but I was unable to obtain a firm date for the event.

Figure 3.1 compares the age distributions of the population in the 1972 and 1986 censuses. These data are approximate because the people do not observe birthdays, and only the youngest are certain of their exact age. No records are kept of births, and so I was forced to accept estimated ages. I cross-checked my estimates with other villagers and compared birth order of siblings, but the ages remain approximate. As we would expect in a growing population, the bulk of individuals are under 14 years of age. In the 1986 count, nearly one-half of the population fell below the 14-year cutoff. I do not have specific figures on infant mortality, but my clear impression is that there is a high death rate before the age of 4 or 5, and thus not all of the children recorded in the census will grow into adulthood. The enormous overrepresentation of people in the lower age brackets is not carried beyond the late teens, after which the chart takes on a more normal pyramid shape.

Anomalies in the age–sex pyramid are caused by two additional factors. First, the data reveal that females outlive males by a substantial margin. In the latest census, 36 females above the age of 50 were counted, as opposed to only 21 males. Second, comparison of the two censuses reveals that there are fewer people in the 30-to-54 age range in 1986. This reflects out-migration and gives an idea of ages at which people are most likely to leave the village. Men leave because they have been widowed or perhaps because they did not inherit enough land to support a household. In some cases individuals have left because of the availability of work in the cities. A more important cause of out-migration is the periodic fissioning of the village in which a large number of younger families leave, usually to begin a nearby daughter village. In sum, the generally uneven contours of this graph reflect the relatively high birth rate of the villagers, differential mortality rates of males and females, and processes of out-migration.

Some additional information from the 1986 census will help complete the picture of who lives in Amatlán. I found 71 married couples

1972 CENSUS

	287 FEMALES	296 MALES	
			TOTAL 583
95+	I		
90-94			
85-89			
80-84	II	I	
75-79			
70-74	III IIII		
65-69	I II		
60-64	II 卌 卌		
55-59	II		
50-54	卌 卌 卌 II		
45-49	卌 卌 III		
40-44	I 卌 卌 IIII		
35-39	IIII 卌 卌 卌 III		
30-34	IIII 卌 卌 卌 卌 IIII		
25-29	卌 卌 卌 卌 卌 卌		
20-24	卌 卌 卌 卌 卌 卌 II		
15-19	卌 卌 卌 卌 卌 卌 卌 卌 卌 卌		
10-14	III 卌 卌 卌 卌 卌 卌 卌 卌 卌 卌 II		
5-9	III 卌 卌 卌 卌 卌 卌 卌 卌 卌 卌 卌 卌 II		
0-4	I 卌 卌 卌 卌 卌 卌 卌 卌 卌 卌 卌 卌 卌		

1986 CENSUS

	260 FEMALES	246 MALES	
			TOTAL 506
95+	I	I	
90-94	I	I	
85-89			
80-84	II IIII		
75-79	I 卌 III		
70-74	IIII		
65-69	I 卌 IIII		
60-64	II 卌 III		
55-59	IIII I		
50-54	卌 卌 I		
45-49	IIII III		
40-44	II 卌 III		
35-39	II 卌 卌 卌 卌 I		
30-34	IIII 卌 卌 卌 卌 IIII		
25-29	卌 卌 卌 卌 卌 III		
20-24	III 卌 卌 卌 卌		
15-19	IIII 卌 卌 卌 卌 卌 卌 II		
10-14	II 卌 卌 卌 卌 卌 卌 卌 卌 II		
5-9	IIII 卌 卌 卌 卌 卌 卌 卌 卌 IIII		
0-4	IIII 卌 卌 卌 卌 卌 卌 卌 卌 卌 卌		

3.1. Age-sex distributions in Amatlán, 1972 and 1986

in residence. Of these, 63 are in what is known in Mexican legal terms as *unión libre*, or common-law marriages. The remaining 8 have been legalized through a civil ceremony. In the earlier census no marriages were of the legally registered civil type. As we left the field in 1986, we were invited to a wedding in the village in which a visiting priest performed the ceremony. This was the first time this had occurred in Amatlán, and it may indicate changes taking place in marriage customs. Traditional marriage customs are inelaborate and will be discussed below.

The average (mean) number of children living at home with parents is 3.8, and the mode or most commonly occurring number is 3. In the absence of birth records it is difficult to get an accurate account of the average number of live births per woman, but I estimate that it is between five and seven. I was not able to get much information on Nahua birth control, but women did tell me about a plant they call *xalcuahuitl* that induces abortions. I was unable to identify this plant botanically, nor was I able to determine if it is effective. However, its existence indicates that the Nahuas are interested in controlling the number of children they have. The average number of people living in a single residence in 1986 (and thus cooperating economically) is 6.2, including adults and children. In the 1972 census the average household membership was 5.3 people. This earlier figure is smaller because it includes many newly married couples with few children who subsequently left Amatlán to form other villages. Virtually all residence groupings reflect the workings of a long-term domestic cycle in which household membership oscillates between nuclear families and patrilocal extended families. As discussed in greater detail in Chapter 4, nuclear-family residence groups account for a majority of village households and average 5.4 people. Patrilocal extended-family households, on the other hand, have an average of 7.5 residents, and the few matrilocal extended-family households in Amatlán have an average of 8.3 members. Thus, as we might expect, extended-family households are significantly larger on average than nuclear-family households.

My 1986 census reveals that there are 33 widows living in the village and 4 widowers. The figures on widows and widowers are probably low because lone surviving spouses sometimes have to leave the village and seek work in the cities or, if old and feeble, go to live with sons who may live elsewhere. Finally, I found that all children under 5 or 6 years of age are monolingual in Nahuatl. Nahuatl is the only language spoken in the home, and children get their first exposure to Spanish when they attend school. About 60 adults are monolingual, and the remainder of villagers possess varying degrees of ability in Spanish. Most of the people above age 55 are monolingual, and even those who are able to speak Spanish can neither read nor write it. Villagers who have attended at least 4 years of school can read and write in Spanish, although they do so with widely varying degrees of fluency. Women are far more likely to be monolingual Nahuatl speakers than men.

While conducting the first census relatively early in my field research during 1972–73, I discovered that the Nahuas have naming traditions that differ somewhat from those found in Western European cultural traditions. When a Nahua child is born, he or she is named by the parents or by a ritual kinsman. Firstborn children are often named after a paternal grandparent. Names of subsequent children are commonly taken from an almanac popular in rural regions called the *Calendario del más Antiguo Galván* that lists all of the dates of the year and associated saints. The child is frequently named after the saint listed on his or her birthday. In many cases the saint is rather obscure, and the names can be multisyllabic tongue twisters. To an urban Mexican, an odd foreign-sounding given name is often a first indication that the person was named from the *Calendario* and is therefore an Indian.

In general, the child is given a second and third name following the Spanish practice. The second name is the surname of the father, and the third name is the surname of the mother. In a significant number of cases, however, this pattern is not rigorously followed. Often one or two siblings have a totally different name from the rest of the family. When I inquired about this, people responded that they simply liked the alternate name or that the child liked it. In one case a man had a totally distinct name from that of his three brothers. I asked him why his name was different, expecting that he was adopted by his family or that his brothers had a different father. He replied that when he was 12 years old he was getting some papers filled out in Ixhuatlán and when he was asked his name he simply made up one. Since that time he has assumed the invented name as his own and uses it on all official documents. Interestingly, some of his children were given the father's original name, and some have taken his chosen name. It is easy to imagine the difficulties an outsider faces trying to trace kinship relations in a society without rigid naming rules.

Each person has a nickname as well. These often follow the traditional Mexican pattern. For example, Jesús will be called Chucho, or Manuel becomes Manolo. However, in addition to the traditional nickname, almost everyone has a completely distinct name that is used in everyday conversation. For example, Luis Magdelena is called Carlos, and Juan Hernández is called Cirilo. Adding to the confusion is the very limited number of surnames in use in Amatlán and, for that matter, in most Indian communities. Probably over three-quarters of the villagers have either Hernández or Martínez as one or both of their names. In addition, virtually all females have the multiple first names María Angelina. Thus the name María Angelina Hernández Hernández belongs to quite a number of people. Unlike in Western European cultures where people identify closely with their name, the Nahuas hold to theirs loosely. They find it perfectly natural to acquire a new name or two during their lifetimes. For example, as discussed earlier, each person has a toponymic name based on the location of his or her house. This confusion of names is of course daunting only to outsiders. Everyone knows who is who in the village. Just as in the case with house names and village-specific names of geographical features, the system of personal naming serves to create a cognitive community for the villagers and to create an information barrier for representatives of the national culture.

MILPA HORTICULTURE AND HOUSE GARDENS

The people of Amatlán live by farming the lands that surround the village on all sides. Farming is the most important productive activity and thus it is not surprising that the cycles of clearing, planting, and harvesting influence all aspects of village life. Men spend a majority of their working lives engaged in the many tasks required by farming techniques that have changed little since pre-Columbian days. Women and children also play their part in the hard work of cultivating the tropical forest. With the exception of sugar production, villagers accomplish all work by hand without the use of machine or animal power. The major tools are the steel machete, which they purchase in the market, and a digging stick used in planting. Farming not only occupies people's time but also their thoughts. It is enthusiastically discussed by villagers in intricate detail, and it provides a focus for symbolic representation during the most sacred rituals.

All men in the village, with the exception of the schoolmaster, earn their living by working their fields. Despite sometimes considerable differences in wealth among villagers, all men view themselves equally as farmers. Farming is basic to life itself, not only for the village as an abstraction but for each individual who lives in it. I will begin by describing the ancient techniques for cultivating corn (*sintli* in Nahuatl), the most important crop grown by the Nahuas. The horticultural cycle starts in mid-May when men make preparations for the rainy-season planting, called *xopajmili* in Nahuatl. Many Nahuas believe that work must be initiated on a Saturday, Monday, or Wednesday to obtain the maximum harvest. Sunday, Tuesday, Thursday, or Friday may be a *cococ tonati*, Nahuatl for a "bad" or "unlucky" day (see Reyes Antonio 1982:85–86). A man organizes a group of assistants (*peones* in Spanish, *tlanejmej* in Nahuatl) to help him clear a new area of forest or, more commonly, the dense overgrowth from one of his fallow fields. Villagers call a fallow field a *milcahuali* ("abandoned field" in Nahuatl). Thick tropical brush called *cuatitlaj* in Nahuatl or *monte* in Spanish rapidly covers any untended spot, often to a height of 15 or 20 feet. It is to the advantage of the man to have the *monte* cut in one or two days so that it will dry uniformly and thus burn more evenly. Each man brings his own machete that has been honed to a razor's edge on a piece of sandstone. The men work together in a row using a crooked stick in the left hand to hold back the brush while striking at the base of the vegetation with full swings of their machetes. Care must be taken to avoid poisonous snakes and spiders that hide in the dense thickets.

After cutting, the piles of brush and trees are allowed to dry for one or more weeks. During this period, the farmer hopes that the rains will not come and soak the drying vegetation. It is during these weeks that an individual repays his helpers by working an equivalent time in their fields. After the vegetation has dried, it is burned in a spectacular fire, flames from which may shoot 100 feet into the air. Following the burning, the earth is left scorched and apparently lifeless but enriched by minerals in the ash. Within a very few days the farmer reassembles his helpers for the planting. Each assistant cuts a dibble pole (*cuatlatoctli* or *cuahuitsoctli* in Nahuatl) of about 7 feet in length and sharpens it at one end. The owner of the field then pours seed into the sisal carrying bag that each man wears slung over his shoulder. The men line up and walk a straight course across the field, plunging the stick in at about 80-centimeter intervals and dropping four or five seeds into each hole. They cover over the hole and lightly tamp the earth before proceeding. Once it has been planted, the field is transformed into a milpa (also *milaj* in Nahuatl).

The corn seed is carefully selected for planting, based on size and freshness. It is often the case that new seed has to be purchased at the market if that which remains from the previous harvest is of insufficient quantity or in questionable condition. Older seed has a powdery appearance, and men told me that fewer of these seeds will sprout. Fresh seed is glossy and has a high rate of germination. Inside each Nahua house there is invariably a bundle of fine maize ears hanging from a roof support that is being saved for seed.

Villagers call the type of corn they grow *criollo* (Spanish for "creole"), and they recognize four varieties by color. They consider the white to be superior for eating, and they grow a surplus of this variety in the rainy season to sell in the market. The yellow is hardy and has a shorter growing period, and so villagers try to plant this variety mainly in the dry season. However, because of the dry conditions, yellow corn often actually takes longer to mature than white. Villagers state that yellow corn lacks the flavor of the white, and, although they sometimes consume it themselves, they prefer to feed it to their animals. It is rarely grown for sale in the market. Rapidly maturing black and red varieties of corn are grown in small amounts and play an insignificant part in village diet or economy. The people are aware of modern hybrid varieties of corn, and several individuals have tried to plant them. They found, however, that they are susceptible to insect damage and, in the absence of costly insecticide, they yield poorly in the region. See Table 3.2 for a summary of major crop varieties grown in Amatlán.

A few weeks or so after planting, a farmer goes to his milpa to determine if it needs to be weeded. Usually it does, especially if there has been rain, and he spends several days cleaning the field using a special hooked machete called a *uíngaro*, or in some cases, a hoe, the steel blade of which has been purchased in the market. The men consider this an arduous task, but they say it is necessary if the newly sprouted plants are to have a chance against faster growing weeds. A second weeding takes place about 5 weeks later, and sometimes a third is required several weeks after that. In the meantime, the maize is growing and blocking out sunlight to the earth, effectively preventing weeds from overtaking it.

Between weedings, a man carefully examines his milpa every few days. If gullies form due to the heavy rains, he dams them with large stones and earth. He may mound soil at the base of each cluster of corn plants to keep water from pooling around the stalk and drowning the roots. Once planted, a field increases its yield in accord with the amount of care expended on it. Milpa horticulture is labor intensive in that output at harvest is directly proportional to labor invested in maintaining the field. Not surprisingly, the milpa is a source of immense pride on the part of men and boys. A well-kept field with a

TABLE 3.2. Varieties of Major Crops Grown in Amatlán

Crop	Varieties	Characteristics
sintli ("corn" general type *criollo*, meaning "creole" in Spanish)		
	1. *chipahuac* ("white")	The most important variety grown for household consumption and to be sold at the market. It is characterized by a relatively long growth cycle and is planted primarily in the rainy season.
	2. *costic* ("yellow")	Villagers state that yellow corn is not as tasty as the white, although they eat it on occasion. It has a shorter growth cycle and is generally planted in the dry season.
	3. *chichiltic* ("red")	Both the red and black varieties of
	4. *yayahuic* ("black")	corn are rarely grown in Amatlán.
etl ("bean")		
	1. *pitsajetl* ("small bean")	This variety of black bean is favored by villagers for household consumption and is also the major type grown for sale. Its growing season is September through December.
	2. *chichimequetl* ("*chichimecaj* bean")	The word *chichimecaj* means "wild," and the name for this variety of bean may come from its resemblance to a wild vine that grows in the region. It comes in black and yellow varieties.
	3. *emecatl* ("bean vine")	The bean produced by *emecatl* is larger than the *pitsajetl* or *chichimequetl*. It comes in black and red varieties.
	4. *patlachetl* ("broad bean")	This is another of the lesser varieties grown in Amatlán for household consumption.
	5. *torojetl* ("bull bean")	The largest bean variety grown, although it is rarely cultivated in the village.
chili ("chile pepper")		
	1. *xoxochili* ("green chile")	This is a medium-sized Jalapeño pepper that is mostly grown for household consumption, although surpluses are occasionally sold at the market. It is the most popular variety of chile and may be consumed fresh or dried.

TABLE 3.2. *Continued*

Crop	Varieties	Characteristics
	2. *pitsajchili* ("small chile")	This variety mostly grows wild in fallowing milpas or along the arroyo, and the seed is distributed by birds. It produces a tiny pepper that is extremely hot, and for this reason it is greatly appreciated by the villagers. Villagers occasionally cultivate this pepper to sell, but most people rely on gathering it from wild plants.
	3. *cuajteco* ("Huatla pepper")	The name derives from the region where it is extensively grown. This is the pepper most often cultivated to sell in the market. The seed has to be sprouted before it is planted in the milpa.
	4. *pico de pájaro* (meaning "bird's beak" in Spanish)	The name derives from the shape of the pepper. It is cultivated for household consumption.
camojtli ("camote")	1. *cuacamojtli* ("yuca")	This root crop is known in two varieties, brown and white. It is grown for household consumption.
	2. *tlalcamojtli* ("earth camote")	This is the sweet camote of which there are white, yellow, and purple varieties. The sweet camote is like a sweet potato and is grown by villagers for household consumption.
ohuatl ("cane" general type *criollo*, meaning "creole" in Spanish)	1. *xolohuatl* ("cane with no spines," from *xolotl*, a scaleless fish)	This is a variety of cane that can be used for making sugarloaf.
	2. *tlapalohuatl* ("painted cane")	This purple variety of cane is grown to be consumed directly. The stalk is cut into pieces, and the sweet juice is sucked out.

(continued)

TABLE 3.2. *Continued*

Crop	Varieties	Characteristics
(general type *caña de azucar*, meaning "sugarcane" in Spanish)		
	1. *ohuatl chipahuac* ("white cane")	White sugarcane is cultivated for making sugarloaf. Informants state that this commercial type of sugarcane is a recent introduction into the village. It is rapidly replacing the creole varieties which were introduced into the region earlier.

After my fieldnotes and De la Cruz Hernández 1982:43–52; see also Reyes Martínez 1982:70–89 and Ixmatlahua Montalvo *et al.* 1982:74–75 for names of additional varieties of beans and chiles grown in the Huasteca. (All names are in Nahuatl unless otherwise indicated.)

high rate of yield contributes to a man's reputation. For the most part, the fields are kept in immaculate condition, and men spend many hours each week lavishing care on them.

Shortly after planting, and then again sometime in September when the newly formed ears reach several inches in length, there is danger of losing the crop to birds. I was not able to identify the species of bird that poses the greatest threat, but they appear to be dark in color and smaller than a crow. The men build platforms that rise about 7 or 8 feet above the ground in the middle of the milpa and station a lookout there to scare off the invaders. Villagers call this period *tlapiya-listli* ("having or taking care of something"). Family members take turns on the platform, manning it day and night for a period of 2 or 3 weeks. Small boys particularly come in handy during this period because they use their deadly accurate slingshots (*tehuitlastli* sing. in Nahuatl) against the birds. Other family members rely on shouting and stone throwing to do the job, or they may make a scarecrow from white clothing.

The varieties of maize grown by the Indians are characterized by hard, flinty kernels that must be processed before they can be eaten. However, in September and early October some immature ears can be consumed, much like we eat corn on the cob. The ears at this stage of their development are called *elotl* (sing., in Nahuatl, *elote* in Spanish) and are savored as a delicacy by the villagers. The main harvest of maize takes place in November and into early December. At this time men or other members of the family may enter the milpa to load up carrying baskets (*cuachiquihuitl*, sing. in Nahuatl) with the ripe ears. They carry the laden basket to the house on their backs by means of a tumpline across the forehead, and there they stack the unshucked ears neatly against one wall. In many instances a farmer harvests only a few baskets a day over a period of several weeks. In this case, he may "double" the corn to prevent it from rotting. In doubling, the corn stalk is bent in half while it still stands in the field, thus preventing water from entering the ears. Doubled corn can remain in the fields for many weeks without harm to the ears (Reyes Martínez 1982:56).

After the harvest, the stalks are allowed to stand, and the field lies unattended until the next clearing and planting. Climatic conditions allow for two crops a year. However, the farmer tries to rotate fields so that no single field is planted twice in the same year. The dry-season planting (*tonamili* in Nahuatl) follows the same basic work pattern as that of the wet season. The fields are cleared, dried, burned, and seeded during December and early January. Shorter maturing yellow corn is the favored crop for his season. If possible, the seeds are planted in fields that are of lower elevation so that the scant rainfall of the dry season will be put to its most efficient use. Fewer weedings are required because of the lower rainfall, and these usually occur at 5 and 10 weeks after planting. Harvest time varies depending on rainfall, but the crop is usually mature by mid-June. The corn on the cob is ready for eating in late April or early May. The watch for birds takes place just after seeding and during elote season. The dry-season planting is a highly uncertain affair; it is not uncommon to lose the whole crop due to drought. In other areas of the Huasteca, conditions allow for a third growing season called the *sehualmili* in Nahuatl. The fields are planted at the beginning of November, and the crop matures over the colder winter months. No one in Amatlán, however, recalls being able to plant a third crop (see Table 3.3 for a summary of the slash-and-burn cycle; also Ixmatlahua Montalvo et al. 1982:76–84,86–87; Reyes Martínez 1982:45–63; and Reyes Antonio 1982:85–91 for descriptions of Nahua corn farming and the growth stages of the corn plant).

Maize is the Nahua staple, and the overwhelming majority of every milpa is given over to its cultivation. The milpa, however, is a complex garden containing many different kinds of cultigens. Sections are always planted in black beans, squash, chiles, amaranth, melons, various herbs for use as condiments such as coriander or mint, along with tomatoes, onions, root crops such as camote, bananas, sugarcane,

TABLE 3.3. Steps in the Slash-and-Burn Horticultural
Cycle for Corn

Operation	Nahuatl
1. Cutting brush	*tlayistli*
Cutting large forest trees	*tlamaximasi*
2. Allowing sun to dry cut vegetation	*ma huaqui*
3. Burning cut vegetation	*tlajchinoa*
4. Planting	*tlatocalistli*
5. Weeding	*tlamehualistli*
6. Guarding the milpa	*tlapiyalistli*
7. Harvesting	*pixquistli*
8. Carrying	*tlatsaquilistli*
9. Piling	*tlatecpicholistli*
10. Shucking	*tlaxipehualistli*
11. Shelling	*tlaoyalistli*

coffee and many other crops (see Reyes Antonio 1982:45). The techniques for cultivating these additional crops are, in almost all cases,
simple variations on the method for planting corn.

Beans (*etl*, sing. in Nahuatl) and sugarcane (*ohuatl*, sing. in Nahuatl)
are important commercial crops that merit separate mention. Beans
for household consumption are often planted among the corn in the
milpa, and their vines climb up the lower stalks. However, beans
grown by individuals strictly as a cash crop are sometimes planted in
their own fields. Men cultivate several varieties of beans (see Table
3.2) but grow for sale only the small black bean called *pitsajetl* in
Nahuatl. They plant seeds in small clusters about 20 centimeters
apart, and thus a milpa can accomodate about four times as many bean
plants as corn. The varieties of beans people grow in Amatlán are
relatively productive, but they are not as hardy as corn. Thus variations
in rainfall affect beans more than corn, and they can only be grown on
a large scale during one season near the end of the rainy period. A
third, important commercial crop is sugarcane. Villagers grow new
plants from cuttings that they place in holes made with a dibble stick.
See below for a description of the procedure for making sugarloaf.

As a supplement to the milpa, most households have small fenced-
in gardens adjacent to the house where herbs, some food crops, flowers, and an occasional banana tree are grown. In addition, privately
owned fruit trees planted in and around the house clearings add variety
to the diet. Villagers favor plums, avocados, *anonas* ("custard apples"),
mangos, *zapotes* ("sapotes," or possibly "mameys"), lemons, limes,

and other less familiar citrus fruits. Some of these trees are quite old and must have been planted by the grandparents of the current occupants of the clearing. Villagers grow tobacco that, after being air-dried, is smoked by the older men and women. They roll short cigars that are tied together with a strip of plant fiber. Nonconsumable plants grown include *ojtlatl* (*otate* in Spanish), a bamboo-like species used as a building material, and many varieties of beautiful and fragrant flowers. Both men and women appreciate flowers and can sometimes be seen walking through the village holding a small bouquet. The most important flower grown is the marigold, *sempoalxochitl* in Nahuatl, which plays an important part in all rituals.

Like farmers everywhere, Nahuas must contend with numerous pests that threaten their crops. I have already mentioned birds that take a heavy toll on yields each year. Apparently, different species of birds attack the growing crops at different stages of their growth. The most destructive wild animal is the racoon (*mapachij* in Nahuatl) that can ruin many plants in a single evening of feeding. Field mice (*quimichij*, sing. in Nahuatl) also attack crops in the field and in storage as well. Domestic foraging animals such as pigs and cattle, however, pose the greatest danger to the milpa. Owners are responsible for destruction caused by their animals, and they must make compensation for lost crops. Another threat is the voracious "elote worm" (*eloocuilij* in Nahuatl) that enters the elote from the top and consumes the young corn. After the harvest, a weevil called the "corn cutter" (*sintequiyotl* in Nahuatl) consumes large amounts of corn as it lies in storage. Another weevil called the "bean cutter" (*etequiuj* in Nahuatl) similarly attacks harvested beans. These and other pests and plant diseases combine to make traditional farming in the southern Huasteca a risky enterprise (De la Cruz 1982:61–64; Reyes Martínez 1982:54–56).

GATHERING, HUNTING, AND FISHING

Most household members, but particularly women and children, engage in gathering of wild products from the lush forest. There are literally hundreds of items collected, ranging from firewood to a delicious substitute for coffee. Most meals are enhanced by some edible a family member found on the way back from the stream or the milpa. These products typically mature at known times during the year, and people are always on the lookout for them. During times of food shortage, families rely more heavily on gathering, and women may be away for hours in search of useful items. By observing food habits of several families in the village, I estimated that nearly 30% of the noncorn diet is composed of wild products. Secondary crops, fruits, and gathered items may be sold in small quantities to other villagers or at one of the regional markets, but for the most part they are consumed at home by the family. However, despite the importance of these sources of food, the villagers consider maize to be the absolute necessity of life, the source of nourishment that takes precedence over all others. When the Nahuas say "corn is our blood," the literal meaning of this metaphor is that it is their most important food. I will show in a later section that growing maize makes good economic sense as well.

Hunting and fishing also play a role in provisioning the villagers. Men rarely hunt these days because of the relative dearth of wild animals in the region. Apparently population increases coupled with deforestation from slash-and-burn horticulture have caused animals to migrate toward the Sierra to the west and south. Older men tell of hunting deer and wild pigs in their youth but are quick to emphasize their scarcity today. Rabbits are hunted by a few of the young men who have access to .22-caliber rifles, but they are not an important food source. Of slightly greater importance is the hunting and trapping of edible birds. Men set traps on artificial perches that snare a bird's head or feet. Small boys assist in this endeavor as well, and they are amazingly accurate with their slingshots, bringing down birds perched in trees or feeding on the ground. The favored catch is a medium-sized bird that resembles a dove.

Fishing plays a more important role in subsistence activities. Hardly a week goes by without some fish or crustacean meal being served in the Nahua household. Interestingly, men teach their sons to fish several years before they teach them techniques of cultivation. Both men and boys devote a good deal of time and employ several techniques in catching fish, large crayfish, and several varieties of shrimplike crustaceans. In the deeper pools of the arroyo, a handmade throwing net is used to ensnare fish. The net is circular and is woven by men from commercial nylon line. Lead sinkers are tied around the edge of the net, and it is cast so as to land flat on the surface of the water. Men tell of past times when nets were handwoven from cotton line and small stones were used as sinkers. In shallower parts of streams and rivers and particularly after rains, a long conical weir (called *achiquihuitl* in Nahuatl) is placed in specially prepared stone formations. The rushing water is funneled through two low walls constructed to flare out at the upstream end and to narrow to a small opening at the downstream end. The fisherman places the weir in this smaller opening and the fish swept downstream become trapped in it and are held there by the force of the water. Additional techniques employed by the people of Amatlán include spearfishing using either pointed sticks, sticks with attached points made from sharpened wire, or using a handmade speargun powered by a large rubberband, hunting large edible tropical crayfish with small bows and arrows, and finally, fishing with the use of oversized firecrackers to stun fish. Most villagers consider this last technique to be an inappropriate and destructive practice because it kills too many fish and it disturbs an important spirit, *apanchanej*, who resides in the water.

VILLAGE ANIMALS

Large numbers of domesticated animals roam the trails and clearings of Amatlán. Unlike most Euro-American farmers, villagers do not confine domesticated animals in enclosures. They take the opposite approach to farmyard organization by fencing only those areas that are off-limits to animals. Thus, house gardens, fruit trees, and sometimes a whole milpa will be fenced in to exclude animals. This practice leaves animals free to explore and forage at will, and sometimes they may wander miles away from their owners' compounds. Once while walking to a distant village I encountered a pig from Amatlán on the trail. I recognized the animal by its markings that were so unusual that the Indians had commented upon them. I was surprised seeing it there, about a 2-hour walk away from the village. That evening the pig returned to Amatlán to receive his ration of corn. When I mentioned the incident to people, they did not seem concerned, and several commented that turkeys will also wander miles from the village. Villagers know their animals' habits very well, and twice-daily feedings always seem to insure their return.

Dogs are ubiquitous and can be heard barking throughout the village night and day. The Indians favor a small variety of dog whose primary function is to warn household members of approaching people or animals. Dogs are not pets in the usual sense of the word, and they cannot be petted or approached by people. They are fed leftovers from the table and are often skinny, mangy, and ill-tempered. Villagers consider dogs to be a nuisance, and they spend considerable time driving them outdoors. A visit to someone's house always involves a commotion in which household members try to control numerous barking dogs that are nipping at the ankles of the approaching guest.

The most important animal in relation to the average family budget is the pig. Each household has several pigs attached to it, ranging in size from small piglets to enormous animals several years of age. They are fed maize and allowed to root for food in the forest during the day. At night they sleep outside under the house eaves or in a nearby wallow. Some animals are reserved to be consumed during special ritual occasions and infrequently one may be butchered so family members can have some meat, but for the most part pigs are raised to be sold at market. A full-grown pig eats more maize on a daily basis than a man does, and so they are very expensive to maintain. However, as will be shown in Chapter 5, a pig serves the family as a "walking bank account," a convenience for storing wealth for later use. Pigs are voracious and at all cost must be kept out of people's houses and out of the gardens and milpas. They can often be seen walking on the trails with sticks tied to their necks to help prevent them from entering fenced-in areas.

Turkeys, chickens and, ducks to a lesser extent are also kept by households. Villagers feed these fowl maize and value them both for their eggs and meat. Since they also wander freely, finding their eggs in the forest sometimes poses a problem. If the family decides to increase the size of its flock, they take the female bird and place her under an upturned carrying basket along with as many fertilized eggs as they can find. Newborn chicks are fed cornmeal until they are old enough to forage on their own. At night, the birds roost on the roof of the house or in a nearby tree to avoid predators.

Other domesticated animals include burros, mules, horses, and finally, cattle. In 1972–73 two families own one burro each, and the animals are used solely for carrying burdens. One of these families also owns a mule, and they use it not only to turn the sugarcane press (*trapiche* in Spanish) during the sugar-making season but also as a means of transporting loads throughout the rest of the year. Three Indian families own one horse each, and another family owns two. Horses are pack animals used to carry produce to and from the market. These animals are rarely fed maize but instead are allowed to graze on land set aside by each family for the purpose. Owning a beast of burden is a definite advantage for the individual farmer, but the purchase price and land required to support it are beyond the means of all but a few. In fact, all of these work animals are owned by families who own cattle as well.

The Huasteca is a cattle-raising area, and one goal of most Indians of the region is to own cattle. Cattle raising allows the individual farmer to move beyond the built-in constraints of growing corn and beans in the traditional way. In a sense it lifts him outside of the local village economy and allows for a far higher level of productivity and accumulation of wealth. However, the incorporation of cattle raising in farming activities has costs that place it beyond the reach of most villagers. In 1972–73, thirteen men in Amatlán raise cattle in addition to their farming activities. Although it is difficult to get exact figures because of the scattered layout of the pastures and the unwillingness of cattle owners to reveal their wealth, the average herd in the village is about 5 head, with the largest reaching 16 head. These figures are corroborated by livestock registration documents I examined in Ixhuatlán that indicate that the average herd is 5.3 head. The herds are small, but they represent considerable wealth by village standards. The advantage of cattle raising for those with the land to support it is that a herd is a self-perpetuating system that depends on grazing. Cattle are never fed corn and so, unlike pigs, they do not compete directly with humans for the staple crop.

Several factors prevent most people from becoming cattle owners. To begin with, the purchase price of a calf is prohibitively high for most Indians. An even greater problem is the cost of feeding and watering an animal. To own even a single head the farmer must have access to pasture land with an adequate source of water. This of course removes valuable milpa land that could alternately be used to grow additional crops. Also, cattle in the tropics are expensive to maintain. They require periodic tick baths, vaccines, and medicine to fight disease, and they are vulnerable to snakebite, vampire bats, jaguars, and injury caused by uneven, sometimes treacherously steep pastures. An additional problem is that cattle have no immediate utility. They cannot be used to carry burdens, and the people never consume milk or dairy products. Beef is eaten only in the rare circumstance where an animal dies prematurely. In sum, although cattle raising is the highest level of economic activity in villages, it seems to contradict the pragmatic, utilitarian character of other economic pursuits.

Because land is supposed to be divided equally among ejido members, it is surprising that 13 families have managed to enter the cattle-raising economy. This fact reveals something very important about life in Amatlán, something that undermines the view that Indian communities are homogeneous. The cattle-owning families form a kind of economic elite in the village. This elite may come into conflict with those who are dependent solely on their crops for their livelihood. An indicator of the high potential for problems between cattle owners and other villagers is the fact that cattle are the only animals enclosed and not allowed to roam. A single animal can devastate a milpa in a few hours and cause tremendous conflict in the village. It is in the interest of the cattle-owning families to avoid conflicts that bring economic differences into the open. Therefore, cattle pastures are carefully fenced and the fences scrupulously maintained. If an animal does invade someone's milpa, compensation is paid to the field's owner with a minimum of argument (see Harnapp 1972 for a discussion of the development of the cattle industry in the Huasteca).

FOOD

All production activities serve to insure that the people of Amatlán have sufficient food. Generally, food is abundant, and the people have a varied and interesting diet. Food shortages have been known, however. People told me about disasterous harvests in the past where villagers were reduced to eating nothing more than tortillas and salt. Occasionally an individual household will become impoverished due to alcoholism, bad luck, or inadequate planning, but this is rare. Poor harvests are most often caused by adverse weather, either too little or too much rain. There are also cyclical shortages. The periods just before the two harvests in the late spring and early fall are called the times of hunger (*mayantli*, sing. in Nahuatl). During these periods of the year, household stores of corn and other staples may decline, forcing people to gather more of their food from the forest or purchase it at the market. It is my experience that preharvest shortages rarely result in people having insufficient food. The 1972 harvest was poor due to drought and a sudden and unexplained increase in the population of field mice that infested every house and milpa. Villagers told me they were worried about food shortages the next year when the inadequate stores from the bad harvest ran out. However, households adjusted to the problem, and I saw no serious signs of hunger that year.

The Nahua diet is based on corn. To call it a staple in the same sense that potatoes are a staple in the North American diet is to underestimate its importance seriously. No meal is complete without corn and regardless of how much rich food a person has eaten, he or she will complain of hunger if the dish lacks a corn component. In addition to supporting people, corn feeds domestic animals, it is the basis of the village economy, and it indirectly underlies village politics. Not surprisingly, it plays an important role in Nahua ideology. In ritual and myth, corn sustains the people physically and spiritually. The corn spirit, *chicomexochitl* ("7-flower"), is both a provider of sustenance and a nourisher of the human soul (see Chapter 6).

The most common way the Nahuas eat corn is in the form of tortillas (*tlaxcali*, sing. in Nahuatl). Women and girls spend a good part of each day engaged in the long process of preparing tortillas. After shelling sufficient corn, women place the hard kernels in boiling water to which has been added a small portion of mineral lime. This cooking is done in a large pottery vessel placed over a fire on the floor of the house. After about 1½ hours, the corn becomes soft and swollen and, at this stage, is called *nixtamali* in Nahuatl. The kernels are then washed thoroughly in the water of the arroyo; women say that repeated washings make a superior, whiter tortilla. The cooled and rinsed kernels are then ground at least three times using the mano and metate. After placing the saturated corn on the metate the woman moves the mano back and forth over it with a slight twisting motion of the wrist. Eventually a wet paste is formed called *tixtli* in Nahuatl. The woman picks up small amounts of the dough, slaps it deftly between her hands into the classic circular shape, and cooks the tortilla on the flat clay *comali*. During any meal, no matter how small or impromptu, the woman of the house prepares a steady supply of fresh tortillas.

Nahua women create a number of other dishes from the cornmeal. Mixed with beans, formed into a thick tortilla and cooked on the comali, the corn dough becomes the basis of a delicious bread called *piqui* in Nahuatl. The women may form the dough around a small piece of meat and a chile pepper, wrap it in banana leaves, and steam it to make a tamale (*tamali* in Nahuatl). Corn porridge, called *atoli* in Nahuatl (*atole* in Spanish), is flavored with raw sugar and is a favorite beverage prepared for celebrations. Variations on cornmeal dishes are endless. The basic tortilla, for example, can be folded plain or around beans, meat, or other foods and covered with one of a variety of chile-pepper-based sauces to make enchiladas. For most dishes the corn is processed into meal first. However, as mentioned above, part way through the growth cycle corn can be eaten right off the cob. At this time women make special tamales directly from the sweet and tender kernels without first boiling them. These are called in Nahuatl *xamitl* (sing., literally "adobe"). At the height of the elote season women often make a giant xamitl called a xamconetsij (Nahuatl for "*xamitl* baby") that is about the size of a newborn baby. The arrival of elotes is a time of excitement and anticipation. When the elotes are ready to eat, harvest time is close at hand.

Black beans are an important source of protein in the Nahua diet. When not cooked in *piqui* bread they are boiled with onions, chiles, and tropical herbs such as coriander or *epazote* and eaten like a soup with the ever-present tortillas. Along with corn and beans, the third major food in the Indian diet is squash. Squash (*ayojtli* in Nahuatl) is grown in several varieties, and it is consumed boiled and sweetened with raw sugar. Root crops such as yuca and camote are also boiled and candied with raw sugar. Onions are chopped and used to flavor sauces. A great variety of tomatoes (*tomatl*, sing. in Nahuatl) are grown and used in Nahua cooking, particularly for sauces, ranging from the familiar, large, red *jitomate* to the green, leaf-covered *tomatillo*, to a tiny green tomato that grows in clusters and resembles grapes. Peanuts are roasted in the shell and eaten. Mangos, bananas, anonas, avocados, zapotes, plums, oranges, and limes are some of the many tree-grown items that are eaten without preparation. The villagers also raise watermelons and papayas, and as mentioned above, collect hundreds of domesticated and semidomesticated items from the forest and overgrown fields. During their season, most of these plant products are available in small quantities at the weekly markets. Household members try to sell their small periodic surpluses to increase family income.

The most common condiment used by the Indians are several varieties of hot chile peppers, called *chili*, sing. in Nahuatl. Many of the prepared dishes, and especially meat dishes described below, are burning hot by North American standards and can cause severe gastrointestinal distress to the unprepared outsider. Interestingly, not all people in Amatlán like chile peppers, although an overwhelming number of women use them liberally in their cooking. Chicken eggs are consumed, usually fried and placed inside a folded tortilla. Domesticated fowl are not cooped, however, and thus relatively few eggs are recovered. Several families keep hives of a stingless variety of bee that makes the honey harvest much easier and safer. Most villagers enjoy the succulent honey as a beverage to drink. As a treat, some people like to suck on a cut section of sugarcane. Women also make a porridge out of amaranth seeds, which they sweeten with raw sugar and serve as a kind of dessert. Amaranth porridge, which is high in protein, is called *alegría* in Spanish. They also prepare a delicious concoction out of squash or fruit in which large pieces are lightly cooked in a syrup made of raw sugar. The dish is eaten when cooled and is called *nectli* in Nahuatl.

Fish and crustaceans caught by the men and boys are cooked whole and eaten folded in tortillas. Fish are generally boiled, wrapped in banana leaves and steamed, or grilled on the comali in corn-husk wrappers. Small shrimplike crustaceans are often eaten whole in tamales, whereas crayfishlike *acamayas* are generally steamed in banana leaves. Meat is rarely consumed in Amatlán. On occasion a family kills and prepares a chicken or turkey as a special treat. Pork is almost never eaten except as part of a ritual observance, and the only time beef is available is when an animal dies of natural causes. Meat is usually boiled and prepared as a soup, flavored with onion, chile peppers, or herbs. It is eaten in tortillas and is often supplemented with fresh red or green chile sauce. On occasion women prepare meat in the form of tamales, but this tends to be a food associated with ritual feasts. The most favored way villagers serve meat of any kind is in a thick, dark chile sauce called *mole* in Spanish. Preparation of this savory sauce is complicated and time-consuming, but it is a high point of Nahua cuisine. Mole is known all over Mexico, with each region preparing it in a characteristic style. In the village it is prepared with a number of ingredients including garlic, several varieties of tomatoes and peppers including dried red chiles and small fresh green ones, and fresh-ground spices such as cumin seed, cloves, and black pepper. There are many local variations on the dish, but it is always extremely spicy. Mole is served in a bowl, accompanied by rice and eaten with tortillas. When villagers visited us in the state capital and I took them to their first restaurant meal, they would invariably order mole, even for breakfast.

Villagers usually eat their meals informally using a bowl that they may hold in their hands, place on a small table, or set on the ground. The only utensil they ever use, even for soup, is the tortilla. As they eat, they tear a small piece from the tortilla and, after forming it into a cone, scoop up the food. This temporary spoon is swallowed with each bite. Frequently, people wash their hands before as well as after eating because of this practice. There are three meals a day that are served by women at dawn, around midday, and again at dusk. If a man is working in the field, his wife sends a stack of hot tortillas or enchiladas out to him at noon via one of the children. Often, men and boys eat first, but this practice is not rigidly followed. During meals, the woman of the household makes tortillas while the others eat. Finally, rules of etiquette stipulate that invited guests eat before family members.

Villagers obtain water for drinking or cooking from the numerous springs found in and surrounding Amatlán close to the arroyo. It is the task of women and young girls to keep two or three containers in the house full of fresh water at all times. People purchase in the market the clay pots used for carrying and storing water. These are specially made with an indented bottom so that they can be easily carried atop the head. They are fired at low temperatures and have thin walls so that water evaporates through the pot and cools the water inside. Women scoop water into these pots with a gourd that they then float on top for the trip home. At any time during the day one can observe numerous women and girls walking to the springs carrying an empty pot or returning to their houses with the filled vessels on their heads. If for some reason the woman is incapacitated or extremely busy, a man or boy will carry the water in a heavy, awkward bucket. Males never attempt to carry anything on their heads.

In general, I conclude that food in Amatlán is plentiful and in its variety, nutritious. Although I have no scientific evidence on the matter, it seems probable that the diet is slightly lacking in protein. Corn is a relatively low-protein grain, and because the lack of milk or its by-products in the diet is coupled with only an intermittent availability of beans, meat and fish, I expect that protein intake may be below an optimal level. This would not pose a problem for the adults, but it may be deleterious for the children. Low protein may account in part for what seems to be a relatively high infant mortality rate. The people in general appear healthy. There is virtually no obesity no doubt due to their active lifestyle. A health problem for some men and a few women is the overconsumption of the very powerful cane alcohol that is popular in the region. Statistics are impossible to acquire, but I think it is likely that alcohol consumption is the key factor in premature deaths among adults in the village. The Indian diet evidenced in Amatlán differs very little from that of rural mestizos of this area. The major difference is that Indians eat far more gathered items and mestizos have more access to and thus consume more meat and processed food such as canned goods, candy, and soft drinks.

CASH CROPS AND WAGE LABOR

All households in Amatlán must raise some cash in their farming operation to pay for machetes, cloth, and other necessities from the market and to cover periodic assessments to support the ejido and school. The amount of money circulating in the village at any given time is very small, but the people do operate in a cash economy. I learned early during fieldwork to carry only coins and the smallest denomination bills. During my entire stay in the village, no one was ever able to change a 20-peso note (worth about $1.60 in 1972). When one looks at the problems North American farmers face in earning a living despite the fact that they employ the most modern technology in the world, it is not hard to understand why milpa horticulturists in Amatlán find it difficult to run a paying operation. In order to earn money, families must produce a surplus to be sold at market. However, individual farmers face virtually insurmountable constraints that are built into the productive and marketing systems. These constraints, which are discussed in Chapter 5, prevent the household from participating fully in the national economy.

Villagers have experimented with growing a variety of crops that can be sold in the marketplace. Several families planted coffee, a crop that has successfully transformed the economies of Indian villages in the nearby Sierra Norte de Puebla. They found that coffee does not produce very well in Amatlán. Some have experimented with tobacco, but to be profitable it must be grown in quantities beyond the capabilities of the villagers. Two or three families tried to grow bananas for profit, but they, too, faced the problem of scale and the difficulty of delivering their product to distant markets. Overall, the most successful crop grown in the village remains corn. Corn growing has many disadvantages, including generally low market value and rollercoaster price cycles that have led some agriculture and development experts to conclude that Indian villagers are irrational to persist in cultivating it. They have concluded that Indians continue to grow corn because of tradition and that they would be better off planting a more profitable crop. From the Indian perspective, however, growing corn makes economic sense, as we will see below (see Kvam 1985 for an account of Nahuas near the southern Huasteca town of Alamo who have become successful citrus farmers; also, Reyes Antonio 1982:28–29).

Black beans command a high price in the market, and they constitute an important source of protein in the regional diet but, as we have seen, growing this crop commercially is risky in Amatlán (see also Chapter 5). All households grow beans for their own consumption, but commercial production of this crop entails many disadvantages. More than corn and black beans, however, villagers see sugarcane as having the most potential for developing the local economy. The sugarcane grown in the milpas is processed into sugarloaf by individual households. Prices paid for village sugar are low, but it can be produced in large enough quantities to earn significant income. Nearly all households have made sugar at one time or another, but fewer than 15 produce it every season with regularity. One problem is that the cane crop takes more than a year to mature and thus ties up valuable planting space in the milpa. A second consideration is that sugar making requires specialized equipment, including copper vessels for boiling the juice, a costly press to extract the juice, and a horse or mule to turn the mechanism. The process of making sugar is an interesting example of Nahua technology at work.

Sugarcane matures in March, and villagers organize for the *tlapats-quistli* ("pressing" in English). The household head and his helpers, usually relatives, begin by building a thatched sunshade in the milpa. This structure is constructed over an embankment that has been excavated to form a deep pit oven. The men cut an opening in the top of the earthen oven to receive an enormous copper cauldron with a capacity of about 250 liters. While this work is being completed, additional helpers set up the wooden sugarcane press. The press is constructed of three large cylinders of wood mounted side by side and connected by wooden gears. When the central cylinder is turned, the two flanking cylinders rotate. A long pole is attached to this central cylinder and to the harness of a draft animal that, by walking in a circle, keeps the press turning. Long cane stalks are passed through the revolving cylinders, and the juice is collected in the copper cauldron. When filled to the brim, the cauldron is lifted onto the oven, and the juice is boiled down. Cloth stretched over a conical wooden frame is suspended above the boiling juice so that the foam runs over it and back down into the cauldron. This ingenious device prevents boilovers that would waste the precious sugarcane juice. Throughout the reducing process the juice is continually strained through a special sieve (*cuahuajcali* in Nahuatl) made from a gourd in order to remove plant fibers. As the juice thickens it is stirred rapidly to increase smoothness and consistency.

When about 80 percent of the juice is boiled away, the remaining thick residue is poured into tapered clay molds about the size of large drinking glasses. These are allowed to cool, and two of the cylinders of sugar are wrapped together, end to end, in dried cane leaves and tied with cane fibers. These are sold in paired loaves weighing a kilogram for between $.16 and $.24 per pair. The sugar, called *xancacaj* in Nahuatl, is dark brown, hard but slightly sticky, and tastes like delicious smoked molasses. Everything must be prepared ahead of time because once the oven is stoked with firewood and the cauldron is heating, the process does not stop until all of the sugarcane has been pressed and the juice rendered. Sugarmaking often takes two or three days to complete, and during this time the family camps out at the site. For children, it is a time of high excitement, and as a treat they are allowed endless tastings of the sweet cane juice. See Chapter 5 for information on sugar productivity and earning potential.

In addition to corn, beans, and sugar as the three major cash products in Amatlán, villagers sometimes sell other crops in minute quantities. Often sales occur within the village or among one or two neighboring communities. For example, a woman may harvest a basketful of chile peppers, far more than she can use herself, and she might sell the remainder to earn a few pesos. This small-scale marketing produces some income for the household, but it represents only a small fraction of total income derived from the major cash crops. Animals, such as chickens or turkeys, may be sold locally or even in the market, but this, too, brings in little. In fact, I argue in the next chapter that raising farm animals appears to be a losing proposition for villagers. The cost of maintaining livestock is high, and villagers are often unable to recover their investment when they sell an animal. I will show, however, that this fact does not mean raising animals is irrational or uneconomic.

Many villagers engage in part-time secondary occupations to supplement their income. The money earned from these endeavors is small, and many people work at them as much for recreation and prestige as for monetary reward. Two men run small cantinas out of their houses that offer a few assorted items for sale. The cantina owners buy items in the market and raise the price a few cents to pay for the trouble of transporting them to the village and to earn a small profit. By far, their greatest income derives from the sale of cane alcohol, which is called *aguardiente* ("burning water") in Spanish, and *xochiatsij* ("flower water") in Nahuatl. This clear rum is extremely high proof and is drunk with gusto by many village men. It is measured out with a dipper by the cantina owner and then poured into a bottle brought by the customer. Often a corncob is used as a stopper. Alcohol consumption is an important part of village life and even has religious significance. Following a pre-Hispanic pattern, however, generally only older villagers indulge in imbibing alcohol (see Soustelle 1961 [1955]:156–57). Every evening after the day's work is completed, one can witness groups of men talking and laughing as they share a bottle of aguardiente.

Several secondary occupations are available in the village to both men and women. An older woman may become a midwife (*tetejquetl* in Nahuatl) or a bonesetter (*texixitojquetl* in Nahuatl). These are honored occupations that trace back to pre-Hispanic days. Although women do all household tasks themselves, they may hire a particularly skilled older woman as a potter or an embroiderer. As a specialist she com-

mands a fee when her services are required. There are some households in which members have built a dome-shaped bread oven out of
mud and stones, and the woman earns money baking and selling
bread. A woman may offer for sale food she has cooked, or she may
peddle loads of firewood she has collected on a more or less regular
basis. A man may be a sawyer (all lumber being cut by hand), carpenter, ritual guitarist or violinist, porter, or day laborer for one of his
neighbors. A more significant amount of money is earned by men who
hire themselves out as day laborers on regional cattle ranches. In 1972
and still in 1986, they worked for about $1 a day. They are usually
hired to clear brush and open up areas for cattle grazing. The rancher
supplies food and at the end of the day may also supply a bottle of
aguardiente for the men. Women sometimes hire themselves out as
cooks on ranches or perhaps to schoolmasters, but these opportunities
are rare. One secondary occupation open to both men and women is
that of curer. Curers can attract wide followings and may be selected
to orchestrate village-wide rituals. Clients pay fairly well for their
services, but, as we shall see, becoming a curer is not totally a matter
of choice (Romualdo Hernández 1982:33–35 lists occupations and
money-earning activities in a Nahua village in neighboring Hidalgo
state).

The people of Amatlán fully realize that they need some money to
survive and that milpa horticulture cannot supply their needs. I have
heard many people state, "You can't earn anything from a milpa, no
matter how hard you work." This should not be surprising because
milpa horticulture was not developed to make money in a capitalist
economy, and it has benefited neither from outside investment nor
scientific research. Also, as both Warman and Stavenhagen have
pointed out (see Chapter 1), numerous factors prevent villages like
Amatlán from participating in the Mexican national economy. Villagers
grow crops for cash in addition to what they need for their own consumption, but they are always looking for service jobs or wage labor
to supplement the family income. Some money can be earned within
the village or in neighboring communities, but people in Amatlán
know that temporary labor in the mestizo world is essential if they are
to survive. And their opportunities are limited indeed. These villagers
do not produce crafts that would be appropriate for the tourist market,
and even if they did they do not have any established access to the
folk-industry market. Some people have responded to the situation
by moving permanently to the cities where wage labor is available.
These expatriates sometimes send money back to the village to assist

family members, but often they do not earn enough in the cities even to sustain themselves. The villagers find that they must rely on the mestizos to survive, and yet they have difficulty surviving because of the system the mestizos represent.

NAHUA SOCIAL CHARACTER

The Nahuas exhibit a range of personality types that one might expect to find in a relatively small group of people anywhere in the world. Some are serious, private, and inwardly directed. Others are outgoing, witty, and charismatic. But there exist in all societies a set of unspoken or rarely articulated guidelines for how a person should present himself or herself to others. Successful individuals express their personalities within these guidelines, and those who deviate too widely experience stress and will be pressured by others to conform. It is these socially shared guidelines that I call "social character." There is no doubt that most villagers possess personalities that fall within the range of Nahua social character, and thus they share many personality traits. It is also clear that Nahua social character is quite different from that of neighboring mestizos and from that of most Anglo-Americans. My observations about Nahua social character derive from my long-term residence in Amatlán where I was able to witness numerous occasions in which individuals, both in public and in private, played their social roles, handled adversity, and discussed the deviations of others. I did not administer psychology tests to the villagers nor employ other methods for gathering systematic data on personality, and so my observations must remain tentative.

Anthropologist Paul Jean Provost conducted a study of a Huastecan Nahua village in which he outlines five basic "cultural principles" that underlie social interaction and reflect something of social character (1975:138ff.). I found these principles to be an accurate description of the interactional patterns in Amatlán. The first principle he calls "indirectness." Nahuas generally value social interaction that is oblique and avoids direct confrontation. Pointed questions, authoritative assertions, commands, or direct requests are considered rude and aggressive. Social interaction requires patience as participants communicate through circumlocution and gentle suggestion. As an outsider I had to learn indirectness before my interactions with villagers went smoothly and I was able to elicit accurate information from them. A second cultural principle, related to the first, Provost calls "attrition." Villagers persuade not by the direct argument that would contradict the first cultural principle, but rather by wearing the listener down with subtle and persistent suggestion. No excuse or evasive action can turn back the tide of entreaties, and in the end the listener is overwhelmed and forced to capitulate.

A third cultural principle among the Nahuas is "informality." Most areas of Nahua life are free from rigid rules and strict procedures, and many village activities are accordingly carried out in a relaxed and flexible way. Religious rituals, village meetings, and communal work crews appear almost disorganized to the outsider. But informality does not mean disorganization, and the villagers are very efficient at accomplishing cooperative tasks. One exception to the principle of informality is in the area of Nahua hospitality. A visitor is always provided with a special chair, food is prepared, and the guest is treated very cordially. The Nahuas are renowned throughout the region for their hospitality, politeness, and the respect they show others. The fourth principle discussed by Provost is "individuality." Villagers view themselves and others as individuals, and each person is expected to behave accordingly. Even in matters of kinship a great deal of individuality is permitted and encouraged within the group. The final cultural principle is "reciprocity." The villagers see themselves at the center of a complex network of obligations and expectations involving other villagers, mestizos, and even the spirits in their pantheon. The idea of exchange permeates the way they think about the world and their place in it. Village life is largely organized around gift exchange, labor exchange, and ritual offerings to spirits in return for health, food, and well-being.

These five principles—indirectness, attrition, informality, individuality, and reciprocity—combine to create a social character that differs markedly from that of the mestizos. To many mestizos the Indians appear dull-witted, slow, and uncooperative. In contrast, once I became aware of their style of interaction I found them to be curious and quick learners. I taught many people a few words in English while I was there in the early 1970s, and they were able to repeat them perfectly in 1986. To the villagers, many mestizos lack proper reserve and are overly direct and blunt. Mestizos thus appear rude, aggressive, demanding, and overbearing. When Indians and mestizos interact with each other, one may easily see that both are acting properly according to the guidelines of their own ethnic groups and yet are reinforcing each other's negative stereotypes.

Manning Nash has made several observations about Quiché Maya social character that also fit very well with what I witnessed in Amatlán (1973[1958]:97ff.) Nash's observations regarding this Guatemalan group and my own regarding the Nahuas indicate remarkable similarities in social character among even diverse Indian groups of Mesoamerica. He notes the high value Indians place on being reserved and on controlling emotion. This is certainly true in Amatlán where people value stoicism and consider most outbursts of any emotion to be undignified. Like the Quiché, the Nahuas strive for a placid and controlled presentation of self even in the face of disaster or shocking news. Among the Quiché and the people of Amatlán there exist certain occasions where strong emotion is permitted. At funerals I have witnessed mourners lose control and wail loudly in their grief. I have observed both men and women weep overtly when individuals part from one another for a significant period of time. The men may also become quite demonstrative when intoxicated. They sometimes laugh loudly, and it is during drinking bouts when men may become violent. I have witnessed machete fights between drunk men that started over some trifling matter. However, in general the Nahuas I know tend to be patient, cautious, and placid, and they seem to favor proceeding with a measured dignity rather than rushing into things excitedly.

Nash mentions that the Quiché he studied are prone to gossip, and this is also true of the Nahuas. They sometimes seem suspicious of the motives of others and ready to believe the worst about them. Villagers almost expect ejido and municipio authorities to be dishonest, and they do not mind revealing their distrust to others in private. Of course, some suspicion may be based on villagers' previous experience with dishonest public office holders. Because being poor is part of Indian identity, wealthier villagers may be suspected of stealing or cheating to get their money. I did not notice a universal resentment against better-off members of the community, but wealth is sometimes attributed to luck rather than hard work or planning. Fear of suspicion on the part of others makes villagers sometimes appear uncommunicative and even secretive. I have also detected a tendency for villagers to play on their status as poor Indians that produces the appearance that they indulge in a bit of self-pity. I am inclined to believe, however, that this is possibly a strategy for dealing with mestizos rather than a feature of Nahua social character.

Nahua women are expected to be modest and to exhibit perhaps even more restraint and reserve in daily interaction than the men. Women occupy a world dominated by domestic and family concerns and are not expected to be interested or become involved in village politics. They may strike the outsider as shy and retiring types who ask little and are satisfied with their lives of working hard for their families. Women, and particularly younger women, appear uncomfortable in public, and prefer to turn responsibility for dealing with an unfamiliar visitor over to a male relative even if he is much younger. At the same time, villagers attribute to women a certain toughness and endurance that makes them excellent hagglers at the market. When women pass the childbearing years they are accorded more freedom to express themselves. Some begin to smoke handmade cigars or drink cane alcohol in public. In general, women do not appear to compete with the men but instead occupy a world that is distinct from the male domain.

I found the Nahuas I came to know to be relaxed and cheerful with a ready willingness to smile and laugh. Although reserved in their behavior, they are generous, tolerant, and extremely polite. They never appear to be covetous, and despite the numerous opportunities they had in the time I lived in Amatlán nothing of mine was ever taken without permission. The villagers are rather puritanical, and I did not detect a trace of machismo among the men in their private talk or public behavior. Groups of men or women crossing the arroyo often encounter members of the opposite sex bathing. They simply avert their eyes, mumble a greeting, and pass by quickly. I have never seen an overt sexual gesture made by males or females, and neither husbands and wives nor sweethearts make public displays of affection. The only exception to this observation is the extraordinary behavior of the masked dancers during the celebration of *nanahuatili* (see Chapter 6). Villagers tolerate adversity with courage and equanimity, and despite many hardships resulting from their position in Mexican society, I have never known them to complain. Although they refuse to rush or establish deadlines, I found that the villagers are self-disciplined and have an enormous capacity for work under difficult conditions.

Family life in Amatlán is warm and supportive. Although the man is considered head of the household, I found that there is much cooperation between husband and wife. On many occasions I have witnessed married couples discussing plans as equals, with each making suggestions and then arriving together at a workable compromise. In and around the house and in regards to the children the woman has considerable authority even over her husband, although this is not true outside the home. Nahua children are highly valued and lavished with attention. I rarely saw a child struck, and discipline is conducted without raised voices. Small children are indulged and learn that they can always turn to either parent to be picked up and held. Children are given responsibility early, and most of them are mature and self-confident by the age of 10 or 11. By this age village girls may be taking care of a baby sibling, and boys may be trusted to walk to a distant market to make the family's purchases. After the evening meal, families sit around the entrances of their houses and talk and laugh quietly until dark. One by one as they become tired the children go inside to unroll their palm mats on the house floor and fall asleep.

THE SCHOOL

The school, with its large clearing maintained by the village for the schoolmaster's horses, stands as a focus of villagewide activities. It is here, outside the high, two-roomed schoolhouse built a generation ago that the authorities hold village meetings and where men gather for the weekly communal workday. The building is constructed from stones gathered from the arroyo, and the roof is made of corrugated iron. To the north and adjacent to the school are a series of low buildings built and maintained by the village for housing the schoolmaster and his family. As the school-age population has grown over the years, a second teacher was assigned to Amatlán who lives in a small oneroom, mud-walled dwelling with an attached kitchen shed. In each schoolroom are a blackboard and benches and desks for the students, all supplied by the government. Maps, scissors, paper, and some books must be purchased by the village using money collected from students' families or earned through village communal work activities.

All children in the village attend school through the sixth grade. Those wishing to continue their education must walk an hour and a half to a school near the market town of Llano de Enmedio. The schoolmaster informed me that none of the children speak Spanish when they first come to school at about age 6. This makes the first few months difficult because neither schoolteacher speaks Nahuatl. By the time they finish school, children have learned to speak, read, and write Spanish and have learned elementary arithmetic. They are introduced through schoolbooks to life in Mexico City and other regions of the country. In essence, the students are taught about the mestizo world, a world that is filled with trains, cars, apartments, and light-skinned children who wear shorts and take music lessons. They are introduced through a foreign language, by mestizo teachers, to an alien world far removed from life in Amatlán.

I asked many parents what they thought of the school and its effects on the children. Almost all replied that they approved of schooling and that they felt that it is important for their children to understand arithmetic and to learn about life in other parts of the country. Most of them worked willingly on the communal work projects in order to support school operations. Just as in our society, each Nahua household is decorated with drawings and papers brought home by the children. None of the villagers I talked to viewed the school as a threat to their values or way of life. In fact, I noted the opposite reaction. Village adults see the school as an important institution through which their children learn about the mestizo world. How else, they felt, could the next generation gain the skills to operate successfully in that non-Indian world? Knowledge gained could prove useful to the child as he or she comes into contact with outsiders. Most villagers consider their mastery of Spanish to be poor, and yet Spanish is essential if the child is to work outside the village, whether on a temporary or permanent basis. Although villagers often distrust the schoolteachers whom they view as self-serving and aloof, they do applaud the benefits they bring to the community.

In 1972, a crack developed in one of the masonry walls of the schoolhouse, which seriously weakened the structure. Villagers worried about the danger it posed to the children, and they feared that bureaucratic delays in replacing the building would threaten the existence of the school in Amatlán. This occurred midway through my fieldwork, and I decided that in order to repay villagers for their hospitality I would try to help them obtain a new building. I traveled to the state capital and, by luck, met the man in charge of new school constructions for the state. I think he was surprised to find a foreigner making the request, and he graciously agreed to inspect the old building himself. A few weeks later he arrived in the village, made the inspection, and submitted an order that a new structure be built. The state government supplied two builders and construction materials. The villagers had to carry everything from a dropoff at the distant road and were required to furnish the construction workers with all needed raw materials such as sand and stone. The men gladly did the work, and everyone in Amatlán was happy at having a modern new building. It was a fortunate turn of events because it allowed me to do something for the village that offered benefits equally to all families and that everyone seemed to appreciate.

CONCLUSIONS

This thumbnail sketch summarizes some of the salient features of Amatlán between the years 1970 and 1977. Up to this point we have seen that villages like Amatlán are the Indians' domain in Mexico, but that even straightforward description cannot hide the fact that it is a world of contradiction and irony. Amatlán presents idyllic features such as tropical streams and luxuriant vegetation, thatch-roofed houses enveloped in the aroma of cooking fires, the glow of beeswax candles at colorful rituals, green corn in the milpa, and people who know how to treat a guest and who are ever willing to laugh at themselves and their circumstances. At the same time villagers face a life where they cannot get decent pay for a day's work; where, as we will see, their crops are made practically worthless by price cycles determined by mestizo middlemen; where land shortages force the breakup of their families; and where harassment and torture by local authorities are accepted methods for dealing with Indians. Despite the fullness of their lives in the village, the people of Amatlán live at the margins of mestizo Mexico, which at times wants to help them but at other times seems to wish that they would just go away.

The village itself is probably an artifact first of Spanish and then Mexican programs of population consolidation where previously dispersed populations were forced together for better administrative control. Even after forced nucleation, the scattered residences in Amatlán, organized by principles of kinship rather than administrative efficiency, probably reflect the pre-Hispanic pattern. Inhabitants clearly identify with their kinsmen and with small, named subsections of the village rather than with the village as a whole. Yet the government has created a legal community through its land-grant policy that transformed Amatlán into an ejido. As we will see, ejido status requires that villagers govern themselves through state-mandated local political offices. Thus the centralized village, where Indians cultivate their ancient traditions in response to the mestizos, is itself more than likely an artifact of the Conquest.

Further contradictions emerge if we examine Nahua technology. I have indicated that the villagers are admirably adapted to living in their forest habitat. They rely on remarkably few tools to supply themselves with food and the necessities of life. With the exception of the steel machete, which is relatively inexpensive, most essential tools can be manufactured locally. The effect of this scaled-down technology is to free villagers from dependence on the mestizo sector of the economy. They cannot be self-sufficient, but they have been careful to avoid an overdependence on mestizos in their productive activities. What Hispanic technology they have adopted, including the steel hoe blade, clothing styles, the cane press, and the stone bread oven, does not significantly increase their dependence on outsiders. Unelaborate technology such as we find in Amatlán creates a degree of autonomy for villagers, but it simultaneously prevents them from competing as equals with mestizo farmers who have access to machinery, fertilizers, hybrid seed, and modern scientific knowledge. Thus lack of money is only part of the problem for Indians. To buy into modern farming methods even at a gradual rate would place the people at the mercy of mestizo middlemen and subject poor villagers to spiraling prices for manufactured commodites. By staying with "Indian" technology, villagers maintain their relative independence but at the cost of full participation in the national economy.

Much of what I have described in Amatlán can be seen as mechanisms for Indians to create and maintain their autonomy in the face of the mestizo threat. Villagers build houses without nails, and they furnish them with very few industrially manufactured items. They gather, hunt, and fish, which further reduce dependence, and they create cognitive communities, effectively cutting off all but the most persistent outsiders. Village autonomy is facilitated by customs that set Indians apart from mestizos and by the Nahuatl language. Through secondary occupations villagers themselves are able to satisfy community needs for medical care, skilled crafts such as pottery making or carpentry, and for religious expression. The features of village life around which the people preserve their autonomy are partly pre-Hispanic in origin, but a significant number are post-Hispanic. Villagers seem quite willing to borrow so long as they do not increase the magnitude of their dependence. Even Nahua social character seems to set the villagers apart from the mestizo majority.

Because of the political and economic position of the Indian community in Mexico, however, Amatlán cannot fully escape dependence on the dominant groups. The agrarian reform laws gave land back to the Indians, allowing them a more independent existence, but at the same time placing them under laws governing ejido operation. Indians must be able to operate in the mestizo world in order to sustain their own quasi-independent existence in the village. This is the reason, I believe, that the people of Amatlán are happy to have a local school. The school gives children the skills necessary to provide them access to the alien mestizo world. But the delicate balance the villagers have achieved between independence and dependence, between the Indian and mestizo worlds, has been disrupted by the final paradox. As the Mexican economy has grown, it has extracted more wealth from the village farmers. At the same time the population throughout the country has grown rapidly. The population figures for the microcosm of Amatlán reflect these national increases as well as the social disruption they are causing as numbers of people are forced to emigrate. When villagers can no longer support themselves as Indians, they must seize more land or lose their independence.

Viewed in this way, the Indian response to mestizo domination appears quite reasonable. The villagers are not trapped in an irrational world that has survived from a previous era, but rather are responding creatively and rationally to the threat of domination and the annihilation of their culture by representatives of the Hispanic elites. As we will see below, villagers are open to change, and they are certainly not averse to economic development. They will, however, reject any new technology that leads them to lose what independence they have. From their perspective, the best long-term plan is to grab what they can from the mestizo sector and retain their Indian and independent status. Within the village itself, as we will see in the next chapter, individuals devise many strategies to make the most out of what they have.

CHAPTER 4

SOCIAL ORGANIZATION AND SOCIAL ACTION

LIKE all persistent human groups, Amatlán is a community in that it is a social system composed of a complex network of mutual obligations and expectations among people that is created and recreated out of people's actions and that simultaneously provides the context for their lives. Like people everywhere, the Nahuas are only partially conscious of their overall social system, but individuals may be particularly aware of their own place in the local network of statuses and roles. Discussions circulate around how much help one can expect from a son-in-law, whether the current Comisariado has an obligation to petition for more land, or what to do with a widowed sister who wants to return home. Like the visiting anthropologist, the people themselves are engaged in a constant effort to understand what is going on and to act appropriately.

In this chapter I will outline the major features of community life in Amatlán, focusing on the formal political organization of the ejido and the Nahua kinship system. As in all human groups, of course, there is a distinction between the formal or ideal social system and actual or real behavior. We have already seen how factions can form around charismatic leaders and how the struggle for land can take place outside official ejido channels. Among the Indians of Mexico, many of the stresses that cause people to deviate from stated norms in social behavior originate from outside the village context. Again, it is the position of the Indian in the nation-state that is decisive. As an example of how exogenous factors affect Nahua social organization, I will present evidence that the breakdown in certain village kin relations can be linked to chronic land shortages. Furthermore, I will show how these stress areas in the kinship system are clearly expressed in Nahua myths and folktales.

150

A WORLD OF TRAILS

The trail (*ojtli* in Nahuatl) holds a special place in the life of the Nahuas. Trails are the connections among houses, and thus they are a kind of nervous system that channels the social interactions of the village. They are literal tunnels in the forest that keep the residence group from being an isolated entity—umbilical cords connecting individual families to the society of the village. Trails are the living, physical proof that Amatlán is a community in the sense of a social system with interacting parts. A trail between house groupings implies a relation among the inhabitants, and a village like Amatlán is a tangle of beaten paths. It is an amazing facet of Nahua life how often the trail system changes to accomodate new and emerging social interactional patterns. In returning to the village after intervals of several years, I had to relearn the system of trails before I could begin research. It was a lesson in the dynamic nature of village life.

Most trails are footpaths kept open by heavy traffic. As a man or woman walks along, he or she may chop off an annoying branch or root with a machete, and thousands of such acts over the months and years help keep the path clear. Larger trails that connect villages to each other are wider and will accomodate a horse and rider. As the horse slowly walks along, the rider occasionally cuts overhead branches that threaten to reach face level. In addition, the larger trails are maintained by village communal work crews. The men cut back the encroaching vegetation and dam washouts by filling them in with rocks and tree branches. In this way individuals and whole villages renew their connection to others in the region and underscore their commitment to keeping the communication lines open.

Trail behavior is an important indicator of status for the people of the Huasteca region. Most footpaths allow only single-file travel. Higher-status people almost always walk ahead. Thus a family going to market will be led by the man, followed by his wife, who is in turn followed by the children in descending order of birth. Although families do not always strictly follow this pattern, one can observe it often, particularly in formal situations. Villagers adhered to the custom, for example, whenever I accompanied them somewhere. As a guest, they expected me to walk first even though I had no idea where I was going. This situation was a frequent cause of hilarity among my traveling companions. As an indication of my ambiguous status in the village when I first arrived, the villagers would send along a child to lead me whenever I walked somewhere alone. It was an indignity I willingly accepted because on two of the occasions when I went out on my own I became lost in the forest. Both times I wandered along unfamiliar trails well into the night before accidently finding my way back to Amatlán. Those were experiences I wished never to repeat.

It is the custom for people of lesser social rank to stand aside when someone of higher status wishes to pass by. Thus, walking on a trail is an interesting lesson in village statuses. Children always stand aside for adults, and younger people always stand aside for the elderly. A woman stands aside for a man, and Indians stand aside for mestizos. One complicating factor is that non-Indians rarely walk on the trails between villages. It is an index of their higher status that they ride on horseback. Thus there exists a general unspoken rule that walkers stand aside for riders, which is both a status statement and a necessity on the narrow trails.

The trail plays an interesting role in Nahua ideology as well. Villagers use it as a metaphor for the course of a person's life. They say, for example, that each individual has his own trail to follow. In the Nahua view, a person walking on a trail is in a state of transition without the usual safeguards of family and hearth. Someone on a trail may see the spirit of death in the form of an owl, an event with potentially dire consequences. The trail is also a common place to encounter dangerous wind spirits that may attack and cause disease and death. During curing rituals, the shaman often symbolically cleanses the trails around a patient's house. This act protects the patient and his family from spirit attack while moving along trails. During Day of the Dead rituals, each household head sprinkles marigold petals on the floor to create a magical trail from the entrance of the house to the special altar constructed for the occasion. They call this pathway in Nahuatl the *xochiojtli*, or "flower trail." The spirits of the ancestors follow the marigold path to receive their offerings.

Trails, then, are far more than a simple medium of travel. They have a social and ideological significance for the Nahuas that is sometimes difficult for outsiders to grasp. In our own culture roads and paths are also used as metaphors. But in general, most North Americans view streets and sidewalks as public thoroughfares that are built and maintained by tax revenues for ease of travel and as part of the necessary infrastructure for economic well-being. For the Nahuas, trails are literal and figurative links between families and villages. They are a kind of model of and model for interactional patterns. Furthermore they are part of the sacred geography that is so important to Nahua world view.

SOCIAL ORGANIZATION

The social organization of Amatlán is uncomplicated compared to that of some tribal peoples or to larger social units such as towns and cities. The division of labor is based on sex and age, and although there are secondary occupations in which individuals specialize in certain skilled tasks, all people support themselves primarily by farming. With no full-time occupational specialization and no internal class structure, the village appears on the surface to be homogeneous in its composition. Each individual household appears to operate much on its own without the necessity of engaging outside specialists or submitting to formal authority structures. To an extent this egalitarian ideal applies to Amatlán, although the people there are still enmeshed in a network of social, political, and economic obligations and expectations that forms a system that is greater than any given individual or household. After discussing the organization of the ejido and Nahua kinship and family organization, I will outline the domestic cycle and include a brief description of Nahua age groupings.

THE EJIDO

The offices and procedures for electing ejido officials are set by laws deriving from the agrarian reform following the Mexican Revolution. But there is an authority structure in most Indian communities that traces to the organization of the pre-Hispanic village. A council of elders, called in Nahuatl the *tetajtlajlamitianij* or simply *tetatajmej* ("elders"), is looked to by villagers for guidance and ultimate authority in village decisions. It is composed of older men who have served Amatlán in a number of capacities, usually as ejido officeholders and organizers of certain religious events. Only men held in the highest regard are considered worthy to be elders. There is no formal installation of new members. A man slowly enters the ranks of the elders as he ages and continues to lead an exemplary life. No formal meetings are held by this group, but its members are present at all village gatherings, and their words carry much weight with those in attendance. In Amatlán, membership in the council of elders varies between six and eight men and their average age is about 70. People told me that the council is not as important now as it was in the past. However, it is interesting to note that when the villagers run into serious trouble, as they did during the land struggles of the 1970s, they turned to the council of elders for guidance (see Chapter 2).

Agrarian law stipulates that the supreme authority in an ejido is the Asamblea General ("General Assembly") composed of household heads who have full rights to ejido land (see Whetten 1948:182–89). The general assembly must meet on a regular basis to discuss and vote upon issues relating to ejido governance and policymaking. This body exercises its collective will through a series of elected committees, perhaps the most important of which is the Comisariado Ejidal ("Ejido Commissariat"). This committee is headed by a Presidente ("President"), who is usually called simply the Comisariado, a Secretaría ("Secretary") for keeping records, a Tesorero ("Treasurer") responsible for financial accounting, two Vocales ("Committee Members") who inform other villagers when a meeting has been called, and a variable number of Suplentes ("Assistants") depending on the needs of each officeholder. The Comisariado Ejidal is responsible for directing many of the internal affairs of the ejido and for representing the ejido to agrarian officials. Boundary disputes, requests for house-building sites, and solicitations for new lands are all handled through this important committee.

The Consejo de Vigilancia ("Vigilance Council") headed by a Presidente ("President"), who is usually called simply the Consejo de Vigilancia and is aided by a set of officers parallel to those of the Comisariado Ejidal, is an oversight committee insuring that the Comisariado and his officers act properly in their conduct of ejido business. This committee has full access to records of the Comisariado Ejidal and may call meetings of the general assembly if it uncovers irregularities. Law stipulates that when two candidates compete for the office of president of the Comisariado Ejidal, people who voted for the losing candidate are permitted to elect the members of the Consejo de Vigilancia.

Another major governing body is the Comité del Agente Municipal ("Committee of the Municipal Agent"). This committee is led by the Agente who acts as a local representative or agent for the municipio government. A large part of his duties revolve around handling village external relations. Certain state government directives are passed through this office and on to the villagers during periodic meetings called by the Agente. Visitors, such as an anthropologist, are the responsibility of the Agente. This official is aided by an assistant, a Comandante de Policías ("Commander of the Police Force"), a Cabo de Policías ("Corporal of the Police") under him, and four Topiles ("Policemen") who are appointed for 1-year terms by the president of the municipio. The Agente also has a treasurer, a secretary for keeping records, and two committee members for calling village-wide meetings. With the exception of the policemen, all of these positions are elected. Both the Agente and Comisariado serve 3-year terms.

An office associated with this committee is the Juez Auxiliar ("Auxiliary Judge") who, together with his assistant, has the responsibility of seeing that people receive care if they become seriously ill, of insuring that people who die are buried properly, and of acting as an informal judge for local civil complaints. He has the authority to lock people in the village jail for small offenses.

An additional important ejido committee is the Comité de los Padres de Familia de la Escuela ("School Parents Committee") that is headed by an official called the Escolar (literally "Scholar"). The committee consists of an assistant, secretary, treasurer, and two committee members to communicate announcements to villagers. This committee is responsible for the smooth running of the school, and it works closely with the village schoolmaster who, for the most part, determines what work needs to be done. When the children need supplies, this committee raises the money to buy them. Committee members help in the construction of a new schoolhouse and repair the building if it should need it. They may also be responsible for supplying the schoolmaster and his family with firewood. There is also a Comité del Desarrollo Integral de la Familia ("Committee for the Integral Development of the Family") composed of women whose tasks in Amatlán include keeping the village and its sources of drinking water clean. Another committee has as its task the maintenance of houses and the system of trails in the village. It is my experience in the years I have spent in the village that both of these committees are moribund. Finally, in 1986 there was a self-appointed Catequista ("Catechist") who, in response to the proselytizing efforts of Protestant missionaries, began holding meetings every so often with young girls in the village shrine to sing songs and discuss issues related to the Catholic faith.

In large ejidos, additional committees may be created by the general assembly to accomplish specific tasks. For example, there may be a committee for barrio governance or one for overseeing parish and church activities. In a small village like Amatlán, however, there are no barrios, parishes, or churches, and so these committees are unnecessary. All ejido offices are voluntary, and any certified adult ejido member may run for office. In Amatlán, however, it is rare for two men to run against each other for the same office. An incumbent whose term is about to expire selects a successor, and if no one raises an objection, the designee is officially elected at the next meeting of the general assembly. The pool of eligible men in Amatlán is relatively small, and this informal system seems to work quite well. No village official is paid for performing public duties. Despite this fact, most officials take their responsibilities seriously, and many work hard to insure the smooth running of the village.

The business of the village is conducted in meetings called by officeholders. These are attended by resident males who are at least 18 years of age, although only villagers with full rights to ejido land are eligible to vote. To the outsider the meetings appear to be remarkably disorganized and fruitless. In reality, they are simultaneous discussions in which each man has a chance to voice an opinion. Rarely is a formal vote held, but by freely talking over issues, unanimity is achieved on most decisions. Part of the village holdings are common lands belonging collectively to the entire community. A perennial discussion concerns how the village should best use this land during the upcoming seasons. Sometimes villagers decide to rent it for pastureland to a neighboring rancher, whereas in other years they may choose to plant a crop on it to earn money for the school. Depending on the business to be transacted, meetings are usually run by the Agente, with the Comisariado always present.

A second major topic of discussion at village meetings is the *faena*. The Spanish word means "labor" or "chore," and it refers to the legal requirement that each male household head, 18 years of age or older, works 1 day per week for the village if requested by the authorities. Men who are ill or who are elderly are excused from the faena. The work is done without pay, and a fine is imposed if a man fails to show up for work. The only way to escape the faena is to pay the equivalent of one day's pay to the official who called it. The money is placed in the village treasury for use on public projects. A faena may be called by the Agente, the Comisariado, or the Escolar. The official discusses the proposed work at a village meeting, and everyone concurs with the plan. Sometimes the faena will hire out to a neighboring rancher who pays a lump sum for the work he wants done. The money may then be used to acquire school supplies or other necessities. At other times the Agente will have the *faena* cultivate corn on the communal field with the idea of selling the produce. A man who persistently fails to attend the *faena* or to pay in lieu of work could be deprived of his rights in the ejido.

Being Agente and especially Comisariado can be difficult work and even dangerous as witness the historical problems of village officials recorded in Chapter 2. When I arrived for long-term fieldwork in 1972 the Agente, Miguel, was almost frantic in his efforts to resign from the position. I remember one night when he arrived at home with his clothes cut to ribbons. He had apparently been attacked by someone wielding a machete and narrowly escaped with his life. His wife was close to being hysterical, and I began to understand the conflicts involved in occupying his office. Village officials are under pressure from their neighbors who want them to solicit the government for more land. On the other side are the ranchers, some of whom may resort to murdering village officials who appear to be successful in convincing the government to expropriate their land. But even in peaceful times, it is difficult to remain popular with your neighbors when you are charged with enforcing government policies that may be resented.

In sum, officeholders are elected by household heads who are fully certified members of the ejido. Females, however, are excluded from the political process unless they are themselves household heads, in which case they attend village meetings and vote on all issues. In my experience, the system works quite well in handling relatively noncontroversial local matters. But again, ejido political structure constitutes a contradiction for villagers. It is significant, for example, that ejido offices completely bypass the traditional council of elders. Although the council retains prestige, it lacks the backing of the state and has no means of enforcing decisions. Ejido officials, on the other hand, have the power of law behind them, and they can summon the police or militia to uphold their rulings. These officials, although elected from among villagers, represent an intrusion of the state into village affairs. Village officeholders must see that government mandates are carried out, and they are held responsible for the ejido by local mestizo elites who occupy all regional, state, and federal positions of authority. In a sense, the ejido political system represents a loss of village autonomy. It is one of the prices villagers pay for the independence they gain from being granted ejido status.

NAHUA FAMILY AND KINSHIP

Nahua kinship can be understood as a product of the interaction between local social structures of probable antiquity and political and economic forces originating at the regional and national level (Hunt 1976:100). The kinship system of the Nahuas, as well as that of many other Indian groups in Mexico, is characterized by flexibility and openness. It is well adapted to respond to the many contingencies that have resulted from their experiences under colonization, independence, serfdom, land expropriation, revolution, and government pro-grams of land reallocation. Nahua kinship is far from a rigid set of rules; rather it is a system by which people can interact with each other in a coherent manner while simultaneously adjusting to the changing circumstances of their position in the larger society. Above all, kinship must be understood in connection with the Nahua system of land tenure that has largely been forced upon them by regional and national power elites.

Gathering information on Nahua kinship is even more difficult than taking a census. The naming problem mentioned above becomes a significant obstacle, patterns of temporary migration lead to un-dercounts of household members, and the layout of the village makes systematic data collection a frustrating experience. To counteract these problems I gathered information over a period of years beginning in 1972. I continually made and revised detailed maps of the village and listed all people in each residence. I took genealogies and traced the histories of each family over the years ending in 1986. Only in this way could I begin to see patterns emerge. Two complications intervened. One is that the village fissioned at least twice during the period of research, once in the mid-1970s and later in the early 1980s. The daughter villages and Amatlán have hostile relations, and so I could not go to them to gather information without arousing serious suspicion. In 1972 I counted 110 independent households in Amatlán. By 1986 there were 81 households with 77 fewer people living in the village. The second complication is that about 3 years before my 1985–86 fieldwork the village consolidated residences into a pattern classified in Spanish as a *zona urbana* ("urban zone") according to instructions from government engineers. The purpose of relocating was to facilitate the introduction of electricity into the village.

Because of these complications I will be using the 81 residential groups living in Amatlán in 1986 as my database. I can trace all of these households back to 1972, and so I have reliable long-term information on the domestic cycle. I will include information on fami-lies that have since left the village, but only when I have confirming data from multiple sources.

First, I will describe some basic features of the kinship system in Amatlán. The Nahuas trace descent bilaterally, that is through both the mother's and father's sides of the family. Similar to most North American Anglos, the Nahuas consider themselves equally related to their matrilateral (mother's side) and patrilateral (father's side) kins-men. Even so, as we will see below, most villagers expect more help from, and want to live near patrilateral relatives. Because of bilateral descent, many villagers are able to trace kinship relations to each other, even though these links may be quite distant. Nahuas observe a rule prohibiting marriage to first or second cousins, and this requires many young men to search for potential wives in nearby communities. The result is that people generally have relatives in daughter villages and in many of the surrounding Nahua villages.

Given the prohibition of first- and second-cousin marriage and the small size of Amatlán, there is no rule of endogamy (a requirement that individuals marry inside the village). Nor does Amatlán have a rule of exogamy (a requirement that individuals marry outside of the community); in fact, for reasons discussed below, there are advantages to finding a spouse within the village. Although many people could claim a relationship to others in the village if they cared to do so, only a core of relatives constitutes the active kin group. Thus, for example, most villagers do not recognize more distant kinsmen outside of the direct parental and grandparental line beyond second cousins as active relatives. Also, it is common among people who have a bilateral system to recall family genealogies back only a few generations, and the Nahuas are no exception. Most people remember back to their grandparents, and occasionally they can speak about great-grandparents. In sum, the Nahuas do not extend their recognized kinsmen to great genealogical distance, either back in time or outside of the direct grandparental and parental lines. The Nahuas call their kinsmen "my family," or *noteixmaticahuaj* in Nahuatl. They distinguish this broader inclusive group from the people who live with them in the same household by the Nahuatl term *nocalpixcahuaj* ("my house family"), the narrower usage of "my family."

Figure 4.1 presents the Nahuatl terms used by male villagers to label their kinsmen. Because kin labels can vary according to sex of the speaker, I have included Figure 4.2 that presents kin terms employed by female speakers. Note that in Nahuatl, kin terms require the first person possessive prefix "no-" that means "my." Thus the term *notata* should be translated "my father." By analyzing the pattern of kin terms a people use, we can reveal something of the mental or cognitive organization of their kinship system. One way that anthropologists have classified different types of kinship terminology systems from around the world is by how cousins are labeled. In order to clarify these systems, anthropologists always list kinship terms of reference from the viewpoint of a hypothetical individual they call "ego." In the Hawaiian system of kinship terminology, ego refers to his siblings and

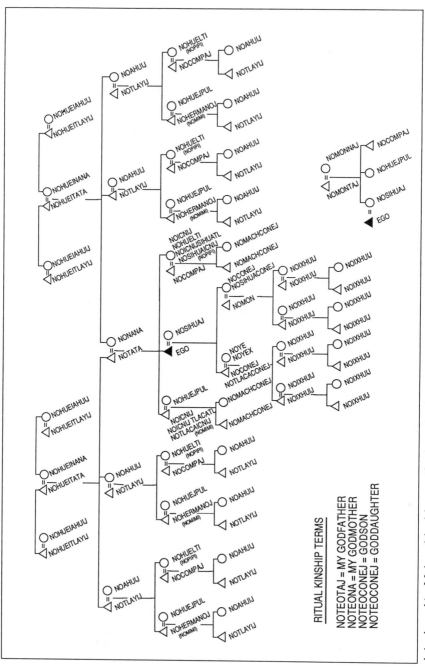

RITUAL KINSHIP TERMS

NOTEOTAJ = MY GODFATHER
NOTEONA = MY GODMOTHER
NOTEOCONEJ = GODSON
NOTEOCONEJ = GODDAUGHTER

4.1. Amatlán Nahua kinship terminology (male speaking)

cousins by the identical term. In other words, in cultures that employ the Hawaiian system we find no distinct terms for cousin. Hawaiian terminology systems generally distinguish relatives by sex and by generation relative to ego. Thus by equating siblings and cousins terminologically, this system emphasizes that these kinsmen are all of the same generation.

A second way of labeling cousins is called the Eskimo system. In this pattern of kin terms, siblings of ego are distinguished from cousins. The Eskimo system of labeling kinsmen indicates generation, but at the same time it distinguishes the more closely related kinsmen (brothers and sisters) from the more distantly related kinsmen (cousins). Eskimo terminology makes the distinction between lineals (grandparents, parents) and collaterals (siblings of lineal relatives or kinsmen outside of the direct grandparental and parental line) in all ascending and descending generations. This pattern of labeling kinsmen also has the effect of separating out members of the nuclear family from the larger kin group through the use of distinguishing terms. Eskimo-type terminology is the same system of terminology used by most Anglo North Americans (see Murdock 1949:223ff.; Fox 1967:256ff.; and Keesing 1975:104–5 for discussion of Hawaiian and Eskimo terminology systems).

In both the Hawaiian and Eskimo systems of terminology, the terms used to label cousins are identical on both the father's and mother's side of ego's family. These systems are, thus, compatible with a bilateral type of descent. If ego is equally related to kinsmen on both sides of his or her family it makes sense to label them identically. The Nahua terminology system appears to be basically Hawaiian in type but with significant incorporated Eskimo features. Because it is the system most familiar to North Americans, I will first describe the Eskimo features revealed in Figure 4.1. Ego's grandparents, called *nohueitata* ("my grandfather") and *nohueinana* ("my grandmother"), are distinguished by sex but not by whether they are related through the father's or mother's side. This pattern of naming also reflects the rule of bilateral descent. In addition, grandparents are distinguished from their own siblings who are called *nohueitlayij* ("my great uncle") and *nohueiahuij* ("my great aunt"). This practice departs from Hawaiian labeling where the same term would apply to all relatives of the same generation.

The terms for parents, *notata* ("my father") and *nonana* ("my mother"), are distinguished from the terms for parents' siblings, *notlayij* ("my uncle") and *noahuij* ("my aunt"). This also departs from

Hawaiian usage. In both Hawaiian and Eskimo systems, however, parent's siblings and their spouses (even though these are not consanguineals or "blood" relatives) may be called by the same terms and are distinguished only by sex. Thus, the Nahua term *notlayij* ("my uncle") may refer to the brother of either of ego's parents or to the husband of either parent's sister (ego's aunt). Ego uses the term *noconej* to refer to his own children, but he distinguishes them from his nieces and nephews (*nomachconej*), and from the children of his cousins (*notlayij*, sing. for males and *noahuij*, sing. for females). These cousin terms are identical to the terms for aunt and uncle and represent a signficant departure from Hawaiian usage since they highlight genealogical relation relative to ego over and above generation. When I asked villagers why they call parents' siblings and parents' siblings' children by the same terms they said that the terms refer to people who are part of the same family. In other words, aunts and uncles with their children are conceived as separate family units and this fact takes precedence in kin labeling over generational considerations. In the Hawaiian system, ego's own children, nieces, nephews, and cousins' children would be grouped under the identical term because they belong to the same generation. Up to this point in our description, the Nahua terminology system, with the exceptions noted, resembles that used by most North Americans. However, as we turn to the terms used for cousins and grandchildren, significant differences appear.

At first glance the Nahuas seem to distinguish siblings from cousins. Ego refers to his brother as *noicnij* ("my sibling" or by the alternate terms *noicnij tlacatl*, *notlacaicnij*, and the affectionate *nomimi*) and his sister also by the general term *noicnij* ("my sibling"), but when wishing to be more specific, by the term *nohuelti* (or by the alternate terms *noicnisihuaj*, *nosihuaicnij* and the affectionate *nopipi*). He refers to his male cousin by the term *nohermanoj*. However, this last term derives from the Spanish word *hermano* meaning "brother." I believe that this term has been adopted relatively recently by the Nahuas to introduce a terminological distinction between male cousin and brother. In the older system the word for male cousin was undoubtedly the same as that used for brother. The word for female cousin is *nohuelti*, the same as that used for sister. So it appears that the words for brother and sister are extended out to include male and female cousins. As further evidence that siblings and cousins are equated in the Nahua system, the term for brother-in-law (*nocompaj*, from the Spanish *compadre*, "co-father" or "ritual kinsmen") is the same one used to refer to a female cousin's spouse. The term for sister-in-law (*nohuejpul*) is also the same one used to refer to the wife of a male cousin. Finally, the affectionate term for brother is *nomimi* and for sister is *nopipi*, the identical affectionate terms used for male and female cousins.

All of this points to an underlying Hawaiian-type cousin-term system that has been modified to include Eskimo features. By equating siblings and cousins terminologically, the Nahuas are stressing the importance of a generational over a genealogical criterion for distinguishing kinsmen. As we have seen, this practice represents a departure from the typical Eskimo pattern where cousins are distinguished from siblings; that is, where genealogical relation of the cousin to ego takes precedence over generation relative to ego. This Hawaiian feature of Nahua kinship terminology appears again when we examine Nahua terms for great-grandchild and grandchild. The Nahuas use the term *noixhuij* for all children below ego's child's generation regardless of specific genealogical relation. In addition, although not shown on Figure 4.1, a cousin's grandchild is referred to by the same term as ego's grandchild. This practice represents another example of terms that base distinctions among kinsmen on generational over genealogical criteria—in short, a Hawaiian-type terminology system. Of course, use of terms such as *nomachconej* for "my niece or nephew," *nohermanoj* for "my cousin," and *notlayij* and *noahuij* for both parents' siblings and cousin's children contradicts stress on generational over genealogical relations. For these and other reasons noted above, it is apparent that the Amatlán Nahuas have a system of naming kinsmen that combines both Hawaiian and Eskimo features. Other students of Nahua culture have reported similar findings among other Nahua groups (see, for example, Arizpe Schlosser 1973:134ff.; Dehouve 1974:56–57, 1978:177ff.; Taggart 1975b:161–66,206).

Figure 4.2 gives kin terms from the viewpoint of a female speaker. It is clear from a comparison of Figures 4.1 and 4.2 that the system of terms used by females overlaps a great deal with that used by males. There are, however, instructive differences. Females do not distinguish uncles and aunts from great uncles and great aunts, preferring to use *notlayij* ("my uncle") and *noahuij* ("my aunt") for both sets of kinsmen. They extend the affectionate terms for brother and sister, *nomimi* and *nopipi*, to label male and female cousins, respectively. This may indicate that females have, or are expected to have, a more informal relationship with kinsmen. The term *nohues* replaces the male term *nohuejpul* for "my sister-in-law," but just as with males, this label is extended to the wives of cousins. For males the term *nohuejpul* is applied to sisters-in-law, but for females it is applied to brothers-in-

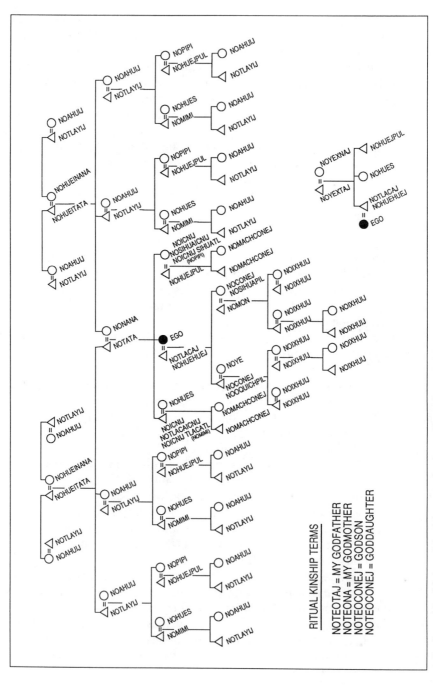

4.2. Amatlán Nahua kinship terminology (female speaking)

RITUAL KINSHIP TERMS

NOTEOTAJ = MY GODFATHER
NOTEONA = MY GODMOTHER
NOTEOCONEJ = GODSON
NOTEOCONEJ = GODDAUGHTER

law. Thus, the deeper meaning of the word *nohuejpul* is "my sibling-in-law of the opposite sex." The terms *noye* and *nomon* for "my daughter-in-law" and "my son-in-law," respectively, are the same for both sexes. However, a male extends the term for son-in-law to refer to his wife's parents. Thus *nomontaj* and *nomonnaj* mean "my father-in-law" and "my mother-in-law." Females extend the term for daughter-in-law to label her husband's parents. Thus *noyextaj* and *noyexnaj* mean "my father-in-law" and "my mother-in-law." These differences between male and female terminology systems, however, do not appear to represent significant alterations of the basic Hawaiian-Eskimo pattern.

Systems of kin terms often reflect social practice. Hawaiian terminology fits well with a society in which individuals form significant groups based on the generation they belong to relative to ego. Terms based on generation, for example, frequently indicate an individual's place in the hierarchy of age groupings and with it his or her obligations and expectations relative to others. The Hawaiian pattern of labeling kinsmen also acts to submerge the nuclear family within a larger kin grouping and is thus compatible with the existence of large extended families or other groupings. No terms of reference distinguish nuclear family members from other kinsmen. Finally, Hawaiian terminology is consonant with the formation of groups of age mates or siblings including cousins, which may unite for common action. It is interesting to note that age groupings, extended families, and long-term sibling cooperation are all important characteristics of Amatlán social organization.

However, as noted, the Nahuas do not label kinsmen using purely Hawaiian rules. They also incorporate Eskimo characteristics in their kinship terminology, such as the practice of distinguishing consanguineals from collaterals on the grandparental and parental generations as well as at the level of ego's children. In addition, there is the incorporation of the Nahuatl–Spanish term *nohermanoj* to distinguish male cousins from brothers. At first I thought that these peculiarities were caused by changes in the kinship system in response to various political, economic, and social pressures. But I was only partially correct. I discovered that the pre-Hispanic Aztec system of terminology contained some similar features (see Gardner 1982; Berdan 1982:66–68; Radin 1925:101). The ancient Aztecs themselves were undoubtedly undergoing modifications in their social organization as they expanded and consolidated their empire, and so social change was a factor in their terminology as well. Nahua kinship terminology basically reflects a flexible kinship system that retains the advantages of both the Hawaiian and Eskimo terminologies. Nahuas live in nuclear and extended families and have age groupings that are supported by Hawaiian terminology. But the extended families are for the most part nonresidential, and nuclear-family residence is the stated ideal for married couples. These factors, combined with the economic independence of the nuclear family, are most compatible with Eskimo terminology. Thus the Nahuas have the advantages of both systems and maintain maximum flexibility to meet future contingencies.

Amatlán is composed of households, and it is important to define this term before proceeding. By *household*, I mean a group of kinsmen who live as a unit, who store corn in common, who share a common domestic budget, and who prepare food in a common kitchen. The Nahuatl term *nocalpixcahuaj* ("my house family") is very close to this concept of household. A Nahua household may consist of either a nuclear family or an extended family. There are several problems, however, in applying this straightforward definition of a household to the real situation I encountered in Amatlán.

Two factors make it extremely difficult for outside observers to isolate households in the village. First, although members of a household may occupy what is technically a single dwelling, they typically live in several contiguous buildings. A Nahua house goes through a life cycle during which it serves many different purposes. Villagers often employ an old house as a kitchen shed and a partially completed house as an open-air porch. Family members may use a new house strictly for sleeping until the kitchen shed becomes too dilapidated and they are forced to make a kitchen in the new dwelling. Thus it is far from easy for the outsider to determine whether a group of buildings is occupied by a single extended family household or perhaps instead, a group of related households.

A second factor making it difficult to demarcate independent households in Amatlán relates to the process by which a newly married couple separates from the patrilocal household. Villagers state that residence after marriage is ideally patrilocal, that is, the young couple initially should move in with the family of the groom and set up a common household. This ideal is reflected in the greater number of patrilocal households operating in Amatlán, as opposed to matrilocal households (where the newly married couple moves in with the family of the bride). Eventually the husband and wife have children and build a house nearby, and over a period of time domestic functions are separated as the new family becomes an independent household. Because the separation is gradual, it is extremely difficult to judge at which point the new household is beginning to operate on its own.

In most cases the new household maintains very close ties with the households of the groom's father and brothers. Most newly forming nuclear families thus become components of larger nonresidential patrilocal extended families (Nutini 1967). Rarely, sisters may live near one another and form a nonresidential matrilocal extended family. In short, the Nahua household is not equivalent to the Nahua family. Households that make up the nonresidential extended family usually try to locate close to one another. The members of a nonresidential extended family participate in family affairs and cooperate in many tasks, but they do not operate as a single household. However, feelings of solidarity among extended family members are often very strong. On several occasions when I inquired about how households cooperate in an extended family, villagers replied that the various households share everything in common. I knew that this was not the case and that these responses reflected the ideal of total family cooperation rather than the reality in which nonresidential extended families are composed of independent households. Statements such as these added another source of confusion as I was trying to understand Nahua households and their relation to the extended family. When I was in doubt about the composition of a household I asked the people involved and checked their responses against the judgments of other kinsmen and neighbors.

In my 1986 survey of households in Amatlán, I found that out of 81 households, 50 contain members of complete or fragmented nuclear families. By these terms I mean an adult male with an adult female and their immature children, or a widow or widower with children. Nuclear families account for 61.7% of total households in the village but only 53.5% of the total population. Another 27 households contain patrilocal extended families. These included one or both parents, possibly with immature children, living with one or more married sons and their wives and children. This type of household accounts for 33.3% of Amatlán households and 39.9% of the population. The last household type is the matrilocal extended family that includes one or both parents along with daughters and their husbands and children. There are 4 such households in Amatlán, representing 4.9% of total households, and this type of extended family accounts for 6.5% of the total population (see Taggart 1972:135–36 for an analysis of household types in a Nahua community of the neighboring Sierra Norte de Puebla; also, Dehouve 1978:173ff. for household types among Nahuas of Guerrero).

Map 4.1 is a plan of village households as they appeared in 1972. Symbols on the map indicate discrete households and not buildings. The households of parents and their male children, or in the event of the death of the parents, the households of male siblings have been circled with solid lines to indicate the links among them. The map shows that sons tend to establish their households close to that of their parents. Single encircled households are those inhabited by parents and an unmarried son, parents and a married son and his wife, generally a temporary arrangement until the son builds a separate dwelling and establishes his own household, or by an old couple or single parent cared for by a son and his family. Occasionally a woman will be able to establish her household near her parents and brothers. In rarer cases, a core of female siblings is able to establish its separate households nearby one another, often close to their parents if they are living. Households linked by these female kin ties are circled on the map with broken lines. The dwellings of the extended family often occupy a single clearing or contiguous clearings in the forest. I prefer to label the households in a single clearing a compound rather than an extended family because not all households in a clearing necessarily belong to kinsmen. Sometimes friendship, economic need, hostile relations with his own family, or any number of factors will lead a man to establish his household among nonkin (see Carrasco 1976:58ff.).

Map 4.1 requires some further explanation. My genealogical information linking households in 1972 was not complete. To some extent I was able to fill in missing information from interviews conducted in 1986 as well as in the intervening years. I omitted, however, all genealogical information that I was unable to confirm with several informants. The effect of these gaps in my knowledge is to underplay the links between households appearing on the map. A second factor that serves to underplay links between households on the map is related to processes of village fissioning. I did not take into account in 1972 that many married younger sons of families were leaving the village to engage in a land invasion. Thus they built their dwellings on the new lands as part of the strategy for gaining legal recognition. The invasion effectively removed families from the village and thus reduced the number of households in compounds that I could document. A final factor that diminishes the number of links among village households is that I did not circle those households of kinsmen that

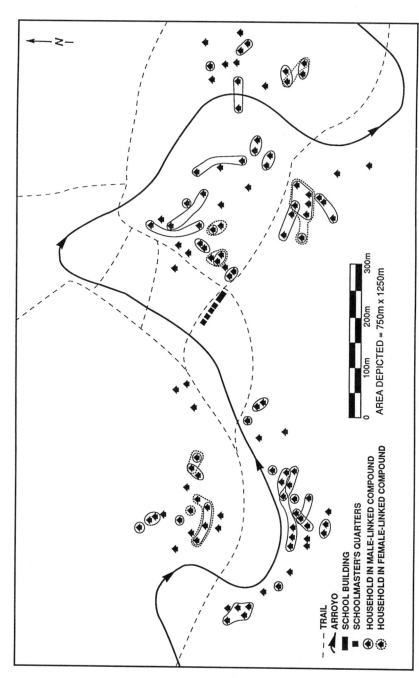

4.1. Village households in 1972 indicating male and female kin ties among households located within 150 meters of one another

are separated by a distance of more than 150 meters. I assumed that at this distance there was no real attempt on the part of kinsmen to live near one another. Distance between residences, however, does not necessarily signify that kinsmen have ceased cooperating with each other. Even among the households I have circled, several appear to be quite distant from each other. In cases where houses of kinsmen approached the 150-meter limit, they often occupied separate clearings connected by a short trail.

Male occupants of a compound have one thing in common: they are work mates. As I mentioned earlier in discussing horticultural practices, there are times in the planting and harvesting cycle when the individual farmer is dependent on the help of a number of other men. The male members of a compound become the core of a work group. An individual may require the help of men outside of the compound to accomplish a specific task but compound co-residents can count upon each other for consistent mutual aid (Taggart 1976 analyzes factors affecting recruitment of corn-planting groups in a Nahua community). In almost all cases, nonkin members of a compound are linked to the others through ties of ritual kinship (see below). The kinsmen in a compound are a man and his sons, or perhaps more accurately, brothers and their father. As the father ages and is less able to work in the fields, he gradually turns sections of his land over to his sons. As will be shown below, when the sons are young they live in their parents' house and contribute to a common budget. After they establish their own residences, they are still regarded as part of the extended family with regard to work cooperation, but as they begin to keep the harvest from their own fields they increasingly take on characteristics of a nuclear family household. In sum, the overwhelming number of individual households in Amatlán are nuclear-family components of larger nonresidential patrilocal extended families.

Occupants of a single household, then, pool their budgetary resources while male occupants of a compound pool their labor resources. For this reason people living in a household are always kinsmen, whereas occupants of a compound need not be. One key feature of Nahua social organization is the sets of brothers who cooperate in their labor. The Nahuatl term for such a group is *noicnihuaj* ("my siblings"). Whenever possible, brothers and sisters try to stay together, and many succeed in doing so throughout their lives. Villagers are particularly explicit about the many advantages of brothers cooperating and remaining neighbors. Not only do they share labor, but they can form a natural group of allies for political advantage or self-defense.

Although these sibling sets may be depleted by death and migration, as their children grow new sets are always forming. In 1986, despite two recent village fissions and a relatively high rate of out-migration, Amatlán was still dominated by sets of siblings. Of the 81 separate households in Amatlán, only eight (9.9%) are not connected in some way to other households through sibling ties. There were 44 sibling sets in all, 41 of which include at least one brother. Twenty-one of the sibling sets contain two or more brothers, and these brothers headed 51 of the village households (or 63%). The village, in sum, is essentially composed of sets of brothers who, despite the odds, have managed to stay together in Amatlán. The groups of brothers range in size from simple pairs to four sets of three brothers each to two sets of four brothers each. All of these brothers headed individual households. Interestingly, even after the residence patterns were broken up and the zona urbana was created, many of these brothers along with their parents managed to continue to live near one another (see Map 4.2 and Chapter 7).

Although villagers repeatedly spoke about the importance of brothers remaining together whenever possible, I found that sisters are also a significant component of sibling sets. However, it is rare for sisters to stay together in the same village in the absence of one or more brothers. Three of the sibling groups I documented in Amatlán are sisters with no living brothers. Two of these three sets of sisters, however, are comprised of old women who have outlived their brothers. Sisters are more likely to remain in the village if they have brothers in residence there. Included in the 21 sets of two or more brothers are 16 of their sisters who have married local men and who have managed to stay in the village. In addition, 20 of the 44 sibling sets I documented are composed of a single brother and one or more sisters. Most of these sisters have also succeeded in finding husbands locally, which has allowed them to remain in the village with their siblings or parents. In some cases the sisters have even managed to live in the vicinity of their brothers or parents as indicated by the dotted lines on Map 4.2. Brothers protect their sisters and look out for their welfare, and so sisters have an interest in staying close by. Cases where sisters remain active members of the family are remarkable because, as we will see below, certain features of Nahua kinship and in particular, the way property is passed down, drive a wedge between sisters and brothers. It is evidence of the strength of Nahua sibling ties that, given all of the difficulties, so many sisters have continued to stay together with their brothers.

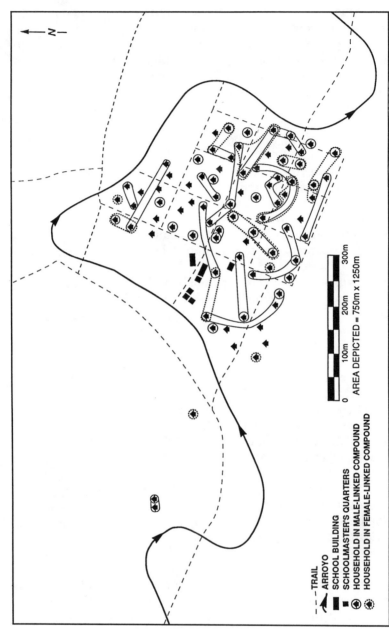

TRAIL
ARROYO
SCHOOL BUILDING
SCHOOLMASTER'S QUARTERS
HOUSEHOLD IN MALE-LINKED COMPOUND
HOUSEHOLD IN FEMALE-LINKED COMPOUND

0   100m   200m   300m
AREA DEPICTED = 750m x 1250m

4.2. Village households in 1986 indicating male and female kin ties among households located within 150 meters of one another

Many of the dynamics of Nahua kinship are connected to the way property, and in particular land, is inherited. Property passes from one generation to the next according to rules that are mandated by Mexican federal law. Theoretically, because the Nahuas determine descent bilaterally, women and men should inherit equally. However, the bilateral system is a set of rules determining kin-group affiliation and is not a set of rules for determining inheritance. By law, females can inherit property, but in fact they rarely do. The milpa is a male domain, and a woman inherits land from her father only in the event that she has no brothers. On the surface this practice may seem unfair, but fathers expect their daughters to marry and in fact, virtually all do. This means that daughters will move away under the rules of patrilocality and will have access to their husband's lands. In fact, when a young husband dies the land usually does revert to his widow and through her to their sons. A young widow without children, however, is in a precarious state and may lose the land to her husband's younger brothers.

Two mutually reinforcing factors have produced a crisis in the Nahua family structure. The first is related to the economic position of the village farmer in Mexico described by Stavenhagen and Warman (see Chapter 1). Villagers have told me repeatedly that, over the years, it has gotten increasingly harder to make ends meet. At first I thought this was due to their growing dependence on expensive industrial goods. However, after having inventoried household possessions and gathered data on household budgets, I could see that this was not so. The possession of manufactured items has changed very little over the years. Villagers complain that the prices paid for corn at the market are increasingly insufficient to cover expenses and that costs of necessities are rising each month. Village households seem to be caught in the grip of market forces that are transferring the wealth they produce to professional middlemen, and through them to the industrial sector of the economy. Given their horticultural mode of production, individual households are faced with ongoing labor shortages as they try to increase output. This situation may be a determinant leading households to increase the number of children born and to place particular value on sons.

The second factor is that the process of land redistribution has apparently reached its limit in the southern Huasteca. Ranchers are mounting an effective campaign with the federal government to halt further expropriations, and judging from news accounts they are maintaining a stepped-up level of violence against villagers who invade private property. The effect of these two factors is devastating to the Nahua household. With no room to expand their milpas, a horticultural technology that requires large amounts of land to be productive, and an increasing population, families are forced to disinherit all but the firstborn son. This has led to the development of a kind of de facto primogeniture. Generally, a father will give a small plot of land to his eldest son when he reaches about the age of 9 or 10. As years go by, the father will shift more of the land to his son who, in turn, is becoming increasingly independent. Some land may be given to second and third sons, but they understand that there will not be enough left for them to support a household of their own. Thus, several factors act in concert to split up the sets of brothers that anchor Nahua social organization. Resentment can easily develop among brothers as we witnessed in the murder case of Lorenzo.

These circumstances that work to divide the family against itself help to explain why the struggle for land is fought with such desperation. Sheer economic deprivation explains much of it, but from the perspective of the Nahuas, the integrity of their families is also at stake. Without additional land, brothers are forced to separate as younger siblings leave the village in search of a livelihood. In some cases the dispossessed brothers clear a particularly remote area of a cattle ranch and commence farming. This is the beginning of an invasion, and often others from similarly land-poor families join them. If they can succeed in farming the area for 3 consecutive years, there is a good chance that government officials will recognize their claims. After this period, the younger brothers move their whole families to the new village, and the father and older brother may actually give up their legal rights in Amatlán and join the new village. Such group relocations explain the paradoxical decertifications that occur periodically, such as that noted for Amatlán in Chapter 2. As they move out, the vacated land is taken up by younger brothers of families that remain behind. Of the 21 sibling sets with two or more brothers in Amatlán, 10 of them include two or more men who have certified land rights in the village. Of these, four actually include three brothers with land rights.

Periodic fissioning of Amatlán leads younger brothers to enter into a kind of holding pattern while waiting for developments. Of the 81 current residence groups in Amatlán, 61 are certifed ejido members with rights to an equal share of the land division. These are called in Spanish *certificados* (short for *certificado de derechos agrarios*, "certified for agrarian rights") by the villagers, and it is a status toward which all younger males are working. The remaining residence groups are classified by villagers as *vecinos* in Spanish, or "neighbors." These people either continue to work in their father's fields, or, depending on the availability of land, the Comisariado allocates to them 2½ hectares of milpa space. This is far below the 7 hectares allocated to certificados. One can barely sustain a family on 2½ hectares, and it is the vecinos who can truly be called the poor of the village. But vecino status is often a temporary strategy employed by younger people anticipating an eventual full share of land. Of the 20 vecinos, 15 are either the youngest of a group of brothers or at least have two or three older brothers. When the percentage of vecinos to certificados approaches 50%, the village becomes unstable and fissioning occurs. In 1973, the number of vecino households grew to near 50%, and they instigated a land invasion that resulted in formation of first one and then, a few years later, a second daughter village (see Kvam 1985 for an examination of Nahua land invasions in a citrus-growing area of the Huasteca).

A land invasion means trouble and often bloodshed. Poorly armed Indians do not undertake such a step unless the situation is desperate. This means that all parents face a crucial dilemma. Given the chronic land shortage, what is to be done with younger sons? The ideal solution is for other sets of brothers from other families to begin a land invasion that would open up new parcels to be distributed to those who remain in the village. No family can count on such luck, and so they must plan for the future. One option, which is available to only a few, is to send a younger son to school so that he can become a teacher. Mexican government officials are anxious to train bilingual teachers, and so they offer various scholarships to Indian children. Several families have sent daughters, particularly younger ones, to the regional school so that they can avoid having to marry a man who does not stand to inherit land. An added plus is that schoolteachers are paid by the government and are considered to be relatively well-off. There are not enough teaching positions in Amatlán itself, but chances are good that these younger sons or daughters could get jobs in the region and thus live fairly close by. Additional options include getting permanent or temporary jobs in a regional town or on a neighboring ranch. In sum, one of the few choices available for the disinherited, aside from invading private land, is to enter the mestizo world.

Occasionally a woman inherits land rights, and a disinherited younger brother from another family has the opportunity to gain access to her fields by marrying her and moving into her household. The

Nahuas call his practice *monticaj* in Nahuatl (literally "he is being an in-law"). Besides its rarity, this option has major drawbacks that make it an undesirable alternative. Villagers are in agreement that a man moving in with the family of his wife is at a distinct disadvantage. He is separated from his brothers, and he is a stranger in his wife's compound. I noticed that when the husband has joined his wife's family, he spends most of his time in the company of his brothers or working outside of the village. Of the four matrilocal families in Amatlán one is completely anomalous and the result of idiosyncratic factors. The three remaining examples have in common that the wife had no resident brothers or brothers-in-law and therefore she had inherited her father's or late husband's land rights. That these women had no trouble finding husbands shows that, although people generally disparage matrilocality, a man's need for land overrides all other considerations. Although I have no case examples due to the small number of matrilocal families, I was told that if the wife dies in such a circumstance, the land bypasses her husband and goes directly to their oldest son. Thus a man in such a circumstance is truly marginal to the family.

Chronic land shortages are hardest on the female members of kin groups. There is much anecdotal evidence in Amatlán showing that sisters-in-law rarely get along together. They are seen by many to be natural enemies who gossip about each other and quarrel. Reasons for this problematic relationship are clarified by examining the inheritance patterns. Once a sister marries, she effectively loses her rights in her own family patrimony. Still, she has an interest in seeing that her brothers stay together, not only for sentimental reasons but because brothers provide some protection against abusive husbands and in-laws. In sum, it is in a woman's interest that her brothers have land. As mentioned above, if she is widowed and has children, she has a very good chance of inheriting her husband's land. However, if her husband had younger brothers, she may end up with nothing because they may try to keep the land in their family. A widowed daughter-in-law or sister-in-law, and particularly one with children, has the right to claim fields that may have been farmed for decades by her father-in-law and his sons.

If younger brothers decide to stay together at all costs and move to join a newly forming village, they would not be likely to include their widowed sister-in-law because she would have no one to work the new land. Widows with children who do retain rights to their husband's land hire young village men to work it for them in return for a portion of the harvest. In sum, a widow is often in a weak position if she has no children or especially if her former husband is not the eldest son. However, regardless of her position, the widow will press for her rights among her in-laws in an attempt to gain sufficient land to live. Should a woman's elder brother die, his widow (her sister-in-law) will most likely inherit part or all of the original family patrimony. The widowed sister-in-law, then, may be seen as an intruder who could potentially remove valuable land from the family. This reduction of the family land base could undermine the ability of the surviving younger siblings to remain together. Thus sisters-in-law are potential and often real-life adversaries.

It is an odd circumstance in a bilateral system that a widowed daughter of the family stands to lose her claim to the most valuable component of the family patrimony, whereas a sister-in-law can suddenly gain rights to the land upon the death of her husband. Only a few events of this nature occurred while I was resident in Amatlán, but it caused much discussion among villagers. The precarious position of widows in Amatlán is reflected in statistics I gathered on people who had left the village. I have documentation on 85 people who left, including information on how they are related to various household heads. Fifty were people related through the wife of the household head, or were younger brothers, or others who left the village for a variety of reasons. Fully 35 of the emigrants (41%) were the sisters of a resident male household head. Eight of these followed husbands who were younger brothers to new villages, but the other 27 were women who, because of the death of their husband or divorce, had no choice but to leave the village. In these circumstances, a woman's brothers may agree to take her and her children in, but the financial burden of supporting two families makes the situation very difficult. An exception seems to be when the sister is elderly or without children at home, in which case a brother may agree to take her in. In several cases where their families helped them, women left their children with family members in the village, traveled to cities to work, and periodically sent money back for their support. The women who leave in this circumstance are forced to participate in the mestizo economy when continued life in the village becomes impossible.

Widowhood is common in Amatlán, and therefore what happens to widows is a crucial question. I have reliable information on 33 women who have lost their husbands. Four of them (and probably many more in reality) have left the village, all but 1 to live with children who have moved to daughter villages or who have entered the mestizo economy. Of the 29 remaining in the sample, 6 live by themselves with their unmarried children. As already noted, they either farm their husband's land through contracted help, or the work is done by their own sons. Of the 23 remaining cases, 12 live with their son and his family. Four of the 11 remaining women live with grandchildren of their sons, and the remaining 7 cases are anomalous. In 3 of these the widow lives with the daughter's family because none of her sons are alive, and in 1 case a young widow went back to live with her own parents. In the remaining cases 1 woman went to live with her in-laws from a previous marriage and the other 2 live with distant relatives. There are 7 cases of men who had been widowers, although at the time of my study 3 of these had remarried. Of the 4 still unmarried 1 lives alone, 1 left the village, another lives with his unmarried children, and the last lives with his married son. Although I have only 3 cases recorded in Amatlán, it seems likely that widowers often are able to select second wives from the large number of widows, some of whom are presumably still youthful. From these figures it is also clear that sons, for the most part, bear the responsibiliy of caring for their parents.

Villagers asserted that the obligation to care for parents falls to the youngest son. I found this hard to understand, since the youngest son has the least chance of inheriting the land and thus of supporting the aged parents. However, of the 12 widows living with sons, 10 of them are indeed living with the youngest. Only twice did I find widows living with their eldest sons, and in both cases their youngest sons had left the village. The reason for this apparent contradiction can be found in the domestic cycle, to be discussed in more detail below. In brief, the youngest son is the last to be cared for by the mother, the last to be living at home with his parents. People explained to me that when he plans to marry, the youngest son builds a house nearby so that the mother will not have to be resettled. Thus, the Nahuas consider it natural that he should continue to care for one or both of his aged parents after he sets up his own household.

THE DOMESTIC AND LIFE CYCLES

The domestic cycle of the Nahua family is not a fixed set of stages that are totally determined by rules. Rather, it is a progression guided partly by cultural rules and partly by the economic and political realities of the village. The nuclear and extended family groupings I found in 1986 are not permanent structures but rather represent steps in the developmental cycle of households (systematic changes that occur in household structure and composition as members pass through stages of their lives). I have traced over a 14-year period the cycles for the 81 residence groups currently living in Amatlán. Needless to say, there are many intervening factors that cause the family to make adjustments. Insufficient land, quarreling, death of the household head, or land invasion may cause changes in the usual progression of family forms (see Taggart 1972:143ff. and 1975b:158ff. for an analysis of factors causing Nahua domestic groups to fragment).

I will begin my description of the cycle at the point when a man and woman decide to marry. The man at this time is usually living in a household headed by his father. The decision to marry signals the beginning of the dissolution of the residential nuclear-family household. To establish his own household, the young man must control enough land to support his wife and future family. Until he has access to sufficient land, the groom may move his bride in with his family, sharing work and the harvest with his brothers and father. This creates a temporary patrilocal extended-family household. However, villagers express a clear preference for nuclear family living, and it is the goal of all newly married couples to set up their own households.

As soon as possible the groom begins to build a separate dwelling near his father's house, usually forming a "compound" in the same forest clearing. If the clearing is already crowded, he moves off and builds in an adjacent area. Taggart calls this splitting of the domestic unit "segmentation" (1975a:348). Soon after the marriage, the man begins the gradual process of separating his corn supply and household budget from that of his father and brothers ("fission" in Taggart's terminology, 1975a:348). Throughout the segmentation and fission processes, cooperation among the father and his sons continues in the cycle of work associated with cultivation and other tasks such as house building. As mentioned, over the years the firstborn son receives the bulk of land, leaving younger brothers too little to support their own future families. Villagers told me that this was not such a problem in times past when there was plenty of land for all. However, because of the restricted land base now, when the oldest son marries, his younger brothers begin to look for alternative sources of land (see below).

The bride initially moves into her husband's house and takes over some of the domestic responsibilites under the direction of her mother-in-law. Women told me that this is a difficult time for a girl because she is a stranger in the family and she can be treated as a kind of servant by the others. Even after the couple moves into their own house, the bride can chafe under the critical eye of her mother-in-law. The problem is made worse if the bride comes from another village and lacks the immediate support of her own family. Cases are known where a new bride returns to her village after a few days, never to return. Assuming the marriage works out, the couple has children shortly following the marriage. Children are highly valued by both parents and are lavished with love and attention. They also legitimize the marriage, give the new wife a sense of independence from her in-laws, and after several years provide helping hands around the house or in the fields. After a second and third child arrive, little girls are particularly valued because they are given responsibility for their younger siblings while the mother engages in domestic tasks.

When a boy reaches 8 or 9 years of age, he receives his first piece of land and assumes responsibility for cultivating it. He is joined in the work by his brothers as well as his father and uncles. In this way he develops close working ties with his kin group and, in particular, with his brothers who are also learning cultivation techniques. When the boy reaches his early 20s he sees himself as increasingly independent from his father and may then begin to search for a mate. Girls usually marry in their late teens, and following the rule of patrilocality will join their husband in his compound. The elderly father usually dies first, leaving his widow in the care of the youngest son. In general, when the youngest son gets married, his mother will occupy the same house or the one next to his, and she will follow him if he joins his brothers in a land invasion. Whenever possible brothers stay together. However, they control the land and its produce as individuals and thus, if need be brothers will go their own way in search of sufficient land or a livelihood in the mestizo world. This is why villagers say that each person follows his own trail through life.

The Nahua family oscillates between patrilocal extended-family households with males working the same land and maintaining a common corn supply and budget, to a nonresidential extended family composed of several households with all adult males maintaining sepa-rate corn supplies and budgets but working together in each others' fields. This pattern is reflected in the seemingly scattered and random layout of Amatlán. As older sets of brothers have sons, new compounds appear in the forest. The extended family shrinks as it spawns nuclear families, but the residential core is destroyed only when the parents die, leaving the youngest son independent for the first time. A village census freezes this process, but it reveals the balance of family types extant at a given time. Over the years, Amatlán has maintained a ratio of about twice as many nuclear-family households as extended-family households. But the sets of brothers in Amatlán who have stayed together despite the odds against their doing so is testimony to the fact that the patrilocal extended family is the preferred kin group.

If we examine household types in terms of level of wealth we find that the cattle-owning families tend to live in extended-family households in somewhat greater proportion than poorer families. The greater resource base of these families may allow the parents to prolong the extended-family phase of the domestic cycle for a year or two. The vecinos, most of whom are the families of younger brothers waiting for an opportunity to acquire land, belong to nonresidential extended families but tend to live in nuclear-family households in somewhat greater proportion than the village as a whole. Because these villagers come from families of more limited resources, they may be forced out of the residential extended family somewhat earlier. Perhaps too, they are simply laying claim to a living site should land eventually become available. With these minor exceptions, the ratio of differing household types does not appear to vary radically according to level of wealth in Amatlán.

The Nahuas mark a person's progress through life by labeling the stages through which he or she passes. At predictable points in the life cycle, the man or woman will be living in different residential groupings. As a child, he or she lives in a nuclear family surrounded by uncles. As an adult, the individual lives in a nuclear family surrounded by brothers or in the case of women, brothers-in-law. As an old person, the man or woman lives in a residential extended family with his or her youngest son and perhaps the son's wife and family. Stages in the life cycle are also partly reflected in the distinctive dress people wear at different times in their lives (see Chapter 2). Most significantly, villagers at approximately the same generational level know a great deal about each other and very little about people in the generations above and below them. Thus, for example, if I wished to obtain information about a specific person, I was forced to ask someone in the same age range. Villagers rarely seemed to know much about people a great deal older or younger than themselves. Table 4.1 summarizes the way Nahuas divide the stages in a person's life.

The Nahuas do not typically mark transitions between levels with elaborate rites of passage. They do hold a small cleansing ritual at birth that is designed more to protect the baby than acknowledge its entrance into the world. The most elaborate rite of passage by far is the funeral. Funeral rituals require enormous outlays of wealth on numerous occasions over a period of several years. Once again, however, the funeral is a rite of passage that serves more to protect the

TABLE 4.1. Stages in the Life Cycle

English	Nahuatl	
	Male	Female
1. Baby-in-arms	*pilconetsij*	*pilconetsij*
2. Toddler	*conetl*	*conetl*
	conetsi	*conetsi*
3. Child (4–14 years old) alternative term for child	*oquichpil*	*sihuapil*
10–14 years old	*piltelpocatsij*	*pilichpocatsij*
4. Youth (14–early 20s)	*telpocatl*	*ichpocatl*
5. Married adult until about age 50	*tlacatl* (may be addressed as *totlayi*, "our uncle")	*sihuatl* (may be addressed as *toahui*, "our aunt")
6. Old person	*huehuentsij* (may be addressed as *tetata*, "father")	*tenantsij* ["mother"]
7. Very old person	*tehueitata* ("grandfather")	*teheuinana* ("grandmother")

Note: the kinship terms are used in Categories 5, 6, and 7 even for nonrelatives.

living than to mark the transition of the deceased (see Chapter 6 for more information on birth and funeral practices). The sequence of stages in a Nahua life are neither rigidly defined nor bound by elaborate rules. Both the life and domestic cycles allow for much free choice on the part of the villagers, which makes the stages of both seem to unfold in a relaxed, unhurried way (for discussions of the Nahua domestic cycle, see Taggart 1972:134ff., 1975b:78ff.; Arizpe Schlosser 1972:42–44, 1973:155–80; Dehouve 1974:56–57; Chamoux 1981b:103–7; for a description of the life cycle in a Nahua village just north of Amatlán see Williams García 1957; for detailed studies of Nahua kinship and family structure see Nutini 1968; Arizpe Schlosser 1973; Taggart 1975a, 1975b; Dehouve 1978; Chamoux 1981b:68–147).

STRESS POINTS IN NAHUA KINSHIP SYSTEMS

After this brief sketch of Nahua kinship organization and domestic and life cycles, I will now provide some examples of how the system has been deformed by factors that derive from the economic and political plight of the Indians in Mexico. The factor I will highlight is the effect of land shortages on key kin relations. In addition, I will give a few examples of how these problematic kin relations are represented in Nahua religious beliefs and myths.

As we have seen, Amatlán is surrounded by other ejidos or by privately owned cattle ranches, and there is little opportunity for the village to expand its land base. We have also seen that population increase has caused the village to fission three times in the last 45 years, and, as in many Indian communities in Mexico, problems of land shortage dominate village politics and social relations. It is no exaggeration to state that villagers consider land to be their most valuable asset and the source of all economic security and well-being.

We have also seen that primarily due to the shortage of land, and despite a bilateral descent system, the Nahuas practice a de facto primogeniture whereby the eldest son inherits the land. Daughters are completely cut off from receiving land, except in the rare event that she has no brothers. From the villagers' perspective there is little choice in this matter because the land is owned in such small units that it should not be subdivided. People explained to me that it is the men and boys who should receive land to support their families when they marry and that women receive access to land when they marry. Thus, they say, it is foolish to divide the family property both among brothers and sisters.

The effect of this system of inheriting property is that sisters are disinherited and younger brothers are left with either no land at all, or at best an insufficient amount. Younger brothers must search for fields to farm just as their sisters must search for husbands with land. Not surprisingly this situation can lead siblings to resent each other, with particular animosity aimed at the eldest brother. This is precisely the situation I encountered in Amatlán. Despite these antagonisms, brothers usually make every effort to stay together, and wise elder brothers (and their parents) work hard to see that younger siblings succeed in gaining access to ejido land (see Taggart 1972:146).

From the information presented earlier it is clear that people who suffer the most from this system are the daughters of the family. They must seek out males who have access to land, but there are relatively few elder brothers available. For a woman, marrying a younger brother may mean a wait of many years in poverty until her husband can acquire land or, more likely, that she will have to leave the village in order to accompany her husband in his quest for land. Worse yet, she will most likely need to move in with her husband's parents for a period of time, and, as I suggested previously, relations between mothers-in-law and daughters-in-law among the Nahuas can be hostile.

Once married, a woman cannot return home again and expect to be supported. Even if a sister's husband dies, brothers guard their own access to land and expect their sister to return to the family of her deceased husband. A childless widow has little chance of inheriting her husband's land, which is often redistributed among her dead husband's brothers. Only if the widow has borne children and particularly sons can she make a realistic case that she should become caretaker of the land until her husband's children become old enough to inherit it.

Dispossessed women or women who have married landless men have little choice but to leave the village. In the end though, most women get their revenge. Women outlive men in an overwhelming number of cases, and widows with children often become caretakers of the property. A widow distributes the land to her sons, but in some cases she can actually retain control until her own death. The implications of this prospect are not lost on the men who sometimes complain that they do not trust their wives to do their bidding when they die. Even in a system of de facto primogeniture like that of the Nahuas, an eldest son may not gain full control of his inheritance until years after the death of his father.

This chronic shortage of land and the way that land is inherited cause particular trouble spots in the system of kin relations among the Nahuas. To illustrate this I will discuss four of these points of potential conflict. First, a wife may be perceived by a man and his kinsmen as a threat to the solidarity of his family. She moves into the parental home and with the birth of a child builds rights in the family patrimony. Should her husband die, she has the right to claim the family fields. Should her husband live a normal life span, she still is likely to gain eventual control of the land and do as she sees fit with it. Besides the normal strains and stresses of married life, the land question can undermine the marriage tie.

A second trouble spot is produced by the system of primogeniture. Elder brothers are alienated from their younger siblings because they receive the bulk of the patrimony. Resentment against elder brothers flares in the open on occasion. I have documented feuds between firstborn males and younger brothers, and in the case reported earlier that rocked the village, it was a younger brother who was accused of murdering his elder brother over a land dispute (see also Taggart 1975a for an analysis of Nahua sibling rivalry).

A third area of difficulty in Nahua kin relations produced by the land shortage is the dilemma of dispossessed sisters. In a bilateral system, a sister may try to claim her right to land should her marriage end. This is a threat to younger brothers who hope that they will eventually obtain land rights. In any event, when sisters marry, their residences and their loyalties shift to their husband. With the birth of children, a woman's claims on her husband's land are strengthened, but simultaneously her ties to her brothers are weakened.

One final area of difficulty is the strained relations that can exist between a widow and the families of her sons. Generally, age is revered among the Nahuas, but antagonisms can still form between a widowed mother and her sons. Sons may be anxious for her to disperse the patrimony. She, on the other hand, may wish to keep direct control of the land as long as possible to keep the family together and to retain her central position in the family. Strains between mothers-in-law and daughters-in-law have already been examined. Even grandchildren are aware that they will receive nothing directly from their grand-mother, and they can be made pawns in the struggle between their parents and grandmother for control of the patrimony.

For the most part, these areas of tension are overshadowed and kept in check by the general sense of solidarity in the extended family. Contradictions in kin relations produced by the unavailability of land remain largely submerged, and families work together to overcome adversity. In particular, I have emphasized that groups of brothers work hard to cooperate and present a united front. Nonetheless, I have documented numerous cases where relations break down at one or more of these four points and the struggles and hostilities come out in the open.

One place where contradictions among kinsmen are unveiled is in the beliefs surrounding supernatural beings and in myths and stories told among villagers. Here are four brief examples that serve to illustrate the four areas of strain outlined above.

The first example is found in a myth concerning *apanchanej*, the female water spirit. In the story, a man goes off fishing each day and brings back the catch for his wife to cook. Unbeknown to him, on each occasion the wife gives some of the cooked fish to another man and this greatly angers apanchanej. She complains that some of her children, the fish, are being injured or killed by the fisherman and that the fisherman's wife, in turn, is giving the catch away. The water spirit sends another of her children, the alligator, who first tells the fisherman what his wife has been doing and then eats him. The fisherman cuts his way through the alligator's shoulder and escapes. In the process of escaping, the man gets alligator blood on his body. He arrives home, and his skin begins to itch from the blood stains. The irritation becomes excruciating, and he throws himself into the cooking fire to get relief and dies.

Here we have a wife illegitimately disposing of a man's property, thereby jeopardizing his relationship to the water spirit, which leads ultimately to his destruction. The wife is portrayed as someone with her own interests who, no matter how innocently, subverts her husband's hard work and frustrates his best intentions. She also outlives him. In short, this story of the water spirit expresses the underlying tension between a man and his wife, a message that would be recognized by most Nahuas listening to it.

The second example involves the alienated elder brother. To illustrate this area of tension in the kinship system, I will recount a belief among the villagers that I heard repeated dozens of times by laymen and shamans alike. The devil, known as *tlacatecolotl* (Nahuatl for "man owl"), is regarded as the elder brother of *toteotsij* (Nahuatl for "God," the "Sun," or "Jesus"). Thus the forces of darkness have the upper hand in the world, and the great battle between God and the devil is explained in this belief as a struggle between younger and elder brothers. This widespread belief also strikes a chord among villagers who face real-life competition with their elder siblings for land and the means of a livelihood.

The third example focuses upon strained relations with the alienated sister. The Nahuas recount a myth about the fire spirit, *xihuantsij*, that reveals the place of the sister among brothers. A woman was unknowingly married to xihuantsij, called in Spanish, Juan Flojo ("John Lazy"). Juan liked to sit around the fire all day to keep warm while his brothers-in-law went to clear the forest and prepare their milpas. The group of brothers complained to their sister about her husband's inactivity, but she defended Juan Flojo. Eventually Juan became angry and lashed out at his wife's brothers. He proclaimed that he would do more work in one day than all of them combined could do in a month and that he would then leave the village. He urinated in the shape of a cross, touched a match to it, and burned a large section of forest for his milpa.

He took fire with him, and the brothers were unable to prepare their fields. Before leaving, Juan Flojo told his sister to make cornmeal in the normal way for her food. When she asked him how she was supposed to heat up the comali without fire, he replied that she should cook the tortillas in her armpit. In the meantime, her brothers were becoming emaciated from lack of food. They asked their sister why she appeared so well-fed while they were starving. She explained that her husband had taken care of her before he left and that it was their own fault that Juan Flojo had disappeared. Eventually she talked them into making an offering to her husband and treating him with respect, and fire was returned to the village.

In this myth we witness a sister who had to choose sides when her brothers accused her husband of laziness. She defended Juan Flojo against her own brothers, and in return her husband provided for her. In pursuing their own interests the brothers alienated their sister. In the end, by forcing them to respect her husband, she was able to resolve the antagonisms that they had caused. The picture presented by this myth is that of a sister caught between the interests of her husband and those of her brothers. Such a marginal position for women is all too real in village life, and unfortunately not so easily resolved.

The final example concerns the alienated grandmother. The Nahuas tell an important myth about the corn spirit, called *chicomexochitl* ("7-flower") in Nahuatl, who is sometimes conceived to be a small blond-haired boy. One day, as chicomexochitl's grandmother is caring for the boy she decides to kill him. First, she tries to drown him, but he miraculously reappears. Next, she kills and buries him in the milpa. Again he miraculously reappears. The myth becomes quite complicated, but the sequence of murder and reappearance repeats itself several times. The myth recreates the planting and harvesting cycle as an instance of aggression between the grandmother and grandchild. Again the myth has meaning to Nahua listeners who have experienced or who at least can understand the potential for hostility between grandparent and grandchild.

Each of these points of friction in Nahua kinship relations can be linked directly to the land shortages faced by Indians in the southern Huasteca and ultimately to the position of the Indian village in Mexico. The land shortage forces distortions in the pattern of obligations and expectations that constitute Nahua kin relations. Nahua kinship must be understood as a product of history, but equally importantly it must be analyzed in relation to the national and regional forces that daily influence even the most intimate Indian family relations. The fact that Nahua kin relations operate as smoothly as they do and that the extended family maintains a high degree of solidarity in the face of adversity might be explained in part by the safety valve provided by these and other myths. By hearing myths whose plots are based on problematic kin relations, people may be able to clarify and externalize their own sometimes ambivalent feelings toward their kinsmen (see Taggart 1977 for an analysis of Nahua narratives related to deviance in family relations).

In the unlikely event that abundant farmland became available, I would expect that younger brothers would each receive adequate fields, sisters would have a good chance of marrying men with sufficient land, and many of these areas of potential tension in the Nahua family would be reduced or eliminated.

RITUAL KINSHIP

Compadrazgo, the Spanish term for the custom of establishing ritual kinship ties with others, is widespread throughout all of Latin America. It is particularly important among the Indians of Mesoamerica. In Amatlán, the compadrazgo complex is not very well developed compared to other communities in Mexico, but it is nevertheless an important factor in village social organization. What I want to emphasize here is how it operates as a system in Amatlán. At first I was perplexed by the existence of a system of fictional kinship operating alongside a bilateral kinship system that relates a person to a large number of people on both the mother's and father's side of the family. What is the reason for having fictional kinship when the real system is so all-inclusive? While I was investigating this question, I was myself constantly being asked to enter into ritual kin relations with many people. Eventually I became *comparej* (Nahuatl from the Spanish *compadre*, "co-father") with many adults and *teotaj* (Nahuatl for "godfather") to dozens of children. I questioned people about compadrazgo many times, and they responded that ritual kinsmen help you when you need it. Ritual kinsmen will offer economic support and a sense of social security for the family. When I pointed out that brothers and other kinsmen do the same, people responded that there are often not enough blood relatives living nearby.

For the villagers then, ritual kinship extends the real kinship system to include people that could not under normal circumstances be called upon in times of need. This reasoning, which was provided by the villagers themselves, reveals an interesting characteristic of their extended family system. Mutual cooperation among kinsmen is limited to brothers, parents, and children. Anyone more distantly related needs an additional motivation to encourage them to act. So, among the Nahuas, the core of kinsmen that one can count upon for mutual aid is really rather small. Of course the advantage of such a restricted network is that the number of people who have a claim on any one person's loyalty or cooperation is correspondingly small. The ritual kinship system allows people to select "kinsmen" with whom they wish to cooperate. There is another advantage of ritual kinship that is sometimes overlooked. Ritual kinship relations can remain inactive for long periods of time. At any given point in time, each person in Amatlán can claim literally dozens of ritual kinship ties. But only a few of these may actually be active and call for mutual aid. The flexibility of the ritual kinship system may be one of its major advantages over real kinship.

The most important ritual kinship role a man and his wife can have is to be made godparents to another couple's child. Godparenthood is always conceived by villagers to be a ritual tie between an adult couple and a child. The couple buys clothes and toys for the child and generally looks out for his or her welfare. Should something happen to the parents, the godparents are obligated to take the child in as their own. It is clear from observation, however, that the key link in the system is forged between the four adults involved. In essence, the couple selected to be godparents becomes co-parents with the child's mother and father. The adults call each other *comparej* or *comarej* (sometimes *compalej* and *comalej*), from the Spanish *compadre* and *comadre* ("co-father" and "co-mother"; Figure 4.1 includes a list of the other terms used by the participants in ritual co-parenthood). In this important relationship, both the child and his or her parents show respect to the godparents.

The way it works in Amatlán is that on special occasions or in association with rituals one person will ask another if he or she is willing to become a ritual kinsman. Such requests come from those who are already friends and have previously engaged in small gift giving and mutual help, usually connected to house building or work in the fields. There is a degree of hierarchy in ritual kinship relations that is expressed in demonstrations of respect. The person asking to enter into the relationship must show courtesy and deference to the person or couple with whom he or she wishes to establish the relationship. This respect relationship continues as long as the ritual link is actively maintained. Because ritual kinship is often entered into in conjunction with an important villagewide or personal occasion, the more important the occasion, the stronger the ritual tie. Every person thus gauges the potential return from each ritual kinsman and regulates the strength of the tie by carefully selecting the appropriate occasion when the link is to be created.

Any ritual may serve as an opportunity to form ritual kinship ties. The period of time following the major offering at the winter solstice ritual (*tlacatelilis*) is a very popular occasion. Fictive kinship ties are usually created in a short ritual cleansing conducted by a village shaman. After the shaman chants and dedicates a small offering, the new compadres and comadres shake hands and call each other by their ritual kinship terms. It is evidence that a ritual kinship tie is being deactivated when people revert to addressing each other by their given names rather than their ritual kinship terms. Apparently most ritual ties fall slowly into such neglect. To keep the relationship functioning requires some effort, not only in using the formal terminology, but in maintaining a flow of small gifts and favors. The greatest test of the health of fictive kinship ties occurs in the period following a ritual occasion called *xantoloj*, which is linked with Day of the Dead celebrations. During this time, ritual kinsmen are obligated to deliver gifts of food—particularly delicacies such as meat-filled tamales—to each other's house. Failure to participate in the exchange is a definitive sign that the relationship is moribund.

It is difficult to specify precisely what fictive kinship obligations entail on the part of the participants. Ritual kinsmen pledge to support each other, but clearly their obligations fall short of the mutual support exhibited by brothers. In the murder trial recounted in the first chapter, the one fact that shocked people almost as much as the act of murder itself is that the victim and the perpetrator were compadres. It may be recalled that Lorenzo felt that no one would suspect him because of his fictive kinship tie to the dead man. A single tie of ritual kinship may vary in the weight it carries, depending on the situation and the people involved. But multiple ties of this sort to members of an individual's family or among a group of related families are far more important and constitute obligations that are difficult to evade. To break multiple ritual ties would imply that the person has no integrity and cannot be trusted by anybody. I witnessed how this works when Raúl beckoned me aside one night to have a private talk.

Raúl and I barely got along. He was a difficult person to talk to, and he had a brusque manner that sometimes seemed rude and overbearing. When slightly intoxicated he became somewhat aggressive, and although I had never had a run-in with him, I must admit that he frightened me. What was curious about Raúl was that although he and I apparently never would establish a bond of friendship, I was welcomed by all of his brothers. In fact, I was already ritual kin to many of the men and women in his extended family and to several of his friends. He called on me one night at 3:00 A.M. following the conclusion of the 4-day winter solstice ritual. I accompanied him silently through the cold, black forest when suddenly he halted on the trail. I was unsure how to interpret what was happening, but I began to feel decidedly uneasy. He turned, brought his face close to mine and in a respectful, barely audible voice asked me to become his compadre. I laughed inwardly at my fright, and with some relief assented to his request. He must have had it planned because his wife and children were ready in the shrine when we entered. The shaman performed the brief cleansing, we turned and addressed each other by our new ritual kin terms, and he and his wife invited me to eat with them on the next day.

Subsequently Raúl became very friendly and helpful to me. Only later did I realize that because I had so many ritual kinsmen among his family and friends it would have been almost impossible for me to refuse his request. This works in other ways as well. For example, if Raúl or one of his brothers wanted to borrow money from me I would have had to think twice before turning them down. A subtle pressure builds with the greater number of links one has with a defined group or faction in the village. To turn down the request of one compadre is to jeopardize a number of other relationships. However, the system works both ways, and ritual kinsmen must be careful not to make unreasonable demands for fear that they will threaten others in the network. All of this points to one of the major functions of the ritual kinship system. If used wisely, it can bind families into powerful coalitions that can influence or even control village political decisions. Individuals must evaluate the political situation in the village before making or accepting requests to enter into fictive kinship relations. This is particularly true due to the hierarchical nature of the links.

Two other uses of compadrazgo are important in Amatlán. The system is frequently used to form men into relatively stable work groups that usually surround a core of two to four brothers. Ritual kinship adds another reason for men to enter into the labor exchange agreements that are an essential part of slash-and-burn horticulture. The existence of a group of men that an individual farmer can count upon for help when he needs it provides an important sense of security. Men who build their houses in the compound of friends are almost always linked to them through ritual kinship. A second feature of compadrazgo is that it is used to link members of the village with outsiders. These can be Indians in other villages, including non-Nahuas, or mestizos in neighboring ranches or towns. Bonds that villagers establish with Indians in neighboring villages open up social horizons that would otherwise be difficult to penetrate. Such relationships provide an excuse for meeting people, a reason to be in an alien village, a potential source of marriage partners, and many other advantages. Links with local mestizos can likewise confer many benefits, not the least of which is to provide a likely source of wages during hard times. A rancher, in turn, likes to have Indian compadres because he can count on them to provide labor when he needs it. It is often the Indian who initiates such a relationship, and this places the rancher in a superordinate position. For this reason rancher–Indian ritual kinship often takes on a patron–client character (see Nutini and Bell 1980, and Nutini 1984 for exhaustive treatments of Nahua ritual kinship in the state of Tlaxcala).

POLITICS, KINSHIP, AND THE LAND QUESTION

Political affairs in a village setting can be exceedingly complex. One of the few clear patterns in Amatlán politics is that most conflicts develop over strategies to obtain more land. These struggles are linked to the kinship system in two ways. First the effort to acquire additional land is an effort to keep the extended family intact. Second, village political action takes place among factions that to a large extent form along kin lines.

The people most active in pressing for more land to open new fields are *vecinos*, villagers who are not certified ejido members and therefore who do not have a full share of land. These vecinos have the most to gain through radical political action, and the majority of them are young and energetic. As their numbers swell, they rally behind local leaders who promise relief. Some work through official channels and hire lawyers to present their cases before the agrarian commission. However, this is a long-term, formal process with many delays that often leads people to suspect that they are being swindled. This solicitation process is financed by payments made by each household to formal and informal leaders. The Comisariado is the official directly in charge of approaching authorities for more land, but this person is, of course, a certificado with land rights and nearly always a member of a more conservative faction that advocates following legal procedures. As discontent increases, other village leaders promise direct action, the most common form of which is the land invasion.

I spoke to many villagers about this process, and they told me that after several years of giving money to support solicitations, most villagers figure that they have paid for the right to occupy unused portions of neighboring cattle ranches. They begin by clearing and planting an area to test what the wealthy rancher's response will be. If the reaction is less than hostile, in the second year several families may actually build houses on the expropriated lands. By the end of the third year, enough people have moved to create a new village. This is the sequence of events that led to the creation of Amatlán's two most recent daughter villages. A few months after an initial violent reaction by the ranch owner, the people returned and again planted crops. These dramas occurred several years ago, and there has been as yet no reprisal by the landowner or his hired representatives. Neither village has succeeded in being recognized as an ejido, but because they have occupied the area for so long, people now expect that they will at least be left alone.

Fighting may break out between villages as well. In 1977, Amatlán authorities made a formal request to the agrarian authorities that an additional 2 hectares to be added to each household's allocation. Following the traditional strategy, when no response was received to this request, a faction of about 20 families simply created fields on neighboring ranch land and began to plant. Problems arose, this time not with the ranch owner but with the people of one of Amatlán's daughter villages. Hostilities broke out between the villages that resulted in the death of one man. It was this death that led to the arrest and near murder of Aurelio recounted in Chapter 2.

This daughter village was also in the process of expanding to accommodate a rising population, mostly the result of individual families moving in from other parts of the region. The former Amatlán occupants welcomed these newcomers because they felt that more people occupying an area would make it less likely that the entire settlement would be forced to move. Unfortunately, this village had no place to expand except in the direction of Amatlán. Two villages expanding illegally into the identical terrain was a formula for disaster. Three brothers, one of whom was Comisariado at the time, led other Amatlán families in asserting their own control over the land. They posted guards in the milpas and patrolled the area with drawn machetes. Because the breakaway village was considerably smaller than Amatlán, its members were forced to back down. In 1986, as I was leaving the village, the issue had apparently been settled in favor of Amatlán. The people from the daughter village had been driven off, and the

Comisariado from Amatlán had once again properly petitioned to have the additional land annexed to the village. No word had been received from the government, but the villagers were growing increasingly confident of a positive judgment with each passing year.

As we can see, even in a small village no one struggles alone. Individuals may die or be incarcerated, but village political process is about faction formation, and factions form around families that are almost always sets of brothers. Occasionally, politics will divide brothers, but this is relatively rare. More typically, battles are fought by brothers in order that they can remain together. The reach of the Nahua extended family is rather limited, and so ties of ritual kinship are called upon to bind additional members to each faction. In sum, it is the formation, dissolution, and realignment of village factions that are forged from family groups over issues of land acquisition that characterize the politics of Amatlán.

When I discussed these battles with the Nahuas, they told me that they have labored hard for land and corn, their metaphor for food. They have paid a price in blood and ceaseless struggle. But lacking central political authority, they have been unable to act in concert to secure their rights. The enemy is whoever is occupying needed land, whether he be Indian or mestizo. The Nahuas often comment upon their neighbors, the rich cattle ranchers, criticizing how much land they control. But they are often equally negative about neighboring Indian villages and the potential threat they represent. Villagers have a clear conception about being Indian in a mestizo world, but they do not identify the enemy as exclusively mestizo. Villagers have forged too many ties with mestizos, through ritual kinship, economic dependence, through the many relatives who live in cities and towns, and through the hopes of finding a place for their youngest children in mestizo society. The Nahuas of Amatlán are in a tremendous bind. To maintain themselves as Indians, they must insure access to the mestizo world. To organize as Indians would threaten that access and undermine their own cultural identity.

The brief sketch of Nahua social organization presented in this chapter serves to highlight the dependent position occupied by Indians in Mexico. The Amatlán council of elders, although still important in village decision making, has been superseded by ejido offices mandated by urban lawmakers. Both of these formal political structures, however, seem almost peripheral to faction formation and the struggle for land that are the true focus of village political activity. We have seen how the Nahua kinship system has been deformed by the subordinate status of villages like Amatlán relative to regional and national political and economic forces. Although Nahua kinship and family organization has proven itself in the face of severe stress, the pattern of obligations and expectations that guide interactions among kinsmen has become internally distorted. These distortions permeate all of Nahua social organization and can be observed not only in the domestic cycle, which places strains on new marriages, but also in village fissioning, which theatens to tear the Nahua family apart. As we have seen, Nahua women pay a heavy price for these pressures. They are the sisters, wives, and mothers who must depend on family members, husbands, and in-laws for their survival, and yet conflicting loyalties and competition over land marginalizes them from the support they require. In order to clarify more of the dynamics of life in Amatlán, we now turn to examine the local and regional economic factors that most influence villagers as they strive to benefit themselves and their families through a system that seems to work against them.

CHAPTER 5

AMATLÁN HOUSEHOLD ECONOMIC AND PRODUCTION ACTIVITIES

WITH the first four chapters serving as descriptive background, I will now outline major features of the Amatlán economy. As mentioned previously, each of the theoretical formulations presented in Chapter 1 suggests that village life is organized around economic principles that are distinct from those operating in the capitalist sector of the national economy. The theories sometimes contain unstated characterizations of village economies as being based on principles of reciprocity, cooperation, and an imperative to follow tradition, rather than upon strategic decision making aimed at increasing profit. Even Friedlander and Bartra, who claim that Indian culture has been virtually destroyed, base their conclusions on the assertion that Indians have been incorporated into the capitalist system and have therefore lost their distinctive cultural and economic identities. It is not possible for me to resolve in this study long-standing disputes within anthropology about the true nature of noncapitalist economies. My research findings in Amatlán, however, do not support the viewpoint that the Nahuas follow unconscious cultural prescriptions without the strategic choice-making that characterizes the way people supposedly operate in a capitalist market system. My findings suggest instead that the Nahuas, within their own sociocultural context, allocate their scarce resources toward alternative ends according to rational principles. Furthermore, I found that where the village economy articulates with the national capitalist sector, villagers are quite overt in their rational strategic planning (for a report of similar findings among Indians of Guatemala, see Tax 1972 [1953]).

When people in Amatlán chat with one another, the topics that interest them include local politics and gossip, but most of all, they enjoy discussing farming, inflation, and the best ways to beat the system. News travels fast about temporary job opportunities on neighboring ranches, and men enjoy endless conversation evaluating alternative crops or recalling examples of schemes by which other Indians

1. Houses of a patrilocal extended family clustered near the edge of a clearing (photo courtesty Paul Jean Provost).

2. A typical Nahua house in the village of Amatlán.

3. Small girls pose beside the schoolhouse.

4. Nahua boys waiting in front of the schoolhouse for class to begin.

5. A Nahua woman at home with her daughter works on embroidery.

6. An Amatlán woman poses for her photograph in a newly embroidered blouse.

7. Men from Amatlán resting in front of the municipal palace in Ixhuatlán de Madero on market day.

8. Men plant a field using dibble sticks. Note the absence of the traditional white clothing of the Indians in this photograph taken in 1986.

9. An Amatlán woman making a large pottery vessel for boiling corn.

10. A shaman sits before his house altar and cuts paper images in preparation for a curing ritual.

11. A Nahua shaman interprets the pattern of corn kernels during a divination ritual. Note the crystals, coins, and other items lined up on the embroidered cloth.

12. A shaman chants before a ritual offering to *tlaltetata* ("earth father" in Nahuatl). The earth spirit is represented by a small hole in the ground into which the shaman pours the food and drink at the conclusion of his chant.

13. A Nahua shaman divines by crystal gazing.

14. A typical altar set up by each household in Amatlán to observe *xantoloj* ("All Saints"). The lighted candles indicate that spirits of the dead are consuming the food that has been placed on the altar. Note the fruit- and flower-covered arch and the marigold petals on the floor forming the *xochiojtli* ("flower trail") that the dead spirits follow to find their way to the altar.

15. The *mecos* circle the food set out on benches before squatting down to eat. This procedure insures that the potentially dangerous underworld spirits the *mecos* represent will not return to the village.

16. An Amatlán man kneels and prays before an altar at the top of the sacred hill. The altar is constructed on the spot where the morning sun first strikes the ground in the village. Note the weathered adornments and paper figures.

17. Some of the dancers performing for *tlacatelilis*, the winter solstice ritual dedicated to *tonantsij*.

18. Nighttime altar for *tonantsij* during the celebration of *tlacatelilis*, when her image is brought to bless each house in the village. The shaman who presided at the ritual said that the two statues flanking the blue box containing *tonantsij* represent the spirit of work and his wife. Note the barely visible shaman in the foreground chanting before the altar.

19. Closeup of an altar dedicated to the corn spirits *chicomexochitl* ("7-flower") and *macuili xochitl* ("5-flower"). Paper images of 5-flower wearing cloth dresses are visible on the altar.

20. A shaman lays out an array of paper images of wind spirits and sacred herbs in preparation for a curing ritual.

21. In preparing an array of paper images and offerings, a shaman lights cigarettes that he will place in the mouths of malevolent underworld spirits. Note the small folded paper figures with the names written on them that he has laid on top of the blackened images. These smaller cuttings represent the spirits of gossiping neighbors whose behavior has caused the shaman's client to become ill. By folding the hands of the figures over their mouths, the shaman can prevent them from continuing to say bad things.

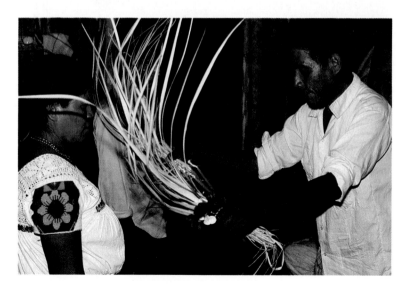

22. A village shaman brushes his patient with sacred palm brooms to rid her body of wind spirits.

23. Pamela and Michael helping to make adornments for an offering to the corn spirit.

24. The author assists a shaman in completing an offering to the earth spirit. After the beeswax candles are positioned, we spread food and drink on the green palm adornments that lie under the small altar table.

25. An adornment called *eloconetl* ("elote child") represents the corn spirit 7-flower. It is made from three ears of corn that have been tied together. The shaman told me that one ear is the spirit's backbone and the other two are its face. After being further adorned, the bundle will be placed on an altar to receive offerings. Following the ritual, the family will remove the bandana and keep the corn adornment on their home altar.

have become "rich." Many people even sought my advice about how they could increase their production or about the best times to sell their surplus. They quickly discovered that my expertise was useless in these areas, but it occurred to me that people who are supposed to adhere to rigid cultural rules would not evaluate economic strategies to such an extent. I do not mean to imply that the economizing behavior and world view of the Indians is identical to that of the capitalist ranchers or mestizo middlemen. Social and cultural factors still make each group distinct. In addition, Indians are nearly always at the bottom of the economic pyramid, and this fact certainly affects their strategic options. Because Indians occupy their own socioeconomic world and therefore have a different style of maximizing their options, Western analysts have tended to misread what they are doing. The success of Japanese economic enterprises in world competition should serve as a warning that the Euro-American model, such as that followed in capitalist urban Mexico, is not the only way to do business.

In Amatlán, men and women work for the benefit of the members of their individual households. In a majority of cases, the household is composed of a nuclear family. Even in the patrilocal extended-family households where a man cooperates with his brothers and parents and where he shares a common budget, he works toward establishing his own independent household. After moving to his own residence, he continues to cooperate with his siblings in the hard work of clearing, burning, planting, and weeding the fields, but he maintains a separate budget from members of the extended family. In addition, land rights are allocated and administered through individual household heads and not through extended families. Cooperation and sharing are certainly important aspects of life in Amatlán, but they are not the sole basis of the Nahua economy or productive activities. In fact, there can be fierce and disruptive competition among individuals and families. The basic units of production and consumption are at the household level. If we are to clarify how the Nahua economic system works both internally and in relation to regional and national forces, we must first determine how households are organized to produce and consume goods.

To understand how households operate in Amatlán, I gathered information during 1972 and 1973 on the weekly price fluctuations of the two major crops, corn and beans. I recorded the dates individual farmers planted their fields and the yields they obtained for both corn and beans. This task proved challenging because yields vary according to the number of consecutive years a field has been planted since the last fallowing. I cross-checked these figures against crop yields reported by the government for the southern Huasteca region and found that my values were within the same ranges. Meanwhile, I questioned individual household heads in detail about the quantities of corn and beans required to support the people and animals of a household. I was surprised to learn that, in most cases, animals consume as much precious corn as people. Finally, in consultation with many household heads, I determined how much cash a family needs to cover expenses for a year. These figures, combined with observations I made about the number of days the household head worked at wage labor, enabled me to determine an average Amatlán household budget.

THE HOUSEHOLD AND CONSUMPTION

Based on data collected in 1972–73, the 110 households in Amatlán can be divided into three broad levels of wealth. At the lowest end of the scale are the vecinos, households headed by individuals who do not have ownership rights in the ejido and that must eke out a living on 2½ hectares or less. Forty-nine, or about 44.5% of Amatlán households are vecinos. A majority of these share lands with a father or elder brother, a temporary arrangement in which extended-family members share poverty while waiting for more land to become available. Household heads in this category must spend a greater amount of time working in the mestizo world to support their families.

The second level of wealth, represented by 48 households (43.6%), is composed of the majority of residence groups that own rights in the ejido and thus farm 5 hectares (a decade later this amount would be increased to 7 hectares). Three households that belong to this group could be placed in the lowest wealth category. Two of these households have been impoverished by alcoholism, and the third is handicapped by a household head who is mentally deficient. I have placed these households in the middle level because, despite their current poverty, they have the resources to regain their prosperity. For example, as we were leaving the village in 1986, the mentally handicapped man's eldest son took over the household affairs, and it looked as if the family would soon be better off. At the upper end of this scale are the 13 households who own cattle (11.8% of village households). These are the wealthier members of the village, most of whom have managed to gain access to extra land (see below).

Romualdo Hernández reports that Nahuas divide fellow villagers into *tlen ijcotsa istocaj* (Nahuatl for "those who have nothing"), *tlen achi tlapijpiyaj* (Nahuatl for "those who make arrangements to live," literally "those who await or expect a little bit here and there"), and *tlen tlatojmihuianij* (Nahuatl for "the rich") (1982:24–25). This division of households fits very well with my findings in Amatlán. However, these distinctions should not be overplayed. Like many North American farmers who maintain seasonal or permanent jobs, all village households regardless of wealth must supplement their incomes by having one or more of their male members work for a period of time each year in the mestizo world.

In 1986, with fewer people in the village and more land available, I was curious to see if the proportions of households occupying the different levels of wealth had changed. Not surprisingly, considering the difficulty of accumulating sufficient resources, the same 13 households continued to be the sole cattle owners in the village (now representing 16% of total households). The percentage of vecino households had halved to about 25% of the total, reflecting out-migration and the formation of daughter villages. The number of households occupying the middle level stayed the same at 48, or just over 59% of the less-populous 1986 village. In sum, the number of households occupying the two highest levels of wealth stayed the same over the years, whereas the number of vecino households fluctuated significantly. I should add here that these levels of village wealth do not represent internal class differences. Households that are able to own cattle can do so basically because they are lucky enough to have access to a source of water or are enterprising enough to acquire use of additional suitable land. Cattle-owning households are not distinguished from other villagers by dress, education, consumption patterns, residence, or access to economic, political, or social resources. They have more wealth (stored in their stock), and they have certain interests in common with other cattle owners, such as preventing animals from destroying fellow villagers' milpas, but they do not appear to constitute a distinct socioeconomic stratum in the village.

Consumption patterns in Amatlán differ significantly from those of mestizo towns and cities and from patterns found in many developed nations. In the village, households exhibit a homogeneous level of consumption regardless of their wealth. Houses are similar in size and quality and, as described in Chapter 3, household furnishings are essentially identical for vecinos and for cattle-owning families alike. Such flattened consumption patterns have been observed by other anthropologists working among Nahuas (Chamoux 1981b:255ff.). Real differences in wealth do exist among households, but the Nahuas diverge from the mestizos in that these differences are less likely to be demonstrated in the goods they choose to buy and own. This fact allows me to generalize about consumption patterns in Amatlán without having to divide the village according to levels of wealth. And it is this tradition of flattened consumption that offers some villagers a distinct advantage over mestizos in their efforts toward increasing production and wealth.

Each man makes initial investments in durable goods that are essential for the successful running of the household. The greatest single expense of starting a household is the construction of the house itself. As mentioned, this enterprise may take many weeks and involves the labor of several men. In general, participants are paid for their labor in constructing a house even if the workers are brothers or ritual kinsmen of the builder. The practice of paying relatives for work is unusual, and I asked a number of people about it. I was informed that building a house is a relatively rare event in a man's life, and for this reason labor exchange, the preferred form of recompense, is not used. Too many years would likely pass before the helper might need the assistance of the man to whom he had lent his labor. Implicit here is the idea that labor is exchanged only for equivalent tasks. Thus, a man who helps build someone's house cannot expect that person to repay his labor by doing work in his fields, for instance. The going rate for day labor within the village in 1973 was $.80 U.S., one meal at noontime, and some cane alcohol at the end of the day. (Note: throughout the text all prices will be expressed in U. S. dollar equivalents for 1972–73).

The second largest investment in the Nahua household is the purchase of a mano and metate for grinding corn. These are bought at the market for about $5.60 and are said to last a lifetime. Just like houses, however, they must be replaced occasionally due to breakage or wear. All other durable items in the house, with the possible exception of pottery, are of secondary importance. Some villagers have come to rely on certain items such as metal buckets, metal hoe-blades, fencing wire for milpas, and several other manufactured items. However, many households do not have any of these industrially produced items, and villagers repeatedly told me that although they may be labor saving and technologically superior, they are not essential.

Once the household is established, there are a series of continuous expenses that must be met. The average household (based on the 1972 average of 5.3 occupants per household) consumes from 2 to 6 *cuartillos* of beans per month. One cuartillo is equivalent to 5 liters and weighs 4 kilograms or 8.8 lb. Thus monthly consumption of beans falls between about 18 and 53 lb. per household. Sufficient space must be allocated in the family's milpa to supply these needs, plus provide for a surplus if the household plans to sell beans at the market. More important is the daily consumption of corn. Members of an average household require about 95 kilograms of corn each month (a remarkable 209 lb. or 39.4 lb. per person per month). Added to this, the animals attached to each household consume close to 100 kilograms of corn during the same period. In sum, it takes just under 200 kilograms of corn to meet the monthly requirements of each household. On a yearly basis (including donations of grain for rituals, food exchange among ritual kinsmen, and other outlays) this amounts to about 2,400 kilograms of corn (about 5,280 lb). This figure does not include seed required for planting, which is saved from the previous harvest, or more often purchased in whole or in part at the market. (In a recent article, Stuart [1990] recommends that maximum per capita consumption of corn in Mesoamerican households should be estimated at about 450 grams based on dietary data (p. 138). My figure from Amatlán is significantly higher at about 578 grams per person per day. Part of the discrepancy is due to my inclusion of storage losses and nondietary uses of corn in the per capita consumption figure. In any event, the difference in the two figures does not undermine my point, which is that households in Amatlán require a substantial amount of corn each year.)

Although corn and beans are the most important food items in Amatlán, other vegetable and animal products play an essential part in consumption patterns. I have already mentioned the cultivation of garden plants. These are planted and harvested in small quantities for use by the individual household, much like we do in backyard gardens in the United States. Once the decision is made to grow a certain amount of a particular vegetable or condiment, there is almost no way of significantly varying the yields to meet contingencies. Gathering and fishing, on the other hand, do provide a degree of flexibility in consumption patterns. In fact, the only cost entailed in these two activities is in the actual amount of time spent on them or, perhaps in the case of fishing, in preparing the implements.

The household must also be able to acquire a series of semidurable items that may either be produced locally or imported via the market system from the industrial sector of the national economy. Locally produced items include pottery, beeswax candles, fishing nets and weirs, baskets, gourd containers and utensils, and other necessities.

Each household may have the capability to produce most of these goods but none produces all of them. Manufactured items include, for example, cloth, thread and needles, machetes, woven straw hats, palm sleeping mats, flashlights and batteries. Each of these consumption items has a limited life expectancy and generally must be replaced on a fairly regular basis. With few exceptions, those semidurables not produced in the household are purchased with cash.

There are also several additional costs entailed in the maintenance of a household. Each adult male is expected to "cooperate" (*cooperar* in Spanish) in the running of the school by paying certain mandatory assessments on an irregular basis throughout the year. This is in addition to his work on the faena (see Chapter 4) and costs the family between $4 and $8 per year. It is also sometimes necessary to send a representative (often the schoolmaster) to the state capital on ejido business. This and other expenses, such as the annual *finca rústica* ("rural farm" tax), must be paid for by the villagers. Whenever possible, village expenses are paid out of profits from the communal milpa that is worked by the faena. Expenses are always greater than income, however, and the difference must be made up by village household heads. In addition, most of the vecinos pay some money each year to cover lawyers' fees and the expenses of local representatives for their efforts to acquire more land. Failure to pay one's share in any but the last of these assessments would result in ostracism and the real possibility of being turned over to the authorities in Ixhuatlán. There, offenders face a possible jail sentence or a period of forced labor on some municipio project. Also each household must budget for recreation costs and for the purchase of personal items. These may include, for example, toys for children, gifts for ritual kinsmen, assessments for village dances, cane alcohol, soft drinks, candy, purchase of luxuries such as a portable radio, batteries, combs, perfume, jewelry, hair ribbons, saints' pictures, personal photographs, and many more small items. If inclined, a man may choose to sponsor a village ritual observance that would cost him anywhere from $4 to $50, depending on the importance of the occasion.

Finally, there are the numerous contingencies that any household might face throughout the year. These usually entail expenditures of money, and the household must maintain solvency to cover them. Probably the most common of these are the costs involved in curing disease. The Nahuas explain most disease by religious causes to be examined in the next chapter, and they first seek cures through the aid of local shamans. Curing rituals vary in size, and the cost can be substantial ($2 to $12 is the general range). If the shaman fails to effect a cure and if the ailment persists, patients may travel to Ixhuatlán or Colatlán to visit a Western-trained doctor as a last resort. The cost of Western medical care is much higher than local care, and often beyond the means of the average household.

After itemizing all of the expenses faced by a household throughout the year, I consulted with several household heads and asked them to estimate how much money is required to maintain their families. For a number of reasons they arrived at various figures. With the exception of a few essential items such as the machete, a household could probably survive with nearly no reliance on purchased goods. Thus, villagers were able to estimate that a relatively small amount of cash is actually required. However, in order to maintain the level of consumption outlined previously, it is clear that the household must participate in the money economy to a greater extent. There is clearly an operating base at which the household must maintain itself if it is to meet the cash outlay requirements demanded to achieve the standard of living visible throughout the village. Based on the costs of operating a household discussed above, including "cooperations," taxes, ongoing purchase of goods, and medical or other contingencies, I estimate that a cash level between $160 and $240 is required each year.

PRODUCTION STRATEGIES AND CONSTRAINTS

In order to provide food, other commodities, and money for their families, household heads must select among a number of production options available to them. All households are supported through a combination of farming, animal husbandry, and temporary wage labor. The mix of these productive activities varies from household to household, depending on choices made by the family.

Amatlán is located in an area where it is feasible to grow two crops in a single year. The rainy-season planting requires less growing time, is more reliable, and produces more than the dry-season planting. Every 2 to 4 years a field must be taken out of use and allowed to lie fallow for about twice the number of years it had been planted. After the first year of planting, the yield significantly decreases on an average plot of land due to heavy leaching of soil nutrients by rain and weed growth, and because of the generally poor quality of the soil to begin with. Thus, although each certified ejido member has use of 5 hectares of land, not all of that can be available for planting at the same time.

TABLE 5.1. Corn Productivity in Kilograms per Hectare (under moderate to optimum conditions)

	First Year	Second Year	Third Year
xopajmili (rainy season)	1,350–1,650	1,100–1,300	900–1,100
tonamili (dry season)	800–1,000	500–700	—

A significant portion is always in fallow, and of the milpas that have been planted in a given year, probably only one is on fully rested land.

In order for an individual villager to increase his level of wealth, he must increase his output of farm produce. Part-time and secondary occupations can never take the place of farming because of the extremely low local wage level. According to villagers I interviewed, crop production can be increased in three basic ways. First, a man can take greater care of each of his fields. Careful weeding, elimination of pests, and care of the individual plants can increase yields, although only within restricted limits. At some point, a man's investment in maintenance tasks exceeds the return he can expect in increased yields. Second, individuals can double-crop their fields. Although the dry-season yield is far below that of the rainy season, planting a field with two sequences of crops can add substantially to yearly production levels. This strategy is particularly effective in situations where there are land shortages, and virtually every man in Amatlán employs it at one time or another. One drawback to double-cropping is that it causes a rapid decline in soil quality and productivity. Table 5.1 gives the average yields of corn in kilograms per hectare in the village for 3 consecutive years of planting in the same field. These figures come from my observations of yields, and they reflect the range of output expected by villagers. The table demonstrates that dry-season production is considerably less than that achieved in the rainy season (compare with similar figures published by Sanders 1952–53:62). Villagers affirm repeatedly that only during the rainy season can they grow a significant surplus to be sold in the market.

The third means of increasing output is to increase the area under cultivation. This simple strategy is the best way to increase production in the long run. The first strategy—giving greater care to crops—always helps in increasing field efficiency but it cannot dramatically raise output. Although double-cropping as a strategy increases output in the short run, its benefits are reduced by accelerated exhaustion of the soil. Two factors make it difficult to increase the size and number of fields under cultivation, however. The first, as has been amply demonstrated, is that very little land is available. The ejido has little hope of expanding without attempting a dangerous land invasion.

A few villagers have been able to increase the land they control within the village by ways that they are usually unwilling to discuss. One example includes a widower who married a land-holding widow with the result that he effectively doubled his land base. Some men and boys have entered into agreements with widows or female heirs to farm their land in return for a percentage of the harvest. Rumors abound of men who have unofficially purchased the rights to land belonging to another. Although law forbids the transfer of ejido property in this way, it is virtually impossible to stop informal deals or to prove that the land has been sold. Other household heads have responded to the land crisis by entering into temporary agreements with cattle ranchers. The ranchers allow individual Indians to clear and plant unimproved land as long as the plot is returned in a year or two. This system gives the villagers some additional land to farm and clears previously unusable areas so that the ranchers can increase their pastures. No money is involved in his type of arrangement, but the opportunity to expand the land base in this manner is limited.

The second factor that makes it difficult to increase farm output undermines the whole strategy of acquiring more land. No villager has enough money to pay field hands on a regular basis, and so everyone relies on a labor exchange system called *matlanilistli* in Nahuatl and *mano vuelta* in Spanish. In this system a man exchanges labor on a one-for-one basis with his brothers, ritual kinsmen, and neighbors. The problem is that there is a fairly strict limit on the amount of labor that this system makes available. If a man arranges for 10 people to work in his field for only 3 days, he must spend 30 days working in their fields in return. Villagers agree that the area of land that can be cultivated using mano vuelta does not exceed a few hectares. Any man who manages to get access to more than this must begin to think of alternative ways for making the excess land productive.

Three related factors further constrain Nahua farmers in their attempts to increase their level of wealth. First, even if land and labor problems were overcome and a household head was able to produce a large harvest of corn or beans, there would be virtually no way to store the surplus. Villagers generally store crops inside their houses after the harvest, although some families build separate storage sheds, called *trojes* in Spanish. Dampness from the tropical climate destroys a portion of all stored produce. A more serious problem is the ubiquitous vermin that feed on corn and beans despite the best efforts to safeguard it. These pests include corn weevils, cockroaches, field mice, and rats. Under conditions obtaining in Amatlán, there is a continuous loss of any produce that is held in reserve. In addition to this problem, both corn and beans rapidly diminish in their ability to germinate under conditions of prolonged storage.

Losses entailed in storing harvested crops are related to a second factor that further constrains villagers. Amatlán is many kilometers from the nearest market town, and villagers have no means to transport large loads of produce. A few households own pack animals that they use for transport, but the majority of men must carry produce on their backs. They do this using a carrying basket and a tumpline that fits over the forehead. This ancient system of carrying is very efficient because it transfers the weight down the back to the legs and the man can walk standing nearly upright. I have seen men carry heavy loads over great distances without resting by using a carrying basket in this way, but the method of transport nevertheless severely restricts the amount of produce they can effectively deliver to market.

A third major constraint on Nahua productive strategies is the fact that Indians are basically cut off from the Mexican financial institutions that provide important services to non-Indian farmers. Banks, for example, could lend money and provide a place for secure savings, and there are indeed federal institutions that are supposed to help ejidos in this way. But the banks have little interest in farmers who operate on such a small scale and who live in such remote locations. Banking establishments prefer to deal with ejidos as a whole, lending money, for example, to buy communally held machinery or to finance community projects. However, the villagers control land individually, and they view themselves as independent farmers. They do not see the ejido as a communal endeavor. Thus, the villagers seldom band together to plan communal projects or try to borrow money for them. Also, villagers have an antipathy to dealing with banks and the feeling appears to be mutual. Indians are clearly marked by dress, motor habits, and speech, and these traits are disparaged by most mestizos. A majority of villagers lack the reading and arithmetical skills necessary to manage a bank account effectively, and they fear, possibly from previous experience, that the bank will steal their money or crops (see Reyes Martínez 1982:103–4,195–96 for a discussion of Nahua views of banks). Thus, the villagers are engaged in farming, which is always a risky endeavor, with no support from the financial institutions of urban Mexico. In comparison, most North American farmers would fail rapidly without federal, state, and private financial backing and the actual payments and subsidies that are a reality of modern agriculture.

In sum, the people of Amatlán, like people everywhere, are subject to factors that constrain their attempts to increase production and maximize their level of wealth. They are small farmers not because of custom or tradition but because they face difficulties in increasing the scale of their production. They face a land shortage that becomes ever more critical as the population increases. The technology available to them makes their farming highly labor-intensive. Labor exchange, which is necessary because of the generally low level of productivity and shortage of money in the village, has intrinsic limits because each individual's time and energy is limited. Even if it were possible to increase production, the problem of how to transport the surplus produce to market would then become critical. Increased production clearly exacerbates the problems of storage that are difficult to solve because of the unavailability of banking and farm cooperative services. Although it is not impossible to overcome these difficulties, it is rare for the villagers to do so. As mentioned, of the 110 households in Amatlán, only 13 have achieved the highest level of production that allows for the maintenance of small herds of cattle.

PRODUCTION PARADOXES

As a way of clarifying economic decision making in Amatlán I will focus on three paradoxes in Nahua productive activities. First, the Nahuas grow corn at the expense of seemingly more profitable crops. Beans bring a far higher price in the market, and it is possible to plant about three times more bean plants than corn on the same land. Why then do the villagers insist on planting corn? The second paradox is that individual farmers plant their crops at varying times throughout the planting season. Some plant early, whereas others wait until the last possible moment. Because seasonal change is marked, why do villagers fail to plant on a fixed schedule? The third paradox involves farm animals. Any villager will confirm that pigs and cattle are a tremendous expense, not only in the initial purchase price but also in their maintenance. Animals require vaccinations, tick baths, and pasture land that could otherwise be used to grow crops. Pigs are a particular burden because they live on corn and thus directly compete with people for food. The Nahuas almost never eat meat, and thus their investment in animals seems contrary to their economic interests. Why do the villagers raise farm animals?

These paradoxes seem to affirm the position that Indians simply follow traditions in their production activities even when these are contrary to their economic well-being. They grow corn, for instance, because it is traditional, even when other crops will apparently earn more money. They plant at varying times, perhaps responding to wavering individual motivation, even though crops that are planted in strict conjunction with the onset of the rainy season will likely produce greater yields. Finally, they invest in animals that not only do not enhance their diet but are clearly a drain on limited resources and a nuisance. Local village schoolmasters and government officials in Ixhuatlán with whom I have talked attribute much of the material poverty of the Indians to these and other seemingly irrational production practices. The schoolmaster in Amatlán tried for years to get villagers to plant more fields of beans so that they could take advantage of higher prices paid for the crop at regional markets. They refused to take his advice, saying that corn had never failed to support them. The attitude revealed in this response, coupled with the central place of corn in Indian myths and religious beliefs, has led some development experts as well as anthropologists to conclude that Indians grow corn for essentially mystical reasons. Some further claim that fundamentally irrational beliefs such as those surrounding corn are hindering economic development in Indian Mexico.

On the surface, the critics of corn appear correct. If villagers are economizing, it is indeed paradoxical that they should grow corn instead of beans. Although corn is a much more important part of the diet, it is also practically the sole crop grown as surplus to be sold at the market. The Indians do not measure land area by surface measure (a practice forced on them by government regulations and employed only in formal situations); rather, they use the much more meaningful measure of how many cuartillos (a 5-liter box) of corn can be planted on a given plot. In general, it takes about four cuartillos of corn to plant 1 hectare of surface area. Because the bean plant takes up less space, over 12 cuartillos of bean seed can be sown on a 1-hectare field. Thus, growing beans would appear to be a more efficient use of a field. In addition, prices paid for beans are uniformly higher than those paid for corn. Prices fluctuated in 1972–73 between $.16 and $.56 per cuartillo for corn and between $.40 and $1.20 per cuartillo for beans.

From the viewpoint of the individual farmer, however, growing beans entails a greater initial investment, involves a greater risk, and requires better storage facilities than does corn (see Reyes Martínez 1982:74,77). One problem with growing beans is that the plants are less productive than corn. On a first-year field, 1 kilogram of corn seed yields approximately 107 kilograms of produce whereas 1 kilogram of bean seed yields only 25 kilograms at harvest. Productivity figures reported from other regions are higher than for Amatlán, but the proportion of bean to corn yield is similar (compare Tax's figures [1972 (1953):52] from a more fertile region of Guatemala, and those of Chamoux 1981b:165–66 from the Sierra Norte de Puebla). Thus, although it is possible to plant three times the amount of beans than corn on a given unit of land, corn still produces more. A second problem is that beans are even more difficult to store in the tropical conditions of the region than corn. Beans are shelled right in the field using an ingenious device made from lashed-together sticks that works like a sieve to separate the beans from the shells. The shelled beans are carried back to the house in cloth sacks. In this state there is really no way to protect them from insects, mice, and damp conditions, and thus the beans rapidly deteriorate. Corn is also difficult to store, but it is far less fragile than beans. It is kept in the husk until ready for use or for sale in the market. The husk protects the cob to a certain extent, allowing for longer storage. But the most important factor that makes corn growing strategically better is the volatile price cycle of beans.

Figure 5.1 presents price graphs that will help to clarify why corn is so central to Nahua productive activities. The first graph shows variations in the price of corn in the region from July 1971 through June 1973. This graph shows that prices have risen greatly over the 2-year period. Prices in 1973 represent an average of about a twofold increase over prices in 1971. The rise can be attributed to inflation and lowered supplies due to a poor harvest in the 1972–73 growing season. This rate of inflation was much greater for manufactured goods during the same period, which supports the contentions of Stavenhagen and Warman that differential inflation serves to transfer wealth from the peasant to the industrial sector of the economy (see Chapter 1). Price data from the period also demonstrate that the relationship of prices from month to month is similar over the years.

I was curious to see what had happened to prices paid for commodities produced in the village during our return in 1985–86. In March 1986 corn was selling for about $.60, a rise of $.20 from the same month in 1973. This increase is significant but far less than the rise between 1971 and 1973. These figures show that the earlier steep rise in prices was due mainly to a temporary supply shortage and not to a long-term trend of price increases. I found that the monthly price cycle that existed in 1972–73 continued to operate in approximately the

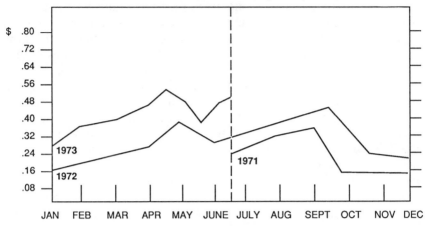

CORN PRICE GRAPH: U.S. DOLLARS (IN 1972) PER CUARTILLO

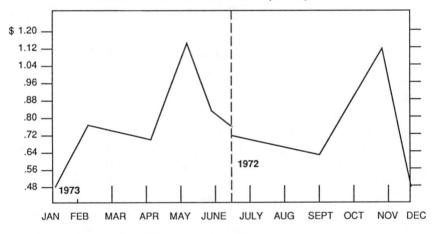

BEAN PRICE GRAPH: U.S. DOLLARS (IN 1972) PER CUARTILLO

5.1. Corn price graph and bean price graph

same proportions in 1985–86. The $.20 rise in the price paid for corn from 1973 to 1986, however, is paralleled by even greater price increases in manufactured goods during the same period. In 1973 a steel machete cost $1.10, but by 1986 the price had risen to about $3.20. Thus, although corn prices increased by half, the cost of a machete nearly tripled during the same period. By 1986 the full impact of the economic collapse of the Mexican economy was being felt throughout the country. The rate of inflation was high, and the economic situation was unstable. Prices in stores and markets had to be adjusted every few days to take into account the rapidly diminishing value of the peso. Unfortunately, the unsettled economic conditions of 1985–86 make fruitless any systematic comparison with the price information I have from the more stable 1972–73 period. We can safely conclude, however, that the more recent economic conditions and prices paid for farming commodities are even less favorable for the people of Amatlán than in the past.

The prices from 1972–73 clearly reflect the buying and selling that occur at different times in the region throughout the year. There is a rise in the price of a cuartillo of corn during January, February, and the first part of March as supply diminishes from the harvest. A rapid rise in prices occurs from about mid-March to mid-April as a result of increases in demand as the Indians in the region replenish their dwindling stocks of food and buy seed for the rainy-season planting. From mid-April to mid-June the price of corn falls as some of the dry season harvest comes in and increases supply. There is a steady increase in price from June to September as stocks dwindle from the dry season harvest, followed by a dramatic decline in September. This last dip is a result of the market being flooded with corn after the rainy-season harvest.

The price graph for beans presents a different picture. Prices are low in January and generally rise until February. During the months of February and March there is a slight decline, followed by a steep rise in the cost of a cuartillo of beans. In May there is a sharp decline followed by a second slight decline from June to early September. From mid-September there is another steep rise in prices followed by a month of rapid decline. The growing season for beans in Amatlán is September through December. We can assume then that the last peak on the graph is caused by the rise in demand as people buy fresh seed, followed by a fall in demand and rise in supplies as the crop is harvested. The first peak is harder to explain because neither Amatlán nor the surrounding villages plant many beans in the dry season.

However, market prices reflect the seasonal nature of crop production throughout the entire region. The first peak in prices therefore is most likely caused by a dry season planting of beans in a different part of the region of which Amatlán is a part.

The slight declines prior to the peaks are somewhat puzzling. Supplies are in fact diminishing over the whole southern Huasteca, and yet prices decline. One possible explanation is that professional speculators influence prices by moving in stores of beans from other regions of Mexico to take advantage of higher prices paid in northern Veracruz. Thus supplies increase at a greater rate than demand. An even more likely explanation is that demand for beans declines at a faster rate than does supply. Indians rarely buy beans for their own consumption because they rely on their own crop to sustain them. If they should run out of beans, the price prevents them from purchasing more. The more important place of corn in the diet, in addition to the higher volume of corn production and its low price, makes additional purchases both necessary and feasible if supplies run low. Thus, a higher overall demand schedule keeps corn prices basically on the rise throughout the year, whereas the secondary importance of beans contributes to a more extreme price cycle.

Examination of the price graphs reveals that the crucial periods for farmers are at planting and harvest times. Just after planting, the price of corn and beans is at its highest because of increased demand for seed. At harvest time the prices are the lowest as supplies increase. Corn peaks at $.56 per cuartillo, and since 4 cuartillos of seed are required to plant 1 hectare, a farmer pays a maximum of $2.24 for each hectare planted. Twelve cuartillos of bean seed are required to plant a single hectare, and the selling price reaches $1.20 per cuartillo. Thus, a single hectare planted in beans can cost $14.40 just for the seed. The initial investment required for beans, then, is significantly higher than for corn, and this is particularly important in a situation where very little cash is available.

At harvest time, prices per cuartillo fall to $.16 for corn and $.40 for beans. Since the villagers cannot store any quantity of harvested beans for more than a few weeks, they end up selling their crop at the $.40 level. Individuals stagger the planting of small quantities of beans and hold back some from the main harvest to keep the household supplied throughout the year. Despite these strategies, however, most families go without beans for several months each year. Corn is kept in reserve until a price of about $.28 is reached. At this point individual farmers throughout the region begin selling their harvest. Each man must

TABLE 5.2. Comparison of Earning Potentials of Corn and Beans

Corn	Beans
a. 1 kg seed yields 107 kg	a. 1 kg seed yields 25 kg
b. 1 cuartillo weighs 3.5 kg	b. 1 cuartillo weighs 4 kg
c. 1 cuartillo yields 375 kg	c. 1 cuartillo yields 100 kg
d. 4 cuartillos plants 1 ha	d. 12 cuartillos plants 1 ha
e. 1 ha produces 1,500 kg	e. 1 ha produces 1,200 kg
f. Sold at $.08 per kg	f. Sold at $.10 per kg
g. Gross earnings $120/ha	g. Gross earning $120/ha

compromise between waiting for a higher price and risking increased loss through deterioration in storage. Table 5.2 illustrates the production and potential profits for 1 hectare of corn and beans on a first-year field.

The figures in table 5.2, which are averaged and rounded to the nearest whole number, illustrate that despite greater planting densities and higher prices for beans, both corn and beans earn about the same market value per hectare. Planting beans, however, requires a higher initial investment than planting corn, and beans are more vulnerable to drought. Cultivating corn, with its greater chance of reaching maturity, entails less risk, making it the best overall value for village producers.

To the outside observer, the Indians' reliance on corn cultivation appears to reflect a deep commitment to traditional patterns of behavior. Corn, the crop with the lowest market value, is grown to such an extent that prices are kept low, and there can be actual shortages of other staples such as beans. From the perspective of the villagers, however, production activities operate under a variety of constraints that make corn overall the most economically viable crop. In the case of Amatlán where the per capita land base is diminishing due to population growth and where there exist serious impediments to increasing production, it is rational that farmers grow corn over other crops. Corn has the greater chance of providing adequate food for household consumption and a surplus for sale in the markets. This reaffirms the observation made by Warman (see Chapter 1) to the effect that as economic pressures increase, villagers respond by planting more corn. When small farmers have an abundance of land to work or have access to other resources, they will be more inclined to experiment with crops or take a variety of other risks. In short, corn is the "rational" crop in Amatlán, strictly from a materialist, economic perspective regardless of the cultural values attached to it. Much of the apparently conservative nature of Nahua society is due not to some innate traditionalism but rather to the lack of adequate resources upon which to increase production of other crops.

This brings us to the second paradox: why do individual farmers vary their planting times? One answer lies in the behavior of villagers in response to certain characteristics of the corn market that are revealed by examining the price graph. The price cycle is relatively constant from year to year, and people in the village monitor it carefully each week. Because the approximate growing time is known for all crops, villagers calculate their chances of bringing in a harvest either ahead or behind the price dips in the market. They plant early or late so that the crop will be ready to harvest when prices are still high. The date of the onset of the rainy season cannot be predicted precisely but can usually be estimated. If the seeds are put in too early, they will fail to germinate, but if they are planted too late, they could rot in the ground. Villagers risk seriously diminishing or even losing their crop by employing this strategy. Although the hardy variety of corn that they grow helps offset the risk entailed, most people vary planting time on only a portion of their crop. The advantages of harvesting early are great. For example, if a farmer were able to harvest the rainy-season planting just a few weeks early, he could nearly double the market value of his crop. Substantial but less spectacular gains could also be made by harvesting late.

As mentioned, prices of beans throughout the year respond sharply to the forces of supply and demand. Corn, on the other hand, exhibits a smoother transition in prices, reflecting more gradual changes in supply and demand. This difference is only partially due to the greater overall production of corn. The absence of extreme price fluctuations is caused, to a large extent, by individual farmers throughout the region varying their planting and harvesting times in order to play the market. Although supply levels still basically reflect the growing seasons, they are spread over a greater time span, thus giving the corn-price graph a smoother appearance. The strategy of varying planting schedules cannot be applied to bean production because, despite even greater fluctuation in prices, beans require such a narrow growing season.

As might be expected, not everyone engages in this particular strategy to the same degree. From my observations, those farmers with the greater resources are more likely to take the risks entailed in varying planting times than are those who are poorer. The point I want to make here, however, is that strategies of this sort, where risk and benefit are calculated and where people modify their behavior so as to take advantage of market conditions, are not to be expected where production is simply a matter of tradition, and the economy is simply an institution for provisioning members of society with little choice and decision making involved.

In a recent work, Sheldon Annis presents an analysis of milpa horticulture in a Cakchiquel Maya town in Guatemala. He concludes that there exists a special "milpa logic" employed by the Indians that is distinct from the market logic of capitalist commodity production. The milpa, according to Annis, "optimizes" family labor input to produce a large variety of crops in small quantities, used primarily in subsistence. Milpa logic protects against food shortages, but it does so by preventing capital accumulation and thus, in the end, it insures poverty. Although he found Cakchiquel families generally "to be shrewd and energetic in exploiting every shred of opportunity" (1987:31), including those deriving from milpa horticulture, he still concludes that milpa production is "antithetical to entrepreneurship" (1987:37). Commodity production for marketing, by contrast, "maximizes" output for profit. Annis sees the milpa as an embodiment of Indian technology that lies at the core of Indian ideology and identity (1987:39). In short, Annis reaffirms the distinction made between rational market production and precapitalist traditional production I noted in the work of the theorists discussed in Chapter 1.

In Amatlán, I found that people engage in milpa production both to provision their families and to create a surplus to sell in the market. I found no reason to divide the logic of the milpa from any of the other strategic planning engaged in by families. Villagers did not view milpa logic as qualitatively distinct from the logic used in cattle raising, owning a cantina, or producing and selling sugarloaf. As we have seen, decisions individuals make with regard to crop choice and time of planting are made with market factors clearly in mind. The same is true for the animal raising discussed below. Annis goes on to assert that widespread Protestant conversion among Indians of Guatemala is in large measure a reflection of antimilpa forces that herald the overthrow of Indian identity and the triumph of the market economy over Indian traditions. This connection between the milpa and Protestantism, however, is not borne out by the information from Amatlán. As we will see in Chapter 7, Protestantism has made inroads in Amatlán as well. I, too, find that Protestantism represents an alternative to traditional Indian identity. However, the converts continue to rely on milpa horticulture, and in no sense does conversion represent a recent penetration of market forces or market logic into the region.

One might suspect that the importance of corn in Nahua religious belief and myth imparts a cultural value to the crop that overrides strictly material economic considerations. It is certainly true that corn plays an important role in Nahua religious belief and that villagers see corn as a crucial aspect of their Indian identity. They use corn as a metaphor to distinguish themselves from non-Indians, as in the phrase "corn is our blood." Corn is the major component of their diet, and growing corn in a milpa is seen by them to be the quintessential Indian activity. However, villagers are perfectly willing to purchase corn for their needs or grow a small amount for their own use and purchase more if they require it. When I interviewed villagers about which cash crops they would like to grow if all constraints were removed, none mentioned corn (see Chapter 7). In short, corn is an important part of Nahua life, and both the plant and grain are sacred in their conception of the universe, but I did not detect such an emotional attachment to corn cultivation that farmers would plant it as their major crop regardless of economic consequences.

The raising of farm animals in Amatlán is the third paradox that seems to support the view that the villagers do not rationally calculate costs and benefits in their productive activities. Pigs are kept by most households despite the high cost of purchasing and maintaining them. Although they are allowed to roam freely and thus can find some food in the forest, pigs must be fed if they are to thrive. Consequently they are given a portion of the same corn supply that feeds household members and generates cash income at the market. An average household has one or two adult animals along with several immature ones, and they consume significant amounts of corn. Despite the expenses involved, pigs are almost never eaten. They are occasionally slaughtered as part of a ritual observance such as Day of the Dead, but in general pork plays a negligible role in the villagers' diet. Pigs present an additional potential disadvantage by being highly destructive to crops should they enter a milpa. Villagers are obliged to build and carefully maintain fences around their fields and to guard their stores against invasion.

Other animals that have importance in village production strategies are chickens, turkeys, and cattle. Chickens and turkeys are raised primarily for their eggs and only on rare occasions eaten. They are allowed to range freely but must be given corn each day to keep them healthy and to keep them from running off. Newly hatched chicks are sometimes taken to the market to be sold. They are sold for a few cents and raised to adulthood by the purchaser. On rare occasions villagers may sell a fully grown bird in the market. For the most part, however, these animals are part of the ongoing system of small-scale buying and selling that operates continuously within the village confines. One major rationale for purchasing chickens and turkeys is to use them as sacrificial animals in rituals. In almost all cases the birds will be eaten by the ritual participants following the offering. In any case, the villagers do not view raising chickens and turkeys as an effective way to earn a great deal of money. Besides the generally low value of adult birds there is constant attrition of the flock by predators such as coyotes, bobcats, and poisonous snakes.

Cattle raising is the elite production activity in Amatlán. Cattle require a reliable water supply, large amounts of land for pasturage during the rainy season, and additional land for growing fodder to sustain them during the dry season. Although cattle are never fed corn, the pastures needed to support them could alteratively be employed for growing crops. Some villagers pay to have their cattle graze on private ranch land, but the cost is prohibitive for all but a few. Cattle are never slaughtered for meat, and the Nahuas make no use whatsoever of dairy products. When I questioned them about this last fact, villagers told me that they do not like milk or cheese and that they would never consume these products. This aversion may be due simply to cultural preference, much like the aversion most North Americans have to eating insects. Nahuas may also share with many different peoples an inability to digest lactose, or milk sugar, as they reach adulthood. Many adults from different parts of the world show low levels of lactase, the enzyme that allows for the breakdown of lactose into products the body can use. I have no evidence that this is the case in Amatlán, but a few villagers told me that milk would make them sick, one sign of lactose intolerance. Members of a government medical team that came to Amatlán once informed me that dairy products in remote areas made from unpasteurized milk often contain bacteria that cause tuberculosis. This may be another reason why Nahuas avoid this food source.

Cattle are not used as work animals, nor is any systematic use made of their manure. Cattle raising is in effect a separate productive activity supported by farming. Because it in fact drains resources from farming and yet is not an efficient means of producing additional wealth, cattle raising is a productive strategy that appears to contradict rational economic behavior. Cattle are rarely bought and sold, although some money can be made by selling young animals that result from natural increase in the herd.

I asked villagers why they expend resources to raise animals when they so rarely sell them or use them as a source of meat. They seemed puzzled by the question and most gave ambiguous responses such as, "What else can we do?" The purpose of raising chickens and turkeys seems clear. The eggs are eaten, they are used for meat on ritual and nonritual occasions, and they are readily bought and sold, even though they earn only a small profit. The pigs and cattle, however, seem like poor investments, and I wondered if the villagers, by raising them, were simply mimicking neighboring mestizo farmers. Then one day, as I was sitting with a friend after dinner in his house smoking the cigars I had brought along as a gift, I observed an interaction that gave me a sudden insight into the problem of Nahua production strategies. My host, Herminio, and his wife were always very kind to me from the early days of my stay in the field. I knew them both fairly well, and they talked freely to each other in my presence. Herminio's wife, Ita, commented to him that weevils had gotten into the corn that was stacked high against the inside wall of their house. In fact, I could actually hear a kind of low, chewing noise coming from that side of the house, and Herminio told me that it was the sound of multitudes of insects eating the corn. As we were discussing the problem, Herminio idly commented to his wife that he would buy a baby pig at the market in two days. It suddenly occurred to me that the paradox of animal raising in Amatlán can be largely resolved if we look at animals not as a means of producing wealth but rather as a means of storing wealth.

In studying Otomí Indians of the Mezquital Valley, Kaja Finkler uses the phrase "living bank accounts" to describe the role of animals in the village where she lived (1969:55). One of her informants stated, "Animals are like having money in the bank. If I were to keep money, I would spend it, whereas if I have animals I have money but I don't spend it." She goes on to say that her informants told her they keep animals for the time when there is nothing to eat (1969:60; see also Tax 1972 [1953]:118–19). I contend that the role of animal husbandry in Amatlán is very similar. One of the major problems faced by villagers is that crop production is seasonal and there is no effective way to store crops or save money. What villagers would like to do is sell their crops and acquire more land with the money. But land is unavailable, and so as villagers manage to increase productivity they begin to look for a means of storing wealth. The common strategy, as revealed by Herminio, is to purchase baby pigs and raise them to maturity. Although pigs consume great quantities of corn, they do not represent a loss of wealth in the eyes of the villagers but rather a means of saving at least some of the value of the corn harvest that would be lost through attrition. Pigs can be sold whenever a need arises. Baby pigs are purchased for about $2, and an adult is sold for between $.32 and $.48 per kilogram. A mature pig of 100 kilos is thus valued at about $40, a substantial sum in Amatlán.

Chickens and turkeys can also provide a means to store wealth until it is needed. Although they produce far less meat than pigs, they have the advantage of consuming less corn. When there is a corn shortage anticipated—and disrupted weather patterns often serve as a warning of this potential disaster—households will increase their flocks by confining their brooding hens or turkeys under a basket in the house so that they will begin to nest. If no breeding animals are available, or if there is a time shortage, villagers buy baby chickens and turkeys at a cost of between $.08 and $.16 each. During these times of shortage, there may be as many as 20 chickens and 7 or 8 turkeys attached to the household. As the need arises, the additional birds are sold at the market. There is such an overall volume of chicken and turkey sales throughout the year that the price does not vary greatly. An adult rooster brings $2 to $2.40 (although the meat is considered tough), and an adult hen sells from $1.44 to $1.60. Adult male turkeys may bring $4.80, whereas an adult female sells for between $4 and $4.40.

If members of a household continue to increase production, and particularly if they manage to gain control of sufficient land, their strategy of storing wealth changes. As mentioned previously, there is a limit on the amount of land that an individual can bring under cultivation because of the *mano vuelta* labor-exchange system. Once an individual manages to acquire access to land that he cannot farm, it is a good strategy to clear the trees, create a pasture, and purchase a calf to raise. Cattle do not consume corn, and thus they have no value as a store of crop wealth, but they are an excellent way of producing wealth from land that cannot be brought under cultivation. A mature animal is worth from $240 to $400 in the southern Huasteca and can be sold at any time throughout the year. The average cattle owner in Amatlán has 5.3 head that could easily be worth $1,500, a very substantial sum in rural Mexico. One household possesses 16 head of cattle, a herd valued at over $4,000. Once cattle begin reproducing, they represent an additional small but potentially steady source of income. Calves are taken from the herd and sold at the market while still fairly young because herd size is strictly limited by land and water resources. Fully mature cattle are retained because of their reproductive ability and because a greater store of wealth can be kept in a mature herd. The basic reason for maintaining a cattle herd, however, is not the income generated by selling calves. Rather cattle are a means of using nonproductive land and as such represent the highest level of investment open to economically successful villagers.

THE HOUSEHOLD AND PRODUCTION

In order to determine how much corn each household produces, I relied on a number of measures. I estimated the weight of corn stacked in each house after harvest, calculated the sizes of fields using a pedometer, and asked individuals how many cuartillos they had planted. Finally, I consulted with a number of village men and asked them to predict harvest figures for different fields. I was surprised at how much agreement there was among the many estimates I recorded. Villagers state that a poor household, by which they meant a non-landholding vecino, plants about 4 cuartillos of maize in the rainy season. A middle-range household, a non-cattle-owning certified ejido member, plants about 8 cuartillos; and the cattle-owning household might plant twice that amount. Most men agreed that 15 or 16 cuartillos is the maximum that could be planted without paying helpers. Of course, determining productivity from these figures is difficult because the harvest from a given field varies according to the stage it is in the fallowing cycle. A further complication is the dry-season planting, which, although not as productive, also contributes to the household food supply. On average, each household plants approximately a 2-cuartillo dry-season corn crop primarily for domestic consumption.

According to villagers, productivity depends on four factors: rainfall, the overall quality of the land, the extent of fallow time previous to planting, and the care given to the growing plants. A farmer must be careful to organize the planting schedule to obtain maximum advantage from his fields, while simultaneously planning field use several years into the future. A common sequence followed by villagers is to plant about half of the rainy-season crop on a newly cleared field and the other half on a second- or third-year field. The dry-season planting is often planted on a second-year field. Following these procedures and providing adequate care of the growing plants produces for each household between 3,000 and 3,500 kilograms of corn per year. Since the average household uses about 2,400 kilograms to supply food for its members and animals, somewhere between 600 and 1,100 kilograms are surplus and may be sold at the market.

Villagers told me that when corn reaches about $.08 per kilogram (about $.28 per cuartillo), people begin to consider selling. At that rate, the household can expect to make between $48 and $88 from their crop. This does not mean that they unload all of their surplus at once, but rather that the rate of selling increases when the $.08 per kilogram threshold is reached. According to my observations, corn is sold to meet specific needs that may arise rather than to generate a large amount of cash all at once. Apparently the general strategy is to hold off buying some desired item until the selling price of corn is optimum, instead of accumulating cash in anticipation of future needs. From the viewpoint of the villagers, it is better to store wealth in the form of corn or animals rather than peso notes. Because prices are basically on the rise after bottoming out in December and because villagers delay selling their surplus for as long as possible, I suspect the earnings reported are probably on the low side.

Assuming that a household earns an average of $80 from the corn harvest, this would leave an $80 to $160 shortfall in meeting typical yearly expenses. To acquire this additional money, members of the household grow secondary crops to sell, market animals, or work at wage labor or secondary occupations. One productive activity that many villagers regard as ideal for supplementing household income, particularly when there is access to additional land, is making sugarloaf from cane grown in the milpa. Evidence from villagers indicates that sugarloaf production was more important in Amatlán in the past than it is today. Villagers report that the price paid for raw sugar plummeted in the mid 1960s, and this, coupled with the shortage of land and draft animals, accounts for the shift. Sugarcane takes more than a year to mature before it can be profitably harvested. It therefore ties up scarce land for several consecutive rainy- and dry-season plantings, and in addition the villagers say it exhausts the soil more than corn or beans. Even if land were available, however, an epidemic of equine encephalitis in the late 1960s so severely reduced the horse and mule population that it became difficult to borrow or purchase draft animals anywhere in the southern Huasteca. Without a horse or mule it is impossible to turn the press and process the cane for market. A slow but steady rise in sugar prices over the past few years has led about a dozen families in the village to resurrect sugarmaking as a supplement to their incomes. Perhaps in part because fewer people have been making sugar, the price of a *mancuerna* of sugar (Spanish for a pair of loaves wrapped together, weighing about a kilogram) has doubled, rising from around $.12 to $.24.

When in full production, three vats (called *pailas* in Spanish) can be processed in a 24-hour period. There are 56 *pilones* of finished sugarloaf in a *paila*, and 2 pilones are tied together to form 1 mancuerna. One day of work, therefore, produces about 84 mancuernas. After one continuous week of work only about 18 pailas are produced due to the need to cut more firewood and because the people must rest. Thus, after a week of arduous work, which is about the average time that a household spends on sugar making, the operation can turn out 500 mancueras of sugarloaf. Throughout the southern Huasteca, sugar is manufactured in late winter or early spring, which causes a drop in prices as the market is flooded with the product. By the end of March 1973, the price dropped down to $.16 per mancuera which is still high compared to the preepidemic prices of $.07 to $.08 for a mancuerna at the same time of the year. Thus it was possible for each of the half-dozen sugarmaking households in Amatlán to gross over $80 during the week.

All other crops account for a much less significant part of total productive activity. A family usually grows coffee, bananas, or chile, for example, in order to use land that would otherwise be wasted. Coffee is planted in small, isolated patches of land that are overgrown with tall, tropical hardwoods. The effort involved in cutting down the trees with machetes and making a milpa is so great that most villagers seek alternative ways of using such terrain. Small-scale coffee production in this setting is ideal because coffee bushes require shade, coffee is moderately productive in this region, and raw coffee beans bring a good price at market (approximately $.72 per cuartillo). Bananas are often planted in cane fields so that some income can be returned from land allocated to the long-maturing sugarcane. Bananas ripen at various times throughout the year, and the fruit can be sold at about $.01 per banana. Finally, chile is often planted on the margins of milpas or on other areas unsuited to corn cultivation. Small green chiles sell for about $.40/liter, whereas larger green or red chiles are priced at $.12/liter.

The family's remaining revenue is earned through the sale of animals. An estimated $40 a year is recovered from corn invested in pigs, in addition to any meat consumed by the household. All other animals combined may produce less than $12 in income. The sale of surplus beans may bring in $12 to $16 at most.

Wages from work as a day laborer on neighboring cattle ranches fills the majority of the remaining gap between income and expenditures. During the month of March, ranchers hire hundreds of field hands for two or three weeks at a time. Other than this brief period of continuous employment, most men work for only 1 or 2 days at a time and then do so only when a specific need arises, such as the purchase of medicine or a new machete. In all, villagers probably work about 30 days each year in this way, earning $1 per day. This brings an additional $28 to $32 into the household annually. Men complain bitterly about the low wages paid by wealthy ranchers for the grueling work of clearing tropical vegetation by hand. Work at this wage barely keeps the Indian household solvent, and it offers the villagers no alternative to milpa horticulture. Once again the contradictions and paradoxes of Indian status are revealed. Villagers require the wage labor to sustain their way of life and, at the same time, aspects of their way of life are made necessary by the unavailability of employment for decent wages.

We have seen that the mestizo sector of the Mexican economy has little incentive to invest in modernizing the agricultural practices of remote villages like Amatlán. Even though the productive activities of villagers have provided the capital for Mexican economic development, they are often seen as a deterrent to national development. The villagers themselves are caught in the contradictions that accompany their status as Indians. To maintain their identity, they must maintain their autonomy and do their best to escape direct domination by mestizos. In order to remain independent, they must continue to rely on a technology based on local resources and local knowledge. The Nahuas are very inclined to accept changes that they perceive will benefit them, but they are not generally willing to embrace these changes at the cost of their independence. As we will see in Chapter 7 villagers enjoy many concrete benefits by maintaining their identity as Indians, and they fight hard to keep from losing their traditions and being incorporated into the lowest levels of the national economy as anonymous mestizos.

The wealthier villagers could supply funds for technological improvements, thus sidestepping the problem of attracting mestizo capital. However, they are unlikely to do so. As we have seen, most technology such as machinery, fertilizers, or hybrid seeds results in a loss of village autonomy. Having a source of investment funds does not eliminate this problem. Moreover, the more prosperous villagers are succeeding to an extent in the system as it is and have little motivation to change it. For this reason it is the least successful villagers, the poorest households, who hold the greatest potential for change. In 1985, when I returned to Amatlán after an extended absence, I found that a few of the poorer households had indeed fomented a revolution. The revolution they created, however, was totally unexpected. Instead of transforming the economy, they altered the basis of their ethnic identity. This surprising turn is discussed in the concluding chapter.

DECISION MAKING IN AMATLÁN

What I have tried to identify in this chapter are the four major features of economic life in Amatlán. The first is that villagers must be able to generate cash income in order to meet the needs of the household. This means that they must grow crops for money and that they must depend on the mestizo-controlled sector of the national economy to supplement their incomes. The second feature is that even inhabitants of remote villages like Amatlán are largely dependent on economic and political forces that derive from the power centers of the nation. Indians work hard to avoid direct domination by mestizo elites, but in the end they can succeed only partially in extricating themselves from being ensnared in the lower reaches of the national socioeconomic hierarchy. In all cases power is wielded by non-Indians, and so the villagers' situation differs from that of most poor Mexicans only in that the power gap is exacerbated by a cultural gap. Third, I have tried to show that the village does not operate communally despite some appearances to the contrary. The household is the focus of consumption and production activity in Amatlán. Finally, like people everywhere, the people of Amatlán are compelled to economize. Villagers must make decisions on how to allocate their scarce means to satisfy diverse ends. They must make strategic decisions all the time, and they are fully aware that they are doing so.

There are three features of Nahua culture that give their participation in production and consumption activities a style that is distinct from that of most mestizos. The first is that consumption patterns are similar from household to household regardless of the unequal levels of household wealth. For the Nahuas, the purpose of wealth is to have a sense of security, or perhaps simply a degree of stability in a changing world. Wealth is not used to prove self-worth, nor is it paraded in any way to impress neighbors. Quite the opposite is true. Villagers feel that displays of wealth cause envy and that feelings of envy can cause disease to spread throughout the village (see Chapter 6). People do like to dress well and to display jewels or adornments and, more rarely, gold dental work, but they always dress within a fairly narrow range of fashion. Clothes that are new and clean are valued, but anything flashy or expensive is thought to invite envy. The same value applies as well to houses and possessions. An image of genteel poverty is the ideal presentation of self in Amatlán.

In fact, in some cases, the wealthier a villager is the more likely that he will make an effort to appear poor. Tomás used to visit me quite often during my research in 1972–73, but I really came to know him in 1986. He is pleasant enough, but he always is the most ragged person in the village. For a long time I attributed his dress to the fact that he drinks to excess, but I learned later that he owns half of a dozen head of cattle. Another friend, Juan, dresses in new Western clothing, wears a silver ring, and plays the guitar for rituals. He is a vecino and among the poorest people in the village. In this case and many others, quality of dress is actually inversely correlated with level of wealth. Demonstrating wealth can not only bring on dangerous feelings of envy, but it also makes one fair game for requests to borrow money. Ranulfo graduated from a teachers' training program, and he now teaches elementary-school children in a neighboring municipio. He once told me that he hates to visit Amatlán because everyone thinks he is rich and they always ask to borrow money from him. Rich people are expected to pay more for things such as village "coopera-tions," and they are expected to be very generous with all visitors.

Wealth invites trouble, and so it is in the interest of those who are better off to conceal their superior positions. This cultural feature has led some scholars to propose that Indians in Mexico have a strong attitude of "shared poverty" (e.g. Wolf 1957:2,5), or that they sub-scribe to an image of "limited good" (Foster 1967:122ff.). Wolf notes that, "In Mesoamerica, display of wealth is viewed with direct hostil-ity" (1957:5). He states that surplus wealth is redistributed within the village and that resignation to poverty is praised. This attitude of shared poverty siphons off surplus wealth and works against the pur-chase of new goods. George Foster holds that villagers in Mexico see a fixed amount of good in the world and that one individual's success is seen by others as reducing their own chances to derive benefits for themselves. Thus, villagers exhibit hostile feelings toward wealthy individuals and assume that those who are better off must have gained their property through dishonesty. This image of the limited good, according to Foster, stymies wealth accumulation and, ultimately, economic development.

These viewpoints only partially describe the situation in Amatlán. Although all villagers identified themselves as poor people, and I did find some jealousy among individuals, I found no evidence that these attitudes contributed to village poverty. Feelings of envy or shared poverty apparently do not stop people from striving to enter the level of wealthier, cattle-raising families in the village; nor others like Julio, described in Chapter 2, from opening up a cantina and becoming a merchant in the market. Generosity is valued and the rich are expected to pay more, but mechanisms for internal redistribution of surplus wealth do not destroy differences in wealth among village families. Despite the fact that everyone knows who is actually wealthy and who is not, the point seems to be to avoid behavior that places one person above another. A cherished value for the Nahuas is a sense of equality and community, and these traits would be destroyed in their view by the show of arrogance and hierarchy that would result if the rich paraded their wealth. In short, villagers strive for economic success, but they are careful not to flaunt it.

I do not wish to exaggerate this egalitarian value nor its effect on people's behavior. Individuals do own items that set them apart from others. A few men have purchased corrugated tarpaper roofing material for their houses. Others have work animals for turning the sugarcane press or for transporting crops to the market. Some households have transistor radios, and I noticed in 1986 that a few people had purchased crank grinders for the first and most difficult step in preparing corn-meal. Small differences do exist among households in quantity and quality of possessions, but the important point is that these differences are not of the same magnitude as the actual differences in wealth in the village.

The second Nahua cultural feature is related to the first. When villagers talk about mestizos, the characteristic they most disparage is how aggressive and hierarchical they are. Many mestizos do indeed look down upon the Indians and do not seem to realize how much the Indians resent it. When villagers leave to work for a while on a local ranch or in a more distant city, they frequently return with stories of how they had to quit because the boss (*patrón* in Spanish) was so bad. In fact, the villagers are generally good employees who are willing to work very hard for what appears to be minimal compensation. And yet I have talked to many local mestizo ranchers who told me that the Indians are lazy and not to be trusted. Part of the cause of this problem of perception is the different attitude villagers have toward work (discussed below), and the fact that villagers resent the way mestizos set up the work situation. Although there are many reasons why Indians leave jobs, the one they talk about most frequently is that they hate working for a boss. The mestizo workplace for them is a contradiction of the democratic and egalitarian values of village life. Of equal importance, villagers resent being dependent on outsiders for their livelihood.

The third feature of Nahua culture that affects their production and consumption activities is more difficult to characterize. It is manifest in an approach to work and an attitude toward time that differs somewhat from that of mestizo Mexico (see Chamoux 1986). The people of Amatlán are task oriented in that they work diligently to finish what needs to be done. They attack and complete projects that appear to the outsider to require almost superhuman endurance. Clearing thick tropical brush in the humidity and scorching heat, or carrying loads of firewood or corn for great distances over steep and broken trails, are two minor examples of the hard work they do without complaint. But for them the purpose of work is to accomplish tasks, and it is not particularly valuable in itself. Although villagers take pride in the work they do, they do not feel lost or empty if, after a task is completed, no further work presents itself. This approach to labor works fine if a person is hired by a local rancher on a temporary basis to complete a specific task. It does not lead to success, however, for more permanent positions where long-term, consistent work for its own sake is required.

Differing concepts of time are another element of incompatibility between mestizo entrepreneurs and villagers. The villagers tend to take the long view of things compared with most Westerners. Like the growing seasons, things unfold in a measured way, and the people of Amatlán have a high tolerance for periods of waiting. Patience is not a virtue for them; it is a way of life. When returning to the village for more research, it always takes me several days to slow down my pace so that it is compatible with theirs. One of the big shocks at returning to the United States after a long stay in the village is how quickly everyone appears to talk and move. People on a city street appear almost comical, like figures gesticulating in a film that has been speeded up. Most American tourists comment on the slower pace of life in Mexican cities, but even the cities are fast-paced compared to life in the villages. This different perception of time sometimes causes problems for Indians in the mestizo workplace.

Individual men may go to the city or surrounding ranches and work on a contractual basis for several months at a time. From the point of view of the employer, the man holds a permanent job and has a responsibility to continue working. The villager, on the other hand, has a long-term plan to return to the village and continue farming. When the time comes to leave, the villager, who always thought that the job was temporary, just quits. The employer is reaffirmed in his judgment that Indians cannot be trusted and that they are too lazy or lack motivation to work. From the point of view of the villager, 3 or 4 months is more than enough time to spend on a job, and the employer is unreasonable in his expectation that it be longer. Additional problems arise over deadlines of any type, the imposition of strict work schedules according to the clock or even days of the week, timetables for beginning and ending work, or any requirement in which timing takes priority over the work itself. From the villagers' perspective, the employers are simply trying to force their will on the workers, and they are usually glad to leave when the time comes.

Some villagers leave Amatlán for good, of course, and they adapt quite well to the alien conditions in the work world. For them, working in the city is no longer a strategy for supplementing farm income but is an end in itself. Changes required for life on the job mean adopting mestizo traits and leaving the traditional culture behind. The villagers know this, and a number are willing to make the changes for the greater opportunities present in the city. Many who leave do so because they have been cut off from land and they have no chance of living a normal life in the village. A few return from the city complaining about air pollution, traffic, and the unpleasant features of urban living. Some of these returnees even become vecinos and begin the long wait for the opportunity to obtain land. Most who make up their minds to leave, however, never come back. Both Indians and mestizos must plan, economize, and work in order to maintain their lives. At the same time, each occupies a different world and, as will be seen in the next chapter, nowhere is that more evident than in the realm of religion.

CHAPTER 6

RELIGION AND THE NAHUA UNIVERSE

XOCHIKOSKATL

Nijkuikatia nititlachixtokej,
nikinkuikatia noikniuaj iuan tlalti-
    paktli,
tonana tlatipaktli;
pampa tlachialistli keuak xochitl
uan keuak kuikatl: xochitl uan
    kuikatl

Nochi santipanoj,
nochi titlakajteuasej;
yeka moneki matitlatlepanitakaj,
yeka moneki matitekitikaj;
yeka moneki matijtlalanakaj,
matijmaluikaj uan matikajokuikaj
tlen ika titlachixtokej:
xochitl uan kuikatl.

NECKLACE OF FLOWERS

I sing to life, to man
and to nature, the mother earth;
because life is flower and it is song,
it is in the end: flower and song.

We are all transient,
all of us will go;
for this reason we must respect,
for this reason we must work;
for this reason we must gather,
respect and conserve
the things of life:
the flower and the song.

By José Antonio Xokoyotsij, pseudonym of Natalio Hernández Hernández,
a Nahua born in the municipio of Ixhuatlán de Madero (1986:45,97).

NAHUA religion creates a universe that differs so fundamentally from that of the mestizos that it creates a community set apart from the national culture. Understanding that universe has proven to be extraordinarily difficult. Nahua myths and rituals are firmly rooted in the pre-Hispanic past, and I have found them to be richly complex and thickly overlaid with levels of meaning. As I mentioned in Chapter 1, for my initial field project in Amatlán I investigated the implications of religious belief and the ritual cycle for the yearly rounds of planting, harvesting, and collecting. I found that information on how the village fit into the regional ecological system was much easier to obtain than data on the people's religion. I had to return again and again to

Amatlán, always with new questions, before I began to understand
how the Nahuas see the world and how radically different their perspective is from that of the mestizos and my own Euro-American world
view (see Mönnich 1976 for a discussion of pre-Hispanic survivals in
Huastecan Nahua religion; see also Martínez 1960).

F rederick Starr (1901,1978 [1908]) was probably the first anthropologist to enter the southern Huasteca and neighboring Sierra Norte de
Puebla. While leading an expedition in 1900, he discovered that
Otomís in the village of San Pablito, in the state of Puebla, continued
the pre-Hispanic practice of making paper by hand from the inner
bark of various species of the fig tree. He also discovered that, just as
in pre-Hispanic times, paper was an important element in religious
rituals. Starr published his findings and stimulated other researchers
to enter the region in search of papermaking and the religious practices
associated with it. After World War I, Nicolás León, a professor in
the National Museum of Archaeology, History, and Ethnography in
Mexico discovered that Nahua Indians in what is now Ixhuatlán de
Madero also made paper and used it in rituals (1924:103). During
World War II, an independent researcher named Hans Lenz entered
the region on horseback and conducted a search for villages where
papermaking had survived. He wrote a few years later that "it is
dangerous to penetrate the sierra de Ixhuatlán beyond a certain point.
This is particularly true if the object of the trip is to gather information
on the pagano-Christian customs of the Indians who live there or to
collect samples of paper they cut for their offerings and witchcraft"
(1973[1948]:139).

From the very beginning, then, we get hints of a mysterious religion
that has survived in the remote reaches of the southern Huasteca and
Sierra Norte de Puebla. In the 1930s, French ethnographer Robert
Gessain and his wife tried to learn more about the paper rituals among
nearby Tepehua Indians. Within a few weeks of their arrival, they
were apparently poisoned by the Indians and were forced to leave the
field. They did manage, however, to collect a small sample of the
sacred paper images used in rituals and published photographs of them
along with a list of Tepehua rituals (1938, 1952–53). An anthropological
reconnaisance in 1955 by Alfonso Medellín Zenil provided tantalizing
glimpses of traditional culture, including religious practices in the
vicinity of Amatlán (1979, 1982). No outsider was able to find out much
about the paper cult religion until Mexican anthropologist Roberto
Williams García spent several weeks in Ichcacuatitla, a Nahua village
less than 30 kilometers from Amatlán. Beginning in the mid-1950s and

continuing to the mid-1960s, he wrote a number of articles on the religion of Ichcacuatitla, but other than mentioning paper images cut by shamans, he was strangely silent on how paper was used by these Nahuas (1955, 1957, 1966a). It is clear that in the short time he was there the Indians did not show him the closely guarded core features of the traditional rituals. In the meantime, other researchers were making some progress in understanding religious practices among the neighboring papermaking Indians, namely the Otomís (Christensen 1942, 1952–53; Christensen and Martí, 1971; Lenz 1973[1948], 1984; Dow 1974, 1975, 1982, 1984, 1986a, 1986b; Galinier 1976a, 1976b, 1979a, 1979b), Totonacs (Ichon 1969), and the Tepehuas (Williams García 1963, 1966b, 1967, 1972). My excitement at having the shaman Reveriano show me his sacred paper cutouts on that cold December evening in 1972 is understandable, given the difficulty researchers have had in obtaining information on the paper cult religion.

I have mentioned that the Indians consciously avoid revealing anything about their religion to outsiders and that they do so in a typically Nahua way. Should a schoolmaster happen upon a ritual, no attempt would be made to cover up the proceedings or eject the unwanted visitor. The people hide ritual activity passively, simply by never revealing where or when a given ritual is held. The thick forest and dispersed village pattern make it easy to conceal ceremonial occasions of any size. One schoolmaster I met, who was generally sympathetic to the Indians and had worked in villages for almost 30 years, had never seen a sacred paper cutting nor witnessed a ritual. So effective is their method of concealment that I had spent almost 5 months in Amatlán before I was aware that there was any ritual activity in the village. I was beginning to wonder whether I had perhaps discovered the first human group without rituals or religion.

There are two major reasons why the Nahuas conceal religious activity. One is historical and derives from the active persecution of Native American religions by European Christians. Sixteenth-century Spanish Catholicism was particularly intolerant of other belief systems, and the Church instituted the Inquisition to assure conformity to its teachings. Many practitioners of the traditional religion were killed by the Spaniards. Interestingly, shortly after the Conquest the Spaniards issued a decree specifying jailing, whipping, and public shearing for baptized Indians caught offering paper at religious sacrifices, so important was this substance to the practice of native religion (Lenz 1984:359). With this level of persecution and given the fact that missionaries moved into the southern Huasteca in the 1520s, it is no wonder that the paper cult religion continues to be practiced with discretion. Active suppression has now ceased, but an occasional itinerant priest will rant at villagers for continuing what he considers to be their pagan beliefs.

A second, and more immediate reason to hide rituals is that participation in religious rites is one of the most important means that people have of affirming their allegiance to the Indian world. Mestizos may speak an Indian language, but they never participate actively in the traditional rituals that give definition to the Indian world view. These rituals offer a means for people to demonstrate their commitment to that which is Indian, and they are therefore held out of the gaze of disapproving mestizos.

The desire on the part of the villagers to keep their rituals and religious beliefs to themselves put me as an anthropologist in an ethical bind. I had a scientific responsibility to document this fascinating religion, and yet I felt my primary obligation was to the people of Amatlán. I could have changed the topic of my research, but I decided to continue to ask about religion until people indicated that my questions were out of bounds. At first, some individuals, and in particular the shamans, wanted to know why I was so interested in the rituals. A few asked if I was planning to make money at their expense. I assured them that I was motivated by sincere interest and that if I wanted to make money there were many far easier ways of doing so. Building confidence and trust was to be a long and difficult process, but I was willing to invest my time and energy in attempting it. Questions I posed were gently evaded with a typical Nahua dodge, "Go ask the shaman." Shamans were either too busy to answer, or they professed ignorance. Only after many months in which I spent literally hundreds of hours first observing rituals and then, little by little, participating in them, did the barriers begin to crumble. People came to know that I was, at worst, a neutral observer and basically harmless. I made many friends who took upon themselves the responsibility of helping me understand the profundities of their religion. As I learned more I became increasingly impressed with the beauty and sophistication of Nahua thought.

In 1975 I mailed a copy of my doctoral dissertation to the schoolmaster in Amatlán, knowing that he would show it to the villagers. Although written in English, it contained many diagrams and drawings and was filled with Nahuatl words. I returned to the village later that same year with a mild feeling of apprehension at what my reception would be after this. To my pleasure, the villagers responded very positively. They told me that they were very happy to have a "book" written about their village. They said that they now realize what I was doing and they wanted to help further in the project. In 1985 members of the council of elders arranged for interviews with shamans, and the Agente Municipal organized a meeting of old people to discuss village history. I was given carte blanche to collect sacred paper cuttings and to take them back to the United States in order to show Americans what they looked like. Most important, villagers made it their responsibility to inform me of each and every ritual event both in Amatlán and in the surrounding area. I became such a fixture at rituals that people would come to summon me if I ever failed to appear.

RITUAL SPECIALISTS

Nahua ritual specialists are men and women who devote their energies to mastering esoteric religious teachings and complex ritual procedures. I will call these ritual specialists "shamans," a term often used by anthropologists to refer to part-time magico–religious specialists who divine the future, heal the sick, and intervene with spirits for the benefit of their clients. In Nahuatl, a shaman is called *tlamátiquetl*, which means "person of knowledge." The major activity of the shaman is to conduct curing rituals, and so he or she is also called *pajchijquetl* or *tepajtijquetl* in Nahuatl or *curandero* in Spanish, terms meaning "curer." A shaman's techniques include divining the cause of disease or foretelling impending events, and so they are sometimes called by the terms *tlachixquetl* in Nahuatl (literally "one who waits, sees, expects something) or *adivino* in Spanish, meaning "diviner." The role of shaman is open to anyone, although very few complete the apprenticeship and still fewer are able to attract and maintain a clientele by compiling a record of successful cures. In the years I spent in Amatlán, the number of active shamans at any one time ranged from four to six.

I have talked extensively with a number of Nahua shamans, and they all recount a similar story of how they came to their profession (see Reyes Antonio 1982:146–51 for a description of how people become shamans in another Nahua village of the region). One sign that curing is one's "destiny" (in Nahuatl, one's *tonali*) is to experience a miraculous cure from a chronic disease. Another sign is a repeated dream involving ritual themes, encounters with spirits, or curing experiences (see Hernández Cuellar 1982:41ff. for additional signs of the power to cure among neighboring Nahuas). These dreams must be interpreted by an established shaman who, after a divination ritual, may recommend that the person undergo training. If a person does have curing powers and yet elects not to undergo the appenticeship, he or she may bring disease and eventual death onto themselves. Thus, to hear the shamans tell it, there is not a great deal of choice in the matter. Some people show little aptitude for becoming a shaman, and others carefully avoid the possibility. Shamans must handle dangerous spirits, and they must orchestrate powerful rituals, and so a masterful personality is required. A more immediate problem is that shamans are sometimes accused of practicing sorcery. Since my first visit to Amatlán, two male shamans have been found murdered shortly after such accusations. The murders occurred far from the village, and people from neighboring communities are suspected of both deeds.

Once a person decides to become a shaman, he or she enters into an apprenticeship with an established master of the art. Apprentices usually initiate their training by making a gift to the prospective mentor, and they continue to offer small gifts of food throughout the training period. The master shaman holds a ritual at the peak of a sacred hill in which the acolyte undergoes a cleansing and is inducted as an assistant. The student accompanies the shaman to rituals and assists, at first in little ways and later by taking over whole sections of the ritual performance. The master imparts his or her knowledge in measured steps, and over many years the assistant picks up the necessary knowledge and techniques to establish an independent practice. Assistants must learn to construct elaborate altars, cut dozens or even hundreds of sacred paper images of various spirits, make appropriate offerings to spirits, memorize long chants, and master various techniques for divination. The training is rigorous and requires tremendous effort and motivation on the part of the student. Shamans agree that the period of training requires between 6 and 7 years. When the shaman perceives that the student has sufficient knowledge to carry on independently, he or she performs an all-night ritual to inform the ancestor spirits of the new practitioner (see Hernández Cuellar 1982:48ff. for a description of this ritual among neighboring Nahuas). During the training period, students have opportunities to prove themselves as effective curers and diviners, and they begin to attract a following of clients. Shamans are paid for their services, and the most successful among them can earn enough to purchase livestock.

Because shamans are the most significant of the ritual specialists among the Nahuas (a group that includes midwives, bonesetters and prayer leaders, for example), I will mention something about their personalities and place in the community. Both male and female shamans possess compelling personalites that are generally marginal to those of the other villagers. One specialist refuses to drink *aguardiente*, even though it is almost a requirement that shamans be intoxicated during rituals. Another sits alone in the corner during gatherings and chortles and talks to himself. Two shamans I have known were reputed to have murdered other men, accusations that are probably not true but that neither took pains to deny. One of the female shamans operating in Amatlán is thought to engage in acts of sorcery for money. Shamans are charismatic people with an air of danger around them. Although they are not exactly avoided by the others, few villagers go out of their way to associate with them. Villagers regard shamans with some antipathy, but they also regard them as valued members of the community whose esoteric knowledge is in some sense the heart of what it is to be a Nahua. It is the shamans who know the myths and rituals, and they are generally respected as warriors in a life-and-death struggle against disease and disorder (see Dow 1986a for a detailed account of the work of an Otomí shaman from the neighboring Sierra Norte de Puebla region).

DIVINATION

Shamans are expected to possess a gift for seeing into the future and diagnosing the hidden causes of clients' problems or ailments. Several methods of divination have been reported for the southern Huasteca, including crystal gazing, casting grains of corn and reading the resulting pattern, interpreting the way grains of corn float in water, and interpreting patterns in incense smoke. I personally witnessed only the first two methods. Each shaman possesses one or more prized quartz crystals that form an essential component of his or her ritual paraphernalia. These are called mirrors (sing. *tescatl* in Nahuatl), and shamans are able to divine by interpreting the faint patterns inside the body of the crystal. The shaman usually interviews the client and then gazes into the crystal while holding a lighted candle behind it.

To divine by casting grains of corn, the shaman lays out a white embroidered cloth on an overturned cuartillo box. This procedure usually takes place on the floor before the shaman's house altar. After smoothing the cloth, the diviner positions piles of coins, crystals, and any other small objects believed to have a sacred association. One shaman lays out two small copper "axes" probably of pre-Hispanic origin, which she said were dropped by the sacred rain dwarfs. Another uses a small pre-Hispanic face carved from green stone. After placing these items along the edge of the cloth, the shaman picks up fourteen grains of corn and holds them in incense smoke. He then chants, asking the sacred hill spirits to guide him. Next, he casts the grains onto the cloth and interprets where they fall. See Figure 6.1 for an illustration of the preliminary layout of divination items and some examples of how the grains are interpreted.

Through divination, shamans are able to specify which spirit is causing problems for a client. Often it is a normally salutary spirit that is feeling neglected or that has been inadvertently offended. Occasionally the soul of a dead kinsman requires ritual attention. The shaman may identify envious neighbors, an angered house spirit, or a sorcerer (a person who uses esoteric ritual knowledge to harm others) as the cause of the trouble. Once the cause has been identified, the shaman can prescribe the type of ritual required to satisfy the offended spirit or counteract the bad intentions of others. Often divination reveals the specific sacred hill where an offering should be made. Clients also ask shamans to foretell the outcome of events or predict, for example, whether a long-absent relative will return home for an upcoming villagewide ritual. The ability to divine accurately is at the heart of the shaman's struggle against discord and suffering. Divination provides the key information that allows the restoration of harmony in the human domain.

ASPECTS OF NAHUA COSMOLOGY

The Nahuas in general, and the shamans in particular, are not very articulate about the philosophical underpinnings of their religion. They communicate with each other through the medium of myth and ritual, through concrete examples in which the basic principles are repeatedly worked out and expressed in religious performance. Nahuas consider direct questions rude in any context and particularly inappropriate in matters connected to religion. This means that as an outsider I was forced to base conclusions on inferences drawn from myths, observations of rituals, and what few interpretations I could elicit from shamans and lay people. My questions were often met with disbelief, and the villagers never seemed to appreciate how profoundly ignorant I was of their world when I began the research. To the Nahuas it is absolutely self-evident that rain comes from caves, human beings have two souls, one of which is subdivided into seven segments, and that Jesus Christ is a manifestation of the sun (see Sandstrom 1975, 1978, 1982, 1983, 1985, 1986, 1989; Provost and Sandstrom 1977; Sandstrom and Provost 1979; Sandstrom and Sandstrom 1986).

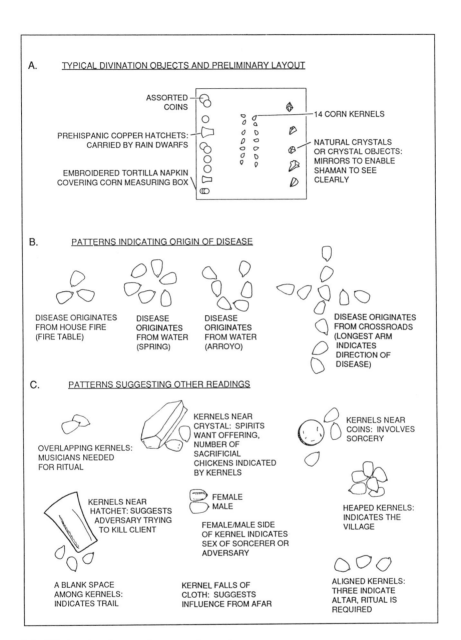

A. TYPICAL DIVINATION OBJECTS AND PRELIMINARY LAYOUT

ASSORTED COINS

PREHISPANIC COPPER HATCHETS: CARRIED BY RAIN DWARFS

EMBROIDERED TORTILLA NAPKIN COVERING CORN MEASURING BOX

14 CORN KERNELS

NATURAL CRYSTALS OR CRYSTAL OBJECTS: MIRRORS TO ENABLE SHAMAN TO SEE CLEARLY

B. PATTERNS INDICATING ORIGIN OF DISEASE

DISEASE ORIGINATES FROM HOUSE FIRE (FIRE TABLE)

DISEASE ORIGINATES FROM WATER (SPRING)

DISEASE ORIGINATES FROM WATER (ARROYO)

DISEASE ORIGINATES FROM CROSSROADS (LONGEST ARM INDICATES DIRECTION OF DISEASE)

C. PATTERNS SUGGESTING OTHER READINGS

OVERLAPPING KERNELS: MUSICIANS NEEDED FOR RITUAL

KERNELS NEAR CRYSTAL: SPIRITS WANT OFFERING, NUMBER OF SACRIFICIAL CHICKENS INDICATED BY KERNELS

KERNELS NEAR COINS: INVOLVES SORCERY

KERNELS NEAR HATCHET: SUGGESTS ADVERSARY TRYING TO KILL CLIENT

FEMALE
MALE

FEMALE/MALE SIDE OF KERNEL INDICATES SEX OF SORCERER OR ADVERSARY

HEAPED KERNELS: INDICATES THE VILLAGE

A BLANK SPACE AMONG KERNELS: INDICATES TRAIL

KERNEL FALLS OF CLOTH: SUGGESTS INFLUENCE FROM AFAR

ALIGNED KERNELS: THREE INDICATE ALTAR, RITUAL IS REQUIRED

6.1. Divination by casting corn kernels

In a previous analysis Pamela Effrein Sandstrom and I concluded that Nahua religion has a pantheistic quality about it (Sandstrom and Sandstrom 1986). After more research and another year of fieldwork, I am more than ever convinced that we are correct. In pantheistic systems of thought, the entire universe and all of its elements partake of deity. Plants, animals, and objects have a kind of spirit or soul that may affect human destiny. But pantheism is not simple animism where each being or object possesses a spirit apart from other beings and objects. For the Nahuas, and probably many other American Indian groups as well, everybody and everything is an aspect of a grand, single, and overriding unity. Separate beings and objects do not exist— that is an illusion peculiar to human beings. In daily life we divide up our environment into discrete units so that we can talk about it and manipulate it for our benefit. But it is an error to assume that the diversity we create in our lives is the way reality is actually structured. For the Nahuas, everything is connected at a deeper level, part of the same basic substratum of being.

In Nahua thought the universe is a deified, seamless totality, but in order to understand its nature better they divide it into four interrelated aspects or realms. The first realm is that of the earth in all its manifestations. The earth in general is called *tlali* in Nahuatl and villagers conceive it to be literally alive. The people say that the soil is the earth's flesh, the stones its bones, and the water its blood. Arching over the earth is the realm of the heavens, called *ilhuicactli* in Nahuatl. Villagers conceive of the sky as a gigantic living mirror, or *tescatl* in Nahuatl, which is filled with the brilliance and sparkle of the sun and stars. In the east are the mirror's feet and in the west its head. Within the earth is the third realm, *mictlan*, Nahuatl for the "place of the dead." Dark and gloomy, it contains the shades of people who died normal, untroubled deaths. The fourth realm is water, the connective tissue of the living universe. This region is called *apan*, Nahuatl for "water realm" (literally "on the surface of the water"). The people talk about the water realm as a kind of pleasant, bubbly paradise abounding with fish and swaying, sunlit grasses.

The four major realms of the Nahua universe, earth, sky, underworld, and water, are more than simply places where human beings and various spirits reside. They, too, are aspects of a deified universe, and in this sense these locations are spirit entities in their own right. For the Nahuas, any thing and any place has a significance in that it partakes of the universal sacred natural order. For example, the hills and mountains in the Nahua landscape are thought by them to be sacred. These are more than residences for spirits; they are living spirits themselves. As a further illustration, I mentioned in Chapters 2 and 3 that the villagers select numerous places in their surrounding environment and attach names to them based on some natural feature. These places can become actual spirit entities in the Nahua pantheon, local expressions of universal deity. Thus in one sense, the Nahua universe contains a countless multitude of spirits. In fact, as we will see below, recognized shamans can actually create new spirits for their rituals. In my confusion about this proliferation I once asked a shaman to explain why there were so many spirits. He replied, "So many spirits? They're all the same." That curt answer contained a wealth of wisdom. All of the numerous spirits are simply aspects of a great unity, a unity that transcends all apparent diversity. The Nahua world is composed of Spirit, the multiple aspects of which fill their pantheon.

THE SPIRIT PANTHEON

With these thoughts on pantheism as background, I will begin this section detailing Nahua spirits with a statement I recorded from the shaman Aurelio. He was trying to explain to me about the sacred nature of the earth:

. . . The earth is alive. We spend our entire lives defiling the earth, pissing on her and that is why she gets annoyed. That's why she wants to forsake us. Some people truly don't know any better. [Human beings] really don't know where they are going. We don't know where we are going to walk, whether we are walking straight or whether we aren't walking straight, but there we are, walking.

Rituals accomplish only what devotion accomplishes. Saying things doesn't make them true. We eat that devotion as corn, we are eating it as tortillas. Where does the corn come from, where does it emerge? It comes out of the earth. All things of value come out of the earth, even money. And yet here we are disturbing the earth, occupying it and planting on it all through our lives. Well, the earth can get annoyed because we disturb it. We plant beans, corn, sugarcane, bananas, and camotes. Whatever it is, we plant it in the earth. We go back and forth to the market on it, and we get drunk on it but we don't give the earth any beer. We don't give her sugarcane, we don't give her bread, we don't give her coffee, and we don't give her joy.

We don't give her what she wants and that is the reason that she forsakes us and doesn't want to produce [for us]. And people say, "Let's go call the father" [a remote unidentified male deity]. But you can't speak to the father. The ancient lord [the creator deity] made her here and the father over there. The earth asks, "When are they going to remember me, when will it be my turn, when will they light a candle? I give them all the things to eat. You are big and healthy because I give you people strength." We are living here and we are born here [on earth]. We sprout like young corn. It is born and sprouts here, and for us it is likewise. . . . You already ate, you're full and you have been [so] all of your life. You've been drunk. Well, likewise the earth also wants its offering. . . . Corn is extremely delicate. Corn is our blood. How can we grab [our living] from the earth when it is our own blood that we are eating?

We can understand from Aurelio's statement that the earth is an important concept in Nahua thought and that humans have a complex relationship to it (see also Romualdo Hernández 1982:148–49 for a quote from a Nahua man on the sacred nature of the earth). Of the four realms that comprise the universe, the earth is clearly the most crucial to these horticultural people. The earth exists in multiple aspects or alter egos, each of which plays a major role in Nahua religion. The male and female aspects of the earth are called *tlaltetata* ("earth father") and *tlaltenana* ("earth mother") respectively; the edge of the earth is called *semanahuac tlaltentle*, and the surface is called *tlaltepactli* (all names in Nahuatl). Interestingly, one personification of the earth is called *montesoma*, a name undoubtedly taken from Motecuhzoma (Montezuma) Xocoyotl, the Aztec emperor at the time of the Spanish Conquest. This spirit entity is conceived by the villagers as a kind of magician who built churches in cities and pre-Hispanic ruins in villages like Amatlán. Montesoma is a frightening figure who consumes dead bodies after they have been buried, and who associates with horrifying underworld spirits. I asked about this spirit repeatedly, but no one connected it to the historical person. The list of earth manifestations could be extended almost indefinitely. Many additional examples have been reported by other researchers from villages in the region (Reyes García 1960:35, 1976:127ff.).

The people of Amatlán have an intimacy with the earth that is difficult for outsiders to comprehend. For the Nahuas, the earth is much more than an entity that grows crops and provides the basis of life. It is, additionally, a powerful spiritual presence with which the villagers are in personal and daily contact. The milpa is a patch of ground that has a sacred quality, and men and boys define their position in the community by how well they care for their fields and thereby demonstrate their respect for the earth. Before planting and following the harvest, gifts are carefully offered to the earth lest it become offended at being disturbed. During curing rituals, people bring a small packet of earth dug from the four outside corners of their house so that the tlaltepactli (the "earth's surface") can also benefit from the cleansing. When men are sitting together drinking after a day's work, each man is careful to let a drop fall on the earth before consuming anything himself. People are considered to sprout from the earth like the corn plant, and they are placed back in the earth when they die. The earth is womb and tomb, the provider of nourishment and all wealth, home to the ancestors, and the daily sustainer of human life.

The landscape surrounding the village in fact is literally alive with aspects of spirit. Every hill, valley, spring, lake, stream, section of river, boulder, plain, grove, gorge, and cave has its proper name and associated spirit. The physical surroundings have been ordered by the Nahuas into a coherent and meaningful system, a "cognized environment," to follow the terminology suggested by Rappaport (1979:5). The features that figure most prominently in Nahua religion are the hills and mountains that are so abundant in the region. Called *santo tepemej*, a mixed Spanish–Nahuatl phrase meaning "sacred hills," they are living entities that are the dwelling places of the seed and rain spirits associated with crop growth, and of powerful spirits who guard over humans. One shaman told me that the hills are the earth's head and face, the ground its body, and the underworld its feet. Shamans make pilgrimages to the peaks of hills and mountains for special offerings. The hills are ranked according to size and importance, and each has a special place in village mythology.

According to the shamans, the most important mountain in Mexico is Popocatepetl (or "smoking mountain" in Nahuatl), a snow-capped volcanic peak near Mexico City. Although none of the village shamans have actually visited Popocatepetl, it nevertheless plays a role in their myths. They tell a story that montesoma was carrying Popocatepetl to the Valley of Mexico when, for reasons that vary according to the version of the story being recounted, he dropped pieces of it that became the other hills and mountains. The most important peak in the vicinity of Amatlán is Postectitla ("broken hill," literally "place next to the base of something that broke lengthwise" in Nahuatl), a huge, basaltic volcanic core jutting over 2,000 feet almost vertically from the surrounding terrain. The rocky core has the appearance of being broken at the top, and this feature has given rise to an explanatory myth. Shamans told me that god (*toteotsij* in Nahuatl, see below for a description) was in his milpa one day at a time when the mountain was still whole. He noticed that ants and other insects were crawling

from earth into the sky, and he ordered that the mountain be broken
and the connection between earth and the sky severed. Ever since,
humans have been trying to reestablish that link through their rituals.
One shaman explained to me that Postectitla is the governor of the
surrounding hills, a mountain in the region called San Jerónimo is the
secretary, and another mountain called La Laguna, with a small lake
at its peak, is the treasurer. Thus the Indians use the metaphor of
municipio political offices as a means of ranking the important sacred
mountains. Map 6.1 shows the important hills and mountains in relation to Amatlán (note that some towns or settlements in the region
take the name of the sacred geographical features near which they are
located).

In the earth realm, the most important spirit besides the earth itself
is *tonantsij* (Nahuatl for "our honored mother"). Tonantsij is a pre-
Hispanic fertility deity that has come to be identified as the Virgin of
Guadalupe in modern Mexico (see Wolf 1958). She is a mother image
for the Indians and a link between Christianity and the pre-Hispanic
traditions of antiquity. She is an important figure for Indian and mestizo alike, and it is no exaggeration to say that she has become the
patroness of Mexico. Most mestizos see the Indian veneration of
tonantsij as a homespun childlike version of their own veneration of
the Virgin of Guadalupe whom they regard as a manifestation of the
Virgin Mary. Actually, in places like Amatlán, tonantsij worship can
be traced to the highly complex and sophisticated religions of the pre-
Hispanic era. Although the shrine to tonantsij in Amatlán is thatch-
roofed and rustic, the ideas she represents and her role in Nahua
religion are anything but simplistic.

People agreed that tonantsij originally came from the sky but that
she now lives in one or more caves located at the peaks of sacred
mountains. She watches over the village and ensures both human and
crop fertility. A statue of the Virgin of Guadalupe is kept in the village
shrine (*teopaj* in Nahuatl) dedicated to her and people give her periodic
offerings so that she will not abandon them. A brief myth recounted
by several individuals establishes her importance to the world. A
villager told me that tonantsij gave birth to four sons. The first was
tlahuelilo, the fearsome figure associated with the underworld. The
second was *sa hua*, the water spirit who lives in the sea and sends
rain. Third was *montesoma*, the earth-realm magician who miraculously
builds churches and pre-Hispanic ruins. The last child was the sun,
toteotsij, who in his Christian aspect is Jesus Christ. Tonantsij, the
fertility mother, thus gave birth to four sons each of whom is associated

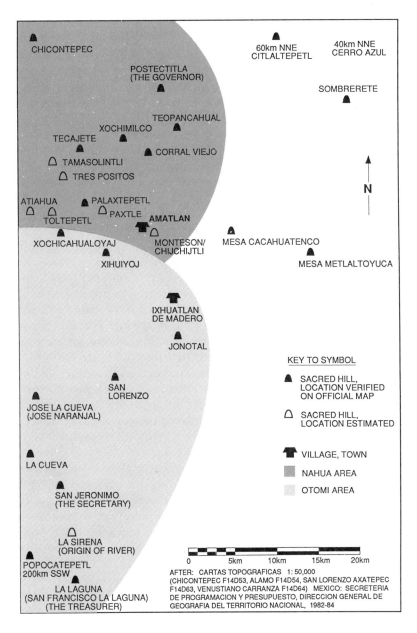

6.1. Major sacred hills in Amatlán Nahua religion

with one of the four realms. Tlahuelilo is from the underworld, montesoma is an earth spirit, sa hua is master of all the waters, and toteotsij rules from the sky. Interestingly, the sun is the last born and thus, according to several villagers, has less power than his older brothers. The myth neatly summarizes a sequence of four past ages when the universe was ruled by the underworld, water realm, earth realm, and sky realm respectively. It also recounts the coming of Christianity as tonantsij gives birth to the sun-Christ who rules our current era. Tonantsij is venerated during an observance called *tlacatelilis* ("birth" in Nahuatl), a fertility ritual held during the winter solstice.

Tonantsij, from her mountaintop cave rules over the seed spirits who villagers believe are her children. These are called *xinaxtli* or *xinachtli* in Nahuatl, meaning "seed," and there is one spirit for each of the diverse crops grown in the milpa. They represent the life force or potential for fertility of each crop, and thus they are in the forefront of villagers' thoughts. I first learned about the seed spirits as I was walking through a friend's compound on my way to witness a curing ritual. I glanced up, and on a clothesline strung between two houses, I saw hanging about 75 tiny girls dresses and boys' pants and shirts, each about 12 inches in length. As I entered my friend's house to inquire, I could see that a ritual was beginning. People greeted me as if I were expected, for it turned out that they had just sent a boy to get me and assumed that I was responding to the invitation. The ritual is called *xochitlalia* ("flower earth," literally "to put down flowers" in Nahuatl), and its central feature is an offering to the seed spirits. I was anxious to find out about the miniature clothes on the line, but I was forced to be patient; the ritual continued without a break for 12 days and nights.

Shamans portray the seed spirits by cutting their images out of paper. These are carefully preserved throughout the year in a special chest made from cedar. Villagers place the chest on an elaborately decorated altar and open it only for this annual ritual. They dress the paper images inside the chest in the tiny clothes I had seen drying on the clothesline outside. In addition to the clothing, they adorn the images with hats, miniature necklaces, earrings, and combs. Along with the dressed figures inside the chest, the shamans and their helpers place miniature items of furniture similar to those found in an Indian house. As part of the ritual, the shaman opens the chest and removes the paper images and furnishings. Helpers wash and dry the clothes and scrub out the inside of the chest before dressing the seed spirits and replacing them for another year. Villagers told me that the seeds have a desire to return to their cave homes in the mountains and that the beautiful chest with its elaborate offerings is designed to make them want to remain in the village. Should the seeds decide to leave, the crops would fail and the people would starve. Throughout the year villagers place periodic offerings before the box of seed spirits and in front of the statue of tonant-sij in her shrine to ensure abundant harvests.

The seed spirits are ranked by the villagers according to their importance. Not surprisingly, corn is paramount. When I was allowed to examine the seed images in the cedar chest, I found that the overwhelming majority were portrayals of varieties of corn. The corn spirit exists in both male and female aspect. The male aspect is called *chicomexochitl* ("7-flower") and the female aspect is *macuili xochitl* ("5-flower" both terms in Nahuatl). I asked why the corn spirit has these names, and people responded that they did not know the origin of 5-flower, but that the name 7-flower is based on a miraculous corn plant discovered growing many years ago which had seven ears of corn. I believe that this explanation is a secondary rationalization, however. Both 5-flower and 7-flower were Aztec deity names. Seven-flower protected seamstresses and painters and was related to Pilzintecutli, the lord of young maize. There was also an Aztec day name called 7-flower that was symbolized by an ear of corn (Berdan 1982:135; Mönnich 1976:143). Five-flower was patron of dances, games, and love and was the sibling of Centeotl, the "God of Corn" (Caso 1958:46–47; Soustelle 1961 [1955]:104). In sum, it seems likely that the names for the corn spirit are pre-Hispanic in origin (see also Nicholson 1971:416–21, table 3).

When I pressed villagers for more details about the corn spirit, they replied that 7-flower and 5-flower are divine twin children with hair the color of corn silk. In fact, when we arrived in the field in 1985 with our blond 3-year-old son, many people commented that he looked like *pilsintsij* (the spirit "little corn" in Nahuatl), an alter ego of 7-flower. Chicomexochitl is the hero-subject of numerous myths, some of which I was able to record during 1985 and 1986. In one story, mestizos spilled corn on the ground and did not trouble themselves to pick it up. The grains, in the guise of chicomexochitl, began to weep at being so badly treated. An Indian passing by carefully gathered up the corn, and from that time chicomexochitl has supported the Indians. I noted with interest that villagers are always very careful to gather up every corn kernel that accidently falls onto the ground.

In an important myth about the corn spirit that exists in many variations, the grandmother of chicomexochitl kills him and tries to hide the body (see chapter 4). No matter what she does he reappears to face her with the crime. The myth seems to describe the symbolic killing of corn at the harvest and its resurrection as it bursts into life after the spring planting. An interesting theme running through these myths is that the deer spirit (called simply *masatl* in Nahuatl or "deer") is always cast as the father of chicomexochitl. Although villagers were not able to explain why this should be so, it is possible that the theme recalls the transition between a hunting way of life, symbolized by the deer, to a horticultural mode of production represented by corn (see Myerhoff 1974:200–201 for an elaboration on this theme among the Huichol Indians).

In one episode chicomexochitl retired to the inside of the sacred mountain Postectitla, and in his absence the villagers went hungry. One day people saw red ants carrying grains of corn emerging from a cave in the mountain. At this point, the water spirit sa hua struck the mountain, causing the peak to break off and allowing fire to escape from inside the earth. Thunder and lightning spirits (*pilhuehuentsitsij* in Nahuatl, literally "honored little old ones") sprinkled water on the fire to prevent the corn from burning, but they were only partially successful. All corn up until that time was white in color. The white corn grown in the village today is descended from the grains that escaped the flames entirely. Modern yellow corn grown is descended from the grains that were just singed, and red corn comes from the grains that were fully exposed to the flames. The black corn cultivated today is descended from grains that were nearly destroyed by the fire. This mythic episode not only explains the origin of the varieties of corn, but it also reveals the basis for ranking them from white, the least burned and most desirable variety, through black, the variety most affected by the fire and therefore the least desirable. In addition, an underlying theme of the myth is that whenever the corn spirit is absent or inattentive, hunger will invade the village.

Chicomexochitl, however, is more than a mythic culture hero symbolizing the central importance of corn in Nahua life. It plays a deeper metaphysical role in the Nahua view of the universe and the place of human beings in the natural order. This is not something villagers are able to articulate with unambiguous clarity but, rather, it is an interpretation I have derived based on listening to myths, observing countless rituals, and isolating underlying patterns in what both shamans and laypeople have told me.

In Nahua thought, human beings are part of the sacred universe, and each of us contains within our bodies a spark of the divine energy that makes the world live. This energy ultimately derives from the sun, toteotsij. Much of the sun's energy comes to us in the form of heat that the Nahuas call *tona* or *tonatl* in Nahuatl and is experienced by us as body heat. In fact one of the souls possessed by human beings is called the *tonali* in Nahuatl, a term that derives from the word for this divine heat (see below for a fuller explanation of souls). Once inside the body, this heat is transformed into *chicahualistli*, Nahuatl for a kind of energy or force that gives humans vigor and the power to act. This energy is carried in the blood (*estli* in Nahuatl), and it is renewed when we consume food, particularly corn. Without corn, the tonali or heat-soul loses energy, weakens (that is, cools), and the person eventually dies. Corn, then, is the physical and spiritual link between human beings and the sun, the life-giving substance that ties people to the sacred universe. This system of beliefs adds yet another layer of meaning to the Nahua saying, corn is our blood.

Tonantsij and her seed children comprise one of the most important spirit clusters in the Nahua pantheon, and two major rituals center on these figures. But it is difficult to isolate groups of spirits for analysis because of the way the Nahuas see spirits in relation to one another. The cave dwelling of tonantsij and her seed children is also occupied by thunder (*tlatomoni* in Nahuatl) and lightning (*tlapetlani* in Nahuatl), spirits who are associated with the rain dwarfs. Thus some villagers assert that it is tonantsij, perhaps in the guise of a water spirit, who actually sends the rain. The earthly abode of tonantsij also puts her in close association with ancestor spirits called *tecutli* (sing.) in Nahuatl who live within the sacred hills and who guard over and generally care for Amatlán. These ancestors, in turn, are linked to pre-Hispanic sculptures (usually small ceramic figurines or faces) that are occasionally unearthed and are respected as power objects by villagers. Called *teteomej* in Nahuatl ("stone gods or spirits") or *antihuatl* (sing., a mixed Spanish–Nahuatl term meaning "ancient one"), they appear to be different from, or perhaps an aspect of, the tecutli spirits. Any line of questioning about the spirits quickly leads to a complex tangle of associations that serves to blur neat boundaries when trying to create a map of the spirit pantheon.

Shamans describe the sky realm, *ilhuicactli*, as a glittery place brilliantly lit by the pure light of the sun and stars. Reigning over the entire universe and casting its life-giving light to the earth is the sun. Called *toteotsij* in Nahuatl, "our honored god," the sun created the universe we now inhabit and presides over his creation with a kind of benign indifference. The sun animates the universe with its heat and light but refrains from interfering directly in human events. Herein resides a paradox in Nahua thought. People agree that the sun is the most powerful of all the spirits, and they even call it *tata sol*, a mixed Nahuatl–Spanish phrase meaning "father sun," but they make few offerings to the sun and seldom direct prayers to it. Villagers maintain a permanent altar at the peak of a nearby hill called *monteson* (a mixed Nahuatl–Spanish word meaning "*montesoma* song"). This site is significant because it is the place in Amatlán where the sun first hits the earth in the morning. The altar, however, is actually dedicated to the hill and earth made sacred by the sun's first rays. In Nahua thought, the sun is Jesus Christ, a spirit entity that dispells the forces of darkness during the day but that must be approached through intermediaries when the people wish to make requests. The shamans told me about a rarely held ritual in which special paper cutouts are prepared and an offering is dedicated directly to the sun. The ritual is held in secret, however, and only the most powerful shamans participate.

The sun provides the energy for the animate universe and also guards over people during the day. At night it passes beneath the earth and out of range. In its place emerge the stars (*sitlalij*, sing. in Nahuatl) which take over the sun's role as guardian. During the night, stones can turn into wild, carnivorous animals, and the stars intercede to protect human beings. The stars shoot arrows in the form of meteors to kill the meat eaters and save humans from a horrible fate. Villagers told me that small stones with holes in them have been killed by the star guardians, and these are valued as power objects by shamans. The moon (*metsli* in Nahuatl), in comparison to the sun, is seen as an inconstant and undependable force (for a discussion of Nahua beliefs about the effects of the lunar cycle on many types of plants, see Reyes Antonio 1982:48–50). Its light is pale and cold, and its image waxes and wanes with the lunar cycle. In fact, the moon is an ambivalent spirit entity in Nahua thought, connected with fertility and tonantsij but also with a terrifying spirit from the underworld called *tlahuelilo* (a Nahuatl term meaning "wrathful one"). Often, paper images of fearful disease-causing spirits are cut with hornlike projections that are meant to portray the crescent moon.

The most important constellation is the Pleiades, called by the Nahuatl terms *miaquetl* (literally "many"), or *chicome sitlalij* meaning "7-stars." The Pleiades has come to stand for the night sky in general, which the Nahuas refer to as *chicome ilhuicactli* in Nahuatl or "7-sky." They call the Milky Way *sitlalcueitl*, Nahuatl for "star skirt" or *Santiago ojtli*, a mixed Spanish–Nahuatl phrase meaning "Santiago's trail."

Villagers consider the Milky Way to be the residence of the Catholic saints. In addition they recognize Venus, which they call *tonquetl* in Nahuatl. Another celestial manifestation of importance is the rainbow, called in Nahuatl *acosejmalotl*. The villagers consider rainbows to be dangerous and to place the people who see them in jeopardy. The Nahuas conceive of the sky as an arch or dome with the various heavenly bodies suspended from it above the earth. In general, the spirits of the sky pantheon are less important than those associated with the earth. The sky and its divine inhabitants play an important role in rituals, but they have little impact on daily life. Even tonantsij, among the most important sacred personages in Amatlán and one who is associated with the moon, has been relocated and is believed by the villagers to have an earthly home in sacred mountain caves.

One particularly important spirit that originates from the sky, along with the sun, moon, stars, and Catholic saints, is fire. In Chapter 4, I presented a summary of the myth in which Juan Flojo (Spanish for "John Lazy," also known as Juan Ceniza, "John Ashes"), an earthly manifestation of *tlixihuantsij* the fire spirit, abandons Amatlán when his brothers-in-law criticize him for being lazy. It will be recalled that in the end, young girls were able to go to the mountains, make offerings to Juan, and coax him into returning fire to the people. Villagers believe that the fire spirit remains in the village and now lives in the three stones that surround the main cooking fire in each dwelling. Shamans cast food and drink into the household fire in the course of all rituals as an offering to tlixihuantsij so that he will never again abandon human beings.

Water is a fundamental element in Nahua world view, and it plays a crucial role in religious belief and ritual. It percolates up from the ground, falls from the sky, and lies in pools on the surface of the earth. Villagers told me that water ties the world together in the sense that it connects the sky, earth, and underworld realms. Shamans often keep a permanent display of paper images portraying the spirit of water on their home altars. The water spirit exists in many aspects, and these figure prominently in village myths. To the east lies the sea (actually the Gulf of Mexico) that is the source of all water and home to sa hua, a name derived from the Spanish San Juan, "Saint John the Baptist." Sa hua dispenses water and controls the animals of the deep. Rain is carried from the sea by the twelve *pilhuehuentsitsij*, the "honored little old ones," sometimes called in the singular by the mixed Spanish–Nahuatl term *antihuatl* meaning "ancient one." These dwarflike spirits appear as elderly little men who wear fine black clothing with rubber sleeves and who carry walking sticks, swords, or chains in their hands. They travel in the clouds that come from the Gulf during the rainy season and, as they proceed inland, strike their implements, creating dramatic displays of thunder and lightning. They carry the water to their cave homes at the peaks of sacred hills where it is then dispensed by *apanchanej*, the Nahuatl name for the spirit of the water or "water dweller." The rain dwarfs appear to be metaphors for the dark clouds that blow in off the Gulf at the start of the rainy season. As the clouds rise to surmount the Sierra they cool and drop their precious moisture. Several people told me that the pilhuehuentsitsij are black, "like the clouds."

Many Nahua beliefs have a basis in close observations of the work-ings of nature. Once when I was walking far from Amatlán with some friends, we rounded a bend on a high trail, and the dramatic sharp peak of Postectitla ("broken hill") came into view. Clouds blowing inland from the Gulf had snagged on the jagged peak of this remarkable rock formation, and this situation caused my companions to state that this is a sure sign that it will rain later in the evening. Just as predicted, by 10 o'clock that night there was a downpour that lasted until morn-ing. Clouds from the Gulf seemed to emanate from the mountain, and their presence around the peak is apparently a harbinger of rain.

Springs, lakes, streams, and rivers are also important manifestations of the water spirit. Apanchanej lives in these locations in the form of a lady with long hair and a mermaid-like fish tail. When speaking Spanish, the villagers call her *la sirena*, "the siren." She rules over freshwater creatures and the souls of people who experienced certain forms of death. Death by drowning or being struck by lightning abruptly diverts the soul from its usual journey to the underworld and assures it a place in the paradisiacal realm of water. One intriguing aspect of apanchanej is *santa rosa*, literally the "sacred rose" in Spanish, but probably named for Saint Rose of Lima, the first New World saint, who was renowned for her visions. Santa rosa is the villagers' term for marijuana, and on rare occasions shamans and selected assistants ingest the ground leaves mixed with cane alcohol. A sober helper guards each participant to insure that no one gets injured. Ritual participants use santa rosa to communicate directly with the water realm in order to ask for the blessing of rain. The Nahuas consider marijuana to be a powerful hallucinogen with strong religious connections, and they never use it except under the supervision of a shaman.

The final realm is mictlan, the underworld and place of dead souls. This realm is part of the earth, but villagers talk about it as if it were a separate region. They describe it as a gloomy place without sunlight, where the crops planted by the inhabitants do not prosper. Those souls not going to the water realm, *apan*, all go to mictlan where they remarry, live in villages similar to Amatlán, and farm for a living just as in this life. Death causes a physical transformation, however, and individuals lose their bodies. Villagers told me that the inhabitants of mictlan are like air, like puffs of wind. The ultimate fate of these souls, however, is not agreed upon by villagers. A few maintain that they are reborn as animals, while others say that as the physical body returns to the earth from which it was born, the soul slowly fades away and disappears forever. Concerning the souls in the water realm, most people had little to say except that even that paradise is not always a happy place. Souls of the dead are sustained by food offerings made by kinsmen during Day of the Dead rituals, and as part of complex funeral observances discussed below.

Threats to the people of Amatlán are not restricted to the secular forces of the police, army, hired gunmen, corrupt government officials, and neighboring villages. From mictlan, *tlacatecolotl* (Nahuatl for "man owl") with his owl messengers leads the beings of the underworld and prowls the trails in search of victims. This creature often appears on earth in the guise of an owl, and for this reason villagers consider owls to be harbingers of death. His colleague or perhaps alter ego is *tlahuelilo* (Nahuatl for "wrathful one"), also known as *hueitlacatl*, Nahuatl for "big man," or *señor de la noche* (Spanish for "lord of the night"). This malevolent spirit is identified with the Christian devil, and it lurks at night around the graveyards and pre-Hispanic ruins. When shamans cut paper images of tlahuelilo and his wife, they blacken the figures with charcoal from the fireplace as a sign of the dark forces they represent. Another denizen of the underworld is *miquilistli* (a Nahuatl term meaning "death") that the people conceive as a living skeleton. When shamans fear that a patient is dying, they cut a skeleton image of this creature from white paper and attempt to divert it through ritual means. Tlacatecolotl is further served in the underworld by a group of hideous masked and painted beings called *mecos*, a word of uncertain origin (see Chapter 2). These spirits of the dead are released on the earth for an 8-day period that coincides with a ritual observance akin to Carnival called *nanahuatili* in Nahuatl. The mecos are impersonated by young men wearing costumes and masks, and they visit each household to perform dances and to behave as disruptively as possible. Only after the household head makes a small donation of money to the lead meco can they be persuaded to move on.

The most dangerous, life-threatening spirits that daily cause concern to the people of Amatlán are the *ejecamej* (sing. *ejecatl* in Nahuatl), meaning "gusts of winds." In Spanish they are called *malos vientos* ("bad winds"), *malos aires* ("bad airs"), *diablos* ("devils"), or *judíos* ("jews"). (The Nahuas, along with other Indian groups of Mexico, use the term "jew" to refer to any number of malevolent spirits, and they have no idea that it refers to a member of a living religious and ethnic group. It is for this reason that I prefer to write the term jew in lower case. The Indians' use of the word jew in this way is obviously a legacy of Christian missionaries who portrayed the historic Jews as Christ killers.) Ejecatl spirits ride in gusts of wind spreading disease, misfortune, and death. The villagers attribute almost any negative event or circumstance to the work of ejecatl spirits including drought, crop or animal disease, mental disorders, illness, bad luck, and infertility. By far, the majority of a shaman's professional activity is spent controlling ejecatl spirits, usually through cleansing rituals (see Adams and Rubel 1967:338–40 for a general discussion of beliefs concerning disease-causing winds in Mesoamerica; also Montoya Briones 1981 and Reyes Antonio 1982:107 for discussions of ejecatl spirits in neighboring Nahua villages).

The idea that bad airs produce disease was common throughout both pre-Hispanic Latin America and Europe. The Nahuas are unusual, however, in the degree to which they have elaborated on this theme. Not only do they give the various wind spirits names and color associations indicating their place of origin, but in the course of curing rituals the shamans cut their images from paper as well. The images are subjected to ritual procedures designed to remove their corresponding ejecatl spirit from the patient's body or environment. Ejecatl spirits are insidious, and they tend to attack newborns or the elderly, people whose *chicahualistli* ("strength" or "force") is diminished. They infest the entire universe but are attracted to the village when people lose their tempers, gossip, become angry, speak badly of others, swear, steal, cheat, lie, or otherwise break the social norms. It took many long months of research before I came to understand what the ejecatl spirits are. The insight came from examining their paper images, many of which are skeleton-like, complete with rib holes. The ejecatl spirits are the wandering souls of people who died bad deaths or who have been forgotten by their kinsmen.

Human beings become ejecatl spirits if they die by violence or if their kinsmen neglect them during funeral rituals or Day of the Dead observances. The true horror of these malevolent spirits, then, is that they are former villagers who have returned to attack their living kinsmen. Leading an exemplary life by avoiding activities that can attract ejecatl spirits helps to protect the village, but only the power and techniques of a shaman can vanquish them. Not surprisingly, a common point of origin for these dangerous spirits is mictlan, the underworld. The fundamental problem is that, being dead souls, they cannot be coerced to stay where they belong. They wander throughout the universe, and some have permanently infested the other realms. Thus, among the hundreds of ejecatl spirits we find names (in Nahuatl) such as *mictlan tlasoli ejecatl* ("filth wind from the place of the dead"), *tlali ejecatl* ("earth wind"), *tonal ejecatl* ("sun wind" or "heat-soul wind"), and *apantlasoli ejecatl* ("filth wind from the water realm"). For reasons unknown to me, shamans often describe these dangerous spirits as creatures who walk on tiptoes or who are severely pigeon-toed. The spirits are apparently good fliers but clumsy walkers.

The shamans agreed that the graveyard and pre-Hispanic ruins are the most common places to encounter ejecatl spirits because these places act as doors connecting the earth's surface to the underworld. Graveyards in particular are thought by the Nahuas to be dangerous places inhabited by wandering spirits who have escaped from mictlan. For this reason, graveyards are always located far from the main concentrations of dwellings in Nahua villages. Pre-Hispanic ruins (called *cubes* in the local dialect of Spanish) abound in the southern Huasteca region. Although villagers state that they are passages between mictlan and the earth's surface, they do not feel that these ancient structures pose any immediate danger, and people do not mind building their houses near them. However, villagers are careful not to disturb the ancient stones for fear that they will inadvertently loose a horde of dangerous spirits. Shamans perform a cleansing rite at the ruins as a step during most curing rituals to remove disease-causing spirits that may have emerged from the underworld.

Sorcery is another major threat to the people of Amatlán. A sorcerer is a *tlamátiquetl* or "person of knowledge" who has gone astray and who now works for *tlahuelilo*. Nahuas use the term *tetlachihuijquetl* to distinguish a sorcerer from a shaman who works for the benefit of humanity. Sometimes these are in the person of an old woman that the villagers call in Nahuatl a *tsitsimitl*. Villagers profess to know little about sorcery, but they acknowledge that sorcerers operate in Amatlán and in neighboring villages. To be recognized by other sorcerers, initiates supposedly undergo a ceremonial induction deep in the forest in the middle of the night. The master makes some use of a large, irregularly shaped camote root in the ritual and has the initiates swear allegiance to tlahuelilo. Sorcerers are able to use paper cuttings to attract ejecatl spirits to the village and direct them to specific victims. The most commonly used figure is that of *miquilistli*, the skeleton of death. Sorcerers perform this service for money at the behest of people seeking revenge. Certain sorcerers can turn themselves at will into animals (often birds) to perform their evil. Villagers call such a dangerous manifestation *tlacueptli* in Nahuatl. They also have the power to transform themselves into a birdlike creature called a *nahuali* or *tlacuapali* in Nahuatl that flies around at night in search of victims. The nahuali sucks blood from people while they sleep and particularly likes the young sweet blood of babies. As mentioned above, all shamans run the risk of being accused of sorcery, and I have recorded two cases where shamans from Amatlán have been murdered following accusations that they used their power for harm.

The degree of insecurity in Nahua life is reflected in the number of spirits whose role is to guard the village and protect individuals from harm. I have already mentioned ancestor spirits, the sun, and the stars in this connection. An added layer of defense is composed of a complex array of spirits called *tlamocuitlahuijquetl, totepixcahuaj*, or *onipixtoc aqui quiixtoc*, Nahuatl names that mean "caretaker" or "protector." These village guardians act in two capacities. First, they warn people or other protector spirits of impending disaster, and second they serve as witnesses who act as intermediaries between shamans and more powerful spirits such as the ancestors. People often hang paper images of these spirits over their home altars to watch over the family. Along with guardian spirits villagers also display inexpensive pictures of Catholic saints purchased at the market. These prints portray various saints and holy figures in guises that are alien and often puzzling to the Nahuas. The saints are dressed in medieval or Renaissance clothing, some have beards or bald heads, and many have glowing halos suspended above them. Villagers informed me that these are pictures of the *mu axcatl* (sing. in Nahuatl), a class of spirits that protect the members and belongings of the household. In short, the pictures have been reinterpreted by the villagers to fit their own vision of the world.

Table 6.1 lists major Nahua spirits along with their realms of origin. The list is not complete and cannot be (see Knab 1979 for a discussion of spirits among Nahuas of the neighboring Sierra Norte de Puebla). Shamans continually create new spirits or revive ones that have not appeared in rituals for many years. They feel free to cut paper images of the life force or spiritual essence of just about anything, including objects such as houses, musical instruments, and candles. During the New Year's celebration held on the evening of December 31st, shamans hold a birth cleansing for a spirit they call in Nahuatl *yancuic xihuitl* ("new year") and a funeral feast for *huehuexihuitl* (Nahuatl for "old year"). Thus the span of a year is a kind of spirit presence that must be given the proper ritual observances for its birth and death. Shamans are also able to cut a paper image of a person's soul and through ritual means manipulate it on command. The most common application of this technique is in love magic where a client pays the shaman to make someone fall helplessly in love with him or her. The technique is also used to make a straying husband or wife again love his or her spouse. In sum, the pantheistic nature of Nahua religion means that the creative imagination of the shaman and the willingness of the villagers to accept innovation are the only limitations on the number of spirits in the pantheon.

But it should not be forgotten that for the Nahuas all of these spirits trace back to the one creator deity, the sun, whose visible presence in the sky affirms the oneness of the universe. The sun not only the provides the heat in our bodies, but it is the animator of the universe as well. Human beings are insignificant in comparison with the sun, and they must take their place alongside all of the sun's other living creations. For this reason the most important human attribute for the Nahuas is respect (*tlatlepanitalistli* in Nahuatl), and the one criticism that the villagers consistently level at the mestizos is that they fail to show respect. By respect, the villagers mean a sense of propriety, or a recognition of the place that humans have in relation to the rest of the world. Respect is expressed by making offerings to the water, the earth, the hills, and the crops. One shaman told me that the devastating earthquake that struck Mexico City in September 1985 happened because people in the cities do not respect the earth. For the villagers, failure to show respect by taking one's proper place in the sun's great creation has very real and clearly negative consequences (see the poem that appears at the beginning of this chapter).

Although the sun is the creator and sustainer of the universe, the Nahuas often use the human body as the metaphor for the animating principle itself. As we have seen, they visualize the sky realm as a mirror in human form, and the earth is thought of as a giant human body with feet in the underworld and head in the mountains. This association of the human form with aspects of the universe is very common in Nahua thought. For example, the corn plant is conceived as having a human body, with the roots its feet and the tassel its hair.

TABLE 6.1. Major Nahua Spirits, Realms of the Universe, and Associated
Spirits

Ilhuicactli (Sky)
  toteotsij (our honored diety, sun, Jesus)
  metstli (moon, also associated with *tlahuelilo*)
  sitlalmej (stars)
  Catholic saints
  tlixihuantsij (fire)
  ejecatl (wind, many different manifestations)
Tlali (Earth)
  tlaltepactli (earth's surface)
    axcatlaltipactli (belongings of the earth)
    tlaltetata (earth father)
    tlaltenana (earth mother)
    montesoma (devouring earth) plus many additional earth aspects
  tonantsij (our sacred mother, Virgin of Guadalupe, associated with the
    moon)
  xinaxtli (seed)
    chicomexochitl (7-Flower, male aspect of corn)
    macuili xochitl (5-Flower, female aspect of corn)
    pilsintsij (little corn, young corn)
    plus many additional seed spirits
  santo tepemej (sacred hills)
  tecutli (ancestor)
  pilhuehuentsitsij (thunder and lightning spirits, rain dwarfs)
    tlatomoni (thunder, aspect of rain dwarfs)
    tlapetlani (lightning, aspect of rain dwarfs)
  tlamocuitlahuijquetl (guardian or witness)
    totepixcahuaj (caretaker or protector)
    onipixtoc aqui quiixtoc (caretaker or protector)
    mu axcatl (house guardian)
  nahuali (sorcerer transformed into bird)
    tlacuapali (sorcerer transformed into bird)
    tlacueptli (sorcerer transformed into animal)
  teteomej (meaning unknown, sacred pre-Hispanic artifacts)
  ejecatl (wind, many different manifestations)
Mictlan (Underworld)
  tlacatecolotl (man owl)
  tlahuelilo (wrathful one, devil, demon); also *señor de la noche* (Lord of the
    Night)
  miquilistli (death)
  mecos (servants of tlacatecolotl)
  yolojmej (hearts, heart-souls, spirits of the dead)
  ejecatl (wind, many different manifestations)

TABLE 6.1. *Continued*

Apan (Water)
  apanchanej (water dweller); also
    sa hua or San Juan (Saint John the Baptist), also Santa Rosa (Saint
    Rose) or marijuana)
  yolojmej (hearts, heart-souls, spirits of the dead)
  ejecatl (wind, many different manifestations)

Shamans describe the pointed end of their divination crystals as the head, the shaft as the body, and the rough lower end as the feet. When shamans cut paper images of spirits, they are usually depicted in the form of an anthropomorphic figure. This human figure is the heart-soul of the spirit, that which makes it a living entity. The human body was an important and highly elaborated metaphor in pre-Hispanic thought as well (Hunt 1977:112ff.; López Austin 1988).

Finally, an important characteristic of Nahua spirits and souls is that they are often neutral with regard to human beings. Most spirits as aspects of a pantheistic universe are not really conceived of as good or evil, and I have avoided the use of these terms in describing them. They are somewhat like our own concept of nature: a thing of wonder but basically indifferent to human welfare. Some spirits are dangerous, such as those associated with the underworld, but villagers do not really see them as evil. They are equivalent to a deadly virus that cannot be conceived as morally corrupt but rather must be thought of as a natural phenomenon that can be injurious to people. Salutary spirits such as San Juan, the sun, and the seeds also have their negative sides, rendering them unpredictable with regard to human welfare. Many Nahua tales and myths recount incidents where a normally beneficent spirit menaces the human population. For example, sa hua constantly threatens to flood the world and drown everyone, and it is only the intercession of tonantsij that prevents him from doing it. The sun threatens to burn up the earth with its heat, and the seeds are always on the verge of abandoning the village to starvation. Only the nearly constant round of ritual offerings made by the people prevents these catastrophes. The Nahua universe is an uncertain place where human existence hangs on the whim of indifferent spirits that require continuous ritual attention.

CONCEPTS OF THE HUMAN SOUL

When Nahuas meet, one greeting they use is, *"Tlen quiijtoa moyoloj?"* (Nahuatl for "What does your heart say?"). The customary response in Nahuatl is, *"Cuali"* ("Good"). Hidden in this interchange is a complex view of the human soul and its relation to the spirit world. The Nahuas say that humans have two basic souls, one of which is subdivided. The first, which is called the *yolotl* in Nahuatl, can be literally translated as "heart" but is closer to the idea of a "life force." Villagers say that this heart-soul accounts for how we can taste or smell things and why we find certain food, drink, or activities pleasurable. The yolotl is the heart or essence of an object, being, or spirit, and everything in the universe possesses one. Physical objects whether living or not have a yolotl by virtue of being part of the pantheistic universe. The yolotl is a piece of the universal deity that inheres in everything in existence. Thus, even objects partake of an animate universe, and they can be said to be alive in this sense. They are alive, too, in the way that they impinge on human thoughts and actions and therefore have a kind of inner dynamic or life force. By asking, "What does your heart say?", a person is inquiring about the other person's state of being and about his or her divine spark as well.

The second soul is the tonali in Nahuatl, a term based on the root word for heat. This soul is something like a person's consciousness or personality, or as one person told me, "It is like your work in life." It is powered by an individual's internal vigor or energy (*chicahualistli*). Villagers told me that the tonali wanders around when people sleep and that we experience this wandering as dreaming. At death, the body turns cold as chicahualistli diminishes and the tonali dissipates and vanishes. Only humans and animals have a tonali in addition to their yolotl. As explained above, this heat-soul is a special gift from the sun that comes to us via that other special gift, corn. What the Nahuas seem to be saying metaphorically is that our bodies are sustained by energy from the sun stored in food that we consume.

Whereas the yolotl has a kind of timeless, impersonal quality in that it is possessed by all objects in the universe, the tonali places humans (and animals) in time and in the stream of events and feelings that we experience as our lives. For the villagers, the concept of tonali has a clear association with the sun, daytime, the passage of weeks and months, and by extension, fate, destiny, and fortune. If a man or woman is beset by tragedy or dies young even after taking the proper ritual precautions, people say that it was in his or her tonali to suffer. When I asked people whether they aspired to be shamans or musicians, most answered that they must wait to see if it is in their tonali. Despite the implications that one's life is in a sense predetermined, I do not regard the Nahuas as fatalistic. Tonali seems to be closer to our concept of talent, aptitude, or even luck. In many Indian communities in Mexico there exists a belief that each person has a companion animal called a *tonal* or *tonali* (Adams and Rubel 1967:341). This is yet another expression of the tonali concept, although I did not find this belief to be widespread in Amatlán (see Reyes Antonio 1982:158 for a further discussion of the tonali in Nahua thought).

The tonali in human beings is composed of seven segments or components that are scattered evenly throughout the body. These seven segments act in concert and do not appear to have separate functions. Because of the composite nature of this soul many Nahuas call it *chicome tonali*, Nahuatl for "7-tonali." It is likely that the segmented character of the tonali accounts for certain ritual practices that one finds among the Nahuas. For example, curing rituals often include a sequence where patients are made to pass through a vine-and-marigold loop seven times in order to be cleansed of disease-causing spirits (see below). It seems possible that the seven passes of the loop are to rid the seven segments of the tonali of disease. I have not been able to confirm this, however. Interestingly, the Nahuas believe that animals have a tonali divided into fourteen segments. When I inquired about this, people told me that animals are generally more powerful than humans. They gave examples of scorpions and snakes that can kill with their venom. The number of segments in the tonali, then, has a direct bearing on an organism's power. This belief reflects the Nahua view that human beings, while part of the universe, are not the master species put here to exercise dominion over it.

When people die their tonali disappears but the yolotl, or heart-soul, remains in the physical body. Death causes the heart-soul to become confused, and it may actually leave the body for short periods of time as it tries to rejoin its living kinsmen. This can be very dangerous because the heart-soul is unaware of its power and it may inadvertently kill some of its living relatives. Of particular danger are the heart-souls of young people that are angry at having lost their bodies prematurely. The purpose of a funeral ritual and subsequent offerings to spirits of the dead is to ensure that the heart-soul is satisfied and that it stays in the underworld with the heart-souls of others who died previously. The family continues to invest heavily in food offerings for the deceased for a period of 4 years following the death. I asked people why they did this for such a long period, expecting them to say that 4 is a lucky or sacred number. Instead they told me that after 4 years the body has returned to dust and the heart-soul is slowly reabsorbed into the earth as the body disintegrates. In other words, the heart-soul rejoins the generalized earth pantheon (see Provost 1981 for a discussion of Huastecan Nahua concepts of soul).

The abstract nature of Nahua religion is brought to a more understandable level through ritual performance and through the shamanic art of portraying specific spirits in cut-paper figures. We know from the records left by sixteenth-century chroniclers that paper and paper cutting were an important part of ritual performance among both highland and lowland civilizations of Mesoamerica. At that time paper was made primarily from the inner bark of several species of the fig tree, as well as from the succulent leaves of the desert maguey, and from other sources of fiber (see Lenz 1973 [1948], 1984 and Sandstrom and Sandstrom 1986). Today, Nahua shamans in Amatlán prefer industrially manufactured paper sold at low prices in regional markets. They cut the paper with scissors as part of the preparations before a ritual performance. They use some cuttings as altar decorations, or as mats, called "tortilla napkins" (sing. *tlaxcali yoyomitl* in Nahuatl) or "beds" (sing. *tlapechtli* in Nahuatl), designed to hold images of the spirits. Even though some of the figures are quite complex, shamans take only a few seconds to complete each one. The paper is stacked and folded before cutting so that multiple images are produced. A medium-sized curing ritual may require about 50 paper images, and I attended one important rain ceremony for which shamans cut over 25,000 images.

The spirits show a remarkable similarity in the way they are portrayed. In most cases, spirits are cut as small human figures, front faced with the hands held by the sides of the head. Some earth-related spirits are cut with the hands turned down. The paper images range in height from about 5 cm to 30 cm (about 2 to 12 inches), and the shaman selects paper of different textures and colors that are appropriate to the spirit being portrayed. These images are called *tlatectli* (sing. in Nahuatl), meaning "cut item" and *muñecos*, "dolls," in Spanish. They are cut only by shamans who spend years practicing the art before they are recognized as professionals. Each shaman develops a distinctive style of cutting and may eventually create new spirits and new paper images for his or her rituals. The paper images represent the heart-soul or yolotl of the spirit and not the spirit itself. The shamans, by making offerings to the spirit's heart-soul, can control the spirit for the benefit of their clients.

The paper images are masterful creations that portray in concrete form some very abstract and sophisticated ideas. The human figure, representing the animating principle or heart-soul, is at the center of all the images. The shaman adds to this core various markers to distinguish a particular spirit from others. These markers include headdresses, clothing, footwear, various patterns cut from the body, and items attached to the sides and legs of the image. Care is always taken by the shamans to cut facial features, fingers, and toes where appropriate, occasionally genitals, and a central V-cut to represent the spirit's heart. This system of representation is an economical expression of the pantheistic nature of Nahua religion. The human form, closely associated with the principle of animation, is the core element common to virtually all paper images. It is a physical representation of the unity that underlies apparent diversity in the spirit world. The variety of spirits can be distinguished by markers, but the core figure impresses upon the viewer what one shaman told me, namely that "they're all the same." See the thirty-five Nahua ritual paper images on pages 262–76 below for a previously unpublished sample of paper images cut by Amatlán shamans and refer to our account of the paper images for a more complete discussion of their meaning and significance (Sandstrom and Sandstrom 1986).

NAHUA RITUAL PAPER IMAGES

The paper cult figures presented here were collected in 1985–86 and represent the work of three shamans. I have used letters to identify the shamans in order to protect their anonymity. Sacred paper figures are almost always cut for use in groups or sets. I have selected individual figures from these sets in order to give an idea of the range of ritual cuttings that shamans produce. Thus, many of the images that follow have accompanying figures that are not reproduced here. Shamans are sometimes reluctant (or unable) to provide certain details about the images they cut or about the spirits they wish to portray. I have provided as much information about each paper figure as I was able to elicit from the shaman who cut it. Names are in Nahuatl unless otherwise indicated.

1. *tlaltepactli* (earth spirit,
    literally "earth's
    surface")
   White tissue paper
   24.5 x 13.5 cm
   Cut by female shaman A

This image is a female aspect of the spirit of the earth's surface. The headdress represents foliage, and the triangular cut beneath the neck is the heart. Flanking the heart are cuts that portray shoulders, and below these are two cuts representing corn. The row of diamond cuts is a belt. The shaman informed me that if one should meet an old bearded man on the trail at night it is most likely the male aspect of this spirit taking his walk. This image is cut to receive offerings during major curing rituals. Only certain earth-related spirits such as this one are cut with the hands pointing down.

2. *tepetl* (hill spirit, literally
    "hill")
   White tissue paper
   18 x 9 cm
   Cut by female shaman A

This portrayal of a hill spirit is cut with a hat surmounted by luxuriant vegetation. The cuts flanking the heart triangle are pockets or possibly representations of corn. Shamans cut this image for curing rituals or to protect a patient from illness.

3. *tepetl* (hill spirit, literally
      "hill")
   White tissue paper
   25 x 11 cm
   Cut by female shaman A

This is the image of a male hill spirit cut with the poncholike *jorongo* worn by Nahua men and boys. Absence of a heart triangle is probably an inadvertent omission by the shaman. The pair of cuts in the body are pockets. The shaman said that when offerings are left on hilltops, spirits like this one consume them. This image is cut for curing rituals and to protect the patient from spirit attack.

4. *tepeseñor* (mixed Nahuatl–
      Spanish term meaning
      "hill lord")
   Manila paper
   24 x 8.5 cm
   Cut by female shaman B

The shaman explained that this figure is the image (*ixcopintli* in Nahuatl) of the heart-soul (*yolotl*) of a male hill spirit. Once sacralized, the image attracts the hill spirit that comes to receive its offerings. She said that hill spirits can also act as witness and guardian spirits. When I asked her to explain the differences among these types of spirits, she stated that all of them are really aspects of the sun (*toteotsij*) anyway. She further explained that only certain hills have a resident spirit and that lightning often strikes those particular hills. The patterns of cuts beneath the heart triangle are clothing decorations, and the image has a simple crownlike headdress. The figure is usually cut as part of a curing ritual or to protect a patient from spirit attack.

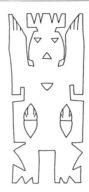

5. *chicomexochitl* (corn spirit,
   literally "7-flower")
   Manila paper
   21 x 9 cm
   Cut by female shaman B

This image of the male aspect of the corn spirit and source of human
energy is portrayed as a relatively inelaborate figure with a headdress,
heart triangle, body cuts representing corncobs, pants with pointed
knees, and roots emerging from the bottoms of the feet. This figure
is cut primarily for crop fertility rituals.

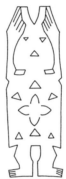

6. *sitlalij* ("star")
   Manila paper
   17.5 x 5.5 cm
   Cut by male shaman C

The forked headdress of this image of a star guardian may be the
bow used by the spirit to shoot flaming arrows at stone monsters that
threaten humans at night. The rosette beneath the heart triangle
represents a star, and the other cuts are clothing decorations. This
image is cut to protect the shaman's client against spirit attack and
other forms of danger.

7. *tlixihuantsij* (fire spirit,
   literally "honorific fire
   John," from the myth
   concerning Juan Ceniza,
   "John Ashes" or Juan
   Flojo, "John Lazy")
   Manila paper
   17.5 x 6.5 cm
   Cut by male shaman C

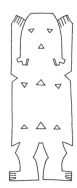

The shaman stated that this is a female aspect of the fire spirit who lives in the three stones surrounding the main fireplace in each house. It also lives in huge mountains and is the most ancient of the spirits. He stated that the paper image is just a "sign" (*seña* in Spanish) of the actual spirit. The figure is cut with earrings, a heart triangle, and other triangular clothing decorations. Shamans cut this image when they are conducting rituals to honor the "ancient ones," rain dwarf spirits linked to thunder and lightning. The fire spirit also acts as a household guardian, and shamans may invoke it to protect family members.

8. *apanchanej* ("water
   dweller," female water
   spirit)
   Manila paper
   23.5 x 5 cm
   Cut by female shaman B

This female aspect of the water spirit originates from the sea but resides in the springs, streams, rivers, and lakes of the southern Huasteca. This rare depiction of the water spirit is cut with a fish tail and with long hair that can trap and drown careless people. The shaman stated that apanchanej is basically good but that she will attack humans if they fail to give her a proper offering. The souls of people killed by lightning accompany this spirit in her watery residence. Shamans usually cut this image as part of curing rituals or to prevent spirit attack.

9. *tlacatecolotl* ("man owl")
   Manila paper blackened
      with charcoal
   23.5 x 17.5 cm
   Cut by male shaman C

Sometimes called *tlahuelilo* ("wrathful one"), this blackened figure commands the spirits who inhabit *mictlan*, "place of the dead." The Nahuas sometimes equate this spirit with the Christian devil (*diablo* in Spanish), although it shares few characteristics with its European counterpart. The shaman stated that this spirit is responsible for releasing disease-causing wind spirits among humans and that the *mecos* who dance during *nanahuatili* (Carnival) are its servants. It is portrayed here in male aspect, and the shaman colors the figure with charcoal from the fireplace to indicate its dangerous nature. The figure is closely associated with death, and therefore the shaman cuts two rib holes on each side and omits the heart triangle. It has a simple crown and bulky clothing that resembles wings. The image is cut during curing rituals to remove wind spirits from the patient's body and surroundings.

10. *tlacatecolotl sihuatl* ("wife
       of tlacatecolotl,"
       literally "man owl
       woman")
    Manila paper blackened
       with charcoal
    20.5 x 15 cm
    Cut by male shaman C

Many Nahua spirits exist in male and female aspects, and people often speak of these as a married pair. Here is the wife of the previous figure who, although similar in appearance to her husband, differs in some details. Her crown is slightly simpler, her clothing is square, and the charcoal is applied with a different pattern of marks. This figure is also cut during curing rituals and is placed beside the image of her husband in the array of paper images and sacred items.

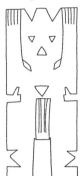

11. *tlahuelilo* ("wrathful one")
Manila paper
22.5 x 9.5 cm
Cut by female shaman B

Tlahuelilo is a manifestation or alter ego of tlacatecolotl, portrayed here as an inelaborate figure with a three-part crown, heart triangle, pointed knees representing pants, and a tail protruding between the legs. This image is cut during curing rituals in which the shaman attempts to control disease-causing wind spirits.

12. *diablo* (Spanish for "devil")
Black tissue paper
24 x 12.5 cm
Cut by female shaman A

The shaman used the Spanish word to label this figure, which she emphasized does not represent the same spirit as tlacatecolotl or tlahuelilo. She stated that this figure is the brother of the following spirit, *miquilistli* or "death," adding that they travel around together at night. The figure is cut with an animal-horn crown, teeth, wings, a V-cut for the heart, pockets, and a hairy tail. The shaman said that the black paper signifies the night and the dark underworld. The image is cut for curing rituals and to prevent spirit attack.

13. *miquilistli* ("death")
    White tissue paper
    23 x 11 cm
    Cut by female shaman A

The spirit of death is cut if the patient is feared to be dying or, according to some informants, for use in rituals of sorcery. White paper is used to represent the color of bones. The wavy line describing the head represents wrinkles, indicating that this spirit is ancient. The irregular arms and legs represent bones, and each foot is cut with three toes. A central V-cut represents the heart, and additional cuts are pockets and a belt. The garment resembling chaps is a skirt made from human bones. The shaman stated that this spirit is very dangerous and that it lives in solid rock or in the forest. She said that it moves by flying around like a butterfly or by walking on tiptoes, which is how it is portrayed here.

14. *miquilistli* ("death")
    White tissue paper
    25 x 11 cm
    Cut by female shaman A

Another version of death by the same shaman, this figure is also cut from white paper, the color of bones. It is depicted with wrinkles indicating advanced age and teeth suggesting aggressiveness. The shaman said that the second in the line of verticle V-cuts is the heart and that the others above and below it are the backbone. The cuts on the elbows are bones and the radiating V-cuts are the ribs of the spirit. The legs are cut with wavy lines reminiscent of bones. The shaman said that the spirit travels around at night and that it attacks and kills whomever it meets.

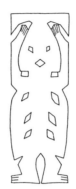

15. *ejecatl* ("wind," disease-
    causing spirit)
    Layered from the top:
    red, green, yellow,
    black tissue paper
    18 x 6.5 cm
    Cut by male shaman C

This is a wind spirit cut for use in curing rituals. The headdress resembles animal horns, and the cuts in the body represent ribs, linking this figure with spirits of the dead. By layering paper, the shaman is able to cut several figures at once. Often the colors indicate the origin of the particular wind spirit. Red or yellow figures originate from the sky, black from the underworld, green or blue from the water, and purple or other dark colors from the earth.

16. *ejecatl* ("wind," disease-
    causing spirit)
    Layered from the top:
    red, black, green,
    yellow tissue paper
    18 x 6.5 cm
    Cut by male shaman C

This is another example of a wind spirit from the same shaman. The headdress is a hat, and the body cuts are rib holes.

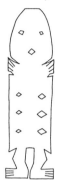

17. *ejecatl* ("wind," disease-
causing spirit)
Manila paper
17.5 x 6 cm
Cut by male shaman C

This inelaborate wind spirit has no crown, small winglike hands, and the typical pattern of rib holes. The shaman stated that this spirit likes to attack people when they are on the trail. By layering the paper, the shaman cuts eight of these figures at once.

18. *ejecatl* ("wind," disease-
causing spirit)
Layered from the top:
red, yellow, black,
green tissue paper
17.5 x 6 cm
Cut by male shaman C

This image is similar to number 17 except that it is cut from four different colors of paper. The winglike hands remind ritual participants that these spirits fly with the wind.

19. *ejecatl* ("wind," disease-
      causing spirit)
   Manila paper
   15.5 x 9 cm
   Cut by male shaman C

   The skeletal appearance of this figure connects it to disease-causing spirits of the dead. The shaman cuts this image for curing rituals to remove the spirit's malignant influence from the patient. In rituals I have witnessed, the shaman often ties examples of this paper figure to bundles of leaves from the *amatl* tree (any number of species of Ficus) and then places them in an arch around the curing array. The shaman who cut the figure said that the spirit travels around on falling leaves.

20. *mijcatsitsij ejecatl* ("corpses
      wind")
   Manila paper
   17.5 x 5.5 cm
   Cut by male shaman C

   This is the portrayal of a spirit of a dead person that travels around on the wind spreading disease and misfortune. The downward thrust of the arms links the spirit to the earth and the winglike hands link it to the wind. The shaman said that the spirit comes from human bones buried in the earth. It is cut for use in curing rituals.

21. *tlasoli ejecatl* ("filth wind,"
    literally "refuse or trash
    wind")
    Alternating double layers
    of purple and green
    tissue paper
    16.5 x 6.5 cm
    Cut by female shaman B

This double-image wind spirit comes from the underworld via the
pre-Hispanic ruins in Amatlán. Once on the earth's surface, it hides
in the forest waiting to attack humans who have become weakened in
some way. The purple color links the spirit to the earth, and the green
color indicates that this spirit may attack people who are bathing or
near the water. The figure has large heart triangles and pants with
pointed knees. Nahua shamans commonly cut paper figures in multi-
ples of two, four, or eight. This is a convention that indicates the
extraordinary power and danger of the spirit portrayed. Shamans cut
this figure for use in curing rituals.

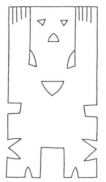

22. *xochiejecatl* ("flower wind")
    Alternating double layers
    of yellow and red tissue
    paper
    18 x 9.5 cm
    Cut by female shaman B

This figure is cut by the curer as part of an offering to protect a
newborn child when the umbilical cord is buried in the house floor.
The offering distracts the wind spirit and removes it from the surroundings. The shaman cuts a prominent heart triangle, pants with pointed
knees, and heavy boots. This spirit comes from the sky realm; hence
its yellow and red color.

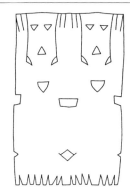

23. *xochiejecatl* ("flower wind")
      Alternating double layers
         of yellow and green
         tissue paper
      16.5 x 11.5 cm
      Cut by female shaman B

According to the shaman who cut it, the fringe at the bottom of this double-image wind spirit represents flowers. The spirit comes from a mountain called Coatitlán and can live in solid rock. It poses a danger to people in or near the water during the daytime, and therefore the shaman portrays it using green and yellow paper. In some cases the color of paper used by a shaman indicates where the spirit is most likely to attack its victims rather than its realm of origin. The figure is cut as part of curing rituals.

24. *tlasoli ejecatl* ("filth wind,"
         literally "refuse or trash
         wind")
      Yellow tissue paper
      14 x 7.5 cm
      Cut by female shaman A

This wind spirit comes from the sky realm but attacks people from its lair in the forest. One shaman suggested that the comblike head-dress that appears on many paper figures represents the open jaws of the earth. In one of its manifestations the earth is a monster that consumes human bodies once they have been buried in the ground. Nahuas link wind spirits with the earth and especially with this fero-cious aspect of its nature. The central heart triangle is flanked by pockets. The word "filth" in the name links the spirit with Nahua ideas of the spiritual pollution that can be caused by disruptive thoughts, emotions, or behavior.

25. *apanxinolaj sihuatl* (mixed
 Nahuatl–Spanish
 phrase meaning "lady
 of the water," literally
 "water lady woman")
 Yellow tissue paper
 12.5 x 6 cm
 Cut by female shaman A

This spirit attacks in daylight and causes people to fall and hurt themselves on rocks in the arroyo. Shamans cut the figure as part of curing rituals to protect their patients against falls. It is depicted with an elaborate headdress and two pockets.

26. *tlamocuitlahuijquetl*
 ("guardian" or
 "witness")
 Manila paper
 24 x 8.5 cm
 Cut by male shaman C

Shamans cut this figure so that the spirit it portrays will watch over a patient and prevent spirit attack. The shaman stands the figure upright on a slotted stick driven into the ground and lays out an offering before it. In 1986 I saw this shaman ritually cleanse a spring where a neighbor watered his cattle, and he set up several of these figures to stand guard after we had left. He said that this spirit is an "earth witness," a witness that guards things of the earth. This may explain the comblike headdress (see number 24). The heart triangle is flanked by pockets.

27. *tlamocuitlahuijquetl*
    ("guardian" or
    "witness")
    Manila paper
    20.5 x 8 cm
    Cut by female shaman B

This image of a guardian spirit has a hatlike crown, heart triangle, and pants with pointed knees. The shaman said that this figure is placed with an image of the patient's spirit (*tonali*) to prevent disease.

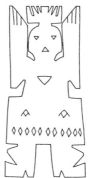

28. *tlamocuitlahuijquetl*
    ("guardian" or
    "witness")
    Manila paper
    20 x 9 cm
    Cut by female shaman B

The shaman said that this is the image of an earth witness (*testigo* in Spanish) that guards over patients. She specified that it cares for things on the earth, which may explain the comblike headdress (see number 24). Below the heart triangle are decorations she called flowers. The figure also has pants with pointed knees and heavy boots. It is placed on a *tlaxcali yoyomitl* ("tortilla napkin"), a sheet of paper decorated with symmetrical cuts, and left with offerings on the house altar of the patient.

29. *tonali* ("person's spirit,"
     "heat-soul," "fate," or
     "destiny")
     Manila paper
     20 x 8 cm
     Cut by female shaman B

This figure represents one of a person's two major souls or spirits and it is cut by the shaman for use in curing rituals. The Nahuatl word *tonali* also means "fate" or "destiny," and offerings are made to the figure to improve the patient's luck. The shaman was careful to state that she uses this image only to help people. She may have been motivated to say that because the figure can be cut as part of sorcery rituals as well. It has a simple crown, a heart triangle, a row of diamond-shaped clothing decorations, and pants with pointed knees.

30. *tonali* ("person's spirit,"
     "heat-soul," "fate," or
     "destiny")
     Manila paper
     21 x 18.5 cm
     Cut by female shaman B

This double image represents the tonali spirits of a woman and a man. The female is on the left with the two rows of diamond cuts representing clothing decorations. The male is dressed more plainly with just two pockets for adornment. By holding a small ritual and making offerings to these spirits, the shaman can make people fall in love. The love ritual is often used when a man or woman suspects that his or her spouse is having an affair or is losing interest in the marriage. In some cases the shaman instructs the client to hide the image under the sleeping mat of the spouse to increase the effectiveness of the ritual. Love magic indicates how much power the Nahua shaman is believed to have to influence the behavior and feelings of other people. This power can be potentially hazardous and I know of cases where shamans have been killed by people who believed they had been victimized by the shaman's rituals.

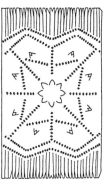

31. *tlaxcali yoyomitl* ("tortilla
      napkin")
    Manila paper
    60 x 36 cm
    Cut by female shaman B

This decorated sheet is used to hold the images of witness and guardian spirits that are left on the tops of sacred hills to watch over patients in the village below. It is cut by the shaman to be a beautiful bed on which to create an array of the paper figures. The central rosette is a guardian star, and the other cuts are described by the shaman as decorations. The name of this class of paper cuttings derives from the elaborately embroidered cloths used to keep tortillas warm during a meal.

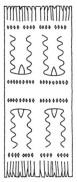

32. *tlaxcali yoyomitl* ("tortilla
      napkin")
    Manila paper
    41 x 17 cm
    Cut by female shaman B

A special witness spirit flies to the sun on this decorated sheet, carrying with it flowers and beautiful prayers. The shaman cuts these images for curings and on occasion as part of the cleansing rituals surrounding a birth. The flowers and prayers are gifts to the sun so that it will watch over the people below. The four wavy cuts represent doors through which beneficial spirits may pass or through which offerings are accepted by the sun.

33. *tonatij* ("sun")
    White tissue paper
    23 x 22.5 cm
    Cut by female shaman A

This sheet is cut to represent the power of the sun, and it is used in particularly difficult cures. During the curing ritual the cutting is placed by the incense brazier or by the household fireplace. The shaman told me that she can cut an anthropomorphic image of the sun's spirit but that she does this on rare occasions and only after much ritual preparation. The anthropomorphic image of the sun's spirit is overwhelmingly powerful and must only be cut when the villagers face a severe emergency, such as drought or epidemic. This sheet is a somewhat less powerful image of the sun that can be employed to benefit individual patients.

34. *metsli* ("moon")
    White tissue paper
    25.5 x 22.5 cm
    Cut by female shaman A

Although the Nahuas see an image of a rabbit in the moon instead of our "man in the moon," this sheet representing the moon spirit is cut with two smiling faces. The moon is an ambivalent spirit in Nahua thought that is linked to the benevolent *tonantsij* but is also associated with the underworld. Shamans cut this image for curing rituals.

35. *sitlalij* ("star")
White tissue paper
50 x 44 cm
Cut by female shaman A

This elaborate "tortilla napkin" is cut for a major curing ritual. At the center is the sun that protects all of the people on earth. The small figures surrounding the sun are called *angelitos* in Spanish, and they are the spirits of innocent, deceased children, each cut with a small crown and heart triangle. In the four corners are the images of guardian stars. During the curing ritual, the shaman holds this cutout over the patient's head while chanting to the spirits. The shaman then walks to the top of a sacred hill and hangs the image from an arch that has been constructed there. Before leaving she places an offering under the arch. The object of this procedure is to invite salutary spirits such as the sun, stars, and angelitos to help watch over the patient. Even a complex figure such as this one takes the shaman only a minute or two to cut.

NAHUA RITUALS

Villagers call rituals *xochitlalia* (sing. "flower earth," literally "to put down flowers") in Nahuatl and *costumbres* ("customs") when speaking Spanish. Attending a ritual in Amatlán is an unforgettable experience. Outwardly, religious events appear as disorganized as village meetings, but just as in the latter case there exists a hidden structure in rituals through which a great deal gets accomplished. Rituals themselves are colorful and filled with action. They often run continuously for several days at a time, producing in participants a dreamlike state of semiexhaustion. Most people consume quantities of potent cane alcohol that adds to the otherworldly quality of these events. Rituals are accompanied by lilting, repetitive guitar and violin music called *xochisones*, a Nahuatl–Spanish term meaning "flower sounds" (for recorded examples from Amatlán, see Provost and Sandstrom 1977). In larger events, lines of dancers perform in ornate headdresses while shaking gourd rattles. Shamans and their helpers construct elaborate altars decorated with greenery and flowers and load them with offerings and rows of lighted beeswax candles. One or more copal incense braziers pour out billows of resinous, aromatic smoke as the shaman sacrifices chickens or turkeys and dances wildly holding bundles of cut paper figures. The rituals are exciting events, but their major significance is what they reveal about Nahua culture. Rituals can express rarely spoken values of how a people see themselves in relation to the universe at large. They are composed of conventional actions that only have meaning in the world created and inhabited by the participants.

In pre-Hispanic times calendrical rituals were often synchronized with the march of the seasons, the cyclical movement of heavenly bodies, or the growth, death, and rebirth of vegetation. Today the Nahuas have coordinated many of their ritual occasions with the liturgical calendar of the Catholic Church. Of course the official church calendar itself is partly based on seasonal changes. The Nahua ritual season begins with the death of the earth as the dry season approaches and many deciduous plants lose their foliage. On October 18 members of households burn copal incense and beeswax candles on their altars to observe the day of San Lucas (Spanish for Saint Luke). After this day, the yolotl heart-souls of the dead roam the earth in search of their kinsmen. These souls are also called the *micatsitsij*, in Nahuatl meaning "corpses" or "honored dead." Villagers show the greatest respect for the souls of their kinsmen throughout this observance. However, it is a time of potential danger, because even the souls of kinsmen can unintentionally harm the living members of their families. Shamans refused to cut paper images for me between San Lucas and the culminating offering on November 2nd for fear that they would attract disease to the village.

On October 30, twelve days after San Lucas, members of each household set up a special altar to receive the dead souls of their ancestors. In preparation, the family often kills a pig in order to have meat for tamales, a special food prepared for this occasion. The women also bake bread in the shapes of men and women, animals, and little baskets that are hung along with bananas, oranges, marigolds, and green fig-tree leaves on a bamboo arch over the altar table. Household members sometimes attach to the arch pinwheel-like adornments they weave out of leaves of the *coyolij* palm and marigold blossoms. These adornments are called *sitlalmej* ("stars" in Nahuatl), and they stand for the guardian stars that protect the village at night.

This occasion is a time of great excitement in Amatlán as women prepare delicacies and the family busies itself by butchering a pig and constructing the house altar. On October 30, the altar is completed, and a member of the household sprinkles a trail of marigold petals on the floor leading from the altar table out through the door of the house. This *xochiojtli* or "flower trail" in Nahuatl is for the yolotl or heart-soul to follow as it searches for its living kinsmen. Three times a day through November 1 the family places hot food on the altar table with care and reverence and lights beeswax candles around the place setting so that the spirit can see and enjoy the meal. After a few minutes, the spirit has finished consuming the essence of the food, and family members may eat what is left. On November 2, called Día de los Muertos ("Day of the Dead") in Spanish, the family packs food in baskets and heads for the graveyard. They clean weeds from the graves of their kinsmen and tie fresh marigolds on the grave markers. The indigenous marigold, called *sempoalxochitl* in Nahuatl (literally "20-flower") or *flor de los muertos* in Spanish ("flower of the dead") has been associated with the earth, death, and the underworld since pre-Hispanic days.

After cleaning the grave site and decorating the marker, the family lays out a rich feast upon brightly colored embroidered cloths. Beeswax candles are lighted as the spirits consume the food offering. It is a colorful occasion as hundreds of villagers dressed in their finest clothes converge on the small graveyard and turn it into a festival with flowers, bright candles, and the tastiest food. Often the village communally hires musicians to play the sacred violin and guitar melodies that accompany all major ritual occasions. Several people told me that 4 days on earth are equal to 1 year in mictlan, and therefore this observance serves to feed the dead souls throughout the year. Failure to make an offering at this time converts normally benign souls of kinsmen into the disease-causing *ejecatl* spirits discussed above. In fact, just to be certain that no soul has been forgotten, a week or so after Day of the Dead people set up a special large altar, complete with food offerings, just outside the village on the main trail. This altar is dedicated to the souls of those unfortunates who may have been neglected by their foolish kinsmen.

Villagers call the final 4 days of this observance beginning October 30 *xantoloj* or *xantojtitlaj*, words meaning "many saints." The terms derive from the Spanish *Todos Santos* ("All Saints"), the traditional Christian holiday celebrated on November 1. The villagers have borrowed the Spanish name for All Saints day and expanded its meaning to include the other 3 days of their observance as well. The final day of their longer observance is All Souls day, celebrated by traditional Catholics on November 2. In Mexico All Souls day is called *Día de los Muertos* ("Day of the Dead"), and villagers have continued this usage when speaking Spanish. However, villagers use the terms *xantoloj* or *xantojtitlaj* to refer to the entire 4-day observance when speaking Nahuatl.

Like all Nahua ritual occasions, xantoloj has internal complexities that add a richness to the sequence of major events. Participants dedicate the final offering in the graveyard to the dead souls of adult kinsmen. Offerings made the day before are dedicated to the *angelitos* (literally "little angels" in Spanish), the souls of children who died before they learned to speak. Speech, which is associated with the fully developed tonali heat-soul, allows humans to lie, gossip, and commit bad deeds that can attract the malevolent wind spirits. Infants who die are thought by the Nahuas to pose no danger to the living, and they are frequently buried right in the family compound. Some people think that infants are reborn as other children and that they do not spend any time in mictlan. Xantoloj is also the time when many ritual kinsmen renew their mutual ties. Throughout the last days of the observance, one can see individuals and sometimes whole families carrying plates of food to the houses of their ritual kinsmen. The favored dish to offer is tamales filled with spicy pork. Failure to exchange food at this time indicates that the ritual tie is moribund. This is also the time when women make or purchase new clay cooking pots for their kitchens. Older women who make pots to sell are busy for weeks prior to xantoloj taking and filling orders. People who can afford it also purchase new clothing during this period. Finally, during the 4-day food offering people carefully sweep the trails and areas around their houses of all forest debris. The village fills with smoke for hours at a time as people burn piles of dried sticks and leaves (Romualdo Hernández 1982:149–52 describes xantoloj in a Nahua community in neighboring Hidalgo state).

The next major calendrical ritual observance occurs during the winter solstice, from December 21 through 24. This ritual is called *tlacatelilis* ("birth" in Nahuatl) and it is the tonantsij celebration mentioned at the beginning of Chapter 1. After the winter solstice the sun begins its migration northward, and the days grow longer. The lengthening days mean that the promise of spring will be fulfilled and that the vegetation will return to life as the dry season comes to an end. Many cultures in the northern hemisphere, including Euro-American cultures, celebrate this occurrence with rituals symbolizing birth. The Nahuas begin preparations for this observance several weeks in advance. Each evening men gather at the tonantsij shrine to practice dancing. They form two lines in front of the entrance and rehearse the complex steps that mimic, among other things, planting, weeding, and harvesting. On the day before the shrine is opened, they prepare crowns made from bent bamboo and decorated with mirrors, colored ribbons, and small folded-paper fans.

Two shamans open the shrine and direct helpers to sweep the interior and clean the two altar tables against the rear walls. They remove a plaster statue of tonantsij (in her guise as the Virgin of Guadalupe) from its place beneath the arch on the altar and carry it to the waiting arms of a young girl. The girl places the statue in a blue wooden box that she loads on her back and carries with the aid of a tumpline. The shamans form a procession with both of them taking the lead positions. Next follow a guitarist and violinist who play sacred melodies as they walk along. Pairs of musicians spell each other so that there can be continuous music throughout the entire 4 days and nights. Following the musicans in the procession is an old lady carrying a smoking copal brazier. She is called the *copalmijtotijquetl* ("copal dancer" in Nahuatl), and she is in charge of the group of about a dozen little girls who follow her in the procession carrying lighted beeswax candles. Next are two or three men carrying cloth sacks to receive the offerings from each household. Last in line come the villagers, including many children, who tag along for all or part of the peregrination.

Members of each household in the village prepare a small altar with a leaf-covered arch in anticipation of the visit from the procession. As the procession arrives, the shamans place the statue of tonantsij on the house altar along with two other plaster statues of lesser significance. The additional smaller statues are of the Sacred Heart of Jesus and the Virgin Mary, which the Nahuas call *tequitl* and *tequitl isihuaj* ("work" and "work's wife"). Nahuas believe that the spirit of work and his wife are necessary if the milpa is to be productive (see Sandstrom 1982). Helpers take the candles from the girls and stand them on the altar and on the earth beneath. Family members bring forward a cuartillo of corn, a liter of beans, and a few coins as an offering. Each of the shamans squats before the little altar and chants as the old woman executes a swaying dance while swirling the smoking brazier. Ritual chanting, called *tlanojnotscayotl* in Nahuatl, is an important component of all rituals conducted by shamans. In their chants the shamans list the offerings being made and entreat tonantsij to bestow her blessing of fertility upon the household. The musicians change melodies and tempo with each part of the ritual, which allows people crowding outside the house to know exactly what is happening. At the conclusion, helpers dismantle the altar and hand the candles and statues back to procession members. They pour the offerings into the sacks, and everyone moves on to the next house. It is difficult to describe the anticipation felt by household members as they await the arrival of the procession. Particularly among the children, the excitement is almost unbearable as they hear the music approaching through the forest from the distance.

At the last house to be visited before dark, the participants leave the altar intact, and men arrive prepared to perform dances until dawn. They dress in new white clothes, and in addition to their colorful headdresses each carries a gourd rattle (*ayacachtli* in Nahuatl) and a flower carved out of wood (*maxochitl*, literally "hand flower" in Nahuatl). They form two lines for the first dance, and the musicians, who had been playing sacred melodies, now switch to dance tunes. The dancers, called *ayacachmijtotijquetl* (sing. "rattle dancer" in Nahuatl), perform the fast-paced and energetic steps under the direction of a leader who dances between the two lines. Many dances have exotic names in Nahuatl such as *coatl* ("snake"), *nopali* ("nopal cactus"), *etocanij* ("bean planter"), and perhaps the most famous of all, *xochipitsahuac* ("slender flower"). The purpose of the dancing is to entertain tonantsij while she rests after her labors of the day. The performance continues until dawn when the participants form a new procession and the peregrination resumes. On the morning of the fourth day, December 24, the dancers continue to perform until noon. By then, all the houses have been visited, and the villagers prepare for a final feast to honor tonantsij.

After chanting and censing the altar with copal smoke, the shamans direct the procession to be formed once more and return to the shrine from which it had started 3 days before. In front of the shrine helpers have erected two leaf- and flower-covered arches. Others are gathered in groups constructing a variety of adornments out of palm leaves and flowers. The surrounding houses are busy with the noise of cooking as women and girls prepare a large feast. The procession arrives and passes through the arches as the shamans shower the marchers with marigold petals. Helpers set up a table outdoors to hold the statues, candles, and adornments while preparations continue. Late in the evening Reveriano, the leading shaman in Amatlán, kills the sacrificial chickens and takes out his sheaf of paper as described in Chapter 1. He cuts out images of several dozen ejecatl spirits and performs a ritual cleansing of the shrine, using techniques explained in greater detail below. At midnight hundreds of people crowd into the shrine as a massive feast is laid out on the altar. Both shamans, exhausted from days without sleep, shout instructions above the music and noise and instruct everyone to gather outside.

There, led by the shamans, musicians, copal incense bearers, and the girls carrying the statues and candles, nearly all of the people of the village swirl around the shrine, encircling it four times. Then they enter the shrine, and the shamans replace the statues where they belong, and the girls carefully line the altar with lighted candles. The altar is about 3 meters long and is spanned by an arch covered with green leaves, marigolds, and eight pinwheel adornments representing guardian stars. The altar table itself has been decorated with leaf and marigold adornments to accompany the food and candles. Beneath the altar on the earth floor helpers have set out adornments, a smoking copal brazier, lighted candles, and cups and plates of food. At a nearby spring, the shamans have carefully assembled another similar offering. As the shaman chants, the music suddenly changes to a driving rhythm. The shaman grabs a smoking brazier and executes a brief wild and high-stepping dance before the altar as an offering to tonantsij. After about half an hour, women bring more food, and everyone in attendance enjoys one of the best meals of the year. By dawn on December 25, only a single lighted candle beneath the main altar is witness to the color and pageantry of a few hours before. The yearly ritual for tonantsij is over, men and women return to their work, and children can be heard once again playing in the forest and on the banks of the arroyo.

Although this observance does share features with Christmas celebrations among mestizos, in Amatlán the occasion has little to do with Jesus Christ per se (except perhaps in its oblique recognition of the return of the sun-Christ); and the date of December 25, Christmas Day, has no ritual significance. The focus instead is on birth itself, or in a broader sense, on fertility. Women and children play important roles in the event, and little girls representing potential fertility are key figures. Villagers pointed out that tonantsij also controls fertility in the milpas, and so the celebration is held for the seeds and for rain as well. This is the largest village-wide ritual and one of the most costly. Tonantsij seems to embody the basic concerns and worries of people, and despite being a major spirit entity she remains accessible to the villagers.

The Nahuas are mother worshippers because fertility is life for horticulturists, and tonantsij, who springs from the pre-Hispanic past, is responsive to human needs. She represents aspects of the earth, sun, and water as they conjoin in fruitful union in the milpa as well as the womb. Offerings are dedicated to the sky, earth, water, and underworld realms as symbolized respectively by the food-laden altar table with its arch, the floor array, the altar set up at the spring, and the initial offering to the spirits of the dead. She also connects the Indian past and the Christian mestizo present, and as such there is no need to conceal her worship. When she appeared as the Virgin of Guadalupe in 1531, tonantsi had black hair, dark skin, and she spoke the Nahuatl language. Indians all over Mexico are proud of her and see in her a symbol of their ethnic and national identity (see Sandstrom 1982 for a detailed description and analysis of the tlacatelilis ritual).

New Year's, celebrated on December 31, is a ceremony with dual themes. On the one hand the rite marks the death of *huehuexihuitl*, Nahuatl for the "old year," and on the other it is a cleansing and welcoming rite for *yancuic xihuitl*, the "new year" to come. The ritual offering is held in the tonantsij shrine, and it begins late in the evening and lasts all night. New Year's Day is not marked as a special occasion, and people go about their business as usual. Villagers told me that as the old year dies, the new one comes into being through a process much like human birth. I was not able to get further details about this intriguing concept, however. For both New Year's and the tonantsij observance the period following the main feast, from about midnight until dawn, is a special time. People wishing to enter into ritual kinship ties make arrangements with the shaman to have the relationship sacralized in a brief cleansing ceremony. After most people have gone home, candidates who wish to forge new ritual kin ties form a line before the altar that sometimes stretches out through the door of the shrine. The ritual itself is nothing more than an abbreviated cleansing where the shaman chants, brushes the candidates with palm adornments, and has them shake hands and address each other by their new ritual kin terms.

Following New Year's, the southern Huasteca enters into the most severe part of the dry season. Sometimes 2 months go by without a drop of rain, and many of the leaves in the forest turn brown and fall. In late February or early March villagers hold a lengthy and elaborate ritual dedicated to the seed and rain spirits. It is called by the generic Nahuatl terms *tlamanilistli* ("offering," literally "the spreading out of something"), or *xochitlalia* ("flower earth," literally "to put down flowers," the general word for ritual), or by the more specific Nahuatl name *chicomexochitl* ("7-flower"), after the corn spirit. This ritual offering is made in anticipation of the spring planting and serves to call up rain for the dry-season crops. The ritual often can last for 12 days and contains many highly complex ritual sequences. It begins with a cleansing for which the head shaman cuts scores of paper images of ejecatl spirits and lays them out in an elaborate array. The shaman ritually banishes these dangerous spirits to keep them away from the offerings dedicated to rain and seed spirits. As part of the preparations, the shaman cuts hundreds of additional paper images for use on a series of altars. In the meantime, volunteers construct many special palm and marigold adornments for the altars while they sit around in small groups chatting.

The main altar is inside a private house and at its center is the sealed box containing the seed images. Helpers clean this altar, and the shaman carefully lays out a large number of paper images of seeds and water-related spirits. The shaman directs assistants to open the seed box and to remove and wash the clothes worn by the paper images. As the clothes are drying on the line, assistants lean the naked seed children upright at various places on the altar table and on the earthen floor below. After the cleansing outside in which he expels dangerous ejecatl or wind spirits, the shaman enters the house followed by helpers carrying live turkeys and chickens. The shaman grabs a large bird, cuts its throat with a pair of scissors, and carefully drips the blood over the large array of paper images laid on the altar. He repeats this with several additional sacrificial birds, taking care that blood falls on to the paper images and adornments on the floor that forms the display to the earth. He then fills a shallow dish with blood, and using a turkey feather as a brush paints each paper image with it. When I asked what he was doing, he replied, "This is their food."

Over the next 11 days the shaman and several helpers build and decorate a number of smaller altars. The most important are dedicated to the fire spirit, the water spirit, and the sun (symbolized by a cross). Each altar is composed of paper images, leaf and marigold adornments, and copious food and drink offerings. For hours at a time very little happens, and some people drift off to their houses to sleep or catch up on work. Then, as if by cue, the action resumes, and a new round of chanting, dancing before the altar, or dedicating of offerings occurs. All the while musicians play the slow melodic tunes that accompany important ritual occasions. During times of activity the music conveys a sense of urgency, and dozens of people arrive, carrying additional food offerings or perhaps more flowers or palm leaves. The copal smoke pours out of numerous braziers, people approach the altars and execute the double bow used on ritual occasions, shamans chant, and a general air of excitement pervades. After an hour or two, the action subsides as rapidly and mysteriously as it began.

On the twelfth day the people are exhausted but buoyant as they prepare for the final offering. Helpers clear away old adornments and replace them with fresh ones. Women cook additional food, and the musicians seem to acquire new life. Men have neatly refilled the seed box with the paper images, now dressed in clean clothes, with many wearing new necklaces and earrings. As women bring out the food offerings and place them on the altars, the shaman chants intensely. In his chant he lists the offerings and implores tonantsij and her children, the seeds, to support the village in the year to come. He chants before each altar, beseeching the sun, water, and earth to be kind to the people even though they often offend the spirits through their activities and occasional evil intentions. At the end, the shaman directs everyone to kneel before the main altar to demonstrate their ultimate respect for a sacred universe that has provided life and the means of living. The adorned altar is left intact, and the seed box remains sealed throughout the year. The other altars are dismantled within a few days. As the adornments surrounding the seed box dry, helpers periodically replace them. On occasion an individual places a fresh container of water before the box so that the seeds will be comfortable. The shamans repeated to me how imperative it is that the village be maintained as a pleasant place so that the seeds will be happy and remain in the village to help the people. Without the reproductive power of the crops as embodied in the seeds, human existence would come to an end. For a more detailed account of this ritual, see Sandstrom and Sandstrom (1986:35ff.) and for a description of chicomexochitl and similar rituals in Nahua villages in the same region, see Williams García 1966a and Ixmatlahua Montalvo et al. 1982:89–92.

The final major calendrical ritual occurs during the Christian celebration of Carnival, the wild days before the austerity of Lent. The dates vary in accordance with the Christian calendar, but it usually falls between mid-February and the end of March. Although Lent is not observed by the people of Amatlán, they have readily adopted their own version of Carnival into their ritual cycle. Ethnomusicologist Charles Boilès (1971) has demonstrated the pre-Hispanic roots of Carnival celebrations among neighboring Otomí Indians, and I am certain that his findings apply to Amatlán as well. The Nahuas call the observance *nanahuatili* in Nahuatl after the name of a dance that is performed during it. The entire occasion is planned and financed by a group of volunteer organizers called in Spanish *capitanes* ("captains"). The celebration lasts for about a week (although its length may vary slightly depending on the motivation of the dancers) and is characterized by the playing of *huapango* music, a vibrant rhythmic and melodic dance form for which the entire Huasteca region is renowned. The guitarist and violinist move from house to house accompanied by raucous masked dancers. These are the mecos mentioned earlier. As the musicians and dancers enter a compound, the inhabitants crowd around to view the event. After several dances, the household head offers money to the lead meco to try to coerce the disruptive troop to move on to their next victims.

All of the dancers are males, although half are dressed as women and girls. Everyone wears a mask or bandana tied over his face and speaks in a falsetto voice. To add to the disguise, participants are dressed in clothing borrowed from someone else. The papier-maché masks are purchased in the market, and they represent pink-faced mestizos, and, for my benefit in 1973, a blond North American girl. During performances the mecos kick dogs, climb trees, mock people, make obscene jokes and gestures, and carry out the roles of pranksters. They are the cause of much laughing and teasing, particularly on the part of the hordes of children who follow them around. Only young males between about 16 and 23 years old, or about the time they marry, become mecos, and the entire occasion is considered a time for younger people to have fun.

This observance is connected to Nahua religious practices in that the mecos are considered to be servants of *tlacatecolotl*, master spirit of the underworld. For about a week they are loosed on the village in what becomes a serious disruption of normal daily affairs. The ritual significance of the mecos becomes clearer by examining how they are served food in the evening. Household members set out a meal for the performers on a long bench while musicians and dancers are performing at the last compound they plan to visit for the day. The hosts also place four additional servings of food on a small table nearby, along with a lighted beeswax candle, a smoking brazier, a bottle of cane alcohol, some bottled soft drinks, and a lighted tallow candle representing the underworld. After the last dance, some of the mecos pick up the food offerings from the table while others take up the candle and brazier. As the musicians switch from dance music to sacred music, these mecos lead the others in a circle around the benches holding the evening meal. The entire group circles four times in one direction and then four times in the reverse direction. The atmosphere has changed from one of levity and practical joking to dead seriousness. The lead meco then pours out the cane alcohol and soft drinks in a circle completely surrounding the eating area. After a short resumption of the dancing, the performers remove their masks, assemble around the bench, and proceed to eat. When they have finished, one meco empties out one of the plates of food, some cane alcohol, and a bottle of soda on the ground near the small table.

This elaborate sequence of acts performed before the mecos are permitted to eat demonstrates their ritual power. The procedure is designed to protect the household from later visitations from underworld spirits who might mistakenly think that the offerings were made on their behalf. The mecos are changed back to normal men before they can eat, and the area is protected by the circles of poured cane alcohol and soft drinks. In addition, they offer food to the earth at the finish to appease offended underworld spirits. I have also seen mecos perform brief cleansings on sick children living in the compounds they visit. They usually brush the child with leaves while chanting a request that the offending underworld spirit depart. Villagers by no means consider the mecos to be evil even though they are servants of a dreaded underworld figure. Rather, they are better described as unpredictable, disrespectful, and humorous. Paul Jean Provost has made an intensive study of nanahuatili in a Huastecan Nahua village, and he concludes that the observance is a rite of reversal, a period when normal cultural rules are suspended or reversed, somewhat akin to our Halloween. He notes that disguised figures break social norms by mocking people directly to their faces, making overt sexual gestures, dressing in women's clothing, making fun of powerful mestizos, and coercing money from households. Provost sees in this behavior a ritualized denial of social norms that may serve as a safety valve for Nahua culture (1975:187ff.).

There is an important secular aspect to this ritual observance. On alternate nights during the week, organizers of nanahuatili hold a dance that is attended by everyone in the village. The first part of the evening is given over to dancing by the mecos, but around 9:00 P.M. unmarried couples may dance. This is the only occasion that I have witnessed people dancing together in ballroom style. Only teenagers and young adults participate while all the others sit to observe and socialize. Music is provided by a regional itinerant band or by a transistor radio. By midnight or 1:00 A.M. the music abruptly stops and everyone goes home, anticipating another day of raucous disorder.

On the last day of nanahuatili people make a mixture of white ashes and water and paint white crosses on their houses and major household items, such as the mano and metate. Participants encircle the trunks of fruit trees in the compound with a white ring of ashes. The mecos have disappeared completely by this time, and their human players, now in normal dress, figure prominently in painting the houses and fruit trees. Nanahuatili thus ends with a return to order symbolized by the white-ash crosses that appear throughout the village.

With the disappearance of the mecos the symbolic reign of the underworld ends for another year. The realm of dead souls regains its significance only after the feast day of San Lucas 8 months away. The rain now returns, vegetation revives, and the spring planting is imminent. The celebrations surrounding tonantsij in December and the late winter dedications to the seeds during xochitlalia both offer the promise of spring. The departure of the last underworld representatives following nanahuatili guarantees that the earth's rejuvenation is not far off. One of the most important holidays in the Christian calendar, Easter, is not celebrated in Amatlán. At most, a few women and girls attend a special Mass held at the church in distant Ixhuatlán. On Easter Sunday, this little town is filled with Indians and mestizos from miles around, and it has the atmosphere of a fair. Villagers I questioned did not seem to attach much importance to Easter Week, and most people dismissed it as a church affair that has little significance for them. With the close of nanahuatili the last major calendrical ritual occasion comes to an end (see also Williams García 1960).

There are numerous smaller calendrical rituals associated with Catholic church holidays that are recognized to varying degrees among village households. An important one is Santa Cruz (Holy Cross Day), observed on May 3. On this day household members put a plate of food, a cup of coffee or chocolate containing bread, and lighted beeswax candles at a site some distance from their house. Sometimes people construct a flower-covered cross using the yellow flower called *santa cruz*, or a leaf- and flower-covered arch over the food. The offering is dedicated to the wandering souls of people who died violently. These souls are dangerous to the living, and so they are offered food away from the family dwelling. Another occasion for which a household might light a candle on their house altar is December 12, Virgin of Guadalupe Day. Other saints' days and holidays that may be observed by villagers are listed in Table 6.2. These official days tend to be ignored by most people, but a man or woman will occasionally light a candle or perhaps fill an incense brazier with hot coals and copal bark as a sign of respect. In the view of the villagers, many saints have counterparts among traditional Nahua spirits, and several people told me that they see no reason for having special days when the important spirits all receive their proper offerings during the normal round of rituals. The identification of Nahua spirits with Catholic saints will be discussed below. Finally, there are several national holidays of a secular nature that are listed in Table 6.2. These are observed by children attending school and not by private households.

The rich religious life of the Nahuas is reflected to the highest degree in their noncalendrical and private observances, which in addition are far less influenced by the outward forms of Spanish Catholicism. For example, I witnessed three rituals occurring at different times in the life cycle of corn. One ritual called *quitlacualtij xinaxtli pilsintsij* (Nahuatl for "he feeds the little corn seed") is held just before planting. Following a cleansing sequence, the shaman constructs an altar that holds an elaborate food offering for the corn seed. The ritual culminates with the shaman blessing a large basket filled with corn seed just before it is carried to the field by helpers. The head of the household then constructs a small altar and makes an offering to the earth in the center of the milpa just before planting begins. This observance is held in the morning and is accompanied by a feast prepared by the women of the house. When the men return from planting they are served another meal consisting of a special sour corn porridge called *axocotl*, followed by turkey mole. The food should be plentiful enough so that many of the workers take home to their families pieces of meat wrapped in tortillas (for descriptions of similar observances in Nahua villages of the region, see Reyes Martínez 1982:49–52 and Ixmatlahua Montalvo et al. 1982:93–95).

When the corn matures to the point where it forms *elotes*, the Nahuas hold a second ritual called in Nahuatl *elotlamanilistli* ("elote offering") or simply *tlamanilistli* ("offering"). The sweet tender corn is much valued by the villagers as a source of food, and this ritual observance can be quite elaborate and expensive. Turkeys, chickens, and pigs

are butchered, and a large array of offerings is assembled by the head
of the household. Family members and friends prepare adornments
and food as young men and women dance before a special altar.
Baskets loaded with elotes are brought in from the fields by helpers
and are set before the altar. Special tamales called *xamitl* in Nahuatl
are prepared from the sweet young corn and are served with mole and
other favorite dishes. During the second night of this observance, the
young dancers hold a performance in which they symbolically remove
raccoons from the fields. Raccoons are a major pest in the milpas. I
have not witnessed this event, but villagers report that individuals
take the roles of hunter, hunting dogs, and the raccoon and that after
the latter is killed, it is symbolically skinned with a maize stalk (for
descriptions of this ritual in neighboring Nahua villages see Hernández
Cuellar 1982:72–80; De la Cruz 1982:85–86; Reyes Martínez 1982:63–
69; Ixmatlahua Montalvo et al. 1982:95–101). The third ritual is called
sintlacualistli (Nahuatl for "corn feeding"), and it is held a few days
following the corn harvest. Floral adornments, food offerings, music,
and feasting are meant to insure future harvests and to keep chicomexochitl ("7-flower," the corn spirit) from leaving the village. Young
performers dance with ripe ears of corn to make chicomexochitl feel
welcome in the household.

There is no rigid form for these rituals, and each shaman varies
them according to his or her own judgment. They do share certain
components, however. Every ritual begins with a cleansing to remove
dangerous underworld spirits. All involve the construction of an arch
or altar and the dedication of offerings to the corn spirit. In addition,
each ritual employs certain specialized adornments that represent corn.
The sacred twins, 7-flower and 5-flower, are represented by two or
sometimes four unshucked ears of corn that are tied together and
wrapped in a new red bandana. These adornments are called the
eloconemej (Nahuatl for the "elote children"). The shaman may cut
paper images of these and other spirits as well. A paired set of floral
adornments resembling ears of corn represent the same sacred spirits.
One is composed of seven rows of flowers and the other smaller one
is composed of five rows. The participants place these on the altar or,
in the case of the planting ritual, in the carrying basket of corn seed.
Not all households take the trouble to sponsor offerings of this type
every season, and some may go years between private crop rituals.
The rituals vary in price between $4 and $20 depending on how
elaborate they are, and many people complain that they cannot afford
them. Several villagers told me that they simply contribute to the

TABLE 6.2. Rituals, Sacred Observances, and Secular Holidays in Amatlán

A. Church holidays recognized by villagers but requiring little or no local ritual activity

Date	Observance	Purpose
November 25	Santa Catarina (Saint Catherine)	Saint's day
November 30	San Andrés (Saint Andrew)	Saint's day
January 6	Día de Reyes (Epiphany)	Saint's day
March 19	San José (Saint Joseph)	Saint's day
May 15	San Isidro (Saint Isidore)	Saint's day
June 13	San Antonio (Saint Anthony)	Saint's day
June 24	San Juan (Saint John)	Saint's day
June 29	San Pedro (Saint Peter), San Pablo (Saint Paul)	Saint's day
July 25	Santiago (Saint James)	Saint's day
August 15	Asunción (Assumption of the Virgin Mary)	Saint's day
August 24	San Bartolo (Saint Bartholomew)	Saint's day
August 28	San Agustín (Saint Augustine)	Saint's day
August 30	Santa Rosa (Saint Rose)	Saint's day
September 10	San Nicolás (Saint Nicolas)	Saint's day
September 21	San Mateo (Saint Mathew)	Saint's day
September 29	San Miguel (Saint Michael)	Saint's day
October 4	San Francisco (Saint Francis)	Saint's day
Movable feast	Semana Santa (Holy Week including Easter)	Women and girls may attend Mass

B. Church holidays observed in the village

Date	Observance	Purpose
October 18	San Lucas (Saint Lucas)	Saint's day, ritual year begins
November 1	xantoloj (Todos Santos, All Saints)	Make offerings to souls of dead children
November 2	xantoloj (Día de los Muertos, All Souls)	Make offering to souls of adult kinsmen
December 12	tonantsij (Virgen de Guadalupe, Virgin of Guadalupe)	Guadalupe day, beings tlacatelilis
December 21–24	tlacatelilis (Navidad, Christmas)	Human and crop fertility
December 31	yancuic xihuitl (New Year's)	Offering to old and new year
May 3	xantojcoros (Santa Cruz, Holy Cross)	Make offerings to those who died violently

TABLE 6.2. *Continued*

Date	Observance	Purpose
Movable feast, February–March	*nanahuatili* (Carnaval, Carnival)	Host underworld spirits

C. Nonchurch ritual observances

Date	Observance	Purpose
Early spring	*xochitlalia* (flower earth), *chicomexochitl* (7-flower)	Insure crop fertility

D. Noncalendrical and private or family rituals:

Observance	Purpose
quitlacualtij xinaxtli pilsintsij (he feeds the little corn seed)	Planting ritual to increase fertility
elotlamanilistli (elote offering)	Ritual to increase harvest
sintlacualistli (corn feeding)	Offering for harvest
nacaspitsalistli (ear blowing)	Birth ritual to make child obey
maltisejcone (the child will bathe himself)	Cleansing of newborn
titeixpiyaj (vigil)	Funeral
quichicuahuitile mijcatsij (wake)	Offering held week following death
tliquixtis (meaning unknown)	Offering held following death to appease spirits
se xihuitlaya (1 year past)	Offering held 1 year following death
tlamanilistli (offering)	Periodic pilgrimage to appeal for rain, also ritual for shamans to honor the sun
momapacalistli (hand washing)	Ritual to affirm ritual kin ties
caltlacualtilistli (house feeding)	Offering to spirit of new house
ochpantli (sweeping)	Curing and cleansing ritual

E. Secular and national holidays observed by schoolchildren

Date	Observance
May 5	Battle of Puebla
May 10	Mother's Day
May 15	Teacher's Day
May 20	Father's Day
September 16	Independence Day
November 20	Revolution Day

Note: Actual observance may vary from official dates given, and religious content often diverges from that of official church holidays.

major villagewide seed ritual described above and they feel that this
is enough to please the seeds.

Rites of passage—rituals marking transitions from one social status
to another—are relatively unelaborate among the Nahuas, with the
exception of funerals. At birth, the midwife (*tetejquetl* in Nahuatl)
performs a brief ritual cleansing to protect the newborn in which
beeswax candles, *coyol* palm adornments, copal incense, and food are
offered to the earth (see Reyes Antonio 1982:49–50 for a description
of Nahua beliefs about dangers to children and pregnant women
caused by solar and lunar eclipses and the steps that midwives take to
protect their clients from these threats). The umbilical cord is cut with
a sharpened piece of reed, and both the placenta and umbilical cord
are buried in the floor of the house. On the fourth day following the
birth, either the midwife or a special ritual kinswoman called in Nahuatl the *axochiteonaj* ("water-flower godmother") bathes the baby in
water in which herbs have been soaked. The woman makes a brief
offering called in Nahuatl *nacaspitsalistli* ("ear blowing"), in which
kinsmen whisper advice into the baby's ear with the hope that as the
baby grows the words will be understood and heeded (see De la Cruz
1982:133; and Hernández Cuellar 1982:59ff. for more information on
these rituals among neighboring Nahuas). A ritual called *maltisejcone*
(Nahuatl for "the child will bathe him/herself) may be held around
this time, which includes a more elaborate cleansing and the creation
of fictive kin ties between the newborn child and friends of the parents.
The new godparents buy gifts for the baby, and they may be asked to
name the child at this time. Godparenthood is a very powerful form
of ritual kinship, and villagers told me that such ties often last a lifetime
(see Reyes Antonio 1982:117–21 for description of Nahua birth procedures and rituals).

There are no formal puberty rituals to mark the achievement of
adulthood. Full adulthood is recognized after marriage and the birth
of the couple's first child. Wedding ceremonies are extremely informal.
In some cases a marriage is arranged through an intermediary, but
typically the couple by prior arrangement simply begins to live together
in the house of the groom's parents. The groom's family may take
gifts to the family of the bride, and in several cases that I have recorded
the bride's family hosted a feast for the groom and his kinsmen. In
the Mexican legal system, Nahua marriage is of the common-law type.
If the boy has built a separate house prior to the marriage, the new
couple often elopes before seeking permission from either set of parents. In these cases, however, the parents often suspect beforehand

what is about to happen and pretend to be surprised or even outraged. Older people told me that during their youth the groom would commonly have to work for the bride's family for up to a year before the marriage was considered valid. However, this practice apparently has been abandoned except for any informal help the son-in-law may provide (see Romualdo Hernández 1982:228–30 for a description of Nahua marriage customs). Divorce is rare and usually results in one partner leaving the village permanently. In this case, divorce and permanent separation amount to the same thing.

The funeral ritual, called *titeixpiyaj* (Nahuatl for "vigil"), is held within a day following the death. Helpers lay out the body on a low platform with the arms folded on the chest and a white cloth over the face. Attendants place marigold circlets called *coronas* (Spanish for "crowns") on the body. They lay out a long garland of marigolds called a *rosario* ("rosary" in English) along the length of the body rising over the face of the corpse to a roof beam overhead. This string of flowers is also called in Nahuatl an *ojtli* ("trail"), over which the heat-soul travels to find its way out of the body. The close association of marigolds with funerals probably accounts in part for their Spanish name *flor de los muertos* ("flower of the dead"). Stakes driven in the ground on three sides of the corpse hold large lighted beeswax candles. A village carpenter is meanwhile building a coffin from boards made from the cedar tree that the Nahuas call *teocuahuitl* ("sacred tree" in Nahuatl). The deceased's relatives stand a 24-hour vigil over the body as preparations are made for the burial.

All through the day and night relatives bring gifts of raw sugar, cane alcohol, corn, beans, soft drinks, candles, and prepared food as musicians play the slow ritual melodies. Women periodically break into high-pitched ululations as both men and women shed tears of grief. Copal incense burns throughout the vigil, and an attendant occasionally sprinkles the corpse using a marigold dipped in water. At various times throughout the night a male relative or a specialist called a *rezandero* (Spanish for "prayer leader") repeats in Latin with a heavy Nahuatl accent a series of incantations taken from a thoroughly worn book of Catholic prayers. Prayer leaders appear to be self-taught, and they are paid for their services. Villagers do not understand the rapidly mumbled Latin, and having these prayers at a funeral seems to be borrowed from mestizo practice. On the day of the burial family members make a cross on the bottom of the coffin in white ashes. Next they lay a white cloth over the cross followed by a set of women's clothes if the deceased is male and men's clothes if the deceased is female. These are clothes intended for the deceased's new spouse in mictlan. Next they place the body in the coffin surrounded by many articles of everyday use. For example, a man will be supplied with cups, plates, folded bundles of clothing, a small tablecloth, a new machete, soft drinks, pieces of bamboo, and a bottle of cane alcohol. Villagers said that the objects were for use by the deceased in mictlan. Before placing the body in the coffin, attendants wrap the marigold rosary around it seven times, holding a series of seven little wooden crosses in place.

In some funerals attendants cut a new door into the house to remove the body for burial. People told me that they do this so that the spirit (yolotl or heart-soul) will not be able find its way back to the house. As the pallbearers leave the house they step on several of the plates and cups used by the deceased, destroying them. This custom also serves to keep the dead soul from returning to its familiar surroundings. The procession to the graveyard is headed by the women, each holding a candle, followed by four men bearing the coffin, followed in turn by the other men and boys. The mourners burn copal as family members open the coffin and place the corpse's hands at its sides. Attendants remove the plates, cups, and machete that were with the body and break them, after which they replace the broken pieces in the coffin and nail on the lid. I was not able to find out why these items were destroyed in this way. I presume that the mourners broke them to release the yolotl souls in the objects so that they could accompany the deceased's soul to mictlan. They lower the coffin into the grave and build an underground platform of wood over the coffin. They then shovel dirt onto the platform, taking care that none scatters on the coffin itself. The mourners erect a small wooden cross covered with marigold blossoms, and as a final gesture they hang the marigold circlets on the flower-covered cross.

About a week after the burial, family members dedicate an offering to the soul of the deceased in his former home. This ritual is called *quichicuahuitile mijcatsij* in Nahuatl, which villagers translate as *velorio* in Spanish or "wake for the spirit of the dead." In some cases the family holds a related ritual at this time called *tliquixtis* in Nahuatl in which a fire is kindled. Both of these observances signal the final departure of the dead soul to the underworld. Following the ritual that marks the entrance of the soul to mictlan, the relatives place a more permanent cross of wood over the grave. The heart-soul or yolotl of the deceased may wander, however, and because it has potential to cause great harm it must be placated with offerings at various times throughout the year. Consequently family members make occasional trips to the graveyard to place fresh decorations or burn candles at the plots of their relatives. One year after the death, members of the extended family and friends gather for a major offering. This observance is called *se xihuitlaya* ("1 year past") in Nahuatl and *cabo de año* ("end of the year") in Spanish. The family butchers pigs and hires a carpenter to construct a new cross, sometimes with the name of the deceased and birth and death dates painted on it. The family calls in a shaman who holds a special cleansing ritual in which offerings are dedicated to paper images of the spirits of the cross (sun), earth, and fire. The shaman asks these spirits to forgive the deceased for offenses he committed while alive.

Attendants keep an all-night vigil during se xihuitlaya before an elaborate altar containing food offerings to the spirit of the deceased. The newly constructed cross lies on a low table perpendicular to the axis of the altar table. Musicians play sacred melodies, beeswax candles line the altar, and aromatic copal smoke fills the room. In the middle of the night, participants raise the cross and set it upright at the end of the small table. This act is called in Spanish *levantada de la cruz*, the "raising of the cross." Early the following morning the participants form a procession with a man bearing the cross at the lead. Each person carries a lighted candle, musicians play as they walk along, and men at the end of the procession carry baskets of food and other offerings. Everyone heads for the graveyard, and on arriving they lay out an offering on the grave similar to the one for xantoloj observances. After the food is dedicated, the ritual marking the 1-year anniversary of the death ends.

For 4 years following an individual's death, family members prepare an extra special offering for xantoloj or Day of the Dead observances. During this period the yolotl or heart-soul of the deceased poses the most danger to family members as it tries vainly to rejoin its former kinsmen. After 4 years the body is believed to have disintegrated, and the heart-soul is weakened and no longer poses a severe threat to the living. Nonetheless, family members will continue to make offerings during xantoloj, as long as there is someone alive who remembers the deceased. Villagers informed me that people who fail to observe these rituals for the dead experience bad dreams and invite spirit attacks.

With the exception of curing rituals discussed below, this list completes the major rituals that I have witnessed in Amatlán. There are, however, additional rituals that I have never been able to observe myself. One is called *caltlacualtilistli* ("house feeding") in Nahuatl and is an offering to the spirit of a newly-completed dwelling (see Hernández Cuellar 1982:83 for a description of this ritual in a neighboring Nahua community). The rarely held ritual to the sun mentioned earlier in this chapter is an important and powerful one, one that apparently involves shamans rather than lay people.

I did witness in 1986 the first day of preparation of an 8-day pilgrimage held every few years to appeal for rain. This remarkable event began in a distant Otomí village, and both Nahuas and Otomís participated. A number of villagers and I accompanied the Nahua shaman Aurelio who co-directed the ritual. The nearly 25 shamans present cut over 25,000 paper images that were wrapped like bales in palm sleeping mats for carrying on the trek. Two sacred walking sticks that are supposed to resemble those used by the rain dwarfs were paraded at the head of the procession, and dozens of carrying baskets filled with food were taken along for offerings. The destination of the pilgrimage was a sacred mountain, San Gerónimo (probably in the state of Hidalgo) with pre-Hispanic ruins and a cave at its peak, from which the spirits send rain to the fields. As the procession left, the participants stopped at a spring to make an offering to the water spirit, and then set off on what must have been an intriguing journey. Unfortunately, although invited to go along, I was unable to accompany the pilgrims further (see Hernández Cristóbal et al. 1982 for a description of a similar ritual in a Nahua village located in the municipio of Ixhuatlán de Madero).

Finally, villagers told me about a ritual they call *momapacalistli* (Nahuatl for "hand washing") in which ritual kinsmen wash each others' hands in a show of respect. They told me that it is sometimes held at the birth of a child when godparental ties are being created. Apparently the handwashing ritual is not held as often now as it was in previous years.

In general, I would conclude that Nahua religion is characterized by an emphasis on ritual over theology. Cosmology, world view, and deep religious principles are encoded in complex systems of ritual symbols rather than being expressed in elaborate formal systems of speech. Thus, in order to increase our understanding of Nahua religion we must have more information on the internal structure of Nahua rituals ranging from the smallest cleansing ritual to the week-long pilgrimages involving dozens of participants and many shamans.

CURING RITUALS

Perhaps nothing better illuminates the world created by a culture than examining how people define, diagnose, and treat disease. Most anthropologists and increasing numbers of Euro-American medical specialists have concluded that the diseases found in a population, who gets sick, and how illnesses are treated are due as much to sociocultural factors as biological ones. The so-called "new medicine" is little more than an attempt to increase the scientific validity of modern medicine by incorporating sociocultural factors in the diagnosis and treatment of disease.

For the Nahuas, most medical problems are treated in one of three ways. The first is to consult a village specialist in herbal cures or, in the case of broken bones, a bonesetter. Herbalists are often practicing shamans or midwives. In the early 1970s I collected a list of over 250 plants known to villagers along with their names and uses (Sandstrom 1975). Many of these are held to have medicinal value (see Reyes Antonio 1982:123–45,114–16 for a list of 46 Nahua medicinal plants and the diseases they cure, as well as a description of how Nahuas prepare medicinal plants). Bonesetters (*texixitojquetl* sing. in Nahuatl) are typically old women who align broken bones through massage, and they are able to do it, according to villagers, without pain. The second means a person has of treating medical problems is to hire a shaman to hold a curing ritual. These rituals are based on the same principles of Nahua world view that underlie all village ritual observances. As a last resort, villagers will travel to Ixhuatlán to consult with medical doctors who staff a clinic there several days each week. People in Amatlán do not perceive any contradiction among these differing systems of treating disease, and most feel comfortable consulting with all three types of specialists.

In the Euro-American medical system most disease is thought to be caused when the body is invaded by a pathogen or when the physiological processes of the body malfunction. Diagnosis and therapy, therefore, are designed to locate and identify the pathogen or malfunction and to remove or correct it through surgery or the administration of drugs. Thus Western medicine focuses on proximate cause. Nahua medicine, by contrast, tends to look for the ultimate causes or conditions that led that particular patient's body to become vulnerable to disease in the first place. Nahua medicine locates these causes in a disharmony or imbalance that has occurred between the patient and his or her physical and social surroundings (for a description of Nahua theories of disease etiology and a Nahua classification of diseases, see Reyes Antonio 1982:106,109). The object of Nahua curing techniques is to eliminate the disease by restoring balance.

In a disharmonious environment a person's *chicahualistli* or energy reserve is dangerously lowered, thus allowing ejecatl wind spirits to invade the body. Curing rituals begin with a divination to find why the ejecatl spirits have infected the patient. Causes include sorcery, gossiping neighbors, an angry house spirit, stumbling, falling, or any occurrence in which a person is suddenly frightened (a condition called in Nahuatl *nemajmatili*, "fright"), or any act or failed obligation on the part of the patient that has angered earth, water, or celestial spirits or the soul of a deceased kinsman. The Nahua shaman must first remove the ejecatl spirits from the patient's body and surroundings, thus allowing the depleted energy reserve to replenish itself. Once the patient's life force has been strengthened, the shaman may recommend that an offering be made at a specified location so that the offended spirit that caused the attack will be satisfied. Where gossiping neighbors are the cause of the disharmony, the shaman may take extraordinary measures to control them, as we will see below.

People hire shamans to perform curing rituals not only for family members but also for their houses, animals, fields, water supply, or their favored bathing area in the arroyo. Disharmony and accompanying ejecatl spirits can turn the whole world against people and destroy them in any number of ways. Curing rituals are called *ochpantli* in Nahuatl, meaning "sweeping" (as in "sweeping clean"), or *limpia* in Spanish, which means "cleansing." Rituals vary in cost, degree of elaboration, and length depending on the seriousness of the problem and the reputation of the shaman. A brief cleansing may last only 2 hours and cost as little as $.80. I have also witnessed cleansings that lasted 24 hours and cost the client more than $20. Villagers are very particular about whom they choose to conduct a cleansing. The effectiveness of the shaman supersedes any village allegiance and even loyalty to Nahua culture. Often, people will call in shamans from other villages, and shamans from Amatlán frequently travel afar to perform rituals. In one instance, a village shaman apprenticed himself to an Otomí master. In turn, this Nahua shaman has trained local apprentices, and thus two discernible variations in curing ritual practice now exist in the village—the Nahua practice and the Otomí variation. I asked people what they thought about this, and they all agreed that the particular Otomí shaman is exceptionally powerful and that it is a sound idea to have him share his knowledge with a local curer. As Pamela Effrein Sandstrom and I have demonstrated elsewhere, the religious beliefs and practices of Nahuas, Otomís, and Tepehuas of the southern Huasteca are fundamentally similar (Sandstrom and Sandstrom 1986:251ff.; see Hunt 1977 and Gossen 1986 for discussions of the fundamental similarities of cultures throughout Mesoamerica). The three groups differ in style and detail, but the core systems of belief are remarkably alike. Thus it is not surprising that individuals would contract with shamans from another cultural and linguistic group.

All curing rituals unfold through a common sequence of steps. As soon as the shaman arrives on the scene, preparations begin. The shaman instructs the family of the patient to gather copal bark as well as certain leaves, herbs, and flowers. They are expected to purchase tobacco, soft drinks, cane alcohol, candles, one or more chickens, an egg, and additional items as requested. Meanwhile, the shaman removes from his sisal carrying bag a stack of tissue papers of various colors and a pair of scissors. The shaman carefully folds and cuts the papers into images of the spirits he wishes to influence. He also cuts decorative sheets called *tlaxcali yoyomitl* (Nahuatl for "tortilla napkin") that he will use to beautify the altar and provide beds for the spirit images. At this point the women of the household begin preparing the food for the offering. For small rituals this may be no more than a simple ball of cooked cornmeal or some coffee. Larger cures require tamales, meat soup, chocolate, a sweetened amaranth or corn beverage, coffee, bread, and stacks of corn tortillas. As food is being prepared, the other household members and friends construct altar adornments from leaves, lengths of vine, and beautiful flowers. The process of constructing floral adornments for rituals is called *xochichihualistli* (literally "the making of flowers") in Nahuatl. The shaman gathers all these items around and checks to be sure everything is at hand before beginning.

The shaman proceeds to fill the brazier with hot coals and copal bark, causing billows of aromatic smoke to perfume the house, and as he begins to chant he takes the sacrificial chickens that are brought before him. He suspends the birds, one at a time, in the smoke and, while continuing to chant, swiftly wrings their necks. He passes them to the women, who will cook them for the food offering. The shaman then begins to lay out a complex ritual array on the floor of the patient's house. There are several basic patterns in which a shaman can arrange the floor array, but all feature a central display of paper images of the ejecatl spirits carefully laid on the decoratively cut sheets. Surrounding this central display may be bundles of leaves arranged in an arch with paper images tied to each bundle, lighted beeswax or tallow candles, small bunches of special leaves or herbs, or a large vine loop with marigolds tied at intervals to it. The shaman then places certain items directly on top of the paper-image display. These include the bottles of soft drinks, cups of coffee, plates of food, special leaf and flower adornments, unlighted candles laid in small piles, a bag of earth from the client's fields or house, and a glass of water from a nearby spring in which has been placed a lighted beeswax candle.

The shaman now begins a long chant in which he names the offending ejecatl spirits, itemizes the offerings being made, and pleads in a poetic and metaphoric way for the health of his patient. He may at some point grab a small stack of paper images along with a bunch of leaf and flower adornments and hold them on the head of his patient while chanting, or he may even rub the patient's body with the bundle. In the course of some curing rituals the shaman and a helper pick up the vine and marigold loop and instruct the patient and his immediate family to step into it. In this ritual act, they raise the loop over the heads of the patients, lower it again to the floor, and repeat the process seven times in total. They then reverse the procedure, bringing the loop down over the huddled family and having them step out of it, again repeating this act seven times in order to remove all ejecatl spirits that have invaded their bodies. In an act called *tlacopalhuilistli* in Nahuatl, the shaman periodically envelops the patient and his family in clouds of pungent incense smoke while chanting, as a further means of entreating the disease spirits to depart.

Following is a chant I recorded in January 1986 during one such curing ritual performed by the shaman Librado, age 70, of Amatlán:

> 1. tlasoli ejecatl
>   mictlantlasoli ejecatl
>   cuatipan ejecatlacatl
>   mictlanxochiejecasihuatl
> 5. tlali ejecasihuatl
>   mictlancuachamancatlacatl
>   ta ticimarróntlali
>   ipan se ojtli
>   ipan se ojmajxali
> 10. ticimarróntlali
>   ipan atl campa nentinemij
>   inin dios itlalchamancahuaj
>   campa moquetstinemij
>   campa tequititinemij

15. nochi tonatij tiyolpoloaj
    ica nopa totonic
    ica nopa xixtli
    ica nopa tlaajmancayotl
    nochi tonatij san tonalcuesijtoc
20. pampa imojuantij inquitlacualispoloa
    inquiatlilispoloaj
    inquiessojpoloaj
    inin tonana dios itlalchamancahuaj
    nojuatic nesi campa quinquiyajquej tonana dios huan totata dios
25. tonana dios quicajtoc ipan inin tescanepantli
    ipan inin tescatlatlanestli
    paraj ma no quipiya tlej iyoloj
    paraj ma no quipiya inemilis
    nochi tonatij quipiyas cuali ichicahualis
30. axcana nopeca intonaltsacualtinemisej
    tla paj se atentli
    tla paj se milasojtli
    tla paj ipan ni calixpamitl
    tla paj ne tlajcocali
35. campa quipixtoc iecahuil
    ax huelis paraj imojuantij
    inquiyolpolosej
    inquiajmantosej
    axcana nicanij
40. ya san ma tlami nopa chichic
    nopa totonic
    nopa ixpoyajcayotl
    nopa tlatsontecocuajcualocayotl
    nopa totonic
45. huan namaj nicanij timechmacaj
    se cuali imoistalpetlayo
    se cuali imoistalnacaj
    se cuali imotragoj
    se cuali imocigarroj
50. paraj ya san paraj san ma
    tlami nopa totonic
    xijmacacaj ya inemilis
    xijmacacaj ya icualnemilis
    ayojcana nopeca inquitonaltsacualtinemisej
55. campa moquetstinemi
    campa ixajcahuetstinemi
    campa tequititinemi
    tla ipaj imilaj
    tla ipaj ipaj se potreroj campa moquetstinemi

60. ax huelis paraj itonal quitsacualtinemisej
    pampa tonana dios quicajqui ipan ni logar
    paraj ma quichihua fuerza
    paraj quitemos tlej ica
    tlej quej motonalquetsas
65. tlej quej motonalpalehuis
    huan yecaj namaj nicanij
    no mosencajquej ica se pilquentsij
    miac ax miac
    peroj no mosencajquej
70. no imechmactilij
    se cuali imoistalnacaj
    se cuali imoistalpetlayo
    se cuali imoistalcandelaj
    yecaj namaj mosencajquej
75. yecaj namaj temactilijqui se quentsij
    ma no quiita ya tonana dios
    ma no quiita ya totata dios
    axcana tlen tlajtlacoli
    quichihua ya no quichijticaj fuerza
80. motemolij tlej ica motonalquetsas
    tlej ica motonalpalehuis
    pampa tonana dios huan totata dios
    ya quimacatoquej icualajlamiquilis
    ya quimacatoquej inemilis
85. ya quimacatoquej itlachiyalis
    huaj ax huelis paraj nopeca inquitonalpechtinemisej
    paraj nopeca itonal
    quinmajmajtinemisej elissa
    seja cuentaj tlen tlajtoli quichihua
90. tlen tlajtoli quiyejyecoa ica yejyectsij
    campa moquetstinemis
    campa tequititinemis
    ayojcana nopeca inquitonaltsacualtinemisej
    ica tlej itrabajoj
95. en el nombre del padre
    del espíritu santo
    amén

1. O filth disease-wind
   O filth disease-wind from the place of the dead
   O disease-wind man from the forest
   O flower-disease-wind woman from the place of the dead
5. O disease-wind woman of the earth
   O forest-sprouting man from the place of the dead

you, you the wild earth
on a trail
at a fork in the trail
10. you are the wild earth
in the water where they go about wandering
these earth-sprouts from god
where they go about standing
where they go about working
15. every day we lose our heart [life]
with this heat [fever]
with this diarrhea
with this bodily discomfort
every day he is in a state of spiritual [*tonali*] sorrow
20. because you take away their hunger
you take away their thirst for water
you take away their blood
they are the earth-sprouts of our mother god
still one observes where our mother god and our father god left them
25. our mother god has left them here in this mirror
in this light reflecting from the mirror
so that he might have his heart
so that he might have his life
every day he will have his good strength [*chicahualistli*]
30. no longer will you go about interfering with his spirit [tonali]
if he is at the edge of the water
if he is on a trail to the milpa
if he is in the areas facing the house
if he is in the middle of the house
35. wherever he has his shadow
it will not be possible for you
to cause him to lose his heart [life]
for you to trouble him
not here in this place
40. so that already bitterness might end
this heat [fever]
this cloudiness in the eyes [dizziness]
this headache
this fever
45. and now here we deliver to you
some of your good white shells [eggs]
some of your good white meat [the white of an egg]
some of your good liquor
some of your good cigarettes [tobacco]
50. so that once and for all
this fever might end
so that you might give him his life

so that you might give him his good life
do not go thereabouts interfering with his spirit
55. where he goes about standing
where he goes about crossing
where he goes about working
be it in his milpa
be it in a pasture where he goes about standing
60. they will not be able to go about interfering with his spirit
because our mother god left it in this place
so that he might have vigor
so that he might search for that
which will raise up his spirit
65. that which will aid his spirit
and thus here now
also they have prepared [an offering] with a little bit
a great deal and a little
but also they have prepared it
70. also they delivered to you
some of your good white meat [the white of an egg]
some of your good white shells [eggs]
some of your good white candles
thus now they have arranged it
75. thus now he has delivered a little to you
so that our mother god might also see it
so that our father god might also see it
it is not a sin
he is also increasing in vigor
80. he had himself looked at [by a curer] to lift his spirit
with that which will aid his spirit
because our mother god and our father god
they have given him his good memory
they have given him his life
85. they have given him his vision
and they will not be able thereabouts to impede his spirit
so that thereabouts his spirit
will not be able to be frightened
it is a story he makes of these words
90. the words that he tries in beauty
where he will go about standing
where he will go about working
no longer thereabouts will you go interfering with his spirit
with that which is his work
95. in the name of the father
of the holy spirit
amen

This translation of the shaman's chant captures some of the meaning of his words but, for the most part, it loses the poetic quality found in the original Nahuatl. Regardless of the ritual occasion, all of the chants that I have heard are similar in function to this one. Although the words may differ from shaman to shaman, in all cases the ritual specialist is stating a definition of the situation both to the relevant spirits and to the patient and his family. In this example the shaman begins by listing some of the offending wind spirits. He then identifies them as being from the wild earth, which is another way of saying that they emanate from mictlan, the place of the dead. The shaman reminds everyone that wind spirits attack people as they go about their daily lives, but he asserts that father and mother spirits who gave birth to humans will protect their children, including the patient. He lists the offerings that are being made to the wind spirits so that the father and mother spirits will "observe" them and give strength to the patient's yolotl or heart (life force). Finally, the shaman asserts that his words and the ritual offering will increase the patient's chicahualistli (force) and strengthen his weakened shade, or tonali (heat-soul). In sum, contained within the chant are statements about the cause of the malady, lists of offerings that will remedy the disease, and declarations that are designed to strengthen and reassure the patient and bring him under the protection of benevolent guardian spirits (for additional texts recorded among Nahuas of the Huasteca, see Reyes García and Christensen 1976:45ff.).

At the conclusion of the chant, the shaman turns to the floor display and prepares to dedicate the offerings. He arranges plates of cooked chicken, tortillas, cups of coffee with bread, bottled soft drinks and beer, and other gifts to the spirits. He may pour cane alcohol in a circle around the floor array as a symbolic means of containing the dangerous wind spirits. After another chant addressed to the wind spirits in which he carefully lists the offerings, the shaman and one or two volunteers pour the offerings on each of the paper images. This procedure is called *quitlatsicuinia* in Nahuatl, which literally means "to sprinkle something" but in this context means to offer food to the spirits. Shamans informed me that the presence of copal incense, candles, and food attracts the various wind spirits and that once present, each spirit feeds from the offerings sprinkled on its paper likeness. While they are distracted, the shaman traps the spirits within the altar array and, after turning the paper figures over, gathers them up a few at a time and violently rips them to pieces. At each tear he blows a puff of air over the shredding paper, and he may spit out commands to the spirits such as *xiyaquej*, Nahuatl for "get out!" or "go away!" Shamans told me that this rough treatment disorients the wind spirits, forcing them to disperse. They pointed out that wind spirits are not killed in a curing, just banished and sent back to their place of origin. The cleansing procedures that follow the offering serve to prevent the spirits from returning to the patient and his household.

In the local Nahua curing tradition, the one not influenced by the Otomí master, the shaman now visits six sites where wind spirits are likely to be lurking about, and at each location he makes a brief offering to get rid of them. These additional offerings are made at the fire table of the house, the house entrance, on a trail, at a place where trails cross, at a place close to where the patient bathes, and at the base of one of the pre-Hispanic ruins in the village. Shamans influenced by the Otomí curing traditions tend to skip these additional ritual sites.

After the offerings have been dedicated, the shaman carefully folds up all the food-stained and sodden paper scraps, leaf and flower adornments, and other items that once made up the display, and he forms a bundle from them. He carefully gathers even the scraps left over from cutting the figures and includes them in the bundle. After the bundle is tied tightly with vines, the patient and his family undergo a series of cleansing procedures designed to protect them from further spirit attack. The shaman may brush the participants with symbolic brooms made from flowers and palm leaves, cense them with copal, rub them with beeswax candles, have participants again pass through vine and marigold loops, or rub the patient with the bundle formed from the floor array. After the ritual is completed and the patient has been given beeswax candles and adornments to place on his home altar, the shaman takes the bundled refuse from the array and carefully disposes of it deep in the forest. The bundle poses a danger because it continues to attract wind spirits, and the shaman must hide it in an inaccessible spot. Reyes Antonio (1982:122,153–54) mentions sucking cures (*tlayejyectili* in Nahuatl) found among neighboring Nahuas in which the curer removes foreign objects from the patient's body. However, I have never observed this curing procedure in Amatlán.

One day in 1986 while I was assisting a shaman engaged in curing a family, I witnessed a ritual episode I had never seen before. The family had been plagued by fevers and various other illnesses, and the shaman determined through divination that neighbors were gossiping and causing wind spirits to attack them. Just before dedicating the major offering, the shaman cut paper images of the tonali soul of each member of the ill-intentioned neighboring family. He carefully inscribed the name of each individual on the body of the corresponding figure and then glued the hands of each figure so that they covered the mouth. He then proceeded with the typical offering sequence, but he included these additional images with the others in the floor array. He told me that the paper images would stop the people from gossiping and harassing his patients. This aspect of a cure is done discreetly because any attempt to control people using ritual means borders dangerously on sorcery. When other people entered the house, for example, I overheard the shaman tell them that the tonali figures were those of his patients and not of the gossiping neighbors. Should these neighbors discover that the shaman had manipulated their tonali souls they could accuse him of sorcery, or perhaps they might even try to harm him physically.

The outline of Nahua curings cannot communicate the powerful drama that unfolds as a shaman does battle with dangerous wind spirits in an attempt to rid his or her patients of their suffering. Glowing beeswax candles surrounding a neat display of colorful but malevolent paper figures, an atmosphere redolent with incense smoke, and the shaman confronting mysterious forces through his actions and murmured chants—all this makes for conspicuous high drama. I found that the dramatic high points in Nahua rituals more than compensated for the tedious task of taking detailed notes of the proceedings. I was not surprised when villagers told me numerous stories of how the shamans were able to cure serious diseases. Both men and women overwhelmingly confirmed that curing rituals always make a person feel better. The sequence of ritual acts in a curing ceremony is designed to make a deep impression on participants, and by and large it succeeds. Put another way, a shaman who can conduct a ritual that makes a dramatic impact on his or her patients tends to attract and maintain a loyal following.

The history of these rituals cannot be traced, but it is clear that they derive from pre-Hispanic ritual practices. Elsewhere I have attempted to demonstrate that curing rituals in the southern Huasteca can be traced back to the pre-Hispanic deity Tlazolteotl (Sandstrom 1989). Worship of this deity originated in the Huasteca region, and her cult was very influential among the Aztecs at the time of the Spanish Conquest (see Vié 1979). She was venerated in the Aztec month of Ochpaniztli (literally "sweeping"; note here the similarity of this name to the contemporary Nahuatl word used in Amatlán for curing ritual, *ochpantli*, also meaning "sweeping"). Among her several other identities, Tlazolteotl is the goddess of filth who consumes human sin and returns people to a state of harmony and balance with the spirit and social world.

Contemporary Nahua curing rituals retain the basic approach of this ancient cult. Disease-causing wind spirits are associated with and attracted by the disruptive misbehavior of people. They are agents of pollution who defile the basic harmony and balance of social life. Shamans describe these foul winds as originating in filthy tangled places, and they often contain in their names the word *tlasoli* (Nahuatl for "filth," literally "refuse" or "trash"). Curing rituals sweep the patient and his surroundings clean of the infectious spirits. The cleansing has the effect of removing the pollutants so that the harmony existing before the patient became ill can be restored. Tlazolteotl herself has disappeared under pressure from missionaries and mestizo neighbors. Often the Spaniards defined pre-Hispanic deities as devils that cause human suffering. In this case Tlazolteotl probably survives in the identities of the elite spirits of the underworld. *Tlahuelilo*, *tlacatecolotl*, and *miquilistli*, all beings mentioned by sixteenth-century chroniclers of Aztec religion, continue to reign over spirits of the dead in Amatlán and are the ones that set loose angry dead souls in the form of polluting wind spirits to roam the earth at night (see Burkhart 1989:87ff. for a discussion of pollution in ancient Nahua thought).

This outline of the Nahua curing ritual contains within it many of the elements that are used in other ritual observances in Amatlán (for more information on repetition of symbolic forms in Mesoamerican ritual, see Vogt 1969:571ff.). Major and minor rituals not connected to curing always begin with a cleansing sequence in which wind spirits are cleared from the area. These preliminary cleansings are similar to regular curings, and the shaman orchestrating the ritual always cuts paper images of the winds as part of the procedure. Next, the shaman dedicates an offering to the relevant spirits. This offering varies greatly in elaboration depending on the resources available to the shaman and the overall importance of the observance. To placate a house spirit, for example, may require a simple plate of food and some tortillas. To satisfy the rain spirits may require a 12-day ritual, the construction of six or more elaborate altars, and many costly supplies. The offering is the core of all Nahua rituals, and this fact reveals a major feature of how villagers relate to the spirits. Rituals are actually a type of exchange in which human beings make offerings in an effort to obligate spirits to conform to their desires. For the Nahuas, humans are engaged in a continual round of exchanges with the spirit world. Whenever the delicate flow is disrupted and the balance is disturbed, people get sick, the rain does not come, and the crops fail. Sometimes rituals take on an air of desperation as villagers try to keep a step ahead of a demanding spirit world.

Ideas of balance and exchange permeate Nahua religious life to a degree difficult for outsiders to comprehend. People share food and drink with the earth before consuming anything themselves. Women sometimes crack a raw egg near the spring after they fill their carrying pot to pay the water spirit apanchanej for the water. Men make a food and incense offering to their fields after planting to repay earth spirits for the disturbance humans cause. If a man cuts down a tree he leaves a gift in payment for disrupting the harmony of the forest. Individual families make periodic offerings so that their daily activities do not anger house and fire spirits. Household heads burn incense as an offering to house guardian spirits so that these beneficial overseers will maintain their vigilance. Many times I witnessed gift and food exchanges among blood and ritual kinsmen before the marriages of their children. Death does not cancel gift-giving obligations as families make periodic offerings on the graves of kinsmen. One of the most important obligations is the exchange of labor among groups of men at critical points in the crop growing cycle. These and many other examples I could list are in addition to the formal offerings made by individuals during the almost constant round of rituals held throughout the year.

The importance of the offering or exchange in people's daily and ritual lives reveals an important element in Nahua world view. Human beings are part of the deified universe, and thus they carry within them the divine energy of life. However, they are capable, more than other creatures, of disrupting universal harmony through their actions, and thus they must constantly placate spirit entities with offerings in order to set things right. Ritual offerings are valued gifts to repay past offenses and to obligate the spirits to continue the flow of benefits that make human life possible. Disruptions caused by human action are transformed into disease or misfortune, always appearing in the guise of attacking wind spirits. In this sense all rituals are curings, formal gestures to reestablish equilibrium with the spirit world, with the avowed purpose of restoring balance and health to the human community.

RITUAL SPONSORS AND THE CIVIL-RELIGIOUS HIERARCHY

One of the most characteristic features of socioreligious organization in traditional communities throughout Mesoamerica is the civil-religious hierarchy. Sometimes called the cargo system, this feature of community organization is often defined by a ranked system of religious sponsorships and political offices, called *cargos* in Spanish. Religious and secular offices are kept separate, but they often intertwine in associated functions and responsibilities. Individual men serve alternate terms of office in the secular and religious hierarchies. In one term they may serve as an unpaid political leader, and in another they will agree to sponsor and pay the major expenses of religious celebrations surrounding saint's days and other holidays. Through the years a man and his family work their way up the hierarchy until they have completed all available cargos. Individual sponsorships can be quite onerous and may plunge a family into debt for years. However, in return for their investment of effort and money they enjoy a high level of prestige in the community, and they earn the right to participate in community decisions. Much has been written by anthropologists and other social scientists attempting to explain this civil-religious hierarchy. Further ethnographic information from places like Amatlán, which has no cult of saints apart from the traditional pantheon of spirits and which therefore does not have a well-developed civil-religious hierarchy, may help to illuminate the cargo system.

For a man in Amatlán to lead an exemplary life and win the respect of his fellow villagers, he must assume civic responsibility. This duty presents itself in two possible forms. In the first, he must agree to be elected to leadership positions in the ejido political structure. A man must first get himself appointed to the lower offices in the hierarchy of political offices. Only then is he eligible to be elected to the two highest positions in the hierarchy, Agente Municipal and Comisariado Ejidal. In a small community like Amatlán nearly all men have a chance at higher office sometime during their lives.

The second avenue to responsibility is through the sponsorship of rituals. Each of the four major villagewide rituals—Day of the Dead, winter solstice, seed offering, and carnival—are organized and sponsored by an individual volunteer. This person is responsible for gathering "cooperations" from the other households and for supplying some money and the food for the major offerings. He also rewards helpers with food or money and takes responsibility for hiring musicians and shamans if they are called for. Although there is no formal hierarchy of sponsorship, the leaders of carnival are young men, and their role is considered less important than sponsors of the other three observances.

In short, to earn the respect of the community and to gain eventual entrance into the council of elders (see Chapter 4), adult men must participate in running village affairs. Although the community expects men to serve in both secular and religious offices, these are not rigidly or formally ranked to the degree documented in other areas of Meso-america. Nor do men alternate between secular and religious offices like they do in other regions. In a setting like that of Amatlán where kin group loyalty is paramount, men of stature must demonstrate a loyalty to the community as a whole. This ranges from active participation in the communal work faenas, to uncomplaining payment of "cooperations," to assuming public office. A kind of ranking from least to most important contribution to the village based on how much money and effort is required of the task is implicit but not codified. No one in Amatlán keeps lists of cargos such as we see reported in other communities.

Reward for participation in communitywide endeavors, then, is probably characteristic of all communities in Mesoamerica. When I described the very formal and highly ranked cargo system found in the Chiapas region of Mexico to the villagers, they thought it sounded quite strange. Several men mused that although it may be good and desirable to help the community, it would be pointless to become impoverished in the process. They commented that people in Amatlán would think such a rigid system very foolish and basically incomprehensible. If we can assume that some kind of reward system for community participation exists in virtually all Mesoamerican villages, then the cargo system can be seen simply as an extreme example of the basic pattern. The explanation for this system, then, may be that rapid acculturation coupled with prosperity has led the traditional system to become involuted and elaborated until it assumes an extreme form. When this occurs, a kind of inflation of the traditional prestige system leads men to spiral higher and higher in their sponsorship investments.

COSTUMBRES AND CHRISTIANITY

The relationship between Catholic Christianity and traditional Nahua religious practices (generally called by the Spanish term *costumbres* or "customs") is always difficult to clarify. Most villagers identify themselves as Catholics. The term was rarely mentioned when I first entered the field, but people use it increasingly to distinguish themselves from Protestant converts, whose numbers are growing (see Chapter 7). To be "Catholic" in Amatlán, however, entails understandings and obligations that would be foreign to Catholics in Mexico

City or the United States. For the Nahuas, to be Catholic is to contribute to and participate in the traditional village ritual observances and to subscribe to the world view associated with them. Thus at one level the villagers equate Catholicism with their traditional religion. This identification of two historically unrelated traditions is not simply an error on their part. Rather, it stems from the fundamentally pantheistic nature of pre-Hispanic religion and world view that lies at the core of Nahua culture.

Following an insight offered by Eva Hunt (1977), I believe that a pantheistic religion like that of the Amatlán Nahuas is able to incorporate Christian elements without disturbing the basic integrity of the indigenous system. Saint John the Baptist becomes San Juan, the Spanish language equivalent of a male aspect of apanchanej; and the Virgin Mary is but one manifestation of tonantsij. The Mass becomes an alternate costumbre, the priest a variety of shaman, and the concept of God, in turn, simply another way of conceiving of the sun or the great spiritual unity underlying apparent diversity. In short, most villagers do not see their costumbres as fundamentally opposed to Christianity. Instead, they see Christianity as an alternate system for dealing with the same underlying reality.

Over nearly half a millennium the Nahuas have borrowed from Spanish Catholicism. Many Nahua rituals are now scheduled basically according to the Christian liturgical calendar. However, the ancient Christian calendar and the pre-Hispanic calendar had certain common characteristics. Worldwide celebrations of Christmas and Nahua celebrations of *tlacatelilis* are held near the winter solstice when the sun begins to journey northward in the sky. Both observances celebrate birth or fertility and reflect the promise of springtime with the return of the life-giving sun. The Nahuas have also borrowed such symbols as the cross (although there was a crosslike symbol in use before the arrival of the Spaniards), statues of saints and Jesus Christ (but again, statues were an important part of Aztec religion), use of certain words in chanting such as "amen," the peregrination featured in tlacatelilis that is probably taken from the Mexican Catholic processionals (although pre-Hispanic religions also made use of processionals), the use of candles, and violin and guitar playing, just to name a few examples. In several cases these symbolic elements have been significantly reinterpreted by the villagers and now fit the traditional Indian system. Finally, as mentioned above, the villagers thoroughly identify as Christians and, in particular, as Catholics. The word Christian (the Spanish *cristiano*), however, is used by people synonymously with human being, as opposed to a sorcerer (in Spanish, *brujo*). The term Catholic, as pointed out above, is generally used to refer to a good person who observes the costumbres.

Thus, in one sense, Nahua religion appears to be a creative blend of both the Catholic and the costumbre religions. At the same time, most villagers with whom I spoke fully realized that their costumbres differ from Church rituals and teachings. One afternoon I was recording myths told by an old man in his eighties, and I asked him if he would recount the story of the Virgin of Guadalupe. He responded with some disdain that this was a story from the Church and that he was not interested in it. In short, he recognized the dual heritage of the village, and he expressed clear preference for the ancient Indian traditions. This did not really surprise me. I had once heard an itinerant priest who was visiting Amatlán lecture to the people vehemently about the need for eliminating pagan elements from their rituals. He asserted, among other things, that the Day of the Dead ritual should be celebrated on one day only and not over the four days prescribed by local custom. When a priest does make one of his rare appearances I noticed that many people take care to hide evidence of traditional ritual practice. For example, on their home altars they conceal the paper guardian spirits behind pictures of saints. The villagers must reconcile the inclusive nature of their own religion with the exclusive character of Christianity. It is this separation between the two traditions that has prevented me from describing the situation purely in terms of syncretism. Syncretism implies a blending of traditions to form a new religion based on the two components. The Nahuas have most certainly incorporated elements of Christian belief and practice into their costumbres, but the core features of their religion, I contend, remain Native American.

Anthropologist John Ingham (1989) reaches a different conclusion in his detailed study of religion and society in the Nahua community of Tlayacapan, Morelos. By combining historical and modern French structuralist analysis, Ingham finds that although "significant elements of the deep structure of the pre-Hispanic world view persist in present-day beliefs and practices . . . they are embedded in, and subordinated to, Catholic beliefs and symbols" (1989:180). In short, pre-Hispanic elements are present among modern-day Nahuas, but they express an essentially Catholic world view (1989:1). Tlayacapan is evidently far more acculturated than Amatlán, and it is possible that pre-Hispanic religion is less in evidence there.

Ingham, however, fails to distinguish clearly between public and private religion. He focuses his analysis primarily on public religious observances surrounding veneration of saints, and indeed the influence of Catholic world view in this domain is overwhelming (although even here Ingham documents the remarkable correspondences between pre-Hispanic and modern practices). However, he neglects the realm of private religion where the pre-Hispanic world view would most likely persist. He mentions, in passing, private witchcraft rituals and shamanic observances in which small clay figurines play an important part, but these practices remain obscure and unanalyzed (1989:173–74). It appears that if these private rituals were included in his analysis, Ingham would probably have found more pre-Hispanic influence in the total religious life in Tlayacapan. Significantly, Ingham notes that the people of Tlayacapan were already losing their Indian identity by the turn of the century (1989:54). Thus it is possible that today the traditional public religion has ceased to be an important element of their ethnicity. In any event, if Ingham is correct, the situation he documents is quite different from the one I encountered in Amatlán.

THE *COSTUMBRE* RELIGION

Huastecan Nahua religion has a sophistication and elegance that contradicts our usual stereotype of a people whose primary social group is the small village. It is true that major concerns of Nahua belief and ritual surround the pragmatic aspects of village life such as curing and crop fertility. The costumbre religion is little concerned with a given individual's attaining personal salvation or going to Heaven after his death, as is Christianity. To the extent that it is concerned with these matters, individuals attain a good afterlife more by fulfilling the village social norms and expectations than by obeying any codified religious commandments. These implied shortcomings simply reflect the fact that Nahua religion is not part of a state apparatus (see below). The Nahuas have no professional theologians and philosophers to regularize beliefs and practices. All of the complexities of the religion must be maintained in people's memories. Knowledge is passed orally from generation to generation, and there is no hierarchy of priests to resolve disputes or maintain a body of authoritative knowledge. The Nahuas are heirs, however, to the complex and sophisticated civilizations of Mesoamerica. The Spaniards largely destroyed the urban religion of the indigenous inhabitants, but they were not able to root out practices in the small and remote villages like Amatlán where the religion continues in modified form today. To this pre-Hispanic base has been added certain elements from both Spanish Catholicism and contemporary neighboring Indian groups. The apparent simplicity of Nahua religious concerns masks a philosophical sophistication that derives from this complex history.

To summarize, Nahua religion is characterized by five key principles that underly the diversity of beliefs and practices. The first and foremost is pantheism, in which the Nahuas view objects and animate beings as reflections of a deified universe. The human propensity to divide up the world into discrete and sometimes incompatible entities is an illusion that is partially corrected during ritual performances. A second key principle is shamanism. Individuals through their training and power of personality acquire the ability to control the unseen forces of the universe, and these charismatic agents are in a constant battle against disturbances that threaten the balance and connectedness of humans with the physical and spiritual world. Shamans are the repositories of the oral traditions that contain the accumulated wisdom of Nahua history, and as such are the focus of what it is to be Nahua. The third characteristic of this religion is its well-developed concept of ritual pollution. This concept is linked to Nahua ideas about disease and curing, and it is linked to village interpersonal relations and human–spirit interactions as well. Fourth, Nahua religion is rich in ritual and symbolism. Rituals are common throughout the year, and they are so densely packed with layers of symbolic meaning that it could take many pages just to describe one of them in proper detail. The final characteristic, and the one that ties the rest together, is the principle of harmony and balance. In brief, the Nahua universe is composed of sacred forces in equilibrium, of a balanced exchange between people and spirits, polluted by disruptions that shamans endeavor to smooth out through elaborate and deeply symbolic ritual offerings.

The costumbres and attendant beliefs serve the Nahuas in the way that any religion serves its adherents. Nahua religion provides a coherent and reasonable view of the universe and how it operates. It places people in relation to the natural and social world and establishes shared attitudes about nature and the human condition. The religion contains the philosophical means of distinguishing what is real from what is illusory, and it provides villagers with formulas for leading a good life. It gives people a set of values to live by and the motivations to live life in accord with the underlying structure of the world. The belief system offers explanations of why things happen and then provides techniques for influencing the course of events. For instance, it explains how and why people get sick and then offers the means to cure disease through the cleansing ritual. Nahua religion provides the mechanism for understanding and facing death and provides ritual means for helping people to cope with their grief. In short, the costumbre religion provides the intellectual and emotional foundation for Nahua society and culture in the same way that Catholicism provides the foundation for mestizo society and culture. But as we have seen, Nahua religion differs in content and form from Christianity and so, in addition to its other functions, it also acts as a refuge for the Indians in an alien and sometimes hostile world.

Religion is an exceedingly complex phenomenon that must be understood on a number of levels. It can be viewed from any combination of psychological, social, cultural, or ecological perspectives. There is one common feature of all religions, however, which helps to clarify the position that the Nahuas occupy relative to the world of the mestizos. Without exception, religion creates a community of believers and sets them apart from others. From this perspective, a critical attribute of the costumbre religion is the degree to which it can be seen as distinct from Mexican Catholicism. The problem of distinguishing Nahua from Christian religious systems is hard to resolve definitively because of correspondences between the systems and because of the insistence by some Indians and mestizos that their religions are essentially the same. Villagers are caught in a paradox when it comes to their religious practices. On the one hand, they have an interest in distinguishing themselves from mestizos and in creating a sense of community as Indians. On the other, they have an interest in appearing not too different from the mestizos so that they can maintain their access to aspects of the mestizo world which they need to survive. Only detailed studies based on long-term participant observation can reveal the profound gulf that exists between the two religions, and consequently the very different kinds of communities they create.

As a final example of how Nahua and mestizo religions diverge, I would like to describe the way each links personal behavior with concepts of the fate of the soul. In many sects of Christianity the ultimate fate of a person's soul after death is linked to the behavior of the person while he or she was alive. Put simply, if a man is righteous in his actions and attitude and believes in the precepts of Christianity, he is rewarded when his soul is allowed entrance into heaven. If, on the other hand, he engages in immoral behavior and strays from Christian teachings, his soul will be forever condemned to hell. In Christianity, each individual is responsible for his own behavior, and he will be rewarded or punished accordingly. Christianity is not the only religion in the world that draws this connection. It is interesting to note that personal accountability in beliefs concerning the fate of the soul is usually found in societies with social classes or significant differences in wealth among people. Disruptive emotions caused by differences in personal wealth and power can be smoothed over by supernatural sanctions for passivity, honesty, hard work, and meeting debts (see Swanson 1960:153ff.). In short, by linking fate of the soul with personal behavior, religion can serve to stabilize potentially explosive social formations.

Among the Nahuas the situation is more complex. As we have seen, immoral behavior such as lying or stealing creates disharmony and attracts disease-causing wind spirits to the village. The person who commits the sin, however, is rarely the one who becomes sick. Wind spirits may infect anyone, and in fact they often attack people with low energy reserves, such as children and the aged. Absence of a connection between behavior and supernatural consequence is even more pronounced in Nahua beliefs concerning the fate of the soul. As discussed above, when a person dies, one of three fates awaits his or her yolotl soul. Those who experienced a natural death proceed to mictlan, the place of the dead. Those who died under certain circumstances such as drowning go to apan, the water paradise. The remainder, those who were murdered or who died prematurely or in a state of anger are doomed to wander all four realms of the universe as wind spirits. Thus, for the Nahuas, it is not behavior on earth that determines the fate of the soul but rather the manner in which a person dies. If, indeed, the most malevolent person in the world died by drowning, he or she would presumably go to the water paradise. If, on the other hand, a saint was murdered by soldiers, the soul would travel with the winds spreading disease and death. From a Christian perspective this would seem grossly unfair because Christian morality is based on individual responsibility, and with the exception of suicide, the means of dying are outside one's personal control.

From the Nahua perspective these beliefs are reasonable reflections of the way the world really works. Sin does draw wind spirits into the village, and therefore bad behavior injures the living. The party attacked by spirits may be the sinner's husband, wife, child, or neighbor. Furthermore, Nahua sins reap immediate punishment and are not simply tallied for a future day of judgment, a belief prevalent in Christianity. Nahua beliefs concerning wind spirits affirm that bad deeds have real, immediate, negative consequences and that people have a collective interest in and responsibility to promote good behavior. Nahua ideas about morality in interpersonal behavior place human beings rather than the deity at the center. Disease-causing wind spirits are themselves former human beings who are delivering retribution on the living for bad deeds. This affirms that bad deeds and wrongful thoughts are the root cause of human suffering. In Nahua thought it is ultimately human beings as a collectivity who are responsible for their own misfortune. Unlike Christianity, which places the moral focus on reward and punishment of individuals, the Nahuas assume a broader social responsibility. Good deeds protect the village from harm, and sin threatens not the sinner directly, but the survival of the entire society. Nahua villages do not have the class structure and vast differences in personal wealth and power found in state societies, and the religion is concerned less with punishing individual behavior than with creating a palpable sense of social responsibility and community.

CHAPTER 7

ETHNIC IDENTITY AND CULTURE CHANGE

AMONG the significant occurrences of our time, it is the most important ones, the ones that future historians will write about, that often go unnoticed and unanalyzed. Caught up in the chain of assassinations, wars, elections, and stock market crashes, most of us miss the universal processes that underlie these events. Anthropologists have long been aware that international economic development and the accompanying spread of industrialization and modernization among the diverse peoples of the world are perhaps the most important of these global features today. Groups of previously independent peoples increasingly find themselves affected by far-reaching regional, national, and international forces. Due to nation formation and population migration, enormous numbers of people throughout Asia, Africa, Latin America, and even in the most economically developed Euro-American countries identify themselves as members of ethnic groups involved in a dynamic struggle to assert their rights and win their share of economic, social, and political gains. One of the most important tasks of social science today is to develop an understanding of how and why ethnic groups are formed and what happens when they become enmeshed in complex processes of economic development.

Ethnic groups often form initially when people who share one or more cultural features come under the domination of a ruling group with different cultural attributes. The subject peoples may not previously have considered themselves to be members of a distinct group at all. Under political domination, however, they develop an ethnic identity to separate themselves from the ruling group and simultaneously to create an alternate social world. People see reasons to band together into ethnic groups in order to preserve cherished cultural values that may be threatened by the dominant group, to increase opportunities for themselves in hostile political environments, to establish an alternate system of rewards for members, or to provide for

323

a common defense against aggressions from members of the dominant group.

Edward Spicer, in his anthropological study, *Cycles of Conquest: The Impact of Spain, Mexico, and the United States on the Indians of the Southwest, 1533–1960*, examines patterns of cultural assimilation and the creation of ethnic identity in numerous Native American groups who live in the American Southwest and northwestern Mexico. He begins from the time each population was conquered militarily by the Spaniards, Mexicans, or Americans. The scope of the study makes his findings useful in understanding ethnicity in other parts of Mexico and the world. He notes that Indian groups exhibited a diversity of reactions following contact, and he analyzes "the connections between the conditions of contact and the patterns of response" (1962:17). He states that the Spanish, Mexican, and American policies toward the Indians were designed essentially to "civilize" native peoples by promoting their assimilation into the European form of society. Each of these dominant groups, however, employed distinctive strategies for accomplishing this end. These different approaches, among many other complex factors, caused the Indians under each regime to respond in different ways.

Briefly, policy in the United States was based on the creation of a reservation system with political control centered in Washington, D.C. Indians were to be assimilated into American society on an individual basis, and thus reservations as a whole were not incorporated into the national economy. This led each tribe to develop its own strongly separate identity based on a sacred attachment to specific tracts of land (1962:574ff.). Spanish (and later Mexican) policy, on the other hand, was predicated on removing the Indians from their ancestral land, gathering them into new communities, and then, under the direction of missionaries and other agents of change, easing the entire community into the local version of European civilization (1962:463ff.,570). Thus the focus of assimilation was on the community rather than the individual. Furthermore, the haciendas recruited labor from these population centers, and mixed groups of Indians were incorporated into the national economy as a temporary rural work force. All the while, under laws of colonization, mestizo settlers were allowed to move into Indian territory with the result that they mixed with the local population. The result has been that "tribal identification lapsed . . . even though the general identification as Indian continued" (1962:573). Thus in a process Spicer calls "suspended assimilation," the aboriginal populations of Mexico largely lost their individual tribal identities and replaced them with a generalized Indian identity.

Spicer concludes that European policies of cultural assimilation have not worked according to plan. In the long run, however, what has resulted is a high degree of assimilation of the Indian populations of both the American Southwest and Mexico into the European cultural system. With regard to Mexico, he states that while rural mestizos and Indians now share many cultural similarities, the Indian still has not gained full acceptance into Mexican society. He reiterates that many of the symbols of Indianness, such as dress, are not aboriginal. "The group identifications of the Indians rested solidly on their historical experiences with white men and were symbolized in elements of their cultures which were, like their experiences, products of contacts between Indians and white men" (1962:579). He concludes that Indian-European contact has been a balance between processes of assimilation and differentiation but that the most common result of programs of cultural assimilation imposed on people by a dominant group is the formation of an ethnic identity (1962:567).

Spicer's formulation fits the situation in Amatlán very well. The village is classified in government documents as a *congregación* ("congregation") in Spanish, which, despite its scattered layout, means that it probably came into being or at least was first legally recognized under the Spanish or Mexican program of concentrating populations into discrete communities. We also have evidence that the village supplied labor for a hacienda and that Mexican settlers have been moving into the southern Huasteca for many centuries. The villagers see themselves as Indian farmers (*masehualmej*), but they have retained less of their specific Nahua or *mexijcaj* (Aztec) tribal identity. Finally, as mentioned earlier, many of the overt symbols of Indian identity such as dress or the steel machete clearly derive from Indian-European contact. Spicer has succeeded in specifying many of the historical conditions and processes that have led Native Americans to forge an identity for themselves and to suggest why that identity takes the form we have witnessed in Amatlán. These broad historical processes are manifested in the specific conditions existing in the southern Huasteca, and it is in response to these conditions that the villagers continue to forge their ethnicity.

With the exception of the mestizo schoolteachers and their families, all of the people who live in Amatlán were born and raised there or in a nearby village. Thus, I was not surprised when people told me repeatedly that they feel comfortable in the village and alienated in the city. The village has its problems, not the least of which are the limited economic opportunities, but it is a familiar place. People speak Nahuatl, they follow known routines, and they share a world view. The food, the pace of life, and the patterns of interaction seem right to people socialized in a small village. Of equal importance, a villager in Amatlán is among his family members rather than alone among strangers in the city. These and many other features of village life provide strong psychological rewards for the people of Amatlán. But these intrinsic rewards alone cannot explain, as I hope to demonstrate below, why villagers work actively to create an ethnic identity that serves to distinguish them from the mestizos. Village life would be comfortable for people socialized there, whether Indian or mestizo, regardless of whether or not they viewed themselves as members of a distinct ethnic group. In the discussion that follows, I emphasize the material rewards that motivate people to create a distinct identity for themselves (Stocks 1989 presents a parallel analysis of ethnic identity among Cocamilla Indians of Peru; see also Siverts 1969 for a similar analysis in southern Mexico; and Castile 1981 for his discussion of a cultural-materialist approach to ethnicity in Mexico and North America).

BEING AN INDIAN

The situation in Amatlán is similar in broad outline to realities faced by villagers in many parts of Mexico and throughout the world. Nahuas are Indians and thus are one of many ethnic groups in modern Mexico. They exhibit linguistic and cultural features that distinguish them from members of the dominant urban society. They are citizens of Mexico, and yet most occupy a position very near the bottom in the social, economic, and political hierarchy of the country. Their economic situation is as marginal to the growing industrial sector of the country as it is to the mechanized agribusinesses that dominate farm production. The villagers, for the most part, have been left out of the tide of economic development that has transformed other parts of the country. But it would be a mistake to conclude that the people of Amatlán have been passive victims of progress who continue doggedly to follow their time-honored traditions even as these become increasingly irrelevant in the modern world.

The Indians of the southern Huasteca have battled for autonomy throughout their long and bloody history. They fought the Spaniards in the War of Independence, the French invaders a few decades later, and the leaders of Republican Mexico on several occasions. They fought as a group, and they fought on even after the major battles were over, not out of loyalty to ever-changing alien elites, but to win for themselves their independence and right to self-determination. Participants in these struggles forged a meaningful group identity not simply as Nahuas, Otomís, or Totonacs, but as Indian farmers in opposition to the *coyomej*, or mestizo outsiders. In-group loyalties do persist, however, and members of each culture retain their own customs and stereotypes of other Indians. While operating among other Indians, for example, an Amatlán villager identifies as a mexijcatl. But in opposition to mestizos, villagers identify primarily as masehualmej, and they see their own interests as tied to that of other neighboring indigenous people.

The people of Amatlán have been far from passive in their efforts to gain access to more land. They struggle not simply for economic reasons but also to keep their families together, thus adding passion to the fight. Their strategies range from filing lawful petitions to outright illegal seizure of land. In some cases these efforts have led to internal factionalism and violence. In others, the villagers have had to band together to protect themselves from external enemies, usually local mestizo landowners. The battle lines are rarely clear in these situations, and some people always confuse their own personal interests with those of the whole village. Conflicts over land have been largely successful, and at least three new villages have been formed by landless citizens from Amatlán. The history of this struggle, as recounted by villagers, makes one thing clear. The only effective way to confront local ranch owners and the entrenched mestizo power structure is for numbers of people to band together. Individuals acting alone have little chance against local elites who are able to hire gunmen or call out the local police or militia to protect their property and interests.

Like most developing countries, Mexico is a land of many contradictions. Most urban people are proud of their Native American heritage, and they speak glowingly of the great achievements of the ancient Mayas, Aztecs, and other pre-Hispanic Indians. But when it comes to contemporary Indian groups they are less enthusiastic, often justifying their antipathy by claiming that noble pre-Hispanic cultures have been degraded and contaminated by Spanish influence. Some mestizos may even feel pathological hatred of the Indians and wish to do them harm. But in general, the mestizos of the southern Huasteca attribute "Indian troubles" to outside agitators, usually believed to originate from the cities.

Many shopkeepers in Ixhuatlán, for example, call villagers *inditos* in Spanish, meaning "little Indians," a slightly patronizing but basically affectionate term. I have occasionally heard villagers themselves use this word in a self-deprecating way when speaking Spanish. In the eyes of the townspeople, Indians are an unsophisticated country folk who are incapable of competing in the fast-paced world that they themselves inhabit. Indians are usually regarded as people of low culture who would rather drink and engage in machete fights than hold steady jobs and save their money. Some mestizos share with many professional social scientists and development experts the image of the Indians as people who follow the dictates of an ancient culture even when doing so goes against their own basic economic interests. Backward, lazy, simple, custom-bound, and carefree—the list of character flaws duplicates the stereotypes held in many countries by the local gentry about those less-privileged people who contribute so much to their support and about whom they know so very little.

At the same time, the ruling political party in Mexico, the PRI (Partido Revolucionario Institucional, or Party of the Institutionalized Revolution) is more or less sympathetic with the plight of the Indians and has set up many programs and allocated considerable money to ameliorate their economic condition. A group of Indians soliciting land is frequently able to get a hearing, and often obtains a favorable, although never prompt, ruling. The PRI was born in a time of crisis over land reform, and party leaders have never totally abandoned these roots.

From the days of the Revolution an Indianist movement (called *indigenismo* in Spanish) has been influencial in Mexican artistic, literary, and political life. Members of this movement have never been unified in their outlook toward Indians, but they have generally moved from an earlier policy of assimilationism to a more recent one of cultural pluralism. The PRI party has been influenced by indigenismo and has established on both the state and federal levels a large number of agencies and programs to help the Indians achieve economic, social, and political parity with mestizos. Such programs are often at odds with each other and contradictory in their goals, they lack sustained funding, and they sometimes fail to follow through with their plans. Nonetheless these programs exist in profusion, and the villagers are very much aware of them. In a sense the government is encouraging people to stress their ethnicity as Indians to receive the benefits from these many Indianist efforts (see Bradley 1988:187ff. for a discussion of government agencies and progams affecting Indians in the southern part of the state of Veracruz).

This is not to say that the government is allocating more resources to help Indians than to help mestizos. Such a policy would be impossible given the political realities of Mexico. Mestizos have a monopoly on government office, they participate more directly in the national economy, and in the eyes of government officials they represent the hope of national economic development. In fact, bowing to political pressure, the government allocates about five times more money to municipios that are primarily mestizo than to municipios that are primarily Indian, according to one analysis (Caso 1971:147). Nevertheless, resources have been set aside for Indians, and the people of Amatlán feel that they have benefited from emphasizing their Indian identity when dealing with mestizos. They point to the schoolhouse built in the early 1970s, the new kindergarten classroom that was being built when I returned in 1985, the electrification project, and many other benefits discussed below. The fact that more actual resources go to mestizo municipios on a national level does not change the perception of the villagers in Amatlán that being Indian can be used to attract government attention and money. Most villagers are acutely conscious of the advantages of Indian identity when it comes to dealing with the government.

When village delegations present their requests to government officials, they frequently stress their Indianness in order to increase their chances for success. This partially explains an anomaly that I perceived in the account of the history of Amatlán presented by the elders. They were emphatic when stating that representatives from Amatlán had walked long distances to meet with officials during the struggle to regain land taken illegally from the village. They reported that on several occasions the men had walked to Tuxpan, almost 100 miles distant. Because inexpensive bus transportation is available for much of the way to this coastal center, I wondered why the delegates chose to walk. One explanation is that villagers opted to arrive exhausted and dirty and thus fulfill their role as downtrodden Indians in order to get a more favorable ruling on their case. The strategy was apparently effective, and the land was eventually restored to the village.

Numerous government services are provided free of charge to rural communities and to Indian communities in particular. Medical teams visit Amatlán twice a year to vaccinate children. Other technicians arrive regularly to spray insecticide in private houses in an effort to eradicate insects and other pests that carry diseases. The villagers organized to take advantage of a government rural electrification program, and they ultimately succeeded in having electricity brought to the village in 1986. The program specifically targeted remote villages like Amatlán, and again being Indian turned out to have its advantages. Finally, in 1986 there was a great deal of excitement in Amatlán over the rumor of a government plan to provide free houses to Indians of the region. Village authorities journeyed several times to the state capital to inquire about the program, but they were unable to obtain confirmation of its existence. Even if the free housing program never materializes, the villagers' reaction is interesting in that it reveals their attitude toward government services. From the villagers' perspective the authorities distribute benefits to poor people, and because they are Indians and by definition poor, they are confident that they will be on the receiving end (see Bradley 1988).

Rural mestizos may also benefit from government programs, but I have the distinct impression, backed by the opinions of many villagers, that, under the influence of indigenismo, Indian communities are often specifically targeted by national development agencies. Officials consider Indians almost as wards of the state. Rural mestizos can be equally poor, but from the viewpoint of government officials they do not suffer from debilitating cultural backwardness like the Indians and therefore should not be first in line to receive government aid. In reality, rural poor mestizos are often more disdained than Indians by many urban people who feel the Indians at least have the excuse of their ancient traditional culture for their poverty. Mestizos, on the other hand, are part of the national culture, and their poverty is less excusable. From this biased perspective, if a person is poor, it is better to be Indian than a lowly member of the national culture.

I do not wish to underplay the suffering inflicted on the Indians by a political-economic system that exploits them and defines them as being less than human. But I think it is important to emphasize that the status of Indian in Mexico can confer certain advantages on people who are at the bottom of the status hierarchy anyway. By standing together as Indians, for example, villagers have a far better chance of gaining legal access to any land they expropriate from mestizo landowners. This is one reason the people of Amatlán are motivated to create and maintain an ethnic identity that separates them from neighboring mestizos. The point I want to make here is that these villagers are not simply rustics who are satisfied to be passive victims of an unfair system. Instead, they develop their own strategies and trust their own methods for obtaining the results they seek. They do not have many cards to play, but they are definitely maneuvering to stay in the game.

Being an Indian can bring tangible advantages to individuals as well as groups. When I first went to work in the southern Huasteca I noted with surprise that many services have a dual-pricing system. Indians often pay one-half of the amount charged to mestizos and foreigners. For example, it cost me $.08 to be poled by dugout canoe across the river on the way to market, but Indians were charged only $.04. Other services such as rides on market trucks or tolls paid to use roads or bridges were priced similarly. At first I thought that I was being cheated, but then I noted that all non-Indians were charged more on the theory that they could afford to pay more. Thus, mestizos (and visiting anthropologists) are subsidizing the costs of certain services that would normally be too expensive for most Indians. In addition, the National Indigenous Institute (Instituto Nacional Indigenista, commonly called INI for short) makes full and partial scholarships available for Indian children to attend secondary school. I know of at least two children from Amatlán who were able to take advantage of this offer during 1985–86 alone, and it is likely that many more children in the village have been supported through this program. Finally, INI also has a program designed to support traditional Indian ritual specialists. Qualifying individuals receive a monthly stipend for keeping ancient traditions alive. No shaman that I met was supported in this way, but several knew about the program and one asked me if I could help him qualify.

We saw in Chapter 5 that Nahua households must supply their members with food and sufficient money to make necessary purchases and to cover various ejido assessments. But most villagers are not satisfied simply to meet expenses; rather, like people anywhere they want to earn as much as they can. To do this they must allocate their time, energy, and other resources in the most productive way possible and must also cut costs. Being an Indian does not prevent a person from accumulating substantial wealth, as witness the cattle-owning Nahua families. Deriving any significant income from slash-and-burn horticulture and animal husbandry is not usually feasible, however. This is particularly the case because the wage scale for available work and the price cycle for village crops seem designed to prevent Indians from acquiring much money. However, compared with small-scale mestizo farmers who face many of the same obstacles, being an Indian can have its distinct advantage.

For one thing, as the French ethnographer Marie Noëlle Chamoux noted among Nahuas in the neighboring Sierra Norte de Puebla region, despite differences in wealth among the Indian villagers they exhibit a marked flattening of their standard of living (1981b:255ff.). This phenomenon of leveling in consumption patterns is not nearly as noticeable in mestizo settlements, where owning a prestige item like a television is a matter of pride and a means of impressing one's neighbor. The Nahuas try to minimize differences among fellow villagers and to stress that they are all members of the same ethnic group. People in Amatlán often say things like, "We are all poor here," or "There are no rich people living in villages." They frequently repeat these aphorisms almost as a way of obliterating the obvious disparity between the local haves and have-nots. People who flaunt their money or who give the appearance of being well-off are often the target of gossip. I was told on many occasions that the reason certain people are rich is because they have found pots of gold and silver or because they stole from public funds. The murder case described in Chapter 1 involved accusations of stealing public money. What is important is that no one is ever believed to get rich through the traditional and legitimate means available to Indians. Indians are defined as poor. For their part, the wealthier villagers do not wish to stir up envy among their neighbors, and so they are careful not to parade their wealth. Strong religious sanctions discourage such behavior. Destructive emotions like envy can summon disease-causing wind spirits or drive neighbors to sorcery.

I have suggested that one reason why richer Indians hide their wealth is that villagers discourage displays of individual achievement or anything else that sets the individual apart from the group. Thus the cultural value of shared poverty is really part of the larger attempt of the villagers to establish a community of Indians who are ideally a unit with little internal differentiation, and who can act together in opposition to the mestizos who oppress them. Flattened consumption does not really mean shared poverty, but it can lead to the appearance of shared poverty. To the extent that it succeeds in discouraging conspicuous consumption, it confers on the Indians a distinct advantage over mestizos. Scarce resources can be invested in animals or perhaps in renting additional land, rather than being squandered in the purchase of nonproductive prestige items. To be Indian, then, is to be committed to values that make it advantageous to appear poor, thus freeing scarce resources that can be applied to the production of additional wealth. At the same time, cutting back on purchases of manufactured items reduces (but does not eliminate) villagers' dependence on the mestizo sector of the national economy.

Being an Indian in Mexico is to live in a world where paradox reigns. To be Indian is to be disadvantaged relative to powerful mestizo elites, but at the same time Indianness confers certain advantages over equally poor rural mestizos. By stressing their ethnic identity as Indians, the villagers affirm their low status and make being an Indian all the more necessary. To understand the dilemma we must observe the situation from the point of view of the villagers. If an individual decides to leave Amatlán and enter the mestizo world, which for reasons discussed below increasing numbers are doing, then he or she has to give up rights in the village. Once away from the village they would never be able to enter the mestizo middle or upper classes but instead would be confined to the mestizo lower classes. This would probably mean living in a slum near a major city and doing poorly paid factory or domestic labor. There are virtually no other options. Local jobs for cowboys (*vaqueros* in Spanish) or ranch hands are scarce and usually seasonal.

I interviewed two villagers who had done factory work but who had since returned to Amatlán as vecinos. They told me about the "smoke" (air pollution), the sleazy living conditions in dangerous neighborhoods, the slick operators who prey on recent arrivals to the city, and the unscrupulous bosses at work. Most emphatically they complained about the high cost of everything and how their meager pay was not enough to support even themselves alone. Some people leave the village and enter the mestizo world, never to return. Others work on a temporary basis in the factories and are able to return periodically to plant their fields and retain their rights in the village. However, after weighing the alternatives available to them, most stay in the village and hope that they can succeed economically in the Indian world.

ETHNIC IDENTITY AS A STRATEGY

Anthropologists, comparative sociologists, political scientists, and others have produced an immense body of published works on the questions surrounding ethnic identity. Many social scientists and most laymen have assumed that membership in an ethnic group is setted at birth and that individuals therefore have little choice in the matter. It is true that when membership in an ethnic group is associated with observable racial markers such as skin color, the element of choice sometimes disappears entirely because ethnic status can be ascribed by the dominant group. However, when members of the dominant and lower status ethnic groups are not easily distinguished by racial or other features, individuals are freer to choose their ethnic group identity.

Scholars have observed that in some situations ethnic group members actively work to maintain ethnic identity and to distinguish their own ethnic group from other such groups and from the dominant group in the society. Many ethnic group members refuse to enter the dominant group even when they could choose to do so, and in fact try to insure that the sociocultural boundaries between groups are strongly maintained (see Barth 1969). One recent work suggests that the concept of tradition (the historically based beliefs and practices that distinguish ethnic groups) should be replaced with the concept of style. The latter concept emphasizes that members of some ethnic groups consciously select elements from their history and actively create an identity separate from other groups (Royce 1982:27–28,147,168). Tradition implies a passive acceptance of the past linked to ascribed status, whereas the concept of style carries with it the element of choice and self-generated identity.

A further example of the dynamic character of ethnic identity can be found in the chicomexochitl ritual observed by most Indian communities in the Huasteca region, including the people of Amatlán. The offering follows the usual pattern of Nahua rituals and the symbolic elements definitely derive from pre-Hispanic antecedents. However, Frans Schryer, an anthropologist working in the western Huasteca, has uncovered evidence that this important seed offering is a relatively new ritual created sometime in the 1940s (1990:182–84). Although ancient in conception, the new ritual reveals that a most traditional facet of Indian culture—religion—is capable of generating new sources of Indian identity (see Huber 1987 for an analysis of how new rituals are incorporated in traditional Nahua fiesta cycles). Tradition should not be viewed as the dead hand of the past intruding into the present. Ethnic group members select from traditional cultural elements and recombine them into new patterns that are faithful to ancient Nahua values but that are also relevant to modern situations. By doing so, they can continue to use their modified culture to enhance and maintain their ethnic identity.

I do not contend that ethnic identity is always or even usually a matter of free choice. In the case of Amatlán, many villagers, particularly those who are older or who do not speak Spanish, have little choice in identifying as Indians. Without mastery of Spanish and considerable knowledge of mestizo culture, Indians have been unable to enter the world beyond the village on a par with the mestizos. In cases such as this where cultural differences prevent assimilation, ethnicity becomes a strategy of last resort to provide a refuge for subjugated groups. The mestizos, of course, are at the center of the problem. They identify the villagers as Indians on the basis of dress, language, or the other markers mentioned above, and they hire the Indians only for temporary, poorly paid, menial tasks. Discrimination against Indians by mestizos is real, and the mestizos play a large role in maintaining by their prejudices the boundaries between Indians and themselves.

Once the above has been stated, however, I would contend that in many places throughout the world the members of lower-status ethnic groups have some degree of freedom in choosing whether to stay in their ethnic group or to try to enter the dominant group. I further contend that in many cases people deliberately choose to stay as members of the lower-status ethnic group, even when this decision seems to an outsider to entail apparent disadvantages. In villages like Amatlán, people actively cultivate their ethnic identity by stressing their Indianness as part of their strategy for dealing with mestizo elites. From the viewpoint of the local society, this decision often confers advantages and is therefore rational.

In Amatlán during the years when villagers had no practical way to learn Spanish, their ability to choose to become mestizo was very limited, and their status as Indians was largely ascribed. They perpetuated their Indian identity in the relative safety of their remote village and interacted with outsiders according to the mestizo definition of the social situation. But the appearance of a dedicated schoolmaster in Amatlán in the early 1960s changed things for the cohort of students who in the late 1980s are approaching middle age and are beginning to assume positions of leadership in the village. This teacher brought his family to live in the village, and he set himself the task of improving the quality and breadth of the education being offered. He added 3 years to the curriculum so that six grades are now avilable to every village child. He taught the Spanish language in earnest, and many of his students became bilingual. He thereby made it possible for certain people, most commonly the young men, to go to the regional towns or cities and obtain temporary work in construction, road building, and industrial hauling. These jobs pay considerably more than machete work, and they offer access to the mestizo domain that had previously been difficult for villagers to enter.

This blossoming of education in Amatlán was short-lived, however. The schoolmaster soon gained a reputation among his superiors and was promoted to inspector for the school district. He moved out of Amatlán to assume his new post and was replaced by a younger man. According to villagers, the new schoolmaster was a disaster. He appeared drunk in front of the children and was ineffective as a teacher. A few months after he arrived, his body was found floating in the arroyo and his horse was located about a mile upstream still wearing the saddle. Apparently he had fallen off the horse in a drunken stupor and hit his head on the rocks. His replacement was another young man whom the villagers found more to their liking. He made friends among the people and was successful in the classroom. Unfortunately he was subject to epileptic attacks and within a few months of his appointment in Amatlán he drowned while bathing. Villagers say that people who die from attacks of this sort are sometimes the victims of sorcery. Many people wondered why both men died in the arroyo and speculated about whether there was a connection between the deaths.

The schoolmaster next assigned to Amatlán was a veteran in his early forties. By this time the children were well behind in each of their grade levels, and he had to spend many months trying to catch up. This schoolmaster and his family had only been in the village a short while when we arrived in 1985 to begin fieldwork. One night after a severe thunderstorm, the schoolmaster's wife ran by our dwelling crying loudly. I investigated and found that her husband had tried to cross the swollen arroyo and both he and his horse had been swept under by the raging torrent. A few minutes later some village men pulled him from the water, still alive but bleeding profusely from a gash in his arm. The horse was found the next day quite a distance downstream, battered but alive. A sense of relief swept through the village, and a shaman held a ritual offering to the water spirit at the place where the schoolmaster nearly drowned. However, their relief was to turn to disappointment. The next year, just a few months after returning home, I received a letter from one of the sons of the schoolmaster informing me that his father had died of a heart attack. Despite these distressing setbacks, the school has generally made it possible for villagers to gain experience in mestizo culture and therefore to become less confined solely to their own. For the people who can operate in both the Indian and mestizo realms, an element of authentic choice enters into ethnic identity (however, for critiques of the education offered in Indian villages written by Nahua schoolmasters see Romualdo Hernández 1982:97–109 and Reyes Martínez 1982:122–24).

The ability to handle themselves with greater skill in urban culture, however, does not relieve the villagers of the need to exercise caution when dealing with mestizos. After I had been in the field for some time, I received a lesson in how villagers negotiate their ethnic status and manage information about themselves to outsiders. One day before dawn, I started out with five men on the 2-hour walk to the main market in Ixhuatlán. As we wound our way along the trails the men joked and carried on animated conversations punctuated by raucous laughter. They made an effort to teach me words in Nahuatl, and they laughed with delight as I recited simple sentences. This pattern of interaction was not unusual, and I had observed it many times back in the village. However, about 15 minutes before we arrived in town the men fell quiet, and they separated themselves from each other and from me. They split up when we arrived, and I noticed that each of them made an effort to avoid me. Gone was the laughter and in place of smiling faces appeared a kind of masklike frown. I approached one of them who had earlier been a good companion, and he pretended not to hear me. I knew something was wrong, and I waited at the edge of town for them to finish their business.

They all arrived simultaneously from different directions and as we left town they resumed their banter and their demeanor returned to normal. They never commented about this, but it was clear what was happening. Upon arriving at the market they put on impassive expressions and their behavior became slow and measured. This was the image they presented to the mestizos in town who, so far as I know, had no idea that they were being fooled. By appearing with me, the men would have drawn attention to themselves, and so they kept away while we were in the town. It was the clearest example of impression management I had ever seen, and I now had an idea where the mestizos get some of their notions about the Indians. During the time I lived in Amatlán I witnessed similar transactions in many different contexts.

By playing the "dumb Indians," the people of Amatlán reproduce behavior engaged in by oppressed minorities all over the world when they interact with the people oppressing them. It is in fact dangerous for Indians to deal with mestizos. I have heard many stories from villagers in which townsmen, ranchers, or cowboys beat and even killed Indians for minor infractions or in drunken rages. According to villagers, mestizos are rarely brought to justice for these crimes. These stories may or may not be true, but they reveal villagers' attitudes toward mestizo character and the effectiveness of the local justice system. The villagers are not cowards and are willing to confront the ranchers' hired guns armed with nothing more than machetes. But when dealing with mestizos, circumspection seems to be the better part of valor. It is startling to see intelligent and energetic people become emotionless and withdrawn in the company of representatives of the local mestizo elite. What they are doing is reaffirming their Indianness in order not to pose a threat to powerful outsiders. In this case, ethnic identity serves the people by providing a defense against potentially dangerous interactions with the mestizos.

Indian status, then, is an identity people in Amatlán are born into but one that, increasingly, they can choose to retain or reject. It is also a status that is to no small extent cultivated by the people themselves. The way that the villagers create and maintain a viable ethnic identity is complex and reaches into every aspect of their lives. To succeed they must create a world in which people can be comfortable and feel essentially in control of their lives. This world must be self-defined and distinct from that of the mestizos whom the villagers uniformly view as outsiders. In addition, they must develop mechanisms for keeping the two worlds apart. This problem is partially resolved by the mestizos themselves, who generally wish to distance themselves from everything they perceive as Indian. As seen below, the Nahuas of Amatlán have succeeded in forging a viable ethnic identity by carefully orchestrating a number of selected social and cultural features.

The recent work of anthropologist John Hawkins on ethnicity in Guatemala differs from the viewpoint presented here in several important ways. Hawkins maintains that aboriginal culture in Mesoamerica and elsewhere in the New World was essentially destroyed by the European conquerers. He states that the sociocultural category "Indian" is a creation of Spanish conquest and a result of the ideology of domination. In this view he is in fundamental agreement with the positions of Friedlander and Bartra discussed in Chapter 1. According to Hawkins, the Spaniards saw their new subjects as mirror images of themselves. The attributes they perceived as Indian were precisely the reverse of those they thought of as Spanish. This caused the surviving aboriginal peoples to react by creating an ethnic identity based on opposition to everything Spanish.

As Hawkins states it, "postconquest Indian culture was largely recast in the inverse image of the Spanish culture" (1984:44). Or put another way, "The Spanish idea of Indian distinctiveness—within the context of forced enslavement—forged an opposite, inverse ideology in the Indian segment of the new colonial society" (1984:349). Indians, then, are a colonial creation, and as such they can only be understood in relation to the essentially European ideology that created them. Thus, both the Ladino heirs to the Spanish tradition (or mestizos in the terminology used here for Mexico) and the Indian populations are simply aspects of a single cultural system. For Hawkins, "The pervasive inverse relationship of Indian to Ladino ideology is the essence of being Indian as well as the essence of being Ladino" (1984:347).

This formulation clearly contradicts the proposition developed here that ethnicity is a type of strategy employed by people to reduce costs and increase benefits to themselves. Hawkins instead regards ethnic identities developed by subjugated peoples as simply inversions of the particular ideologies of their conquerers. As such, he mistakenly reduces processes of ethnicity in all their complexity to an operation in logic. In his formulation the Indians disappear as actors in the great unfolding drama of history, and they again are portrayed as perpetual victims. Furthermore, Hawkins is in error when he removes ethnicity to the realm of ideational opposition because he causes us to lose sight of the local social, political, economic, and other material factors that create the conditions motivating people to forge separate identities.

A significant shortcoming in Hawkins's account is the absence of any treatment of religion, which is one of the most important aspects of Nahua identity and (along with language) provides the clearest evidence of cultural and historical distinctiveness relative to the mestizos. Nahua religion has a history and coherence of its own and in no sense can it be understood as an inversion of Spanish Catholicism. From the viewpoint of the villagers, the costumbre religion incorporates much of Christianity in its pantheistic, universalistic world view. In fact, few of the symbolic or ideological elements of Nahua identity in Amatlán are point for point opposites of mestizo culture. They need only be different in some way to serve to disinguish the Nahuas from the mestizo dominant group. On the contrary, some features of village life are best seen as accommodations to mestizo expectations. Any attempt to clarify ethnicity will fall short unless the individual actors, their motivations, and the context in which they find themselves are major components of the analysis. Finally, although it may be an error to overplay the pre-Hispanic features of contemporary Indian culture, it is equally fallacious to assume that these features are insignificant.

AMATLAN CULTURAL FEATURES AND THE CREATION
OF INDIAN IDENTITY

In describing the cultural features of Amatlán, I have referred the
reader throughout this work to published sources in which identical
or similar cultural features have been documented in other Nahua
communities. I have not systematically compared Amatlán to other
Nahua communities because this would have resulted in a somewhat
different book from the one I intended to write. I want to affirm,
however, that most of the cultural features I describe for Amatlán are
duplicated or exist in modified form in Nahua villages throughout
Mexico. Examples include reliance on maize horticulture, a patrilocal
extended family with a characteristic domestic cycle, stress on male-
sibling solidarity, intergenerational conflict, the central place of the
earth in religious belief, numerous spirits including the sun, tonantsij,
a rain spirit and disease-causing winds, an underworld realm, stress on
harmony and equilibrium between the human and spirit communities,
reliance on shamans to cure disease and foretell the future, entire
myths or mythic motifs, and many other cultural features described
throughout this book.

The people of Amatlán have retained many of their ancient traditions, and it is not surprising that a significant portion of these are
shared by other Nahua groups living at quite a distance from the
southern Huasteca. Specific conditions existing in the region have
caused certain cultural features to assume crucial importance. For
example, I have shown that the land shortage has exacerbated intergenerational conflict, sibling rivalry, and the marginal position of female family members among villagers. These are features found in
other Nahua villages, but due to local conditions they take on particular
importance in Amatlán. In sum, what I have described in Amatlán
should be understood as one regional variant of a general Nahua
cultural pattern that has been shown to exist in many different social
and natural environments throughout Mexico. In my focus on the
role of ethnicity in the perpetuation and, as I will show shortly, the
transformation of Nahua culture, I have not found it necessary to
itemize cultural correspondences among various Nahua communities.
Of greater importance for my purposes is to identify cultural features
that play a significant role in Nahua ethnic identity.

The single most important cultural activity in Amatlán that both
creates a world view for the villagers and defines the ethnic group to
which they belong is participation in the costumbre rituals. The ritual

observances are based on a cosmology that is completely alien to that of the mestizos. No mestizo participates in village ritual life, except possibly on a rare occasion in the more secular observances such as carnival (nanahuatili). Unless they are themselves former members of an Indian community, mestizos have no knowledge of the Indian spirit pantheon, the sacred geography, concepts of soul and spirit, disease etiology, ritual procedures, sacred symbols and icons, or ritual specialists. Many of these Indian religious beliefs, practices, and understandings derive from their pre-Hispanic past. By participating in rituals, villagers are affirming their commitment to Indian culture, and they are actively assuming an Indian identity (see Crumrine 1964 for an analysis of how Mayo Indians of Sonora, Mexico, use the house cross as a symbol of ethnic identity).

Two of the core features of costumbre belief and ritual are the ideals of balance between humans and their environment, and of self-control in interacting with others. People must repay the earth, water, seeds, and all the other elements that support their lives. They must also avoid bad deeds and control feelings of envy, anger, or ill will toward others in order to avoid attracting malevolent wind spirits to the village. One of the most important roles of the shaman is to divine the causes of calamity and disease and to battle the forces of imbalance and disharmony by conducting ritual offerings. Interestingly, many of the human shortcomings that in Nahua belief cause disharmony are precisely those traits that villagers attribute to mestizos. Disrespect for the earth and all of its gifts, accompanied by arrogance, aggressiveness, violence, and dishonesty, practically define mestizo character according to villagers. Thus, the costumbre religion, in addition to creating a community, also helps rid Amatlán of perceived dangerous mestizo character traits and behavior that are felt to threaten the integrity of the community. Religion helps create a focus of ethnic identity for the Nahuas, but it also stands as a bulwark against the erosion of Nahua values.

In the words of a Nahua villager from the neighboring state of Hidalgo who became a schoolteacher and ethnographer, "To maintain our religion is one of the demonstrations of our cultural identity. [It is an identity] different from that of the mestizo population and from that of other Indian groups in Mexico. Also, religion is a means of expressing our resistance. Although at times we have to hold our rituals in secret, we will continue to hold them because they are uniquely ours" (Hernández Cuellar 1982:140). Most people I know are less articulate about the role of religion in Nahua life. However, as we will see below, with the coming of Protestant missionaries into the southern Huasteca, many villagers have become militant supporters of the traditional beliefs and rituals.

I do not mean to imply that people in Amatlán participate in their rituals solely to demonstrate their Indianness or out of a cynical attempt to forge an ethnic identity and thereby gain economic advantages. Most people conveyed to me that they attend rituals out of a deep sense of piety and a sincere desire to establish and maintain links with the ultimate spiritual powers of the universe. It is for these reasons that many individuals make significant investments to sponsor rituals. Thus, devotion to Nahua religion is an end in itself for most participants regardless of social consequences. However, participation in costumbre rituals is also an affirmation of Indian identity, an act that most clearly binds a person to the indigenous culture and separates that person from mestizo identity.

Participation in the costumbres is in many ways the ultimate test of Indianness because it is based on a view of the universe and a body of knowledge not shared by most mestizos. As I discovered for myself, it is not an easy task for an outsider to penetrate Nahua religious thought. Even the shamans are none too eager to explain the more abstract concepts. Villagers learn the precepts of their religion through a lifetime of participating in rituals, through hearing myths recounted, and through informal discussion. Because their theology is not written down and the shamans rarely make systematic explanations of religious principles, a person has to have lived in an Indian community for a long time before he or she can master even the fundamentals of Nahua religion. Most mestizos, of course, would have no desire to participate in Indian rituals even if they possessed the requisite knowledge. For the majority of them the costumbres are the remnants of a pagan past characterized by childlike beliefs that contradict their own urbane Christianity. Thus the barrier between Indian and mestizo is maintained from both directions.

In most social situations, knowledge is power, but when a subordinate ethnic group has dealings with a dominant group, knowledge can mean the difference between survival and extinction. By linking ethnic identity to the costumbre religion, the Nahuas effectively exclude mestizo participation in their lives. It is significant that the Indians have come to know a great deal about the mestizo world, but many mestizos, under the illusion that they already know everything about Indians, continue to operate with the false assumptions and stereotypes that derive from ignorance of the Indian way of life.

Knowledge in rural Mexico is often a one-way street, from the bottom up. An increasing number of people from the village could pass into the world of the national culture and become mestizos, but most mestizos could never return to being Indians.

In short, Indians often have a clearer picture of the realities of Mexican society than the mestizo elites who run everything. Their views of mestizo character are often likewise false and stereotyped, but their knowledge of the mestizo domain is detailed and largely accurate. The mestizos, of course, do not want to become Indians, and Indians for the most part have no interest in becoming mestizos. Even as opportunities arise, relatively few villagers choose to enter the mestizo world permanently, and most of those who do are widows or others with no viable means to support themselves in the village. In any case, villagers must preserve access to government channels and to temporary jobs provided by mestizos to supplement their farming activities. In this situation, knowledge is power, and the Indians can use this knowledge to extract from the mestizo world what they need to survive better in their own.

The basic strategy for Indians is to find out as much as possible about the mestizo world while simultaneously blocking mestizo knowledge of the Indian world. Knowledge in the hands of superordinates is always potentially dangerous. Villagers learn about mestizos by going to school, by working outside the village, by being keen observers of marketplace dynamics, and by asking for information. When I first went to Amatlán, I was amazed at the number of questions people constantly asked me. The questions were indirect in accord with Nahua etiquette, but it was not long before I was able to interpret precisely what they were asking. I believe they were genuinely curious about me and my world, but as the months went by I began to suspect that they were using me as a source of information about the outside world. It was a role I was glad to play as one way of paying them back for my own intrusions. Among other things, they always wanted to know how much everything cost, from shoes to tape recorders to airplanes. They wanted to know how radios, cameras, batteries, or watches worked. People questioned me about the reasons satellites stay up, the principles by which an airplane flies, and how a person driving a car finds his way on the roads. I was asked what foods people in the United States eat, how much money a fieldhand was paid for a day's labor, and why people from my country do not like Mexicans.

The Nahuas were curious about the United States, but they were far more interested in Mexican urban life. Here I was not as much help, but I answered as best I could. Sometimes my questioners clearly did not believe me. No one could accept that most people in the United States do not eat tortillas regularly, nor that a person can buy drinks on an airplane. Once, in 1985, when my wife got involved in an explanation about Tupperware parties with a group of women (the women admired her gift of the plastic lidded bowls), they listened politely, but shook their heads and gently changed the subject. The idea of inviting people as guests to your house in order to sell them plastic goods was pushing their credulity too far. Most people carefully evaluated what I told them and systematically rejected what they thought could not be true. Villagers wanted to know what people outside of the village ate and how they lived, not because they envied other lifestyles but rather because knowing is a good thing in itself. It was clearly partly a matter of gaining familiarity with the mestizo world, but the Nahuas also enjoyed a sense of sophistication at knowing all about how the rich people lived and how advanced technology worked. Individuals took pleasure in telling me about long bus rides to the south of Veracruz state, or of their experiences in Mexico City. After hundreds of hours of conversations with the villagers, I can state that their knowledge of the mestizo world is indeed extensive. By contrast, in all of my interactions with neighboring mestizos I was never asked any question of substance about the Indian way of life.

The people of Amatlán are privy to an enormous body of local knowledge that is not available to any outsider. In this sense the village is closed to outside scrutiny. For an outsider to gain access to this information he or she must be prepared to spend many months of continuous residence in the village. For example, I have already mentioned difficulties with the way people are named. A young school-teacher who had been in residence in Amatlán for about 3 years and was herself a Nahuatl-speaker from a nearby mestizo town tried to take a census of the village. She made of list of names, but when we checked her list against the census we took we found that about one-third of the entries on her list were incorrect or misleading. On several occasions she had apparently listed people two or three times under different names. Added to the name confusion is the idiosyncratic way that houses and house sites are labeled. Without a knowledge of local history and terrain, it is impossible to follow directions in the village or fully comprehend a conversation among locals. The same involution of local knowledge exists for the naming of the geographical features of the whole region. Each village has a slightly different set of names for surrounding mountains, lakes, gulleys, and streams.

Members of all human social groups create their own insider knowledge, for it is one way they distinguish themselves from other groups. However, in small, relatively isolated villages like Amatlán, the process of creating in-group knowledge is carried to an unusual degree. Furthermore, I believe that the proliferation of names and the potential for confusion is so great that the system amounts to a deliberate evasive tactic on the part of villagers. Their system for naming people and places probably derives in modified form from the pre-Hispanic era. By continuing to adhere to it villagers reaffirm their past, create a sense of community, and present almost impenetrable confusion to outsiders. Put another way, the villagers have made no effort to regularize their naming patterns to ease the administrative task of local government officials. People seem quite aware of the effect their complex system has on outsiders. On several occasions I heard people laughing about how officials in Ixhuatlán went after the wrong person or how they had mixed up names on paperwork. To a lifelong inhabitant of Amatlán, of course, the naming patterns are comprehensible and references to people or places are rarely misunderstood.

As might be expected, when they are among themselves the villagers have many ways of overtly asserting their Indianness in opposition to the mestizos. They enjoy sitting around in small groups recounting experiences to each other, and in these situations mestizos are often characterized as aggressive and incompetent compared to the more respectful and knowledgeable villagers. An example of this portrayal is found in the story of the corn spirit presented earlier. A crude and unconscientious mestizo allowed grains of corn to go to waste, and it was a wise Indian who rescued the kernels and was rewarded with the means of a livelihood. This type of plot or theme serves to characterize mestizos and affirm the essential correctness of Indian culture. During the celebration of the carnival rite of nanahuatili an even clearer picture of mestizos emerges in the reversal of social norms. Young men mock the social hierarchy and dress as mestizo men and women, wearing masks with pink faces and mustaches to mimic the men or dresses and long-haired wigs to impersonate mestizo women. As they move from house to house these theatrical "mestizos" shout orders, act in a rude and brusque manner, make overt sexual gestures, and are generally disrespectful and lacking in dignity. The message is clear to all present. During the observance, the world is turned upside down, and the mestizos are exposed for what they really are.

It would be dangerous for Indians directly to attack either the Mexican social hierarchy or the mestizos who occupy the elite positions in the hierarchy. Local political agitators are labeled troublemakers by authorities, and many are murdered outright. At the very least they may be harrassed by the police or army and perhaps even tortured. Criticism of the system is for this reason redirected toward safer targets. For example, the villagers developed elaborate critiques of the city and of city dwellers. In some cases individuals would regale me with horror stories of urban life, and I later found out that they had never set foot outside of the municipio of Ixhuatlán de Madero. One might expect these rural people to hold urban centers in low esteem. However, many of their remarks can be understood as general criticisms of mestizo lifestyles that have been carefully redirected so that even local mestizos would be inclined to agree with them. The villagers speak about aggressive and demanding city dwellers who move fast and rudely shove others aside. They say that city people lack respect, that they have lost touch with the earth and fail to exhibit the spiritual resonance human beings should have with their surroundings. Women in the cities are aggressive and shrill, and villagers suspect that many of them must be prostitutes. People rob you, dishonesty is rife, and the pace of life lacks dignity and the measured calm of the village. Some of these characterizations reflect actual harsh experiences, but I suspect most are thinly veiled criticisms of mestizos in general.

Despite the associated low social standing and relative poverty, the people of Amatlán are generally proud to be masehualmej, cultivators of the land. Like most people they value their culture and would like to see the villages prosper and Indian values prevail (see this sentiment expressed in the poem written by a Nahua that appears at the beginning of this book). One Nahua schoolmaster writes in eloquent support of *masehualchicahualistli*, a Nahuatl neologism that means "Indian power" (Martínez Hernández 1982:92). Villagers do not feel ashamed to declare their Indianness through the way they dress and by other observable signs. A man always carries his machete in a leather sheath, which marks him as a slash-and-burn farmer. They wear crude and heavy sandals on their feet and the straw hats that identify the region and sometimes even the village where they live. The women walk to market in bare feet and wear the brightly colored clothing that are sure signs of Indian status. Villagers feel free to speak in their native language to one another even in the presence of mestizos. With the possible exception of people hiding ritual items when a priest enters the village, I have rarely found signs of Indians concealing their status before outsiders. This fact is consistent with the idea that an element of choice exists in Indian ethnic identity. Being identified as an Indian is only a good idea if that identification entails advantages for the individual.

Up to this point I have been describing various advantages of ethnicity for the Nahuas and some of the means by which they achieve their status. Part of the reason that villagers are permitted and even encouraged to develop a distinct Indian identity is because local mestizo elites see an advantage in the process for themselves. Ranchers can justify paying Indians less for their work because of perceived cultural differences and needs. As long as Indians are confined to ejido land, they pose little threat to the majority of ranchers' property. The land invasions around Amatlán have usually occurred in remote areas of ranches that were not being profitably used at the time. Ranchers who are invaded always put up a show of resistance, but it is relatively rare for a newly established village to be removed by force. In fact, I have heard of only one local incident that occurred in the late 1970s in which the army burned a village, shot all of the animals, and forcibly removed the people. The ranchers and their political allies seem almost willing to give up small, irrelevant patches of land on occasion to calm a potentially explosive situation. It is also far easier to dominate people socially, politically, and economically if they exhibit marked cultural differences. In sum, from the point of view of mestizo elites, having well-behaved Indians around can also offer advantages.

Ironically then, in a situation where one cultural group dominates another, the development and maintenance of ethnic identities can serve the interests of both groups. Although the subject groups will always be at a comparative disadvantage, they are better off than if they lacked any separate ethnic identity. Members of subject ethnic groups must not go too far, however. They must remain docile and familiar enough to members of the dominant group that they do not appear to pose a threat to the dominant group's basic values or world view. If they overly emphasize their distinct historical and cultural heritage, Indians risk becoming scapegoats and targets for dominant group violence. On the other hand, by appearing to share certain fundamental cultural elements with mestizos, Indians at once become less alien and more worthy of sympathy and understanding on the part of the elites. Also, Indians must work for mestizos at times during the year, and therefore they must be able to handle themselves in situations where mestizos are in control. Here again the Indians find themselves in a paradox. They must be sufficiently distinct to create an ethnic identity, but at the same time they must appear familiar enough to mestizo elites so that they can maintain working relations with them.

The need to avert mestizo violence and to remain on amicable terms with mestizos are two reasons that Indians seem, at times, to blur the boundary between themselves and the mestizo elite. The villagers have accepted some of the outward trappings of the national religion and, notably, they call themselves "Catholics," but at the same time their religion remains the principle activity that separates them from the mestizos. In the situation where local elites are basically ignorant of Indian life, appearances can help to reassure those in power that villagers are simply rural, powerless versions of themselves. Thus Indian ethnic identity is expressed overtly only in areas such as ritual, music, dress, language, and a docile and nonaggressive general demeanor, none of which poses a threat to the way powerful mestizos see the world. As numerous stories from villagers testify, attempts on the part of Indians to organize politically at all, much less participate in a radical political movement—in short, to threaten local mestizo elites—is the surest way to invite violent suppression.

In sum, in the years since the Revolution when modern Mexico was born, the Indians of the southern Huasteca have developed a modus vivendi for dealing with the mestizo elites. Many Indians have been confined to ejidos, although a substantial number manage to farm lands to which they have no legal right. Most of the profits they make from farming are siphoned off by the price cycle, inflation, and low wages paid for temporary work. The monied classes do not invest in Indian agriculture, and consequently technology has changed little from pre-Hispanic days. Indians have adjusted to their position in Mexico by creating and maintaining an ethnic identity in opposition to mestizo elites. Ethnic identity confers certain advantages on villagers that would be lost if they simply assimilated into the lowest ranks of rural mestizos.

A coherent Indian ethnic identity is constantly threatened by changes at the national and regional levels. Despite stereotypes held by urban dwellers, Indian culture itself is far from static. In fact, as more young people travel back and forth from village to city in search of temporary employment they bring back with them new ideas and material items that can accelerate change. As the horizons of villagers slowly shift from the villages, ranches, and towns of the southern Huasteca to the cities of Mexico and the world at large, Indian ethnic identity becomes increasingly irrelevant. Put another way, the rewards of being an Indian are diminished as one begins to compete for employment in the urban setting. Young people, then, are becoming less wedded to the traditional strategy of creating an Indian ethnic identity because this strategy is ceasing to be useful in mediating their interactions with urban mestizos. Presumably the identity is not cast off in a decisive moment but gradually loses its utility.

As I left Amatlán in 1973, I was convinced (following Redfield) that the villagers would undergo an incremental loss of ethnic identity as they were engulfed by the expanding Mexican economy and increasing urban influences. My wife and I returned for short visits over the next couple of years to renew old friendships and to document the more visible changes in the village. Just as predicted, changes appeared to be gradual and to be centered on cultural elements that were used to identify individuals as Indians. A number of young men had given up wearing traditional dress and had switched to mestizo clothing. Fewer men wore the traditional straw hat, and more of the children had learned Spanish. After an absence of almost 10 years I returned to Amatlán in 1985 for a yearlong stay, this time accompanied by both Pamela and our 3-year-old son, Michael. I expected to witness further changes in the village and in the people there, but I was totally unprepared for what we found when we arrived.

THE NEW AMATLÁN

Late in the afternoon on a summer day in 1985, I guided our four-wheel-drive vehicle slowly over one of the trails leading to Amatlán. The heat was stifling as dark clouds gathered, and the impending rain threatened to force us back. A downpour would mean that we would not be able to cross the many arroyos that lay between us and the village. Even more worrisome was the prospect of mud. Travel over rain-drenched trails is hazardous enough by foot, but it is absolutely impossible by vehicle. Rain would prevent us from proceeding or turning back, and I knew it would be dangerous to spend a night encamped in the forest. We crested a hill and got a panoramic view of the valley in which Amatlán lies. The trails had changed somewhat from the last time I was there, and I was unsure where we were. As I looked upon the valley, I saw an unfamiliar village. The houses were built in a large rectangle as if arranged along streets. Scattered in a regular pattern throughout the village were poles carrying electric lines. Off in the distance I could see the corrugated tin roof of a familiar-looking schoolhouse.

We proceeded slowly as the trail became steeper and more treacherous. I was filled with a combination of excitement and dread as we crawled along. Was this really Amatlán up ahead? Would anyone remember me after all of these years? I wondered if anyone I knew well had died or if any of my closest associates had left the village. Most of all, I was worried whether or not they would allow us to stay. I knew to expect an awkward reception, as according to Nahua custom we would be virtually ignored for several hours after our arrival while arrangements were being made behind the scenes. After crossing the last arroyo, we entered the village, and I stopped at the first thatch-roofed house and asked which place this was. A man whom I did not recognize said that it was Amatlán. He added that a few years previously the people had petitioned the government to have electricity brought to the village. The state engineers told the people that they would have to move their houses into a grid pattern so that the lines could be distributed more efficiently. As he spoke, I wondered why I did not know him and why he did not appear to know me. He added as an afterthought that he was from elsewhere and was just visiting his aunt in Amatlán. We resumed driving in the direction of the schoolhouse as my anxiety grew.

As we left the forest and entered the school clearing, I noticed that about 15 men were seated at the side of the old schoolhouse. I was surprised to see that all but 2 of them were dressed in mestizo-style clothing. We drove up and I got out of the vehicle and walked toward the men. Following local custom Pamela and Michael stayed behind until I had made first contact. Nobody looked up or made a sound as I approached. As I drew near, several men glanced at me simultaneously and broke out into broad smiles. I was much relieved to see someone recognized me, and I addressed these men by name and touched their fingertips in the traditional greeting. Participant-observation research is such an intense experience that even after an absence of many years I had no trouble remembering at least some portion of each person's multiple names. No one said much, and they all continued to sit quietly by. I knew that it could be 2 or 3 hours before everyone would acknowledge my presence and come talk to me. One man sent a boy to get the Agente Municipal, and once he arrived I proceeded to make sleeping arrangements. After a brief conversation with several men, the Agente decided that we could occupy one of the two rooms in the old dilapidated schoolhouse. After the appropriate amount of time had finally passed, a group of the men came over and greeted me with, "We thought you were dead." They added ominously, "When you came just now we were afraid you were *hermanos.*"

The word *hermanos* in Spanish means "brothers," and I had no idea what they meant. I knew I would have to wait to find out because a direct question at this point would be considered rude and would not elicit the answers I sought. As we adjusted to our new circumstances during the first week, almost everyone in the village came to greet us, bringing fruit or prepared food. I was pleased at our warm reception and at the way the people welcomed our child. They asked where we had been and why we had not visited them sooner. They brought me up to date on recent events in the village. All the while, however, I sensed that many people were worried and that something was wrong. The people seemed fit, in fact more prosperous than I remembered, and they had not lost their fine sense of humor. They asked me what I thought of the new village layout, the electric lines (which were in place but not to be connected for almost another year), and the new style of clothes most people were wearing. I began to suspect from the way they asked these things that many villagers were not too confident about the changes in their lives. But the problem was more serious than I first suspected.

The first week was marred by the deaths of two children within days of one another. They died of whooping cough, and we were invited to attend their funerals. We learned that several children had succumbed to this disease over the previous 3 or 4 years. I was very surprised to hear this. Whooping cough was a major killer of Indian children until government-sponsored health teams began visiting villages to administer free vaccines against common childhood diseases. I asked whether government health workers were not still visiting Amatlán. People answered yes, but then added that the parents of the children who had died had hidden them whenever a medical team arrived. I was shocked. I thought everyone in the village knew the danger of whooping cough, and I remembered how grateful villagers were to be able to protect their children from the dreaded disease. The medical teams were welcomed, and families anxiously lined up to be sure that each child received treatment. When I asked what would cause parents to hide their children, people lowered their voices and whispered, "*Hermanos.*"

We settled in, and over the next several months the story of the hermanos slowly unfolded (see Sandstrom 1987). According to villagers, in 1983, a small truck drove into Amatlán loaded with equipment including a generator powered by a gasoline engine. Three North

Americans and a Mexican emerged and asked permission of village authorities to address a village meeting and show a movie. Most of the people had never seen a movie before and although some were suspicious, permission was granted. That night the Mexican man addressed the village in Nahuatl, telling the crowd that the visitors were bringing a new religion called *agua viva* ("living water") in Spanish. He told villagers that their own religion was devil worship and that the new Protestant religion brought by the strangers would bring salvation. He distributed some pamphlets and small cartoon books, all written in Nahuatl, which explained aspects of the new religion. He spoke for a long time and said that all who wished to become Protestant converts would have to renounce not only "Catholicism" and all traditional rituals but also cane alcohol and tobacco. Furthermore, villagers were to destroy all pictures of the guardian saints on their home altars and to buy Nahuatl Bibles that the men sold for a relatively modest price. Finally, followers of the new religion were not to have their children participate in any school activities other than attending class, and they were to renounce all medical intervention. The visitors said that people who convert and have true faith in the new religion would never again fall ill.

The strangers then set up a portable movie screen and connected a projector to the generator. The villagers had little experience with movies, although they were familiar with still photographs. Among their possessions, many people treasured black-and-white pictures of family members, taken by me on previous visits or by itinerant photographers who visit Indian markets. They thus interpreted the movie as being similar to a photo portrait, perhaps posed, but basically a true representation of reality, in much the same way that we might view a newsreel. They were not fully aware that movies are often artificial constructs with sets, costume designers, and actors playing roles and reading scripts.

Actors spoke Nahuatl in the movie, and one scene depicted Indians burning in hell. Overseeing this horrifying spectacle was a devil figure laughing malevolently. In other scenes, Jesus was shown instructing Indians in the new religion and saving the condemned from fiery torment. Based on statements I recorded 2 years later, the movie made a dramatic impact on many people. When the film ended, the missionaries informed the audience that virtually all North Americans are Protestants and it is because of their religion that God has rewarded them with such great wealth. Indians are poor, they said, because the costumbre religion is of the devil. Finally, the men told the villagers that communists will soon be coming to murder everyone and that God will save only the hermanos. This last statement perhaps reveals some of the underlying political motives of the missionaries.

Every week or so for the next year the missionaries returned to proselytize among the villagers. They won about half a dozen converts who agreed to undergo baptism in the waters of the arroyo. Among the first to convert was a group of three brothers who formed the social core of the new religion. Interestingly, the people who embraced the new religion were from the most impoverished households in the village. Three were alcoholics, one was a suspected thief, and another was known as a deadbeat who did not cooperate in village affairs and who refused to pay people money he owed them. In sum, they were villagers who had lost hope that they could succeed in the prevailing socioeconomic system. These men brought along members of their extended families, and slowly the number of converts began to grow.

One of the early converts was selected by the missionaries to undergo training in the new religion and was to have become pastor (*pastor* in Spanish) of the new congregation. However, he was caught committing adultery shortly thereafter, and the task of leading the new flock fell to his younger brother, a reformed alcoholic. With financial help from the missionaries, the converts soon constructed a thatch-roofed building about twice the size of a house for their chapel. Every Sunday and Wednesday evening the Protestant converts gather to sing hymns in Spanish and Nahuatl and to have passages read to them from the Nahuatl Bible. Following the admonitions of the missionaries, church members and their families do not engage the services of any medical specialists, nor do they participate in traditional village rituals nor allow their children to be involved in extracurricular school events.

I was curious who the missionaries were and what sect of evangelical Protestantism they represented. Villagers told me that according to statements from the strangers themselves, they came from Texas and Louisiana. I collected some of the literature they passed out, and it appeared to be fundamentalist, but no specific group was mentioned. One day in 1986 near the end of our fieldwork stay, a boy came to tell me that the missionaries were once again in the village. I waited on the porch of the schoolhouse, which I knew they would have to pass in order to get to their chapel. After about half an hour three tall, thin men, two in their late teens and one in his early twenties, walked rapidly past me with their heads down. I called out to them in English, and they looked up and waved, but when I started walking toward them they turned and ran away. I followed and saw them get into a four-wheel-drive pickup truck they had parked a mile or two down the trail. They started the engine and drove away rapidly before I could approach.

On another occasion I spotted their truck on the road about 15 miles from Amatlán. I signaled them to stop, and they pulled up and the driver rolled down his window. I asked what they were doing so far from the paved road, and the youthful driver replied, "We're bringing a little Christ to the Indians." I then asked what group they represented, and they would not answer. Then I asked if they were telling people in the villages not to have their children vaccinated. They replied by rolling up the window and spinning their tires in hasty retreat. I was never able to find out firsthand which official organization they represented. Village converts call their religion "living water," probably named after the baptism ritual. Most people, however, refer to both the missionaries and their followers as simply the "*hermanos*" ("brothers") in Spanish. The origin of this name is unknown.

About 15% of the people of Amatlán had converted to Protestantism by 1986, a small but significant minority. Considering the accommodation that the traditional religion had made with Catholicism and the importance of the religion in establishing Indian ethnic identity, I was surprised by this change. Most converts I talked to have a difficult time reading the Bible even though it is written in Nahuatl. Replacing the sophistication of the traditional religion are half-understood ideas written in a book originating from a historical tradition alien to that of the Indians. Supplanting the colorful rituals in which complex symbolism unites people with their physical and social environments are prayer meetings in which unconnected and incomprehensible Biblical formulas are sung or read.

The introduction of a new religion in Amatlán has been accompanied by other nearly universal changes in village life. Most of the men have forsaken their traditional dress in favor of styles worn by mestizos. Interestingly, however, the women continue to make and wear the colorful costume associated with their Indian status. Far more Spanish is spoken today, particularly by young people. Nahuatl remains the language of choice, but people are now more confident in their use of Spanish. The urban grid pattern has replaced the old village layout based in part on the patrilocal extended family. In addition, over half of the houses now feature relatively expensive corrugated tarpaper or sheet-metal roofs, a far greater number than before. As strange as it may seem but fully congruent with their changed lives, the people now call their village of just under 600 individuals a *zona urbana* in Spanish, an "urban zone."

The change in village layout was accomplished in the early 1980s in a series of village meetings. Household heads following the leadership of village authorities decided to consolidate the houses on land demarcated by a broad loop of the arroyo. The impetus was electrification, but people told me that by placing houses close together precious land was also freed for cultivation. The electrification project was begun by a group of younger men under the leadership of the Agente Municipal. These men are the new generation who have had greater experience in the cities and who speak Spanish more fluently. The rural electrification program, which is administered through the states, supplies the technical expertise and about half of the money for each project. The villagers were thus required to raise for them the tremendous sum of about $2,000 to pay their part. It was the young men who organized the collection of the funds and handled negotiations with government representatives. At the last minute officials of the program assessed the villagers the equivalent of another $600, and this new obligation represented a setback for the young leaders. While we lived in Amatlán in 1985–86 villagers heatedly debated what they should do about the problem. Eventually, the community managed to raise the money, and the power was turned on in the late spring of 1986.

Villagers decided that each household was to be allotted a house site measuring 30 by 50 meters. This allocation allowed plenty of space for a house, a garden, and some fruit trees. Professional surveyors from the electrification program laid out the new village. Wide "streets" were cut from the forest between the blocks of house lots, and a broader north–south main thoroughfare was cut between the village proper and the school complex (see Map 7.1). According to informants, house sites were assigned by means of a lottery. I was curious as to what effect this change in residence had on the traditional family structure because presumably the patrilocal compounds had been broken up. I found that by trading house sites among themselves, many sets of brothers managed to build houses nearby one another. Because the consolidated village is relatively compact anyway, I found that these changes in village layout had no discernible effect on the Nahua family. (Map 4.2 shows male and female links among households in the new village.)

Examination of Map 7.1 reveals additional changes in the village. Far more families now own separate kitchen and sleeping structures. In previous years a separate kitchen was an artifact of the building

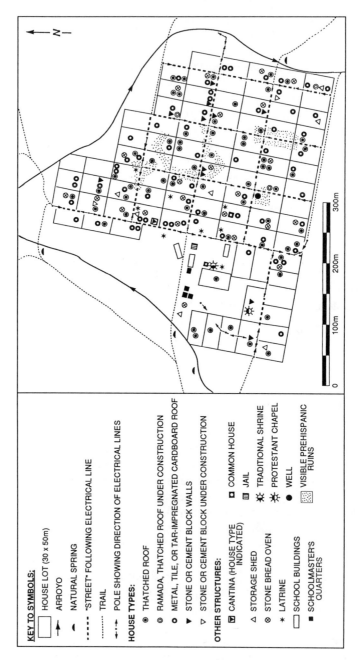

KEY TO SYMBOLS:

☐ HOUSE LOT (30 x 50m)

↑ ARROYO

◖ NATURAL SPRING

–··– "STREET" FOLLOWING ELECTRICAL LINE

······ TRAIL

–·+· POLE SHOWING DIRECTION OF ELECTRICAL LINES

HOUSE TYPES:

◉ THATCHED ROOF

◎ RAMADA, THATCHED ROOF UNDER CONSTRUCTION

○ METAL, TILE, OR TAR-IMPREGNATED CARDBOARD ROOF

▼ STONE OR CEMENT BLOCK WALLS

▽ STONE OR CEMENT BLOCK UNDER CONSTRUCTION

OTHER STRUCTURES:

▣ CANTINA (HOUSE TYPE INDICATED)

◫ COMMON HOUSE

△ STORAGE SHED

▥ JAIL

⊗ STONE BREAD OVEN

✳ TRADITIONAL SHRINE

✳ LATRINE

✲ PROTESTANT CHAPEL

☐ SCHOOL BUILDINGS

● WELL

■ SCHOOLMASTER'S QUARTERS

▨ VISIBLE PREHISPANIC RUINS

7.1. Amatlán "urban zone" in 1986 showing location of houses and other structures cycle. Now, however, people are increasingly building single-function structures. This development appears to be modeled on mestizo practice. Several households and the school complex now have crude outhouses built nearby that serve as toilets. In some cases people have even painted the word *baño* ("bath") in Spanish in whitewashed letters on the outhouse door. Few people ever used these outhouses so far as I could observe, but they are one symbol of the commitment of younger villagers to modernize. Government construction workers completed a new one-room kindergarten school building while we were there. This expansion represents a continuation of village efforts to augment the education of the children in the mestizo world. Under the direction of a schoolmaster, several villagers dug a well in the hopes of securing a convenient water supply through the dry season. They dug down about 25 feet before they struck solid rock. The well goes dry in the winter months, and so its promise remains unfulfilled, although villagers are able to use it when the water returns in the rainy season. I also noticed many more stone-and-mud bread ovens in the new village. Households built these so that the women would have an opporunity to sell bread and earn extra money.

The change in dress was instigated by the group of young men who had worked in the cities. Older men told me that their sons and nephews convinced them that the traditional dress was old-fashioned and marked them as being opposed to progress. Wishing to cooperate with the new generation of village leaders, about 80% of the older men now wear essentially mestizo-style dress. This willingness to change clothing perhaps signals the breakdown of the traditional relationship between Indians and mestizos because previously villagers saw a benefit in proclaiming their ethnic identity. Other small but notable changes have also been brought back from the urban world. The traditional Nahua handshake, a light touching of fingertips, has been replaced by our familiar pumping handshake, following which the men hook thumbs and shake again. This practice is very much in vogue among young people in the cities. Also, the young men and boys often wear a kind of bathing suit when they bathe in the arroyo now. Previously, boys from about 6 to 13 years of age would spend the entire day by the water either playing or fishing in the nude. During 1985–86, I saw children wearing swimming suits and plastic goggles, apparently emulating their mestizo counterparts.

These changes, with the exception of the conversion of the hermanos and the accompanying rejection of the costumbre religion, are all within the dynamic potential of Nahua culture. All cultures change, and it is reasonable for the Indians to be influenced by urban mestizo elites who, in fact, are the most powerful elements in the society. One can shake hands like an urban dweller, own an outhouse, wear a bathing suit in the arroyo, and have a bare bulb suspended in one's house and still be an Indian. Being an Indian is not a state of wealth, nor is it tied to a specific technology, dress style, level of formal education, or ability in the Spanish language. To be Indian does not require that a person be backward, however that is defined. It is instead a matter of ethnic identity, and as I have tried to show in this account, ethnicity is one of the strategies by which individuals survive and thrive in hierarchical societies. But the pattern and directionality of the changes we witness in Amatlán indicate that something is occurring that is more profound than simple cultural borrowing. Unleashed processes are threatening the very core of what it is to be an Indian.

THE CRISIS IN INDIAN IDENTITY

Shortly after we arrived in the village in 1985 an incident occurred that made me suspect that all was not well. Early one evening three village elders arrived at our schoolhouse abode for a formal visit. They were well dressed, carried their machetes, and wore hats, sure signs that the visit was official. They asked if I had everything I needed and made small talk for the requisite 2 hours or so before getting down to business. They wanted to know if I was going to write a book about Amatlán as I had before. I assumed that they were referring to my doctoral dissertation that I had sent to the village following my first lengthy fieldwork in 1972–73. I said I was recording information about village customs and that I hoped to publish it so that others might know about life in Amatlán. They already knew all of this, and I waited for them to reveal the real purpose of the visit. Once again I showed them my notes, maps and kinship charts, along with some of the photos that I had taken earlier. It grew dark, and as I lighted a candle one of the elders announced that they now understood what I was doing in the village. They said that they would like me to write down the customs so that children in the future will know how life once was. The younger people, they said, are not much interested in the old ways any longer. What they had come to do that night was to offer their help and lend their authority to my project of documenting life in the village. I was of course gratified and accepted their offer. But I also realized how extensive their worries were that recent changes had gotten out of control and that the villagers stood to lose more than they would gain in the bargain. I had the distinct impression that a crisis had occurred or that a turning point had been reached.

In an effort to uncover what was happening in the village, I conducted structured interviews with several dozen men and women. I asked each person to tell me what had changed since my last visit, to trace when these changes began, and to make a judgment about whether the changes were beneficial or harmful. Most people had a very clear idea about what was happening, and they were willing to talk about it and give their opinions. Nahuas generally avoid making negative statements about events, and they do not like to criticize or affix blame on other villagers. Not only do they consider it rude to do so, but they also do not wish to invite retaliation from aggrieved parties or wind spirits. It is no doubt for this reason that the situation they depicted was generally positive, but it is significant that most people revealed some worry about the future as well. Villagers were in accord that the evidence they see of "progress" is good and that Amatlán should move forward. But they complained about a number of things, for example that the new clothing made from polyester is uncomfortable and shoddy and that corrugated tarpaper or sheet-metal roofs make the houses too hot. Many people lamented that fewer young villagers now know the old myths, and shamans in particular worried that the ancient rituals would someday no longer be observed.

Most villagers agreed that many changes could be traced to a period of several months between the end of 1982 and the late spring of 1983. During this period three major events happened. First, the federal government approved an increase in per capita land allocations from 5 to 7 hectares for each household. Villagers had been struggling for this *ampliación*, Spanish for "enlargement," for years before it was finally approved. The additional land meant that average household income rose significantly in 1983. Many villagers had already been planting part of the area since claiming it as their own, but only after the final official approval were they able to take full advantage of it. The second factor for change is the general collapse of the Mexican national economy in 1982 (see Chapter 1). Ranchers, who were hit harder by the depression than small-scale horticulturalists, could offer little temporary work for Indians. Suddenly, with more land to plant and potentially more income, the old symbiotic relationship between Indian villager and mestizo rancher broke down. At this same time the first generation of students who knew Spanish well were discovering greater opportunities for temporary wage labor in the cities. During this period a third factor for change arrived as Protestant missionaries moved in to take advantage of regional instability caused by the economic collapse.

Paradoxically, the economic situation in Amatlán seems actually to have improved as the Mexican national economy deteriorated. Because the village represented only a marginal part of the national economy, it was somewhat protected from the collapse occurring in the industrial and agribusiness sectors. The added land helped to increase production for those with full ejido rights. Of equal importance, groups of vecinos, those who were not full members of the ejido, left Amatlán to join the effort to form a new village on neighboring ranch land. Thus there were 77 fewer individuals supporting themselves on a larger land base in 1986 compared to 1972. These pressure-relieving factors, to which was added the higher pay earned by the young men traveling to the cities, caused a minor boom in the Amatlán economy. The increased earnings were used to purchase roofing material, corn grinders, sugarcane presses, and some of the other goods now in greater evidence throughout the village. By itself, this upturn in level of wealth merely accelerated the purchase of manufactured items from the mestizo sector but did not cause fundamental changes in the ways the village relates to the larger society nor in the ethnic identity of the Indians.

By all accounts it was the young men returning from their temporary employment in the cities that provided the greatest and most conscious stimulus for change. It was not so much the new ideas they brought back nor the money they were able to earn. Much more crucial was the fact that by their actions of leaving the region and finding work in urban centers they changed the relation between the village and the mestizo elite. In the city, being an Indian is a liability, and all motivation to create and maintain an Indian identity is undermined. As we have seen, as long as villagers were forced to search for work exclusively on local ranches, being Indian had its advantages. These advantages disappear in the city. Urban work requires language skills and other abilities to operate successfully in the mestizo world.

When the young men returned to Amatlán, they encouraged their elders to discard the clothing and some of the customs that signaled their Indian status. They organized, brought in electricity, and recast the village in an urbanized image. They dug a well, built outhouses, petitioned for a kindergarten building, and subtly discouraged nude bathing. Their suggestions and their efforts were directed not at boldly destroying Indian identity, but rather at obscuring or blurring the boundary between themselves and mestizo outsiders. But in effect, because ethnic groups are known and kept to a large extent by their boundaries, they unknowingly weakened the symbolic means by which Indians establish their separate identity (see Dehouve 1974 for an account of political and economic changes in a Nahua community in the state of Guerrero).

Obscuring boundaries between Indians and mestizos poses little threat to the solidarity of the subordinate group as long as no alternative identities are available. In 1982, however, an alternate identity did become available, provided by North American missionaries. The people attracted to the new religion tended to be the ones who were marginal to the village, those who benefited least from their Indian status. That is, the converts were the poorest villagers who had the least to lose. In contrast, by 1986 no members of wealthier cattle-owning families had converted. Suddenly, a new option opened for the village poor that was completely outside the range of traditional choices. They no longer had to be either Indians or rural mestizos. They now had the possibility of being hermanos. Best of all, the missionaries promised that God would reward them with wealth, health, and everlasting life in return for doing little more than having the proper (albeit alien) faith. The new religion forbade drinking, and so alcoholic individuals did benefit directly, and their families probably even enjoyed new prosperity. All at once the relatively down-and-out had a new lease on life with the promise that they would be the ones to lead the others to a new millennium. The new status is achieved magically with a few sprinkles of water and an avowed rejection of the Nahua religion. In essence, the Protestant converts are becoming a third ethnic group that owes little to its Indian heritage or to the mestizo elites (see Sexton 1978 for an analysis of a somewhat similar process of modernization and Protestant conversion in Guatemala; see also Warren 1989[1978] for an interpretive analysis of the role of the pro-orthodoxy Catholic Action movement in the changing ethnicity of a Cakchiquel Maya town in Guatemala).

When we returned to Amatlán in 1985, I was surprised at the visible changes the village was undergoing. I was also surprised to find that despite these changes, the core of Nahua society remains intact. The kinship groupings remain strong, although a greater number of people than before have left the village more or less permanently. The traditional rituals were still being held, attended by all but the Protestant converts. Production activities remain little changed except that they are supplemented with higher urban wages. But even among the hermanos the kin groupings, production technology, and daily life have not changed dramatically. So long as they remain substantially in the minority, they will not be able to reshape village life. Yet the hermanos represent a disturbing trend that has many villagers worried.

Being an Indian with a coherent view of the world, a set of values, and a distinct identity is not seriously threatened by prosperity, poverty, education, technological backwardness, electricity, or television. It can be seriously threatened, however, when increasing numbers of individuals do not find it to their advantage to work at creating and maintaining their identity. None of the changes I charted in the village during 1985–86 derived directly from the Indian cultural heritage or were new ways of creating or demonstrating Nahua identity. There were no new rituals, myths, or emblems of Indianness that I saw or that people acknowledged. In fact the number of symbols used to distinguish Indians (such as dress) had declined. The fear expressed by people and in particular by the elders is that being Indian, being masehualmej, will no longer be of value to anyone and that the circumstances that have allowed for the persistence and viability of their culture are being swept away by men adopting mestizo traits so they can find temporary work in the city and by villagers who forsake the costumbres for Protestantism.

The hermanos, for their part, are engaged in creating a separate identity for themselves. They form a kind of enclave in the village and participate minimally in village affairs by giving money when there is an assessment and by fulfilling their obligations in the weekly faena work cooperative. Most of the males have adopted mestizo dress but, for reasons that I was not able to determine, they appear to confine themselves to working for local ranchers. I have no information on what effect their new identity has on the ranchers or even if ranchers distinguish hermanos from other villagers. Perhaps because they generally are the poorer members of the village they do not travel to the city as much as the others. However, they do travel frequently to other villages in the region to attend Protestant services, and many people likewise walk long distances to Amatlán to attend services here. They maintain contact with the North American and Mexican missionaries and periodically invite them to the village to perform baptisms. In general, the hermanos are an active group who often hold feasts and gatherings at their church in addition to their twice-weekly prayer meetings.

To a large extent the hermanos are creating a distinct identity for themselves within Amatlán in much the same way that the villagers have created an identity for themselves relative to the mestizos. Hermanos are building separate lives for themselves centered on participation in alien religious beliefs and practices. They are outwardly cooperative, but their identity is created and maintained largely relative to the dominant majority. Just as much of Indian identity can be understood as a response to low status and economic standing relative to a dominant majority, so the creation of hermano identity can be understood as a reaction to the more successful villagers. It is this paradoxical situation more than the preaching of North American missionaries that explains why the hermanos have rejected the free vaccines offered by the Mexican government. By allowing their children to be vaccinated, the hermanos would be in a position of receiving a traditional benefit that derives from being Indian. To accept medical treatment would be tacitly to accept being defined as Indians. By rejecting the vaccines, the hermanos simultaneously reject Indian identity, demonstrate their new identity, and flaunt their new faith that, in any case, teaches that vaccines are obsolete.

My own relations with the hermanos were problematic. They associated me with the traditional rituals that I attended so regularly, and with the way of life as it was when I was first there in the early 1970s. Most of my friends were among the "Catholics," and so I soon became defined as a nonhermano. It was a bad situation for me because, as the villagers defined it, no compromise was possible and I was forced to choose sides. I tried to maintain friendly relations with the hermanos, and they invited me to church meetings and social events. But, as I continued to interact with other villagers and accept invitations to traditional rituals, it became clear that I was no ally of theirs. A few men tried to convert me in a kind of desultory way and, when they failed, my relations with the hermano community cooled. I further alienated the hermanos when I answered questions posed to me by nonhermano villagers. In all cases I did my best to tell the truth and to give an accurate portrayal of reality as I knew it. In response to questions, I told them that the people in the movie were actors and that the scenes of hell and heaven were sets created by the filmmakers. Furthermore, I denied the missionary claim that all or even a significant number of North Americans are hermanos and that communists are coming to kill all people who refuse to convert. In short, I forsook my scientific role as Olympian observer and became a participant in the village struggle. I continued to talk to the hermanos, but I could no longer count on them for reliable information.

I further compromised my scientific objectivity near the end of

1986. After spending months evaluating the situation in Amatlán, I visited the head of the local hermano community. He was just a boy when I first went to the village, and so I knew him slightly. He was friendly but guarded, and we talked together all of one afternoon. I did my best to convince him that the Bible does not forbid vaccinations nor prevent a person from seeking medical attention. I sounded like a television evangelist myself as I tried to quote half-remembered Bible passages and invoked homilies like, "God helps those who help themselves." I asked him to point out the places in which the Bible banned medical treatment (he could not), and I questioned him about why the children of the hermanos were dying (he responded that they clearly did not have proper faith). I countered by asking how a 3-year-old child could possibly possess such faith. I tried to convince him that being innoculated does not lessen faith in religion nor in any way contradict being a sincere hermano. He listened and came to see me a few weeks later to continue the conversation. He finally said that he would discuss the issue with the missionaries and that he would rethink the matter. As we have seen, however, the problem is complex and goes far beyond a single theological question. Refusal of medical care has become an important aspect of hermano social identity as well. We left Amatlán before the medical team visited again, and so I do not know if my efforts changed their policy about childhood vaccinations or whether it simply alienated me further from the hermano community.

WOMEN'S IDENTITY IN AMATLÁN

During my initial fieldwork in the village in the early 1970s it was virtually impossible for me to gather information on the lives of the women. Because I was a bachelor, the unmarried women were not comfortable talking with me, and married women always referred me to their husbands. They were never rude, but they made it clear that I should be talking to male family members and not to them. We have already seen that a woman would delegate even to her 10-year-old son or brother the burden of dealing with me if no older male were available. Because I was accompanied by my family in 1985–86, the women were far more open in their interactions with me. Still, I could not get them to take seriously my questions about changes in the village. They would laugh when I asked them something or respond noncommittally, "Who knows?" with a shrug of the shoulders. Even my wife had a hard time getting them to give their opinions on village changes despite her excellent rapport with several women.

The position of women in Amatlán society differs considerably from that of the men. In many ways the men and women operate in different worlds that overlap only minimally. The men represent the family to the outside world, and thus changes in ethnic identity, religious affiliation, or economic standing are generally effected through them. It is almost as if the status of being a woman overrides all other identities. Thus, the overwhelming majority of women continue to wear their traditional dress. Even female hermanos do not distinguish themselves outwardly from other women. Most women who do assume more of a mestizo identity, for example by wearing manufactured one-piece dresses, are making a statement that they are about to leave the village and seek work in the city or have returned from there. This option is usually taken by younger women who have lost their husbands and have no access to land.

The status of women in Amatlán is difficult to evaluate without better interview data from them. I would say that although they do not have an access to the social, economic, and political resources available to men, they are far from oppressed. They exist in a different domain from the men, and they have clear rights of their own. The status of women in mestizo society, by contrast, appears in many cases to be far lower relative to the men. The much discussed macho complex is evident among rural mestizos of the southern Huasteca, but I have never seen anything like it operating in the Indian villages. A Nahua man is expected to be in charge, but if he were to boast, become aggressive, or abuse his wife he would be seen by the other men as foolish and mestizolike. Indian males are rather reserved and puritanical and would never, for example, make overt sexual gestures toward a woman. In sum, perhaps the women of Amatlán wish to retain their sexual identity in the Indian context rather than become identified as mestizos and have to face a loss of position relative to men. By retaining both traditional roles and dress, they emphasize their femaleness over other potential identities (see Taggart 1979 for a discussion of Nahua men's views of women as revealed in oral narratives).

HOW SOME OF THE VILLAGERS VIEW CHANGE

Following are excerpts from interviews I conducted with a sample of villagers in 1986. I asked people to express their views of the changes that have occurred in the last several years, and I inquired about what they would like to see happen in the future.

ETHNOGRAPHER: Why are more of the young men going to the city to work?

ALFONSO (an older man): [On the cattle ranches] they pay 500 pesos per day (about one dollar), which is very little. It doesn't amount to anything. It hurts the young men. And it is only after much struggle that the ranchers agreed to pay 500 pesos. If you are going to buy, say, a bar of soap it amounts to nothing. With 500 pesos you can't feed yourself.

ETHNOGRAPHER: What do people around here want?

ALFONSO: I have no [young] children, but the parcels of land are running out. They are drying up and the earth gets tired and the corn doesn't thrive in the milpa very well. I want the village to apply for an additional parcel even if we have to pay for half of it. What is lacking in this village is cooperation. We need more people to pull their weight. What is missing is a person to orient us, to lead us.

We need an elected leader who will give us a straight path to follow, who will tell everyone how it should be in the village. He will guide us to work well and make sure people do not get angry. He will convince everyone that we will have a nice village and God will be pleased with the village. . . .

I would like people to plant sugarcane. The land we work is depleted. The place where we plant our beloved corn, our beloved beans, our beloved chile is wiped out. All of the moisture is gone. It seems that the earth is sad and nothing wants to reproduce. Sugarcane can be planted in a small area and it is worth money.

ETHNOGRAPHER: Has anyone ever tried to plant sugarcane on a large scale before?

ALFONSO: Yes, some time ago several of us planted sugarcane fields. There were quite a few in the village. But because the price dropped, the people lost money, and they didn't want to plant cane anymore. Now it has climbed, and it is at a high price. Some people are beginning to plant it again.

ETHNOGRAPHER: What about cattle raising?

PATRICIO (a young man): Yes, but here the parcels are too small. There isn't enough land for us even to eat. It's 7 hectares. Therefore, there is not enough. What we should do is make application to the government to promote something like sugarcane, something. Coffee plantations aren't possible here because there are no mountains.

ETHNOGRAPHER: Wouldn't cattle raising be better?

PATRICIO: But there is nowhere to let them out to pasture.

ETHNOGRAPHER: Aren't you soliciting more land?

PATRICIO: Yes. To raise cattle we would have to take land away from the ranch owners. An animal needs water and here on the hillsides there isn't any. Any animal needs water, even baby pigs seek water. Some of the parcels that make up Amatlán have water. The land was distributed by lottery, and it was my lot not to have water. Now we can't just settle anywhere; you have to settle on your own parcel. We have put in an application for a parcel that has water. I want a parcel that can be used for cattle. But then where am I going to feed them? The land around here is depleted, and so I want more land for the village so that we can have more life. We would like to get [a neighboring private ranch] but that is only good for sugarcane.

ETHNOGRAPHER: Can you get more land for the village?

ATILANO (a young man): The land is for us today and the children tomorrow. You have to be careful how you tread. You can't go around angering the rich because the rich help each other. The *masehualmej* likewise help each other but a single *masehuali* must not just wander around anywhere because they will kill him. You must not pick a quarrel with the rich but must solicit land correctly, according to law.

ETHNOGRAPHER: What do you want to see happen?

PATRICIO: To have the village wake up. We will start with electricity and later make application to the government for more land or to plant sugarcane. That will be a way to wake up the people. The people can then have their things in a refrigerator. They can have this and other benefits. For starters, one might say *hielitos* (flavored frozen treats), ice cubes, tractors, machinery. That is what sugarcane can do for us because it is worth more.

People here are not aware. There are some, but they are few. I would like to make it like it is in Pánuco [in the northern Huasteca] where they raise sugar.

ETHNOGRAPHER: But, isn't it the case that the people here are not united, that there are enemies and religious sects?

ENRIQUE (an hermano convert): That won't be a problem, that can be worked out in some form, like overtime chores. Let the village authorities carry out the plans. The authorities can say, "Establish your cane field, establish your cane field." And it will be done because we don't go pushing them around.

ETHNOGRAPHER: What about sugarcane?

FELIPE (a young man): A gentleman from [a neighboring village] went to Xalapa [the state capital] and inquired about planting sugarcane. They told him, "Sugar is the most valuable—sugarcane!" He told me that they were thinking of setting up a mill to make the sugar in [a nearby village on the road]. He says that sugarcane makes money, there will be no need to make your own sugar with a press. That is what that gentleman told me, and he is a member of a federal government committee.

ETHNOGRAPHER: What would you like to see happen?

ANTONIO (a middle-aged man): I want them to fix the bridge over the Vinazco River at Oxitempa. [A long cement bridge was built across the river permitting travel to Ixhuatlán, but it washed away in a violent storm within months of its completion.] I want to fix it, I want to pursue the matter in Xalapa. That's what we would like. People are asking for a lot of things, but they don't know what they are asking for.

ETHNOGRAPHER: How would you transport the sugarcane to the mill if there is no road?

OCTAVIO (an older man): Well, that is a matter of concern for the government. It is my understanding that if we plant sugarcane, there is a government bank or co-op that is obligated to have the cane carried by truck to the mill. They could throw gravel on the trail [and make it into a road].

ETHNOGRAPHER: What will you eat during the time it takes for the cane to mature?

SÉRGIO (a middle-aged man): Well one doesn't do everything at once. Go a little bit at a time. Plant so that some is maturing each year. One must always plant corn, too.

ETHNOGRAPHER: What about the costumbres?

AURELIO (a shaman): The old costumbres, we are never going to forget them. We receive communication from God [toteotsij], the ancient one, through his children here on earth. The masehualmej are sprouts on the earth, and yet some do not respect it. Some say they don't believe it. Everything in our lives is a gift, and a costumbre is an offering in return for a favor. For my part, I want my village to be in good shape. I will spend my money on costumbres because everyone always benefits in that way.

The lord [toteotsij] himself sometimes requests a turkey and chickens so that he can eat like a rich person. I am happy to go deliver these gifts because then everyone will eat next year. I am happy because I know where my food and life come from. I want to tell the Lord that people are bathing [being baptized] with the evangelists. When the time comes to pay, let them then try to pay, ha!

Some offend the costumbres and say they are not true, that they are like stories. They say that some who hear the stories later create problems for the village. Many outsiders are disturbed because they see the costumbres as wrong. They are very much afraid that we are doing something ancient, something evil because we have gathered in one place. They think this because sometimes people are disorderly at gatherings.

Here in Mexico there is a mountain called Popocatepetl and from there comes all lightning and thunder. From this mountain emerges all of the spirits given by the ancient ones and which we cut from paper. It is the center of the earth, the center of the earth like a spring of water. Popocatepetl is perhaps the very center of Mexico, and one lights candles for those lords from there so that they can smell them, breathe them in. They say the bad thing [referring to the earthquake of September 1985] happened there because the people are not respectful, they do not follow the costumbres. They are not respectful towards anything, truly they are the rich.

The hermanos have lost respect and they say we are doing evil in our costumbres. They are disrespectful, and they may bring devastation on us. I can't say if we are to be granted another year . . . to eat what we have planted now. If we are granted more life we shall see if it is true. When the lord comes to see the costumbres, it is lovely to see how he receives the offering. That is why I want everybody to do something. The hermanos do not see the costumbres with good eyes. That disrespect destroys the world.

[When I interviewed the women of Amatlán they did not speak of the destruction of the Nahua world. They had far more pragmatic concerns.]

ETHNOGRAPHER: What would you like to see happen in the village?

MARÍA FRANCISCA (a middle-aged woman): I want to see a fountain built where we could get water. Sometimes when it floods in the rainy season we have to walk almost to [another village] for water. We need a place closer to the houses to wash the corn.

ETHNOGRAPHER: What has changed in Amatlán?

MARÍA ANGELINA (a young mother): We moved the houses which is a good thing. Now there is more room to plant and bigger pastures for the animals. The electricity is a good thing, but it cost a lot of money. I want to see more scholarships for the children to go to secondary school. We don't have enough to send the children [to the market town where a secondary school is located].

ETHNOGRAPHER: What changes would you like to see?

ROSA (an older woman with grown children): The biggest change has been the electricity. I would like to have a television so we could all sit and watch it. A television is expensive, but I would also like a refrigerator. With a refrigerator I could make *hielitos* and sell them.

ETHNOGRAPHER: Why are people becoming hermanos?

CATALINA (a young hermano woman): Many people were frightened when the hermanos came to Amatlán. They showed a movie and people were afraid. They said that the costumbres are from the devil. But after a while people liked what the gringos were saying. They said we are poor in Mexico because of our religion. They said we should read the Bible and stop drinking aguardiente. My husband Sérgio became an hermano and stopped drinking. He doesn't get drunk anymore, and he goes to the church to sing and listen to the pastor.

The women generally responded to my questions about changes in the village by claiming they did not know or that they had no opinion. It was impossible for me to get them to talk at length on processes that must be affecting them profoundly. My wife, who spent hours with women and girls and made friends with several of them, reports that they rarely talked about changes or village politics. When asked their opinions they tended to switch the topic to their families or

relatives. Several older women expressed regret that their sons were
going off to the cities and were sometimes absent during ritual observances. For example, some women worried that their sons would fail
to return for xantoloj (Day of the Dead) and thereby neglect their
obligations to deceased family members. Although I have very scant
information on what women think about recent events, I suspect from
what they do say that although they may look forward to owning certain
labor-saving appliances, at the same time they worry about the effects
changes will have on their families.

In Chapter 1, I introduced five theoretical perspectives developed to
clarify the place of the Indian village in Mexican society and the world
economy. I will now briefly evaluate these perspectives in light of the
data from Amatlán.

Amatlán does not fit Robert Redfield's definition of a little community very well. The village is not as homogeneous as his model implies.
It is internally divided between the vecinos with their 2½ hectare fields
and the certificados who control 7 hectares. Furthermore, the cattle-
owning households form a wealthy elite relative to other villagers.
Internal factionalism is so pronounced that on several occasions in the
last few years it has led to violence. Another division includes a kind
of generation gap between older villagers and young men with greater
urban sophistication. The subcommunity of hermanos in opposition
to the traditional "Catholics" represents an additional deep division in
Amatlán.

Redfield underestimates the degree to which Indian identity is
created and maintained by the villagers as a means of struggling against
domination by mestizo elites. By creating rituals such as the chicomexochitl seed offering, for example, the Indians use their traditions to
generate an identity that differs from that of the mestizos. The Redfield perspective also underplays how much rural villagers know about
mestizos and urban life, and how they use this knowledge to survive
and in some cases to amass substantial wealth. Nor does it illuminate
how or why villagers play on their status to obtain benefits from
the government. In short, the folk–urban continuum overlooks the
mechanisms by which rural villagers are dominated by mestizos and,
equally important, it downplays the active resistance inherent in maintaining an Indian identity.

Eric Wolf proposes that the essential character of Indian villages and the nature of their relationship to the nation is linked to factors that have caused them to become closed corporate communities. As we have seen in Amatlán, the village does present a barrier to outsiders that can be very difficult to penetrate. Naming customs, esoteric religious beliefs and rituals, the Nahuatl language, and other features effectively seal off the village to most mestizos. But in many ways Amatlán does not act like a closed corporate community. Individuals work for themselves and their families and not for some fictitious corporate group. Land is allocated to communities but it is controlled and passed to succeeding generations by individual families. Villagers establish sometimes long-term relations with mestizos that may even be formalized through ritual kinship. Many of the criticisms of the folk-urban continuum apply here as well. Indian villages are really heterogeneous, and differences in wealth among households are common. Outsiders may have a difficult time in joining Amatlán (in the unlikely case they would want to), but the Indians, by contrast, are able to create new villages, work for mestizos, travel to the city to work, travel to the centers of political power to assert rights and request resources, emigrate to urban centers, hold social events and invite people from great distances, and send their children away to secondary school. Indian communities give the appearance of being closed, but that appearance is probably due more to land shortages and the need to keep mestizo elites in ignorance about community life than any intrinsic, historically drived core feature of the village.

The perspectives of Redfield and Wolf also do not explain why certain things changed in the village when they did. Why, for example, did most of the men of Amatlán suddenly adopt new clothing? The change could not have been due solely to new information coming in about city life. Villagers had known about mestizo clothing, and it has been available in the markets for decades. Is the change simply a product of acculturation, or is it more likely connected to the collapse of the Mexican economy and the diminished utility of demonstrating Indian identity? Both Redfield and Wolf underestimate the internal heterogeneity and flexibility of village life. The people of Amatlán, working through the village political hierarchy and successfully playing up their Indianness, managed to convince the government to underwrite an electrification project. The project was conceived by villagers as a way for their community to participate in progressive change. People did not feel that by supporting electrification they were abandoning their Indian heritage or identity, nor that the project was a step toward becoming mestizos. When the younger village men with urban experience convinced people that they could accomplish the project, everyone supported it. Once again, being Indian does not require people to be passive or backward. A community is closed when being so confers advantages to the inhabitants, but it opens up and changes when opportunities present themselves.

The perspectives of Warman and Stavenhagen sketched in Chapter 1 are based on analyses of regions or of the entire nation. These researches focus on macrosystems, asserting that they are set up to serve the capitalist sector of the economy at the expense of villagers. By focusing on the microsystem of a single community, we have seen how wealth is transferred from Amatlán to the mestizo elites through the pricing of Indian produce and low wages. The Indians are dependent on mestizo elites in a similar way that the Mexican economy as a whole is dependent on the developed European and North American economies. Macrosystem analysis serves to establish the context in which villagers operate, and in this sense the approach is extremely useful. In this account I have illustrated some of the ways that villagers manage their interactions with representatives of the larger socioeconomic environment. By optimizing their ethnicity, villagers have tried to create some advantages for themselves in a system that is stacked against them. Macroscopic and microscopic perspectives deal with different social realms, but they must be reconciled if we are to understand fully the situation of the Indians in Mexico.

Both Warman and Stavenhagen recognize that even villagers have their own strategies in dealing with the dominant powers surrounding them. Warman showed that the emphasis among villagers on raising corn can be understood as a response to intense poverty. When the economy improves, he predicts, peasants will begin to experiment with more profitable cash crops. In this regard, I myself wondered if the reliance on corn in Amatlán would be reduced as the village became more prosperous. I asked some of the men in the village if they were planning to switch from corn to some other crop. Interestingly several indicated that they were seriously considering growing sugarcane on their additional land. Four men had already planted cane and had even purchased expensive cane presses in anticipation of producing sugarloaf to sell. Thus, the prediction of Warman seems to be confirmed in Amatlán.

Aguirre Beltrán's focus on processes of domination to account for the position of the Indian community in Mexico overlaps with the perspectives of Redfield, Wolf, Warman, and Stavenhagen. His insistence that village economies are qualitatively different from the rational economy of the capitalist mestizos, however, does not coincide with what I found in Amatlán. The villagers are always busy planning strategies to take advantage of their opportunities so they can enhance their incomes and advance their interests. They rationally allocate their scarce resources among competing ends to try to maximize the returns they seek. In this they are similar to the mestizos who operate in the national capitalist economy. The realities of their low-energy technology, an abiding family orientation, the existence of ancient beliefs and rituals, and life in a village with no running water does not alter the maximizing character of Nahua behavior.

Friedlander and Bartra see the Indians as the ultimate victims whose ethnic identity has been forced upon them by ruthless elites. In their view, Indian culture did not survive the events of the Conquest, and Indian identity is simply part of the ideology created by the ruling mestizos to exploit rural populations. If local mestizos have imposed an alien Indianness on the people of Amatlán, then the villagers seem to have taken to the identity readily. I have shown in this book that the Indianness of the people of Amatlán is not a recent creation nor an alien import, but it is ancient and authentic. True, Nahua myths and rituals have been influenced by Spanish Catholicism, but they are based solidly on pre-Hispanic cosmology, symbol classes, and spirit entities. Furthermore, Indian culture differs greatly from that of surrounding mestizo neighbors in other elements such as language, interactional patterns, motor habits, beliefs, and many other aspects of daily life. The Nahuas value being Indian and disparage mestizo traits. Many villagers have the opportunity to enter the mestizo world permanently, and yet relatively few do. The villagers do not easily fit the definition of rural mestizos forced to accept Indian identity. Most people of Amatlán constantly work to maintain their Indian identity, not least because doing so has brought them solid material, as well as psychological, advantages. In fact the ethnic identity forged by the Nahuas can be understood, at least in part, as a rational response to their subordinate position in Mexican society. In sum, the position of Friedander and Bartra does not apply to the Nahuas of Amatlán, although it might conceivably be valid in other areas of Mesoamerica.

My research in Amatlán shows that one of the biggest obstacles to understanding the place of the village in the nation and its relation to processes of economic development is the very common view that people in small traditional communities are passive players or even purely victims in the drama of culture change. The minor scale of their production activities, the urban stereotypes about rustic, backward villagers, and the distinctive traditions of the Indian village have led scholars and laymen alike to undervalue the strategies that villagers themselves employ to satisfy their wants. The interpretations presented here demonstrate that the Indians are not responsible for their own poverty but that it is the national and regional mestizo economic system that must be blamed for so ruthlessly extracting wealth from Mexico's Indian farming villages. My work is a tribute to the Indians who, through centuries of dehumanizing exploitation and despite overwhelming odds against them, have managed to survive and forge a viable lifestyle for themselves.

The question of whether people in other cultures act rationally on their own behalf is of central importance in our attempt to understand the nature of culture itself and the ways in which village societies have responded to processes of economic development. If culture causes people to follow established paths toward established ends regardless of costs and benefits, then members of traditional cultures are trapped within their own past histories. But observations from the field do not support this view of culture. When outsiders conclude that the Nahuas of Amatlán simply follow the dictates of their traditions, they are mistaken. My data show them experimenting with new cash crops, playing the price cycles of the markets to make the best profits they can, struggling to get more land, working part-time and raising cattle to augment their incomes, and trying to insure an education for their children so the next generation can take advantage of future economic opportunities. In short, the Nahuas act much like Euro-Americans in trying to maximize returns from their decisions even though of course in Amatlán they have a different technology and other variables with which to contend. In this sense, both Nahuas and Euro-Americans act rationally.

It is obvious that some of the goals that Nahuas aim to achieve by their allocations of scarce resources, for example keeping the malevolent wind spirits from the village by making elaborate and costly offerings to them, are not shared by outsiders such as mestizos. But these goals can be judged neither rational nor irrational by outsiders. These aims are in fact cultural givens that the Nahuas believe are desirable to pursue, and it would be ethnocentric of outsiders to dispute this. Many of the goals of the mestizos no doubt appear outlandish or entirely without value to the Nahuas. From the Nahua perspective, characteristics of our own complex economy such as planned obsolescence, product degradation, pollution of the environment, and participation in an international arms race would probably appear remarkably irrational and dangerous. But both Nahuas and mestizos make conscious decisions about how best to allocate their limited resources to achieve the ends they have decided are worthy of attainment, and it is this process that is rational for both groups.

The Nahuas are small players in the international economic arena, but players nonetheless. I have shown in Chapter 5 that they, too, compete for profits, albeit on a relatively modest scale. They grow corn because it is economic to do so in the materialist sense of that word. They raise animals to store wealth, and they try to buy cheaply and sell dear. Like us, they engage in calculations, and they strive to get the best for themselves and their families. However, the Nahuas are heirs to a remarkable cultural tradition that is historically unrelated to that of Europe, and although they have been highly influenced by centuries of contact with the Spaniards, they have not yet been overwhelmed. The people of Amatlán remain Indians both on a conscious and an unconscious level. As Indians they occupy a position near the bottom of the modern Mexican socioeconomic hierarchy, and this fact distorts the opportunities and strategies open to them. The major strategy shared by the people of Amatlán and villagers throughout Mexico, the one that influences virtually every aspect of village life, is the use they make of their own ethnicity. I believe this study has shown that to be an Indian in Mexico (and by extension, to be a member of an ethnic group in any nation undergoing economic development) can in part be understood as a tactic used by people to increase benefits, cut costs, and, ultimately, to secure a life of quality for themselves.

THE VILLAGE IN TRANSITION

What is happening in Amatlán is happening in similar villages all over the world. People who live in industrial societies commonly believe that villages are static, whereas modern economies are always changing. Yet a good argument can be made that the most profound sociocultural changes occurring throughout the world today are taking place in the villages. Much of the change we experience in modern societies is superficial, merely fads and fashions with an occasional technological innovation thrown in. By contrast, many villages throughout Mexico and the rest of the world are undergoing profound and rapid changes in their social organization, world view, religion, and, most fundamental of all, their self-identity. As previously independent peoples become dominated by national powers, one typical reaction that we can expect is the formation and increased importance of ethnic group identity.

As I am writing these lines, the news media are filled with stories of ethnic unrest and violence. In the Soviet Union, several ethnic nationalities are demanding and gaining greater independence from central control. In Eastern Europe, ethnic unrest threatens the stability of national boundaries established after World War II. Hispanics and blacks (now African Americans) in the United States are beginning to form viable voting blocks that may transform the American political scene. In the Middle East, Arabs, Jews and Christians are locked in struggle. In Sri Lanka, the Tamils and Sinhalese are engaged in a bloody conflict, and Sikh extremists are demanding a partition of northern India. The presence of African students in China has recently led to riots. Almost everywhere in the world, groups formed around ethnic identities are demanding rights and threatening the status quo. News accounts have less to say about nation-states and more about Armenians, Slovenians, Croatians, Kurds, Quebecoises, ethnic Chinese, Moskito Indians, Bretons, Basques, Tibetans, Tutsis, Hutus, Eritreans, and Puerto Rican nationalists.

What this study of change and continuity in Amatlán has shown is that processes of Westernization, industrialization, and modernization are mediated through ethnic identity. For the Nahuas (and for many other peoples as well) the creation and maintenance of an ethnic identity is the means by which they deal with domination by more powerful elites, and simultaneously it is the means by which they retain control over their lives in times of social and cultural change. Ethnic identity may act sometimes as a barrier to change, and in other circumstances it is an avenue for the incursion of outside influences. In either case people recognize the advantages of assuming a shared cultural identity in the face of the acts of injustice and uncontrolled forces that threaten values and social order. When conditions alter, old identities can be discarded, new ones assumed, or traditional ones modified. It is a mistake, however, to conclude that cultivating an identity is simply a game people play, a kind of masquerade for the benefit of outsiders. In the end, ethnic identity is self-identity and self-identity is linked to self-worth and ultimately to the meaning of a human life. It does not admit of a lie. Ethnic identity defines the essence of a person for all the world to see.

The Nahuas, in their abiding wisdom, say of themselves, "Corn is our blood." These words link them to their horticultural way of life, the powerful spirits in their pantheon, the animating principle of the universe, and their vision of the beautiful green earth that gives them life. These words express the essence of what it is to be an Indian, to be a member of a community of people who understand and respect how the world works. But no culture is static, and as the conditions of the world continue to change around them the villagers look for advantages in their perpetual need to adjust. Nahua culture has proven its resilience over the last 500 years. In an unknown world of the future, the increasing numbers of people who have a choice in their ethnic identity may no longer find it of value to be Indian. Only then will the Nahua vision of what it is to be human finally cease to exist.

EPILOGUE

AFTER this work was written, Pamela, Michael and I returned to Mexico for five months in the spring of 1990 to visit old friends and document additional changes in Amatlán. Following the traditional low-keyed Nahua greeting that lasted several days, people began to visit to fill us in on events since we were last there and to hear if we had any news to report. One shaman repeated the greeting I was waiting to hear, "We thought you were dead." The rainy-season harvest had been excellent, and people's houses were stacked high with corn. However, a strange epidemic had all but wiped out the pig and chicken population. No medicine seemed to prevent or cure this disease, and we could see by the numbers of baby pigs and chicks that people were just starting to rebuild their stocks. The freeze of December 1989, which swept across the United States reached Amatlán with devastating results. Friends told us that villagers built large fires and spent their days trying to keep from freezing to death. One day it actually snowed in the village, the first time this had happened in living memory. The dry-season planting was a total loss, including the sugarcane crop. People did not seem discouraged, however, and almost all of the milpas had been replanted by the time we arrived. Apparently the increased movement of men to urban centers for temporary work has caused a small labor shortage among ranches in the region. Men informed me that ranchers were now paying the equivalent of between $2 and $3 U.S. per day—a two- to threefold increase over previous years. Even with the pay hike, however, men told me these wages do not compare to what they can earn in the cities and towns.

Many other characteristics of Amatlán today are due to the acceleration of changes described in this work. Even fewer men wear traditional clothing, and no one (except me) wore the traditional *huarache* sandals. Even a few more women have changed to mestizo-style clothing. Amatlán now boasts about ten television sets and one household

even owns a videocasette player. Several more men are building con-
crete-block houses with corrugated iron roofs. When I asked why,
because everyone acknowledges that the traditional thatch-roofed
houses are more comfortable, many replied that it is now extremely
difficult to obtain the raw materials for an old-style house. The deforestation that appears to have increased since we were last there is now
creating a scarcity of resources. One odd development is that the new
Agente Municipal is an hermano and upon attaining office he went to
Ixhuatlán de Madero to obtain permission to forbid the sale of alcohol
in the village. Permission was granted, and for the first time in memory
Amatlán is dry. Devotees of aguardiente now must journey to neighboring villages to make purchases.

The bad luck that villagers had with their schoolmasters appears to
have come to an end. Four teachers are now assigned to Amatlán, of
whom three live in the village with their families. Three teachers are
bilingual in Nahuatl and Spanish, and the director was born and raised
in a nearby village thus giving him an understanding of the local
conditions and problems. The state has recently informed village
authorities that they plan to construct a wing on the new schoolhouse
within the next year. The new director is quite active, and there has
been an increase in the number of school programs. Regional school
officials have even set up a system of sporting events in which children
travel to different villages to participate in challenge matches. However, many of these programs are conceived by city planners and, as
I will describe below, some appear positively absurd in the context of
village life.

We wanted to contribute to the village in some unobtrusive way,
and the school program seemed the logical choice. Pamela, who is a
librarian, had the very good idea of founding a small lending library
in the village. In consultation with village leaders and the school
director we conceived a plan to purchase books in both Spanish and,
if possible, in Nahuatl and to keep them in the director's house so
that he could oversee circulation. Books are a rarity in remote villages
like Amatlán, and adults and children often spent hours leafing through
books that we brought along. Often the books were in English and
had no illustrations, so it was difficult to know what people could have
gotten out of them. We purchased a large number of books, mostly
containing stories, information on travel to other countries, or information on science. Most of the best books we could obtain were published
by the Mexican government, and we even found several written in
Nahuatl. We dropped off the books on the day we left the village and

were gratified to see a large number of children and adults crowding around the school director's house to examine books from the new Amatlán lending library.

The number of hermanos or Protestant converts seems to have stabilized at about 40% of the village. Interestingly, the hermanos have somewhat lost their fire, and they have split into two factions. The original "living water" sect has been reduced to about 8 families who continue to condemn all other religions and to resist medical interventions such as vaccines. The majority of hermanos now belong to what appears to be a Pentecostal group that seems more flexible and encourages parents to seek medical help and have their children vaccinated. An epidemic of measles that has claimed the lives of several children in neighboring villages may have played a part in increasing the attractiveness of the Pentecostals for many families. Interestingly, the Catholic segment of the village has risen to the Protestant challenge and is now quite active. Under the leadership of Lorenzo, whose trial for murder I recounted in Chapter 1, the Catholic majority now has an active program of chapel activities, and they regularly celebrate major church holidays. Both the Protestants and Catholics reject the traditional costumbres, and so very few families now participate in the old rituals. Two shamans remain active, but they are serving a handful of families who continue the ancient traditions.

But underlying these observable changes in the village we still find evidence of the violence and misunderstanding that has characterized Indian–mestizo interactions since colonial days. I would like to recount briefly a tragedy that befell Julio and his wife as an example of the difficulties facing people like the Nahuas of Amatlán as they try to overcome historical patterns and enter the modern world on an equal footing with others in their respective nations. Julio is the pseudonym for a villager whose example of economic success within the Indian world formed part of Chapter 2. By 1988, Julio was experiencing significant success in his various enterprises. His market stall was doing very well, his farming and cattle raising were highly productive, and his village cantina was booming. In that year he and his wife decided that they needed to buy a pickup truck to use for hauling their goods. It would be the first vehicle purchased by a resident villager. After much searching and negotiation, a used truck was located and purchased. It served well for several months and increased the efficiency of Julio's operations.

Julio's success, however, did not go unnoticed by local mestizos. One morning at about 6:00 A.M. Julio and his wife were in their truck slowly crossing the arroyo below their house when they were confronted by three men wearing masks and mounted on horseback. They were armed with pistols and one had a shotgun. As Julio stopped the truck the men opened fire through the windshield. After a few seconds the firing stopped, leaving the windshield shattered and the truck pocked with bullet holes. Miraculously, Julio's wife was not hit, although she was covered with broken glass. She opened the truck door and in a fear-induced frenzy ran screaming toward the three mounted men. Incredibly, they saw her coming and turned and ran. Julio was not so lucky. He had been shot through the pelvis and was bleeding badly. His wife ran for help, and villagers hurriedly carried him to a medical doctor in Ixhuatlán de Madero. He lived through the ordeal, but clearly he was a broken man. He refused to leave his house for many months following the tragedy, and he abandoned the truck to a relative in a neighboring village. In 1990 when we arrived in Amatlán he was just beginning to move about normally. He walked with a bad limp and had a look of fear on his face. When I questioned him about the attack he said that mestizos did it. He puzzled about the fact that everybody knew he never carried money with him, and yet robbery was their apparent motive. The lesson was not lost on others who concluded that people like Julio invite attack from outsiders.

I would like to end this brief epilogue by describing an event that further reveals the paradoxical position of the Indian in Mexican society. A month or so after we arrived in 1990 one of the schoolteachers came to inform me that the children from the fifth-grade class were preparing an authentic Indian dance for the next school program. He told me that as an anthropologist I should be interested in this glimpse into real Indian culture. There was some excitement about this program, and several villagers said that they, too, were eager to see this traditional dance performed. Finally the day arrived, and the audience waited through the various announcements and preliminaries before the dancers were to appear. At last, from around the corner of the school building appeared the dancers. I was dumbfounded. The children were dressed in cardboard moccasins, loincloths, and had turkey feathers sticking out of their paper headbands. In their hands they carried cardboard tomahawks. These purportedly authentic Indian costumes were conceived by planners in Mexico City, and must have been based on a stereotype of Plains Indian culture from the United States! As I sat there and watched the children shuffle through a simple dance to taped tom-tom music it occurred to me that it is hard to be optimistic about the future of Nahua culture. On the other hand, that same thought might have crossed the mind of an observer on that August day in 1521 when Cortés and his allies crushed the last Aztec military resistance.

Kemantika Nijmachilia Nimiktojka uan Nojua Niyoltok

Kemantika nijmachilia nimiktojka uan nojua niyoltok
pampa ayojkana na:
nijtemoua notlakej uan ayok nikasi.

Kemantika nijmachilia nimiktojka uan nojua niyoltok
pampa ayojkana na:
nijtemoua nomila uan ayok nesi.

Kemantika nijmachilia nimiktojka uan nojua niyoltok
pampa ayojkana na:
nijtemoua xochitlatsotsontli uan ayok nijkaki, kemantika
san uajka kakisti.

Kemantika nijmachilia nimiktojka uan nojua niyoltok
pampa ayojkana na:
nikintemoua noikniuaj uan ayokueli nikin asi,
sekij motlakenpatlakejya uan sekinok moyolpatlakejya.

Kemantika nijmachilia nimiktojka uan nojua niyoltok
yoltok noyolo, nijneki nitlachixtos, nijneki nimochikauas,
sampa nimoyolchikauas.

Sometimes I Feel Dead in Life

Sometimes I feel dead in life
because I am no longer myself:
I search for my clothes and they no longer appear.

Sometimes I feel dead in life
because I am no longer myself:
I search for my milpa and it no longer appears.

Sometimes I feel dead in life
because I am no longer myself:
I search for the flower music and I can no longer hear it,
sometimes I can perceive it in the distance.

Sometimes I feel dead in life
because I am no longer myself:
I search for my brothers and I no longer find them,
some have changed clothes, others have changed their heart.

Sometimes I feel dead in life
but my heart lives, I want to live,
I want to heal myself, I want to return to having a strong heart.

By José Antonio Xokoyotsij, pseudonym of Natalio Hernández
Hernández, a Nahua born in the *municipio* of Ixhuatlán de Madero
(1986:60–61).

GLOSSARY

ACCULTURATION. Changes that occur when two cultures come into contact.

ASCRIBED ETHNICITY. Ethnic group affiliation to which one is assigned by other people.

BILATERAL DESCENT. Tracing descent through both the father's and mother's sides of the family.

CARGO SYSTEM. Ranked system of religious and political positions found in many Mesoamerican Indian communities.

CLOSED CORPORATE COMMUNITY. According to Eric Wolf, rural Mexican communities that have collective control over land, mechanisms forcing the redistribution of wealth, prevention of the formation of social ties outside the community, and mechanisms for forbidding outsiders from joining the community.

COMPOUND. A number of households, the heads of which are not necessarily related, that are located near one another in a Nahua village.

CONSUMPTION UNIT. Social group such as a nuclear family that consumes goods and services in common.

COSMOLOGY. Culturally determined ideas about the origin and nature of the universe.

CULTURAL MATERIALISM. Theoretical approach in anthropology that seeks to explain worldwide cultural similarities and differences by examining techno-environmental factors in differing modes of cultural adaptation.

CULTURE. Evolving totality of ideas, behavior, and values that is shared by members of a social group and that is transmitted through learning. Also, a term applied to the social group itself whose members possess a given culture.

CULTURE SHOCK. Mental disorientation and inability to function that sometimes occurs when a person raised in one cultural tradition interacts intensively with people raised in a different cultural tradition.

DEBT PEONAGE. Economic system in which peasants are kept in a constant state of indebtedness to landlords or bankers.

DEVELOPMENTAL CYCLE OF HOUSEHOLDS. Systematic changes that occur in household structure and composition as household members pass through stages in their lives.

385

DOMESTIC CYCLE. See developmental cycle of households.

DOMINICAL PROCESS. According to Gonzalo Aguirre Beltrán, the process by which the economically and technologically advanced segments of Mexico dominate the Indian groups living in "regions of refuge."

DUAL ECONOMIC SYSTEM. Economic system in which people in an advanced capitalist economy dominate poor peasants or traditional communities within their own society whose productive techniques and economic arrangements differ from those of national elites.

EGO. In anthropology, the conventional term for designating the central person in a kinship diagram to whom all the other positions in the diagram are related.

ENDOGAMY. Cultural rule urging or requiring members of a society to marry within a designated group.

ESKIMO SYSTEM OF KINSHIP TERMS. System in which ego refers to his siblings with a different term than is used for cousins on both sides of the family.

ETHNIC GROUP. Group whose members identify themselves for purposes of political, social, or economic advantage as a distinct group based on cultural markers that are recognized by members and outsiders alike.

ETHNIC GROUP MARKERS. Traits of speech, dress, behavior, or physical appearance used by individuals to assign themselves or the people they meet to an ethnic group.

ETHNIC IDENTITY. Feeling of identification and common destiny with other people who share the same ethnic group markers.

ETHNOCENTRISM. Scientific and logical fallacy in which one culture is judged by the standards of another.

ETHNOGRAPHY. A systematic, scientific description of a culture.

ETHNOHISTORY. Branch of anthropology that attempts to reconstruct cultures from the past using documentary and other sources.

EXOGAMY. Cultural rule urging or requiring people to marry outside of a designated group.

EXTENDED FAMILY. Multigeneration family composed of nuclear families who are related by male or female links.

FICTIVE OR FICTIONAL KINSHIP. Ties of kinship that are assumed to exist between people who are not actually related.

FISSION. According to James Taggart, a gradual process in which a married son separates his family budget and corn supply from that of his father as preliminary steps to becoming an independent nuclear family.

FOLK COMMUNITY. According to Robert Redfield, communities in Mexico like Amatlán that are small, isolated, homogeneous, and family-based.

FOLK-URBAN CONTINUUM. According to Robert Redfield, the idea that communities in Mexico form a developmental series from isolated folk communities to large cities.

HAWAIIAN SYSTEM OF KINSHIP TERMS. System in which ego refers to his siblings and his cousins on both sides by the same kinship term.

HOUSEHOLD. Group of people who live together in the same or nearby houses and who share a common budget and store of corn.

INDUSTRIALIZATION. The changes that may occur in a small-scale traditional culture when industrial plants and other modern means of production are introduced to them.

LIMITED GOOD, IMAGE OF. According to George Foster, the idea that many people in traditional communities feel there is only a limited amount of desirable goods and services in existence and therefore individuals always gain at the expense of other people.

MATRILOCAL EXTENDED FAMILY. Multigenerational family composed of a man and his wife and unmarried children, plus one or more married daughters with their husbands and unmarried children.

MODERNIZATION. All the changes that for various reasons can occur in the behavior and beliefs of small isolated communities to make them become more like large-scale, urban, and economically advanced societies.

MYTH. A sacred tale about spirits, gods, or culture heroes that is often set in the remote past but which is told to validate and explain certain aspects of contemporary society.

NONRESIDENTIAL PATRILOCAL EXTENDED FAMILY. A man and his married sons who live in nearby houses and work each other's fields, but who do not form a household because they do not keep a common budget or store corn in common.

NUCLEAR FAMILY. Family composed of a husband, wife, and unmarried children.

PANTHEISM. The idea that the universe and everything in it partakes of a living spiritual essence so that at a higher level everything and everyone is spiritually united.

PARTICIPANT OBSERVATION. Approach to the study of human behavior in which the researcher lives for an extended time with the social group being studied and takes part in the group's daily activities.

PATRILOCAL EXTENDED FAMILY. Multigeneration family composed of a man, his wife, and unmarried children, plus one or more sons with their wives and unmarried children.

PEASANTS. Rural groups that live in a state of subordination to more powerful and economically advanced urban populations; peasants produce most of their food by traditional methods and sell some crops to the urban populations to whom they must pay some form of rent.

PENNY CAPITALISM. According to Sol Tax, the idea that peasant populations are motivated by profit in their economic exchanges and that their economic behavior thus differs from that of urban capitalist societies only in the scale of their transactions.

PRODUCTION UNIT. The social group in a society that produces goods and services in common.

REGIONS OF REFUGE. According to Gonzalo Aguirre Beltrán, the remote and economically undesirable areas of Mexico where traditional pre-Hispanic Indian cultures survive.

REVERSE CULTURE SHOCK. Difficulty in readjusting to one's own culture after returning from a prolonged period of fieldwork in a foreign culture.

RITUAL. Stereotyped set of physical and verbal behaviors which make visible the abstract principles of the religious system of a given culture.

SEGMENTATION. According to James Taggart, a process in which a married son splits his household from that of his father after establishing his own budget and corn supply.

SHAMAN. Part-time magico-religious specialist who divines the future, heals the sick, and intervenes with the spirits for the benefit of his or her clients.

SLASH-AND-BURN HORTICULTURE. Farming technique in many tropical areas in which vegetation is cut and burned to give nutrients to a farming plot. After a few crops the farmer often must move to another area and begin the process again.

SORCERER. A shaman who uses his or her power to harm individuals or the social group.

STYLE. According to Anya Royce, the idea that members of some ethnic groups consciously select elements from their history and actively create an ethnic identity separate from that of other groups.

TRADITION. Beliefs and practices that distinguish ethnic groups from each other, which are more or less passively inherited from the past rather than consciously selected.

WESTERNIZATION. Processes that cause traditional cultures to change their beliefs and practices to become more like the beliefs and practices of the urban populations of Western Europe and North America.

REFERENCES

Adams, Richard N., and Arthur J. Rubel. 1967. "Sickness and Social Relations." In Manning Nash, ed., *Social Anthropology*, pp. 333–56. Vol. 6 in Robert Wauchope, gen. ed., *Handbook of Middle American Indians*. Austin: University of Texas Press.

Aguirre Beltrán, Gonzalo. 1979. *Regions of Refuge*. Society for Applied Anthropology Monograph Series, No. 12. Washington, D.C.: Society for Applied Anthropology.

Annis, Sheldon. 1987. *God and Production in a Guatemalan Town*. Austin: University of Texas Press.

Anuario estadístico de Veracruz, 1984. 1985. 4 vols. México, D.F.: Secretaría de Programación y Presupuesto, Instituto Nacional de Estadística, Geografía e Informática.

Arizpe Schlosser, Lourdes. 1972. "Nahua Domestic Groups: The Developmental Cycle of Nahua Domestic Groups in Central Mexico." In special issue produced by I. Green, M. Hill, M. J. Schwartz, T. Selwyn, J. Webster, and J. Winter. *!Kung*, pp. 40–46. London: published as the "magazine of the L.S.E. Anthropology Society."

———. 1973. *Parentesco y economía en una sociedad nahua*. México, D.F.: Instituto Nacional Indigenista y Secretaría de Educación Pública.

Barth, Fredrik. 1969. *Ethnic Groups and Boundaries: The Social Organization of Culture Difference*. Boston: Little, Brown and Company.

Bartra, Roger. 1977. "The problem of native peoples and indigenist ideology." In *Race and Class in Post-Colonial Society: A Study of Ethnic Group Relations in the English-Speaking Caribbean, Bolivia, Chile and Mexico*, pp. 341–54. Paris: UNESCO.

Beller, Ricardo N., and Patricia Cowan de Beller. 1984. *Curso del Náhuatl moderno: Náhuatl de la Huasteca*. 2 vols. México: Instituto Lingüístico de Verano.

Berdan, Frances F. 1982. *The Aztecs of Central Mexico: An Imperial Society*. New York: Holt, Rinehart & Winston.

Bernal, Ignacio, and Eusebio Dávalos Hurtado, eds. 1952–53. "Huastecos, totonacos, y sus vecinos." *Revista Mexicana de Estudios Antropológicos* 13(2–3):1–567.

Bernard, H. Russell. 1988. *Research Methods in Cultural Anthropology*. Newbury Park, Calif.: Sage Publications.

Boilès, Charles L. 1971. "Síntesis y sincretismo en el carnaval otomí." *América Indígena* 31(3):555–63.

Bradley, Richard. 1988. "Processes of Sociocultural Change and Ethnicity in Southern Veracruz, Mexico." Ph.D. diss., University of Oklahoma, Norman.

Burkhart, Louise. 1989. *The Slippery Earth: Nahua-Christian Moral Dialogue in Sixteenth-Century Mexico*. Tucson: University of Arizona Press.

Carrasco, Pedro. 1976. "The Joint Family in Ancient Mexico: The Case of Molotla." In Hugo G. Nutini, Pedro Carrasco, and James M. Taggart, eds., *Essays on Mexican Kinship*, pp. 45–64. Pittsburgh: University of Pittsburgh Press.

Caso, Alfonso. 1958. *The Aztecs: People of the Sun*. Translated by Lowell Dunham. Civilization of the American Indian Series. Norman: University of Oklahoma Press.

———. 1971. *La comunidad indígena*. SepSetentas, 8. México, D.F.: Secretaría de Educación Pública.

Castile, George P. 1981. "On the Tarascanness of the Tarascans and the Indianness of the Indians." In George P. Castile and Gilbert Kushner, eds., *Persistent Peoples: Cultural Enclaves in Perspective*, pp. 171–91. Tucson: University of Arizona Press.

Chamoux, Marie-Noëlle. 1981a. "Les savoir-faire techniques et leur appropriation: le cas des Nahuas de Mexique." *L'Homme* 21(3):71–94.

———. 1981b. *Indiens de la Sierra: la communauté paysanne au mexique*. Paris: Editions L'Harmattan.

———. 1986. "The Conception of Work in Contemporary Nahuatl-Speaking Communities in the Sierra de Puebla." Paper read at the 85th annual meeting of the American Anthropological Association, Philadelphia, Pennsylvania.

Christensen, Bodil. 1942. "Notas sobre la fabricación del papel indígena y su empleo para 'brujerías' en la Sierra Norte de Puebla, México." *Revista Mexicana de Estudios Antropológicos* 6(1–2):109–124.

———. 1952–53. "Los Otomís del estado de Puebla." *Revista Mexicana de Estudios Antropológicos* 13(2–3):259–268.

Christensen, Bodil, and Samuel Martí. 1971. *Brujerías y papel precolombino [Witchcraft and Pre-Columbian Paper]*. México, D.F.: Ediciones Euroamericanas.

Collier, John. 1967. *Visual Anthropology: Photography as a Research Method*. New York: Holt, Rinehart & Winston.

Cook, Sherburne F., and Lesley Byrd Simpson. 1948. *The Population of Central Mexico in the Sixteenth Century*. Ibero-Americana, Vol. 31. Berkeley: University of California Press.

Crumrine, N. Ross. 1964. "The House Cross of the Mayo Indians of Sonora, Mexico: A Symbol of Ethnic Identity." *Anthropological Papers of the University of Arizona*, No. 8. Tucson: University of Arizona Press.

De la Cruz Hernández, Juan. 1982. *La comunidad indígena de Tizal, Veracruz, y su lucha por la tierra.* Cuadernos de información y divulgación para maestros bilingües, Etnolingüística 43. México, D.F.: Instituto Nacional Indigenista y Secretaría de Educación Pública, Programa de Formación Profesional de Etnolingüístas.

Dehouve, Danièle. 1974. *Corvée des saints et luttes des marchands.* Paris: Klincksieck.

———. 1978. "Parenté et mariage dans une communauté nahuatl de l'état de Guerrero (Mexique)." *Journal de la Société des Américanistes*, n.s. 65:173–208.

Dow, James. 1974. *Santos y supervivencias: Funciones de la religión en una comunidad Otomí, México.* Colección SEP-INI, No. 33. México, D.F.: Instituto Nacional Indigenista y Secretaría de Educación Pública.

———. 1975. *The Otomí of the Northern Sierra de Puebla, Mexico: An Ethnographic Outline.* Latin American Studies Center Monograph Series, No. 12. East Lansing: Michigan State University.

———. 1982. "Las figuras de papel y el concepto del alma entre los Otomís de la Sierra." *América Indígena* 42(4):629–50.

———. 1984. "Symbols, Soul, and Magical Healing among the Otomí Indians." *Journal of Latin American Lore* 10(1):3–21.

———. 1986a. *The Shaman's Touch: Otomí Indian Symbolic Healing.* Salt Lake City: University of Utah Press.

———. 1986b. "Universal Aspects of Symbolic Healing." *American Anthropologist* 88(1):56–69.

Finkler, Kaja. 1969. "The Faunal Reserve Hypothesis: Living Bank Accounts among the Otomi." In H. Russell Bernard, ed., *Los Otomis: Papers from the Ixmiquilpan Field School*, pp. 55–62. Washington State University Laboratory of Anthropology Report of Investigations, No. 46. Pullman: Washington State University.

Foster, George. 1967. *Tzintzuntzan: Mexican Peasants in a Changing World.* Boston: Little, Brown and Co.

Fox, Robin. 1967. *Kinship and Marriage: An Anthropological Perspective.* Baltimore: Penguin Books.

Friedlander, Judith. 1975. *Being Indian in Hueyapan: A Study of Forced Identity in Contemporary Mexico.* New York: St. Martin's Press.

Galinier, Jacques. 1976a. "La grande vie: Représentation de la mort et practiques funéraires chez les indiens Otomís (Mexique)." *Cahiers du Centre d'Etudes et de Recherches Ethnologique, Université de Bordeaux* 2(4):2–27.

———. 1976b. "Oratoires otomís de la région de Tulancingo." *Actas de XLI Congreso Internacional de Americanistas, México, 1974* 41(3):158–71.

————. 1979a. "La Huasteca (espace et temps) dans la religion des indiens Otomís." *Actes du XLIIe Congrès International des Americanistes, Paris, 1976* 9B:129–40.

————. 1979b. "La peau, la pourriture et le sacré champs sémantique et motivation dans un exemple Otomí (Mexique)." *Journal de la Société des Américanistes*, n.s. 66:205–18.

Gardner, Brant. 1982. "A Structural and Semantic Analysis of Classical Nahuatl Kinship Terminology." *Estudios de Cultura Náhuatl* 15:89–124.

Gerhard, Peter. 1972. *A Guide to the Historical Geography of New Spain.* Cambridge Latin American Studies, Vol. 14. Cambridge: Cambridge University Press.

Gessain, Robert. 1938. "Contribution a l'étude des cultes et des cérémonies indigènes de la région de Huehuetla (Hidalgo)." *Journal de la Société des Américanistes*, n.s. 30:343–71.

————. 1952–53. "Les indiens tepehuas de Huehuetla." *Revista Mexicana de Estudios Antropológicos* 13(2–3):187–211.

Gossen, Gary H., ed. 1986. *Symbol and Meaning Beyond the Closed Community: Essays in Mesoamerican Ideas.* Studies on Culture and Society, Vol. 1. Albany: Institute for Mesoamerican Studies, The University at Albany, State University of New York.

Harnapp, Vern R. 1972. "The Mexican Huasteca: A Region in Formation." Ph.D. diss., University of Kansas, Lawrence.

Hassig, Ross. 1988. *Aztec Warfare: Imperial Expansion and Political Control.* Norman: University of Oklahoma Press.

Hawkins, John. 1984. *Inverse Images: The Meaning of Culture, Ethnicity and Family in Postcolonial Guatemala.* Albuquerque: University of New Mexico Press.

Hernández Cristóbal, Amalia, Rogelio Xocua Cuicahuac, Aurora Tequihuactle Jiménez, y Benito Chimalhua Cosme. 1982. "Las ceremonias del Cerro Xochipapatla: Huitzizilco, Ixhuatlán de Madero, Veracruz." In Maria Elena Hope y Luz Pereyra, eds. *Nuestro Maíz: Treinta Monografías Populares*, Vol. 2, pp. 45–66. México: Museo Nacional de Culturas Populares.

Hernández Cuellar, Rosendo. 1982. *La religion nahua en Texoloc, municipio de Xochiatipan, Hgo.* Cuadernos de información y divulgación para maestros bilingües, Etnolingüística, 51. México, D.F.: Instituto Nacional Indigenista y Secretaría de Educación Pública, Programa de Formación Profesional de Etnolingüístas.

Hill, Jane H., and Kenneth C. Hill. 1986. *Speaking Mexicano: Dynamics of Syncretic Language in Central Mexico.* Tucson: University of Arizona Press.

Horcasitas de Barros, M.L., and Ana María Crespo. 1979. *Hablantes de lengua indígena en méxico.* Colección scientifica lenguas, No. 81. México, D.F.: Secretária de Educación Pública y Instituto Nacional de Antropología e Historia.

Huber, Brad R. 1987. "The Reinterpretation and Elaboration of Fiestas in the Sierra Norte de Puebla, Mexico." *Ethnology* 26(4):281–96.

Hunt, Eva. 1976. "Kinship and Territorial Fission in the Cuicatec Highlands." In Hugo G. Nutini, Pedro Carrasco, and James M. Taggart, eds., *Essays on Mexican Kinship*, pp. 97–153. Pittsburgh: University of Pittsburgh Press.

————. 1977. *The Transformation of the Hummingbird: Cultural Roots of a Zinacanteco Mythical Poem*. Ithaca: Cornell University Press.

Hunt, Robert. 1979. "Introduction." In Gonzalo Aguirre Beltrán. *Regions of Refuge*, pp. 1–3. Society for Applied Anthropology Monograph Series, No. 12. Washington D.C.: Society for Applied Anthropology.

Ichon, Alain. 1969. *La religion de Totonaques de la Sierra*. Paris: Editions du Centre National de la Recherche Scientifique.

Ingham, John M. 1989 [1986]. *Mary, Michael, and Lucifer: Folk Catholicism in Central Mexico*. Austin: University of Texas Press.

Ixmatlahua Montalvo, Isabel, María Martínez Gertrudes, Manuel Orea Méndez, Benito Martínez Hernández, y Juan Antonio Martínez Aldrete. 1982. "El cultivo del maíz y tres rituales asociados a su producción: Cacahuatengo, Ixhuatlán de Madero, Veracruz." In Maria Elena Hope y Luz Pereyra, eds., *Nuestro Maíz: Treinta Monografías Populares*, Vol. 2, pp. 67–101. México: Museo Nacional de Culturas Populares.

Keesing, Roger M. 1975. *Kin Groups and Social Structure*. New York: Holt, Rinehart & Winston.

Kelly, Isabel, and Angel Palerm. 1952. *The Tajin Totonac, Part I: History, Subsistence, Shelter and Technology*. Smithsonian Institution, Institute for Social Anthropology, Publication No. 13. Washington, D.C.: Smithsonian Institution.

Kimball, Geoffrey. 1980. *A Dictionary of the Huazalinguillo Dialect of Nahuatl with Grammatical Sketches and Readings*. Latin American Studies Curriculum Aids. New Orleans: Tulane University Center for Latin American Studies.

Knab, Tim. 1979. "Talocan Talmanic: Supernatural Beings of the Sierra de Puebla." *Actes du XLIIe Congrès International des Américanistes, Paris, 1976* 42(6):127–36.

Kroeber, Alfred. 1948. *Anthropology: Race, Language, Culture, Psychology, History*. New York: Harcourt, Brace, and Company.

Kvam, Reidar. 1985. *Oil, Oranges and Invasions: Economic Development and Political Mobilization in Eastern Mexico*. Ph.D. diss. University of Bergen, Norway.

Lenz, Hans. 1973 [1948]. *El papel indígena mexicano*. SepSetentas, No. 65. México. D.F.: Secretaría de Educación Pública.

————. 1984. *Cosas del papel en Mesoamérica*. México, D.F.: Editorial Libros de México.

León, Nicolás. 1924. "La industria indígena del papel en México, en los tiempos precolombinos y actuales." *Boletín del Museo Nacional*, época IV 2(5):101–105.

Lewis, Oscar. 1951. *Life in a Mexican Village: Tepoztlán Restudied*. Urbana: University of Illinois Press.

Lopez Austin, Alfredo. 1988. *The Human Body and Ideology: Concepts of the Ancient Nahuas*. 2 vols. Translated by Thelma Ortiz de Montellano and Bernard Ortiz de Montellano. Salt Lake City: University of Utah Press.

Madsen, William. 1960. *The Virgin's Children: Life in an Aztec Village Today*. Austin: University of Texas Press.

———. 1969. "The Nahua." In Evon Z. Vogt, ed., *Ethnology*, Part 2, pp. 602–37. Vol. 8 in Robert Wauchope, gen. ed., *Handbook of Middle American Indians*. Austin: University of Texas Press.

Marino Flores, Anselmo. 1967. "Indian Population and Its Identification." In Manning Nash, ed., *Social Anthropology*, pp. 12–25. Vol. 6 in Robert Wauchope, gen. ed., *Handbook of Middle American Indians*. Austin: University of Texas Press.

Martínez H., Librado. 1960. "Costumbres y creencias en el municipio del Ixhuatlán de Madero, Veracruz." *Boletín del Centro de Investigaciones Antropológicas de México* No. 8:9–13.

Martínez Hernández, Joel. 1982. *Análisis comparativo de las dos escuelas que funcionan en la congregación de Cuatzapotitla perteneciente al municipio de Chicontepec del Estado de Veracruz*. Cuadernos de información y divulgación para maestros bilingües, Etnolingüística 14. México, D.F.: Instituto Nacional Indigenista y Secretaría de Educación Pública, Programa de Formación Profesional de Etnolingüistas.

Medellín Zenil, Alfonso. 1979. "Muestrario ceremonial de la región de Chicontepec, Veracruz." *Actes du XLIIe Congrès International des Américanistes, Paris, 1976* 9B:113–19.

———. 1982. *Exploraciones en la región de Chicontepec o Huaxteca meridional*. Jalapa, Veracruz: Editora del Gobierno de Veracruz.

Melgarejo Vivanco, José Luis. 1960. *Breve historia de Veracruz*. Xalapa: Universidad Veracruzana.

Mönnich, Anneliese. 1976. "La supervivencia de antiguas representaciones indígenas en la religión popular de los Nawas de Veracruz y Puebla." In Luis Reyes García and Dieter Christensen, eds., *Das Ring aus Tlalocan: Mythen und Gabete, Lieder und Erzählungen der heutigen Nahua in Veracruz und Puebla, Mexiko; El Anillo de Tlalocan: Mitos, oraciones, cantos y cuentos de los Nawas actuales de los Estados de Veracruz y Puebla, México*, pp. 139–43. Quellenwerke zur alten Geschichte Amerikas aufgezeichnet in den Sprachen der Eingeborenen, Bd. 12. Berlin: Gebr. Mann Verlag. (in German and Spanish)

Montoya Briones, José de Jesús. 1964. *Atla: etnografía de un pueblo náhuatl*. Departmento de Investigaciones Antropológicas, Publicaciones No. 14. México, D.F.: Instituto Nacional de Antropología e Historia.

————. 1981. *Significado de los aires en la cultural indígena*. Cuadernos del Museo Nacional de Antropología, No. 13. México, D.F.: Instituto Nacional de Antropología e Historia.

Murdock, George P. 1949. *Social Structure*. New York: Macmillan.

Myerhoff, Barbara G. 1974. *Peyote Hunt: The Sacred Journey of the Huichol Indians*. Ithaca, New York: Cornell University Press.

Naroll, Raoul, and Ronald Cohen, eds. 1973. *A Handbook of Method in Cultural Anthropology*. New York: Columbia University Press.

Nash, Manning. 1973 [1958]. *Machine Age Maya: The Industrialization of a Guatemalan Community*. Chicago: University of Chicago Press.

————. 1989. *The Cauldron of Ethnicity in the Modern World*. Chicago: University of Chicago Press.

Nicholson, Henry B. 1971. "Religion in Pre-Hispanic Central Mexico." In Gordon F. Ekholm and Ignacio Bernal, eds., *Archaeology of Northern Mesoamerica*, Part 1, pp. 395–446. Vol. 10 in Robert Wauchope, gen. ed., *Handbook of Middle American Indians*. Austin: University of Texas Press.

Nutini, Hugo G. 1967. "A Synoptic Comparison of Mesoamerican Marriage and Family Structure." *Southwestern Journal of Anthropology* 23(4):383–404.

————. 1968. *San Bernardino Contla: Marriage and Family Structure in a Tlaxcalan Municipio*. Pittsburgh: University of Pittsburgh Press.

————. 1984. *Ritual Kinship: Ideological and Structural Integration of the Compadrazgo System in Rural Tlaxcala*. 2 vols. Princeton N.J.: Princeton University Press.

————. 1988. *Todos Santos in Rural Mexico: A Syncretic, Expressive and Symbolic Analysis of the Cult of the Dead*. Princeton, N.J.: Princeton University Press.

————, and Barry L. Isaac. 1974. *Los pueblos de habla náhuatl de la region de Tlaxcala y Puebla*. México: Instituto Nacional Indigenista y Secretaría de Educación Pública.

————, and Betty Bell. 1980. *Ritual Kinship: The Structure and Historical Development of the Compadrazgo System in Rural Tlaxcala*. Princeton, N.J.: Princeton University Press.

Ochoa, Lorenzo. 1979. *Historia prehispánica de la Huasteca*. Serie Antropológica, No. 26. México, D.F.: Instituto de Investigaciones Antropológicos.

Pelto, Pertti J., and Gretel H. Pelto. 1978. *Anthropological Research: The Structure of Inquiry*. 2nd ed. Cambridge: Cambridge University Press

Provost, Paul Jean. 1975. "Culture and Anti-Culture among the Eastern Nahua of Northern Veracruz, Mexico." Ph.D. diss., Indiana University, Bloomington.

————. 1981. "The Fate of the Soul in Modern Aztec Religious Thought." *Proceedings of the Indiana Academy of Science, 1980* 90:80–85.

Provost, Paul Jean, and Alan R. Sandstrom. 1977. "Sacred Guitar and Violin

Music of the Modern Aztecs." Ethnomusicological recording with ethnographic notes, FE 4358. New York: Ethnic Folkways Records.

Puig, Henri. 1976. *Vegetation de la Huasteca, Mexique: Étude phyto-géographique et écologique.* Etudes mésoaméricaines, Vol. 5. México, D.F.: Mission arquéologique et ethnologique francaise au Mexique.

———. 1979. "Contribution de l'écologie à la définition de la limite nord-est Mésoamérique." *Actes du XLIIe Congrès International des Américanistes, Paris, 1976* 9B:13–27.

Radin, Paul. 1925. "Maya, Nahuatl, and Tarascan Kinship Terms." *American Anthropologist,* n.s. 27:100–102

Rappaport, Roy A. 1979. *Ecology, Meaning, and Religion.* Richmond, Calif.: North Atlantic Books.

Reck, Gregory. 1986 [1978]. *In the Shadow of Tlaloc: Life in a Mexican Village.* Prospect Heights, Ill.: Waveland Press.

Redfield, Robert. 1930. *Tepoztlán, A Mexican Village: A Study of Folk Life.* University of Chicago Publications in Anthropology, Ethnological Series. Chicago: University of Chicago Press.

———. 1934. "Culture Change in Yucatan." *American Anthropologist,* n.s. 36:57–69.

———. 1941. *The Folk Culture of Yucatan.* Chicago: University of Chicago Press.

———. 1950. *A Village that Chose Progress.* Chicago: University of Chicago Press.

———. 1953. *The Primitive World and Its Transformations.* Ithaca, N.Y.: Cornell University Press.

———. 1960. *The Little Community and Peasant Society and Culture.* Chicago: University of Chicago Press.

Reyes Antonio, Agustín. 1982. *Plantas y medicina nahua en Matlapa indígena.* Cuadernos de información y divulgación para maestros bilingües, Etnolingüística 21. México, D.F.: Instituto Nacional Indigenista y Secretaría de Educación Pública, Programa de Formación Profesional de Etnolingüistas.

Reyes García, Luis. 1960. *Pasión y muerte del Cristo sol: Carnaval y cuaresma en Ichcatepec.* Xalapa: Universidad Veracruzana.

———. 1976. "Introducción: los Nawas actuales de México." In Luis Reyes García und Dieter Christensen, eds., *Das Ring aus Tlalocan: Mythen und Gabete, Lieder und Erzählungen der heutigen Nahua in Veracruz und Puebla, Mexiko; El Anillo de Tlalocan: Mitos, oraciones, cantos y cuentos de los Nawas actuales de los Estados de Veracruz y Puebla, México,* pp. 123–35. Quellenwerke zur alten Geschichte Amerikas aufgezeichnet in den Sprachen der Eingeborenen, Bd. 12. Berlin: Gebr. Mann Verlag. (in German and Spanish)

———, und Dieter Christensen, eds. 1976. *Das Ring aus Tlalocan: Mythen und Gabete, Lieder und Erzählungen der heutigen Nahua in Veracruz und*

Puebla, Mexiko; El Anillo de Tlalocan: Mitos, oraciones, cantos y cuentos de los Nawas actuales de los Estados de Veracruz y Puebla, México. Quellenwerke zur alten Geschichte Amerikas aufgezeichnet in den Sprachen der Eingeborenen, Bd. 12. Berlin: Gebr. Mann Verlag. (in German and Spanish)

Reyes Martínez, Rosa. 1982. *La comunidad indígena de Tlacolula, Veracruz: La tierra y sus problemas.* Cuadernos de información y divulgación para maestros bilingües, Etnolingüística 45. México, D.F.: Instituto Nacional Indigenista y Secretaría de Educación Pública, Programa de Formación Profesional de Etnolingüístas.

Romualdo Hernández, Joaquin. 1982. *Relaciones políticas entre indígenas y mestizos en Xochiatipan, Hgo.* Cuadernos de información y divulgación para maestros bilingües, Etnolingüística 46. México, D.F.: Instituto Nacional Indigenista y Secretaría de Educación Pública, Programa de Formación Profesional de Etnolingüístas.

Royce, Anya Peterson. 1975. *Prestigio y afiliación en una comunidad urbana, Juchitán, Oax.* Colección SEP-INI, No. 37. México, D.F.: Instituto Nacional Indigenista y Secretaría de Educación Pública.

—————. 1982. *Ethnic Identity: Strategies of Diversity.* Bloomington: Indiana University Press.

Rudolph, James D., ed. 1985. *Mexico: A Country Study.* Area Handbook Series, DA Pam. 550-79. Washington, D.C.: American University Foreign Area Studies; Government Printing Office.

Sanders, William. 1952–53. "The Anthropogeography of Central Veracruz." *Revista Mexicana de Estudios Antropológicos* 13(2–3):27–78.

—————. 1971. "Cultural Ecology and Settlement Patterns of the Gulf Coast." In Gordon F. Ekholm and Ignacio Bernal, eds., *Archaeology of Northern Mesoamerica*, Part 2, pp. 543–57. Vol. 11 in Robert Wauchope, gen. ed., *Handbook of Middle American Indians.* Austin: University of Texas Press.

Sandstrom, Alan R. 1975. "Ecology, Economy and the Realm of the Sacred: An Interpretation of Ritual in a Nahua Community of the Southern Huasteca, Mexico. Ph.D. diss., Indiana University, Bloomington.

—————. 1978. *The Image of Disease: Medical Practices of Nahua Indians of the Huasteca.* University of Missouri Monographs in Anthropology, No. 3. Columbia: Museum of Anthropology, University of Missouri.

—————. 1982. "The Tonantsi Cult of the Eastern Nahua." In James Preston, ed., *Mother Worship: Theme and Variations*, pp. 25–50. Chapel Hill: University of North Carolina Press.

—————. 1983. "Paper Dolls and Symbolic Sequence: An Analysis of a Modern Aztec Curing Ritual." *Folklore Americano* No. 36:109–26.

—————. 1985. "Paper Cult Figures and the Principle of Unity: An Anaylsis of the Sacred Iconography of the Indians of East Central Mexico." *Proceedings of the Indiana Academy of the Social Sciences, 1984* 19:12–19.

—————. 1986. "Paper Spirits of Mexico." *Natural History* 95(1):66–73.

———. 1987. "Winds of Change Over Puyecaco." *Indiana Alumni Magazine* 49(6):24–26.

———. 1989. "The Face of the Devil: Concepts of Disease and Pollution among Nahua Indians of the Southern Huasteca." In Dominique Michelet, ed., *Enquêtes sur l'Amérique moyenne: Mélanges offerts à Guy Stresser-Péan*, pp. 357–72. Etudes Mésoaméricaines, Vol. 16. México, D.F.: Instituto Nacional de Antropología e Historia, Consejo Nacional para la Cultura y las Artes (et) Centre d'Etudes Mexicaines et Centraméricaines.

———, and Paul Jean Provost. 1979. "Carnival in the Huasteca: Guitar and Violin Huapangos of the Modern Aztecs." *Ethnodisc Journal of Recorded Sound* 11:1–19 (with cassette)

———, and Pamela Effrein Sandstrom. 1986. *Traditional Papermaking and Paper Cult Figures of Mexico*. Norman: University of Oklahoma Press.

Schryer, Frans J. 1980. *The Rancheros of Pisaflores: The History of a Peasant Bourgeoisie in Twentieth-Century Mexico*. Toronto: University of Toronto Press.

———. 1986. "Peasants and the Law: A History of Land Tenure and Conflict in the Huasteca." *Journal of Latin American Studies* 18(2):283–311.

———. 1990. *Ethnicity and Class Conflict in Rural Mexico*. Princeton, N.J.: Princeton University Press.

Sexton, James D. 1978. "Protestantism and Modernization in Two Guatemalan Towns." *American Ethnologist* 5(2):280–302.

Siverts, Henning. 1969. "Ethnic Stability and Boundary Dynamics in Southern Mexico." In Fredrik Barth, ed., *Ethnic Groups and Boundaries: The Social Organization of Culture Difference*, pp. 101–16. Boston: Little, Brown and Company.

Soustelle, Jacques. 1961 [1955]. *Daily Life of the Aztecs on the Eve of the Spanish Conquest*. Stanford: Stanford University Press.

Spicer, Edward H. 1962. *Cycles of Conquest: The Impact of Spain, Mexico, and the United States on the Indians of the Southwest, 1533–1960*. Tucson: University of Arizona Press.

Spradley, James P. 1979. *The Ethnographic Interview*. New York: Holt, Rinehart & Winston.

———. 1980. *Participant Observation*. New York: Holt, Rinehart & Winston.

Starr, Frederick. 1901. "Notes upon the Ethnography of Southern Mexico." *Proceedings of the Davenport Academy of Sciences* 8:102–98.

———. 1978 [1908]. *In Indian Mexico: A Narrative of Travel and Labor*. Chicago: Forbes and Co.; reprint, New York: AMS Press.

Stavenhagen, Rodolfo. 1975. *Social Classes in Agrarian Societies*. Translated from the Spanish by Judy Adler Hellman. New York: Anchor Books.

———. 1978. "Capitalism and the Peasantry in Mexico." *Latin American Perspectives* 5(3):27–37.

———. 1980. *Problemas étnicos y campesinos: ensayos*. Serie de Antropología Social, Colección No. 60. México, D.F.: Instituto Nacional Indigenista.

Stiles, Neville S. 1976–79. "Nahuatl: A Course for Beginners: Units 1–13." *Survival International Review* (London). [1- to 2-page lessons included in vols. 1–4.]

Stocks, Anthony. 1989. "Ethnicity and Praxis: The Cocamilla Case." Paper read at the 87th annual meeting of the American Anthropological Association, Phoenix, Arizona.

Stresser-Péan, Guy. 1952–53. "Les nahuas du sud de la Huasteca et l'ancienne extension méridionale des Huastéques." *Revista Mexicana de Estudios Antropológicos* 13(2–3):287–90.

———. 1971. "Ancient Sources on the Huasteca." In Gordon F. Ekholm and Ignacio Bernal, eds., *Archaeology of Northern Mesoamerica*, Part 2, pp. 582–602. Vol. 11 in Robert Wauchope, gen. ed., *Handbook of Middle American Indians*. Austin: University of Texas Press.

———, ed. 1979. "La Huasteca et la Frontière nord-est de la Mesoamérique." *Actes du XLIIe Congrès International des Américanistes, Paris, 1976* 9B:1–157.

Stuart, James W. 1990. "Maize Use by Rural Mesoamerican Households." *Human Organization* 49(2):135–39.

Swanson, Guy E. 1968 [1960]. *The Birth of the Gods: The Origin of Primitive Beliefs*. Ann Arbor: University of Michigan Press.

Taggart, James M. 1972. "The Fissiparous Process in Domestic Groups of a Nahuat-Speaking Community." *Ethnology* 11:132–49.

———. 1975a. " 'Ideal' and 'Real' Behavior in the Mesoamerican Non-Residential Extended Family." *American Ethnologist* 2(2):347–57.

———. 1975b. *Estructura de los grupos domésticos de una comunidad nahuat de Puebla*. México, D.F.: Instituto Nacional Indigenista y Secretaría de Educación Pública.

———. 1976. "Action Group Recruitment: A Nahuat Case." In Hugo G. Nutini, Pedro Carrasco, and James M. Taggart, eds., *Essays on Mexican Kinship*, pp. 137–53. Pittsburgh: University of Pittsburgh Press.

———. 1977. "Metaphors and Symbols of Deviance in Nahuat Narratives." *Journal of Latin American Lore* 3(2):279–308.

———. 1979. "Men's Changing Image of Women in Nahuat Oral Tradition." *American Ethnologist* 6(4):723–41.

———. 1983. *Nahuat Myth and Social Structure*. Austin: University of Texas Press.

Tambiah, Stanley J. 1989. "Ethnic Conflict in the World Today." *American Ethnologist* 16(2):335–49.

Tax, Sol. 1972 [1953]. *Penny Capitalism: A Guatemalan Indian Economy*. New York: Octagon Books.

Vié, Anne-Marie. 1979. "Traditions huastèques dans la fête aztèque d'Ochpaniztli." *Actes du XLIIe Congrès International des Américanistes, Paris, 1976* 9B:77–85.

Vivó Escoto, Jorge A. 1964. "Weather and Climate of Mexico and Central

America." In Robert C. West, ed., *Natural Environment and Early Cultures*, pp. 187–215. Vol. 1 in Robert Wauchope, gen. ed., *Handbook of Middle American Indians*. Austin: University of Texas Press.

Vogt, Evon Z. 1969. *Zinacantan: A Mayan Community in the Highlands of Chiapas*. Cambridge, Mass.: Harvard University Press.

———. 1974. *Aerial Photography in Anthropological Field Research*. Cambridge, Mass.: Harvard University Press

Warman, Arturo. 1976. *"We Come to Object": The Peasants of Morelos and the National State*. Baltimore: Johns Hopkins University Press.

Warren, Kay B. 1989 [1978]. *The Symbolism of Subordination: Indian Identity in a Guatemalan Town*. Austin: University of Texas Press.

Werner, Oswald, and G. Mark Schoepfle. 1987. *Systematic Fieldwork*. 2 vols. Newbury Park, Calif.: Sage Publications.

Whettan, Nathan. 1948. *Rural Mexico*. Chicago: University of Chicago Press.

Wilkerson, Jeffrey K. 1979. "Huastec Presence and Cultural Chronology in North-Central Veracruz, Mexico." *Actes du XLIIe Congrès International des Américanistes, Paris, 1976* 9B:31–47.

Williams García, Roberto. 1955. "Ichcacuatitla: Vida en una comunidad indígena de Chicontepec." Unpublished ms., Instituto de Antropología, Universidad Veracruzana, Xalapa, Ver., México.

———. 1957. "Ichcacuatitla." *La Palabra y el Hombre* No. 3:51–63.

———. 1960. "Carnaval en la Huasteca veracruzana." *La Palabra y el Hombre* No. 15:37–45.

———. 1963. *Los Tepehuas*. Xalapa: Universidad Veracruzana, Instituto de Antropología.

———. 1966a. "Ofrenda al maíz," *La Palabra y el Hombre* No. 39:343–54.

———. 1966b. "Plegarias para el fruto. . . la flor. . . ." *La Palabra y el Hombre* No. 40:653–98.

———. 1967. "Algunas rezos tepehuas." *Revista Mexicana de Estudios Antropológicos* 21:287–315.

———. 1972. *Mitos tepehuas*. SepSetentas, No. 27. México, D.F.: Secretaría de Educación Pública.

Wolf, Eric. 1955. "Types of Latin American Peasantry: A Preliminary Discussion." *American Anthropologist*, n.s. 57:452–71.

———. 1957. "Closed Corporate Peasant Communities in Mesoamerica and Central Java." *Southwestern Journal of Anthropology* 13(1):1–18.

———. 1958. "The Virgin of Guadalupe: A Mexican National Symbol." *Journal of American Folklore* 71:34–39.

———. 1959. *Sons of the Shaking Earth*. Chicago: University of Chicago Press.

———. 1960. "The Indian in Mexican Society." *The Alpha Kappa Deltan* 30(1):3–6.

———. 1967. "Levels of Communal Relations." In Manning Nash, ed., *Social Anthropology*, pp. 299–316. Vol. 6 in Robert Wauchope, gen. ed., *Handbook of Middle American Indians*. Austin: University of Texas Press.

X Censo General de Población y Vivienda, 1980. 1983. Tomo 30, 2 vols. México, D.F.: Secretaría de Programación y Presupuesto, Instituto Nacional de Estadística, Geografía e Informática.

Xokoyotsij, José Antonio (pseudonym for Natalio Hernández Hernández). 1986. "Sempoalxóchitl veinte flores: una sola flor." *Estudios de Cultura Náhuatl* 18:41–97.

MAPS CONSULTED

México, D.F.: Secretaría de Programación y Presupuesto, Coordinación General de los Servicios Nacionales de Estadística, Geografía e Informática, Dirección General de Geografía del Territorio Nacional.
1980. Carta de climas 1:1,000,000 (México)
1983. Carta de evapotranspiración y déficit de agua 1:1,000,000 (México)
1981. Carta de humedad en el suelo 1:1,000,000 (México)
1980. Carta de precipitación total anual 1:1,000,000 (México)
1980. Carta de temperaturas medias anuales 1:1,000,000 (México)
1982. Uso potencial agricultura 1:1,000,000 (México)
1982. Uso potencial ganadería 1:1,000,000 (México)
1983. Carta edafológica 1:250,000 (Pachuca F14-11)
1983. Carta hidrológica de aguas superficiales 1:250,000 (Pachuca F14-11)
1985. Carta uso del suelo y vegetación 1:250,000 (Pachuca F14-11)
1983. Carta topográfica 1:50,000 (Alamo F14D54)
1982. Carta topográfica 1:50,000 (Chicontepec F14D53)
1984. Carta topográfica 1:50,000 (San Lorenzo Axatepec F14D63)
1983. Carta topográfica 1:50,000 (Venustiano Carranza F14D64)

INDEX

403